STUDIES IN THE EARLY HISTORY OF BRITAIN

General Editor: Nicholas Brooks

Pastoral Care Before the Parish

Pastoral Care Before the Parish

Edited by John Blair and Richard Sharpe

Leicester University Press   1992
Leicester, London and New York

© Editor and contributors 1992

First published in Great Britain in 1992 by Leicester University Press
(a division of Pinter Publishers Limited)

Editorial offices
Fielding Johnson Building, University of Leicester,
Leicester, LE1 7RH, England

Trade and other enquiries
25 Floral Street, London, WC2E 9DS

British Library Cataloguing in Publication Data

A CIP catalogue record for this book is available from the
British Library

ISBN 0 7185 1372 X

For enquiries in North America please contact
PO Box 197, Irvington, NY 10533

Library of Congress Cataloging in Publication Data

Pastoral care before the parish/edited by John Blair and Richard
    Sharpe.
        p.   cm. - (Studies in the early history of Britain)
    Includes bibliographical references and index.
    Contents: Church and diocese in the West Midlands/Steven Bassett
- Pastoral care in early medieval Wales/Huw Pryce - The pastoral
role of the Church in the early Irish laws/Thomas Charles-Edwards
- Churches and communities in early medieval Ireland/Richard
Sharpe - Early Christian religious houses in Scotland/Alan
Macquarrie - Monks, preaching, and pastoral care in early Anglo-Saxon
England/Alan Thacker - 'By water in the spirit'/Sarah Foot -
Pastoral care and conciliar canons/Catherine Cubitt -
Anglo-Saxon minsters/Sarah Foot - Anglo-Saxon minsters/John
Blair - The cure of souls in English towns before 1000/Gervase
Rosser.
    ISBN 0-7185-1372-X
    1. Great Britain - Church history - To 449. 2. Great Britain -
Church history - Anglo Saxon period, 449-1066. 3. Pastoral
theology - Great Britain - History. I. Blair, John (W. John)
II. Sharpe, Richard. III. Series.
BR747.P35   1992
253'.0941'09021-dc20   91-36009
                                                                          CIP

Typeset by Mayhew Typesetting, Rhayader, Powys
Printed and bound in Great Britain by Biddles Ltd of Guildford and Kings Lynn

Contents

List of figures

Foreword

The aim of the *Studies in the Early History of Britain* is to promote works of the highest scholarship which open up virgin fields of study or which surmount the barriers of traditional academic disciplines. As interest in the origins of our society and culture grows while scholarship yet becomes ever more specialized, interdisciplinary studies are needed more urgently, not only by scholars but also by students and laymen. The series therefore includes research monographs, works of synthesis and also collaborative studies of important themes by several scholars whose training and expertise has lain in different fields. Our knowledge of the early Middle Ages will always be limited and fragmentary, but progress can be made if the work of the historian embraces that of the philologist, the archaeologist, the geographer, the numismatist, the art historian and the liturgist – to name only the most obvious. The need to cross and to remove academic frontiers also explains the extension of the geographical ranges from that of Leicester University Press's previous *Studies in Early English History* to include the whole island of Britain. The change would have been welcomed by the editor of the earlier series, the late Professor H.P.R. Finberg, whose pioneering work helped to inspire, or to provoke, the interest of a new generation of early medievalists in the relations of Britons and Saxons. The approach of this series is therefore deliberately wide-ranging. Early medieval Britain can be understood only in the context of contemporary developments in Ireland and on the continent.

This volume is the third collaborative study to appear in the series. The ten scholars brought together by John Blair and Richard Sharpe bring very different skills to the task of understanding how the church tackled its fundamental pastoral obligations in early medieval Britain. Differences of nomenclature and of historical tradition, the unevenness of the extant evidence and the extreme difficulty of some of it, have hitherto exaggerated the contrasts between the Anglo-Saxon, British, Irish and Scottish churches and have discouraged any overall synthesis. A new look at the evidence was therefore needed, not in order to impose a new interpretative model, but to see whether by examining common problems on a wide geographical front similarities could be detected and differences defined.

N. P. Brooks
University of Birmingham
July 1991

List of abbreviations

Note: In abbreviating less frequently cited periodicals the commonly accepted usage of *J.* for *Journal*, *Proc.* for *Proceedings*, *Soc.* for *Society* and *Trans.* for *Transactions* has been followed. Other abbreviations are listed below.

Antiq. J.	*Antiquaries Journal*
Archaeol. J.	*Archaeological Journal*
BAR	British Archaeological Reports
Bede, *HE*	Bede, *Historia ecclesiastica gentis Anglorum*
BCS	*Cartularium Saxonicum*, ed. W. de G. Birch (3 vols., 1885-93)
BHL	Bibliotheca Hagiographica Latina
CBA	Council for British Archaeology
CCSL	Corpus Christianorum Series Latina
CIH	*Corpus Iuris Hibernici*, ed. D. A. Binchy, 6 vols. (Dublin, 1978)
Haddan and Stubbs, *Councils*	*Councils and Ecclesiastical Documents relating to Great Britain and Ireland*, ed. A. W. Haddan and W. Stubbs, 3 vols. (1869-78)
JBAA	*Journal of the British Archaeological Association*
JRSAI	*Journal of the Royal Society of the Antiquaries of Ireland*
Med. Arch.	*Medieval Archaeology*
MGH	Monumenta Germaniae Historica
RCA&HM	Royal Commission for Ancient and Historic Monuments
S	P. H. Sawyer, *Anglo-Saxon Charters: an Annotated List and Bibliography* (Royal Historical Soc., Guides & Handbooks, 8, 1968)
VCH	*Victoria County History*

Introduction

JOHN BLAIR and RICHARD SHARPE

As historians, the ten contributors to this volume are concerned with the role of the church in society at large.[1] Before attempting to treat the church as an institution, however, we have tried to consider something of its theological agenda - its spiritual aims, demands, expectations - and how these were fulfilled both for those who devoted themselves to the religious life as monks, nuns or clergy, and for the lay people who formed the majority of the population. In considering the early development of the church in the different parts of Great Britain and Ireland, we have tried to place the pastoral ministry at the centre of our thinking.

Pastoral care took various forms, all ultimately coming under the responsibility of bishops. Communities of religious depended on a bishop for their spiritual welfare as much as did the laity, but in turn they could contribute to the extension of the ministry by teaching or preaching. The formal elements of pastoral care, however, especially baptism and the provision of the sacraments, necessitated men in the orders of priest and deacon working both among seculars and among religious not in orders. The supervision and administration of this ministry led in time to the development of a pastoral organization: its emergence is one of the central themes of this book. Pastoral care, however, began in the British Isles with only the loosest of structures under episcopal jurisdiction. Churches of different kinds contributed to the mission, but most tended to have a communal life in these early centuries of insular Christianity. What unites them is not a specific set of pastoral duties but their approach to achieving their theological aims. Organization is of secondary importance.

None the less, questions of organization have for many years dominated discussions of how the church functioned. In Ireland this has taken the form of a debate over whether the organization was 'episcopal' or 'monastic', with the latter view prevailing until recently. Largely because of the expectation of close parallels between 'Celtic' churches, similar questions have lain in the background whenever the early British or Scottish churches have been discussed. Features supposed to be peculiar have been highlighted, and often overemphasized. In contrast, English historians of an older generation believed that the development of the parish system in the

---

1. This introduction is largely based on ideas in the chapters which follow. As well as to the contributors, we are grateful to Nicholas Brooks, Wyn Evans, Richard Gem, Richard Morris, Clare Stancliffe and Kathy Swift for comments made during the discussion at the end of the conference. Our grateful thanks are also due to Kate Tiller for her help and support in organizing the conference.

late Anglo-Saxon and Norman period was the natural outcome of a dynamic
already at work in the eighth century: the provision of pastoral care
originated with the seventh-century bishops and dioceses, and was brought
progressively nearer to the laity settled in manors. The assumption in the
one case of oddity, in the other of anachronistic norms, led the study of the
Irish and English churches in contrary directions to reach different positions, neither of which satisfactorily made sense of the contemporary
evidence.

Most of the present contributions were read at a conference held in the
Department of Continuing Education, Oxford, on 3-5 November 1989,
which took as its theme that central concern of all early medieval churches, the cure of souls. The stimulus for this gathering was a sense that,
as our work on the early English and Irish churches diminished the
contrasts between them, an investigation of pastoral care was now needed
to clarify how these churches functioned. This approach would contribute
also to understanding how far the distinction between a pastoral role and
a contemplative one was relevant in the early Middle Ages, and how far it
was anachronistic. These studies of the early insular churches therefore
seek to compare rather than to contrast. In this they depart from that long
historiographical tradition dominated by the stereotypes of monastic
parochiae and wandering monks in Ireland, and of territorial dioceses,
manorial churches and parish priests in England. Probably none of the
authors would place any confidence in the distinctions which generations
of scholars have taken mostly for granted, while hypotheses which would
have seemed eccentric only ten years ago have their near-unanimous
support. If the book has a unifying message it is that the quest for sharply
contrasting 'national churches' is doomed to failure.
  This change in outlook is startling, and would have been impossible but
for work published during the last ten years. First, studies of the economic
and territorial basis of kingship have emphasized the strong similarities of
local organization in England, Wales and Ireland,[2] opening the possibility
that the circumstances in which the church took institutional shape in
these societies were basically rather similar. Second, a series of English
local studies has drawn attention to superior or 'mother' churches which
exerted control over groups of lesser churches from the eleventh century
onwards, and which had probably once served great 'proto-parishes'
(sometimes called *parochiae* by historians) from which the parishes of the
lesser churches were formed. Several scholars have gone further, identifying
the mother-churches with seventh and eighth-century *monasteria* or
'minsters' staffed by pastorally active religious communities, and

---

2. See especially, P. Wormald, 'Celtic and Anglo-Saxon kingship', in *Sources of
   Anglo-Saxon Culture*, ed. P. E. Szarmach and V. D. Oggins (Studies in Medieval
   Culture, 20, 1986), 151-83; S. R. Bassett, 'In search of the origins of Anglo-Saxon
   Kingdoms', in *The Origins of Anglo-Saxon Kingdoms*, ed. S. R. Bassett (1989), 3-
   27; T. M. Charles-Edwards, 'Early medieval kingships in the British Isles', in
   ibid, 28-39.

postulating that a network of 'minster parishes' was established in each of the Anglo-Saxon kingdoms within two or three generations of conversion. Third, work on early Irish sources has found the traditional view of church organization seriously inadequate and has moved towards a more complex model which includes parochial mother-churches resembling those now identified in England. The validity or otherwise of this 'minster model', and the nature of the communities which minsters housed, are issues tackled in the succeeding chapters.

The sources make a degree of chronological bias hard to avoid. Evidence for the distribution of churches, and for the nature of their ministry, is not available in Ireland until the second half the seventh century, perhaps 200 years after the first phase of Christian conversion. The written sources are heavily concentrated in the seventh and eighth centuries, the plentiful field evidence is extremely difficult to date, and it can be tempting to extrapolate from later periods. Sources for Wales and Scotland are still more fragmentary, and the English evidence, like the Irish, tends to divide between valuable but limited literary texts dealing with the late seventh and early eighth centuries, and field evidence whose interpretation depends on much later records. Most of these essays have a centre of gravity in the seventh and eighth centuries, though several writers use fragmentary evidence to sustain their arguments to the end of the first millennium, while Rosser's discussion is rooted in the tenth and eleventh centuries.

This introduction tries to pick out themes of central importance which recur in all or most of the chapters. It does not attempt to review the whole subject, and for the background to current controversies and preoccupations the reader is referred to the works cited in footnotes. Nor does it pronounce upon disagreements or offer final answers. Only recently have scholars working in the various fields attained sufficient common ground to be able even to argue sensibly: this book records the first extended airing of a debate, not its conclusion. The reader will observe some disagreements, notably the differences in both emphasis and interpretation between Sarah Foot, Alan Thacker and Catherine Cubitt. None the less, the questioning of received definitions is already bringing specialists in different regions and disciplines much closer together than once seemed possible. Students of the Irish, British and Anglo-Saxon churches may still labour within the often unperceived constraints of their separate historiographical traditions; it may still be the sin of topographers to neglect change over time and the diversity of institutions, and of legal historians and theologians to assume that theoretical structures were followed closely by reality. But at least there is now a dialogue between the specialists in these different areas, and there are signs that they are starting to learn from each other.

A problem which confronts all studies of this kind is that the words used by different sources - different authors, different societies, different languages - have to be understood and interpreted through our own terminology. Much of the inherited model depended on the use of the word 'monastery' with all its Benedictine connotations to translate the Latin *monasterium* or to describe British or Irish church communities. The modern word has tended to influence the course of historical interpretation, when it should rather reflect the fruits. The monastic organization long taken for granted by Irish historians, and often imposed on British ones through the notion of 'Celtic' parallels, has been shown to derive from misplaced assumptions. In the chapters by Thomas Charles-Edwards and Richard Sharpe the life of the Irish church is discussed without recourse to any notion of a characteristically monastic organization, and Huw Pryce makes it clear that the differentiation of monastic and pastoral functions is not possible for Welsh churches. Discussing the evidence from late seventh- and early eighth-century England Alan Thacker makes it clear that the *monasteria* of the period conformed to no type: the same word is used for communities of either sex or both, whose members might include one or more priests, or none. While the sacramental functions reserved to bishops and priests were clearly defined, pastoral functions could be shared with clerks or monks, who were expected to be able to preach and teach. Sarah Foot's more extended study of the words used in Anglo-Saxon texts, whether Latin or Old English, confirms that, although *monasterium* in Latin or its English derivative *mynster* were by far the commonest expressions, the words could be used of any religious community large or small. The only exception to this usage is that, where a church housed a bishop, this aspect tends to override more generalized language. She advocates the use of 'minster' as a comprehensive term for any Anglo-Saxon *monasterium*, not just those with territorial *parochiae* attached. On the other hand, when a site is discussed with reference to its status as the head church of a *parochia*, rather than to the character or functions of its personnel, the term 'mother-church' seems preferable.

The territorial structures of the church were delimited at different times in different areas, and display different levels of continuity. Their study is bedevilled by problems of scale: before different systems are compared, we must decide what kinds of unit can be regarded as comparable. The small size of Irish and British dioceses is often contrasted with the huge size of Anglo-Saxon ones, but the similarities between Irish and British dioceses and English minster *parochiae* may be more relevant. As Charles-Edwards and Sharpe both show, the direct Irish equivalent of the Anglo-Saxon minster is the head church of the *túath* or 'people'. In England, *parochiae* were characteristically based on secular *regiones*, perpetuated as the units of late Anglo-Saxon local government, which often originated as fifth- and sixth-century tribal kingdoms. The Irish *túath* and the Anglo-Saxon *regio* were thus of like kind: the substantive difference is that the head church of the former had a bishop, whereas the head church of the latter normally did not. To a considerable degree this must result from the fact that Christianity arrived some 150 years later in England, during a period when both countries were experiencing the aggregation of social-political groups.

In the size of dioceses it was the English who were anomalous. The territories controlled by Irish episcopal churches were similar in scale to those controlled by the urban sees of sixth-century Gaul; a Gallic structure of episcopal government is in fact advocated by the Irish legal compilation known to canonists as the *Hibernensis*. Among the present contributions, Steven Bassett, Huw Pryce and Alan Macquarrie argue respectively that the minster *parochia* of Worcester may have originated as a British diocese; that the head-priests of the greater Welsh churches may have possessed episcopal status; and that most of the Scottish mother-churches with *parochiae* eventually became cathedrals. The peculiarity of the English dioceses was that they were founded under the patronage of the great kingships which emerged during the late sixth and early seventh centuries: the king who had a bishop was the king who controlled *subreguli*. Once established in great dioceses, English bishops resisted their fragmentation. Thus, while the foundation of *monasteria* proceeded apace from the 660s onwards, building a pattern very similar to that now identified among the British and Irish, the episcopal structure could hardly have been more different: in contrast to the multiplicity of Irish and Welsh bishops, the English episcopate in 669 was reduced to the simoniac Wine, the uncanonical Chad and the uncontrollable Wilfrid.

Thus English minsters were often relatively remote from their diocesan bishops (the burden of one of Bede's complaints to Ecgberht), and their relations with them were ambivalent. Many were founded by kings on the advice of bishops, or by the bishops with the patronage of kings. On the other hand, influences might pull a minster away from its bishop's grasp: the desire for autonomy in choice of lifestyle, the hereditary interests of aristocratic proprietors, or loyalty to a monastic federation. In England, relationships of dependence between *monasteria* are very poorly recorded, but there are signs that they existed in certain areas (notably County Durham and the West Midlands),[3] as well as in the federations associated with Peterborough and with St Wilfrid. Anglo-Saxon practice, then, may not have been so unlike the model which Sharpe proposes for Ireland, where mother-churches with *parochiae* were subject to the control of still greater churches; the incidence of bishops is the one real contrast.

It is the contention of most of the present authors that the organization of pastoral care was based everywhere on mother-churches. Charles-Edwards emphasizes the reciprocal relationship between a mother-church and the folk of its *túath*: the church owed mass, baptism and prayers for the dead, and if it failed to provide these the people could withhold their tithes and first fruits. For the mother-churches of Wales and Scotland, Pryce and Macquarrie suggest pastoral functions resembling those proposed in recent studies for those of Anglo-Saxon England; at Deer especially, an exceptional source shows a monastic community much involved in the lay world and concerned with the ministration of the sacraments.

The importance of *monasteria* for pastoral care among the Anglo-Saxons is emphasized by Thacker, who considers that 'the whole point of [Bede's] eulogy [of Aidan] is to stress the pastoral impact which a properly-constituted *monasterium* could make upon its environs'; by Foot, who argues that religious communities were never isolated from surrounding lay

---

3. E. Cambridge, 'The early church in county Durham: a reassessment', *JBAA*, cxxxvii (1984), 65-85; P. Sims-Williams, *Religion and Literature in Western Britain, 600-800* (1990), 87-143; below, p. 144.

society; and by Blair, who stresses the centrality of minster sites within their localities. Cubitt's chapter, however, questions some of the premises of the 'minster model' and offers a useful corrective to any tendency which it may be showing to fossilize into a new orthodoxy. The canons of the 747 Council of *Clofesho*, she observes, like other contemporary sources, discuss the pastoral work of the church almost entirely in terms of the bishops, priests and deacons whose sacramental offices carried with them the pastoral burden. They are not concerned with structures but with the ecclesiastical personnel through whom the ministry was provided. The canons' references to *monasteria* presuppose institutions with a variety of origins – episcopal, royal, proprietary – founded in many cases with a devotional purpose: pastoral care was not necessarily their prime concern in the first instance. It has to be acknowledged that *monasteria* housed communities which were both varied and complex in their composition and functions, and that the details of these are in most cases irrecoverable.

The present chapters on Ireland, Wales, western Britain and Scotland must strengthen the claim that early Anglo-Saxon pastoral care was based on regional mother-churches, since anything else would now seem anomalous. Precisely when a formal, stable structure of mother-churches with large *parochiae* emerged is still a matter for debate, and opinions vary between the seventh and tenth centuries. The strongest argument for the early formation of English *parochiae* is based on continuity of site: it is hard otherwise to see why so many *monasteria* recorded in the seventh and eighth centuries should re-emerge as parochial mother-churches in the eleventh and twelfth. On the other hand, the inference by topographical historians that, because only one *monasterium* can now be identified in a well-defined territory, it was always so, and was so by design, ignores the possibility of *monasteria* which did not serve *parochiae* and have disappeared precisely for that reason. Cubitt's point that 'much of the evidence for monastic territories used by topographers is late' is a fair one: the first clear statement that any new church must reckon with 'the old minster to which obedience pertains' comes no earlier than the 960s.[4]

Cubitt also draws attention, however, to Canon 9 of the 747 Council, with its reference to *regiones* assigned to priests by their bishop: the first literary evidence for territorial pastoral units smaller than dioceses, which may or may not already imply an organized network. The gradual extension of bishops' control over minsters during the eighth and ninth centuries to provide a comprehensive pastoral structure for their dioceses, along lines recently proposed for the West Midlands,[5] may have been an important part of the process. But bishops could already have had such ideas in the seventh century; there is nothing to show that ecclesiastical *regiones* were a new phenomenon in 747, and the secular *regiones* on which they were

---

4. II Eadgar, 1-3.1.
5. Sims-Williams, *Religion and Literature*, 172, 394-5. For comparable efforts to exert control in Canterbury diocese, see N. Brooks, *Early History of the Church of Canterbury* (1984), 175-206.

often based were certainly older.[6] The system which emerges in sources of the tenth to twelfth centuries was built on a distribution of *monasteria* which were able to meet some or all pastoral needs, and which had in many cases long done so. It was not built at a stroke, but the building began early.

This problem of the chronology of mother-churches is inseparable from that of the chronology of smaller, more local churches. Did the system develop from below upwards, through a minority among existing religious sites acquiring superior status, or from above downwards, the foundation of minsters being followed by the establishment of satellites within their *parochiae*? Did minsters always coexist with lesser churches, or was there a time when they were the only functioning religious sites? These questions are less easily answered for the Anglo-Saxons than for the other insular peoples. In western and south-western Britain, Professor Thomas proposes the 'enclosed developed cemetery' as the normal origin of early churches both great and small.[7] In the present book, Pryce cites the Llandaf charters for a dense provision of churches in Gwent and Ergyng by c. 600, while Charles-Edwards and Sharpe show that seventh-century Irish sources already assume a multiplicity of small local churches.

Discussion of the English evidence on this point has been hampered by a tendency to equate *local* churches with *private* or aristocratic churches. As recent work shows, there are strong grounds for believing that manorial churches of the kind recorded in their thousands from Domesday Book onwards, and perpetuated as the majority of rural parish churches, were a new phenomenon of the tenth and eleventh centuries. This is not to deny that local churches of a different kind, linked to central churches rather than to local territorial lordships and perhaps associated with cult sites such as holy graves or wells, may have existed much earlier. Such is the implication of Bede's incidental remarks that *oratoria uel baptisteria* had not *yet* been built in the time of St Paulinus, and that Dryhthelm went *ad uillulae oratorium* on awakening from his vision.[8] It is in the nature of some Irish texts to mention small ecclesiastical sites, and of the undeveloped Irish landscape to preserve their traces. Given the other close parallels with Irish organization in the seventh and eighth centuries it would be strange if sites of this kind were uncommon in England, but written sources ignore them and quantification is impossible (unless perhaps eventually through archaeology).

The primary aspects of pastoral care need not have depended on the existence of either structures or buildings. As Christianity spread through the pagan kingdoms of Ireland and England, the first baptisms required only

---

6. For the argument that late seventh-century kings, advised by bishops, established *parochiae* based on existing royal territories, see especially P. H. Hase, 'The mother churches of Hampshire', in J. Blair (ed.), *Minsters and Parish Churches* (1988), 45-8.
7. For a recent statement of this view see C. Thomas, 'Christians, chapels, churches and charters', *Landscape History*, xi (1989), 19-26.
8. Bede, *HE*, ii.14, v.2.

the availability of natural water. As the faith took hold on a whole society, the sacrament of baptism developed by stages. The first adult converts were baptized with little preparation, but the more Christianity replaced paganism the greater the emphasis placed on preparation. In the Western church infant baptism was by now usual, but in newly-converted lands adult baptism must inevitably have remained widespread for a generation or so, and the change imposed new demands. Whereas adult catechumens could travel to the episcopal see for baptism and confirmation at one of the canonical seasons of Easter and Pentecost, the baptism of infants only days or weeks old was of necessity performed throughout the dioceses and throughout the year. Confirmation by the bishop came later, but he had to consecrate the chrism used in baptism; the distribution of this chrism by the bishop was a major bond linking churches where baptism was performed to the episcopal see.

Baptism has left remarkably little physical evidence. As Foot and Blair show, the rarity of separate baptismal churches is one of the few real contrasts between the great religious sites of Britain and Ireland and those of Italy and Gaul. Very few Anglo-Saxon fonts remain, and none need be earlier than the tenth century. This negative evidence is striking, and suggests that open-air baptism in rivers, springs and pools may have remained the norm, perhaps at established places of assembly.[9]

Burial, unlike the other sacraments, has left substantial archaeological evidence. Eventually this should provide information about the origins of *parochiae*, since the centralization of burial at mother-churches must bear some relationship to the growing importance of their role. At present, bias in the recovery of data and the cessation of grave-goods mean that we know far more about 'pagan' Anglo-Saxon cemeteries of the fifth to seventh centuries than about 'Christian' ones of the seventh to eleventh. 'Final-phase' cemeteries of the mid to late seventh century show a falling-off in numbers of people buried and a decline in grave-goods, combined with the appearance of new and sometimes explicitly Christian items. Cemeteries of furnished graves were then abandoned, while the first graves in and near churches were (so far as we know, and in striking contrast to Gaul) unfurnished.[10]

Studies of these changes in England have been too preoccupied with grave-goods and have taken insufficient account of the Irish and Welsh evidence: developments may have followed very similar lines. In seventh-century Ireland, secular people were buried in the traditional burial-place of the family or community. Thus Christians lay among pagans; one text

---

9. Cf. R. Morris, 'Baptismal places, 600-800', in *People and Places in Northern Europe 500-1600: Essays in Honour of Peter Hayes Sawyer*, ed, I. Wood and N. Lund (1991), 15-24.

10. For some recent work on this area see R. Morris, *The Church in British Archaeology* (CBA, Research Rep. 47, 1983), 49-62; D. A. Bullough, 'Burial, community and belief in the early medieval West', in *Ideal and Reality in Frankish and Anglo-Saxon Society*, ed, P. Wormald *et al.* (1983), 177-201; A. Boddington, 'Models of burial, settlement and worship: the final phase reviewed', in *Anglo-Saxon Cemeteries: a Reappraisal*, ed. E. Southworth (1990), 177-99.

mentions crosses distinguishing Christian graves from the others, surely reminiscent of the graves with Christian objects in 'final-phase' English cemeteries.[11] By the same token, to transfer one's family burials to a church affirmed a new hereditary allegiance to it. Early medieval Wales also contained many graveyards without churches, progressively abandoned through what seems to have been a general movement towards churchyard burial. The same opposing forces may have operated in all three societies: the allegiance claimed by a new mother-church, and the spiritual advantages accruing from burial among the holy, pulling against the traditional associations of a family graveyard. Two major questions are still unanswered: first, how often, if at all, were churches built during the seventh and eighth centuries on 'pagan' Anglo-Saxon cemeteries? The evidence is slight in the extreme, but intensive burial is one of those activities which destroys its own archaeological traces. Second, how quickly did the monopolistic minster graveyards recorded in tenth- and eleventh-century sources develop? The general antiquity of circular graveyards seems inherently likely, but still needs clearer demonstration. The archaeology of insular burial in the eighth and ninth centuries remains largely unexplored, and is unlikely to advance except through a large and expensive programme of radiocarbon dating.

How far, in fact, were the pastoral needs of the laity fulfilled? The early Irish church may be regarded, in Sharpe's words, as 'one of the most comprehensive pastoral organizations in northern Europe'. The texts reviewed by Charles-Edwards and Sharpe suggest that the reciprocal relationship between a *túath* and its chief church involved high expectations on the part of the laity, with sanctions if the church failed to provide baptism, mass, prayers for the dead and preaching. In the light of this analogy, it seems possible that historians have been overpessimistic in their speculations on the quality of Anglo-Saxon pastoral care. By 800 few settlements in lowland England can have lain further than five or six miles from a minster, and the evidence considered by Foot suggests that concern at least for baptism was reasonably widespread. If the pastoral theology of Theodore and Bede, discussed by Thacker, was austere to the point of excluding most laity from full participation, the cults of local saints provided foci for popular religion in the same centres from which pastoral care was dispensed. The intensely localized forms of devotion which were based on obscure shrines, often thought a peculiarity of the 'Celtic' churches, may in fact have been no less important among the English. Alcuin's complaint that people 'wish to have sacred things round their necks, not in their hearts, and with these holy words of God or the relics of the saints go to their filthy acts',[12] is itself testimony to the absorption of Christianity into lay culture. By the late tenth and eleventh centuries, as Rosser shows, the growth of towns around many minsters and the proliferation of

11. Below, p. 82.
12. Below, p. 168.

small churches had consolidated contacts between church and people within existing structures.

Much of this book emphasizes the secular context of pastoral organization: *monasteria* were founded by rulers, they often adjoined (and sometimes themselves served as) centres of royal power, and their areas of responsibility were defined according to tribal, political or economic territories. One reason why the early insular church eludes the canon lawyer's definitions is that it was articulated to the diverse forms of early insular lay society, and changed with them. The seventh century saw huge political, economic and social changes, of which the progress of Christianity was merely one aspect. These changes were perhaps most decisive among the Anglo-Saxons: the rapid submergence of tribal kingdoms into great ones, the concentration of wealth and its sources into fewer hands, the reintroduction of coinage and the growth of emporia for international trade. None the less, there are many ways in which the English, British, Irish and Gallic peoples were part of one evolving social and cultural whole.

If the church was moulded by lay society, it came in turn to influence it profoundly. One of its most tangible, and in the end most lasting, contributions was to provide stable centres for settlement, production and exchange in a developing world. 'Monastic towns' have been chiefly recognized in Ireland, where the primary character of many towns as complex ecclesiastical settlements is only thinly disguised. Yet in England too, as Blair and Rosser argue below, minsters formed the nuclei of many towns and continued to direct and stimulate their growth up to the eleventh century. The influence of a great church spread far out into its territory, for its clients had a special status and might occupy a wide area. Already in the seventh and eighth centuries there seems to have been a large lay population in both Britain and Ireland whose lives were profoundly affected by their dependence on minsters: they can be glimpsed in the Irish *manach*, in the 500–600 *fratres* at Wearmouth-Jarrow, in the shepherd and *frater* Hadwald who belonged to the abbess of Whitby's *familia*, and in the 'monks' whom Æthelbald of Mercia conscripted for public works.[13] Despite the transformation and eventual destruction of their communities, minsters remained central places. It is a remarkable testimony to the early medieval pastoral system that in most of the ancient towns of Britain and Ireland, the earliest-recorded component is a *monasterium*.

---

13. Below, pp. 67, 102, 141.

Part 1 Celtic Britain and Ireland

1 Church and diocese in the West Midlands: the transition from British to Anglo-Saxon control

STEVEN BASSETT

> To other unspeakable crimes, which Gildas their own historian describes in doleful words, was added this crime, that they never preached the faith to the Saxons or Angles who inhabited Britain with them. Nevertheless God in his goodness did not reject the people whom he foreknew, for he had appointed much worthier heralds of the truth to bring this people to the faith.[1]

The main purpose of this chapter is to attempt to answer two questions. First, what did the pagan Anglo-Saxons find in the way of Christianity and an organized church when they reached the West Midlands in the sixth century? Second, how much of it did the Anglo-Saxon church retain when eventually, in the later seventh century, it managed to extend its activities that far west?

The chief difficulty we face in trying to answer these two questions is that there seems to be hardly any evidence which can be brought to bear on them. Very occasionally, however, an absence of evidence is significant in itself. That could prove to be so on this occasion, for it may be that the very silence of our accustomed sources about the origins of Christianity among the westernmost Anglo-Saxons is telling us something important. We may, moreover, be able to uncover enough evidence of a less familiar sort to allow a little progress to be made with these questions.

For any aspect of the conversion of the Anglo-Saxons to Christianity we immediately turn to Bede's *Ecclesiastical History*. He is our chief, and often our only, source for how the Anglo-Saxons of eastern, central and southern Britain became Christian. He omits none of the kingdoms in those areas, even if his descriptions of the missions to some of them are rather thin. Almost last of all to be converted were the Mercians.[2] Bede tells us nothing, however, about the Anglo-Saxons to the west and south-west of them. He does not mention missions to the Hwicce, the Magonsæte or the Wreocensæte. Yet these were substantial peoples. All three were important enough to carry assessments of 7,000 hides in the later seventh

---

1. Bede, *HE* i. 22. Translation from *Bede's Ecclesiastical History of the English People*, ed. B. Colgrave and R. A. B. Mynors (1969), 69.
2. *HE* iii. 21, 24.

century - the same as those of, for instance, the South Saxons and the people of Lindsey.[3] The Hwicce and the Magonsæte, if not the far more shadowy Wreocensæte, had indigenous kings and, by 680, their own bishops as well.[4]

Why then does Bede tell us nothing about their acceptance of Christianity or about episcopal provision for them from the time of their conversion up to Theodore's reforms? The obvious answer may be that it is because he knew nothing: what had happened on the western fringes of Anglo-Saxon settlement in the seventh century was beyond his and his informants' reliable knowledge.[5] However, he does not even tell us that Theodore created sees for the Magonsæte and the Hwicce, let alone that they were situated at Hereford and Worcester respectively. Surely he knew that much; so it is hard to resist the conclusion that the information did not seem particularly important to him.

What Bede could not tell, or chose not to tell us about the early history of the Anglo-Saxon church in the West Midlands will be hard to find from other reliable sources. Little progress has been made so far in that direction. Instead, as a result of our own almost complete ignorance on the subject, a myth has grown up to fill the vacuum. It runs as follows: when in 655 the Mercians at last became Christian and gained a see, their bishops had responsibility for the peoples to the west and south-west of Mercia as well, until Theodore made separate arrangements for them.[6] The myth rests on an untested assumption. It is to the effect that, since the Hwicce, Magonsæte and Wreocensæte all, sooner or later, came wholly to be absorbed by their powerful neighbour, they were probably already under the Mercians' thumb in the mid-seventh century to such an extent that they counted as part of Mercia for diocesan purposes. Some have gone so far as to say that these three peoples *must* by that date have been subject to direct Mercian control, on the grounds that otherwise the first stage of their Christian history would have been separately reported by Bede, as was that of the Middle Angles and Lindsey.

The earliest bishops of the Mercians certainly did have the extra task of looking after the Middle Angles and the people of Lindsey. In reporting this, Bede says that they were not yet able to have bishops of their own because of a shortage of suitable men.[7] We know enough about these two peoples

---

3. B.L. MS Harl. 3271, f.6v; printed as *BCS* 297. For a critical edition, see D. N. Dumville, 'The Tribal Hidage: an introduction to its texts and their history', in *The Origins of Anglo-Saxon Kingdoms*, ed. S. Bassett (1989), 225-30. The Magonsæte are termed *Westerna* in the Tribal Hidage.
4. A. H. Smith, 'The Hwicce', in *Frankiplegius: Medieval and Linguistic Studies, In Honour of Francis Peabody Magoun, Jn.*, ed. J. B. Bessinger and R. P. Creed (1965), 56-65; H. P. R. Finberg, 'The princes of Magonsæte', in *idem, The Early Charters of the West Midlands* (1961), 217-25; K. Pretty, 'Defining the Magonsæte', in *Origins of Anglo-Saxon Kingdoms*, ed. Bassett, 171-83.
5. Bede seems to have had no Mercian informant: D. P. Kirby, 'Bede's native sources for the *Historia Ecclesiastica*', Bull. John Rylands Lib. xlviii (1965-6), 341-71.
6. E.g. J. Godfrey, *The Church in Anglo-Saxon England* (1962), 133; H. Mayr-Harting, *The Coming of Christianity to Anglo-Saxon England* (1972), 131-2.
7. Bede, *HE* iii. 21, 24.

in the seventh century to see that both were already subject to Mercian overlordship, if only intermittently in the case of Lindsey; so there was an obvious political context for their sharing a bishop. To do the job properly the bishops of the Mercians may at first have been peripatetic, or at least of no fixed see: the see was not established at Lichfield until the time of the fifth bishop, Chad, and we are not told of any previous site.[8]

By contrast there is no reliable evidence that either the Hwicce or the Magonsæte (or perhaps even the Wreocensæte) were as yet dominated to that extent by the Mercians, let alone so subordinate to them that they were effectively part of their kingdom.[9] In view, then, of Bede's inability, or disinclination, to tell us anything about the conversion of these western-most Anglo-Saxons, and in view of our relative ignorance of their political status, we should not make simplistic assumptions predicated on an absence of evidence. It cannot be taken as read that they shared in the conversion of their Mercian neighbours which was effected from Northumbria in the mid-650s.

Conversely, there are clear signs that the West Midlands was an area in which the incoming Anglo-Saxons had found Christianity already established, with an ecclesiastical organization which was both widespread and well organized. First, there is the evidence of archaeology. Burials with grave-goods allow us to trace the steady movement of Anglo-Saxons into the West Midlands proper from the end of the fifth century.[10] There seem to have been two main routes of entry. One was via the Trent valley, a route taken by immigrants who had moved along it from the Humber or else had crossed the intervening divide from the valleys of the nearer rivers which drain into the Wash. These Anglo-Saxons colonized the area which was to become the heartland of the kingdom of Mercia.

The other main route of entry was along the Warwickshire Avon. Some of those who began to use it from the early sixth century onwards had come from the Trent valley and some from the Cambridgeshire region.[11] By the later part of the century the Anglo-Saxons had penetrated the Severn valley itself. There they met others who in much smaller numbers had crossed the Cotswolds from the Thames valley,[12] and together they settled the area east of the Severn, doubtless intermarrying with the local Britons to produce the hybrid population known by the seventh century as the Hwicce.

---

8. Bede, *HE* iii. 24; iv. 3.
9. S. Bassett, 'In search of the origins of Anglo-Saxon kingdoms', in *Origins of Anglo-Saxon Kingdoms*, ed. Bassett, 6–17.
10. A. Meaney, *A Gazetteer of Early Anglo-Saxon Burial Sites* (1964), *passim*. For more recent discoveries, see in the first instance the annual summaries of archaeological work in *Med. Arch.*
11. K. B. Pretty, 'The Welsh Border and the Severn and Avon Valleys in the Fifth and Sixth Centuries AD: An Archaeological Survey' (unpubl. Ph.D. thesis, Univ. of Cambridge, 1975).
12. J. M. Cook, 'An Anglo-Saxon cemetery at Broadway Hill, Broadway, Worcestershire', *Antiq. J.* xxxviii (1958), 76–81; Meaney, *Gazetteer of Early Anglo-Saxon Burial Sites, passim*; D. M. Wilson and D. G. Hurst, 'Medieval Britain in 1969', *Med. Arch.* xiv (1970), 156, for a more recent discovery at Bishops Cleeve.

By the early part of the seventh century they must have reached the region beyond the Severn, as their northern neighbours also seem to have done by moving westwards from the Trent valley. It is hard to be sure if the lands beyond the Severn and the head-waters of the Trent were in effect conquered by military élites, or if they were colonized by migrant farmers. Our sparse and unreliable written sources have traditionally, if unconvincingly, been interpreted in terms of the first alternative. Yet, placename evidence plainly supports the second alternative: both the quantity and the geographical extent of Old English placenames in the region point to its having been settled by a quite substantial farming population.

Archaeology, however, has nothing to say on the matter, for before the end of the sixth century the Anglo-Saxons who had entered the West Midlands by these various routes suddenly become invisible to it. Few later sixth-century burials with grave-goods have been found in any part of the region east of the Severn, and none to the west of it. It has yielded no identifiable seventh-century burials at all. In other words the Anglo-Saxons seem to have undergone a radical and lasting transformation in their mortuary practices within a generation or so of their arrival in the region, and a good while before a similar change occurred in many of the older-settled areas of lowland Britain.

We cannot of course be sure how far the colonization of the West Midlands had proceeded by the time of this transformation. Only in the middle Trent valley have migration-period settlements been found and excavated;[13] even the distribution of burials with grave-goods may not reflect the full extent of Anglo-Saxon penetration of the region by the later sixth century. But in any case we should not doubt that since then, if not before, the Anglo-Saxons were moving out of the Trent and Avon valleys, and were pushing westwards beyond the Severn and its south-flowing tributary, the Tern. Placenames and the meagre written sources show us what archaeology does not: that by the middle decades of the seventh century the whole West Midlands region had been colonized and politically dominated by Anglo-Saxons.

No direct equation can be safely made between the changes which the immigrants made in their burial practices in the later sixth century and their being converted to Christianity. Doing away with grave-goods and becoming a Christian are not the same thing, not even theoretically. Yet the changes were rapid and wholesale enough for us to conclude that they must reflect the Anglo-Saxons' coming into contact with organized Christianity. Although we cannot gauge the speed of their conversion, we need not doubt its occurrence or its lasting effect on them. It was happening well before the arrival of the Augustinian mission, and a century or more before these people were first brought under the control of Canterbury. Their

13. H. M. Wheeler, 'Excavations at Willington, Derbyshire, 1970-2', *Derbyshire Archaeol. J.* xciv (1979), 58-220; S. Losco-Bradley and H. M. Wheeler, 'Anglo-Saxon settlement in the Trent valley: some aspects', in *Studies in Late Anglo-Saxon Settlement*, ed. M. L. Faull (1984), 101-14.

sixth-century contact with Christianity can, therefore, only have been through the British church.

That should come as no great surprise to us. We know very little about Christianity in western Britain in the first two post-Roman centuries, but what we do know clearly demonstrates that there was a thriving church there, complete with bishops and monastic communities. It was a church which was 'structurally entirely consistent with that of Roman Britain' and which is likely to have been its direct descendant, if one which had acquired some new blood on the way.[14]

The survival of organized Christianity in the lowland areas of western Britain was doubtless made possible by an effective continuity of both political and agrarian life occurring there in the centuries after 400. We can see political continuity of sorts through a variety of sources; the agrarian continuity we know of partly from the Llandaf charters, partly from fieldwork and cartographic studies made of a number of quite widely separated areas of the West Midlands.[15] The socio-economic transformation of Britain in the earlier fifth century may well not have affected the less intensively Romanized areas of western Britain too seriously. The more vulnerable elements in the population there, such as the inhabitants of Wroxeter and the landed aristocracy of the Cotswold villas (or the people who ousted them), seem to have adapted as required to the changing circumstances.[16]

The wholly negative evidence we find in the West Midlands in the early disappearance of Anglo-Saxon burials with grave-goods has been supplemented so far by very little actual physical evidence of Christianity being practised there before the later seventh century (though it must be said that there is hardly any *less* archaeological evidence of Christianity during that time than we have for the following 200 years). There is the putatively early Christian use of the site of a Roman town-house at Gloucester, on which a timber-framed building – arguably the first phase of the church of St Mary-de-Lode – was symmetrically placed.[17] At Worcester two orientated, unaccompanied burials found under the cathedral refectory are alleged to be British. However, because the newly calibrated radio-carbon dates from one of the bodies centre on the seventh century, it is not safe to assume that the graves predate the establishment of the Anglo-Saxon see (by 680).[18] Wenlock in Shropshire may also have been a centre of British

---

14. W. Davies, *Wales in the Early Middle Ages* (1982), 170.
15. *ibid.*, 94-5; W. Davies, *The Llandaff Charters* (1979); S. R. Bassett, 'Medieval Lichfield: a topographical review', *Trans. S. Staffs. Archaeol. & Hist. Soc.* xxii (1982), 95-8; idem, 'The Roman and medieval landscape of Wroxeter', in *From Roman Viroconium to Medieval Wroxeter*, ed. P. Barker (1990), 10-12.
16. R. White, 'The Roman city of Wroxeter' in *ibid.* 3-7; K. Branigan, 'Villa settlement in the West Country', in *The Roman West Country*, ed. K. Branigan and P. J. Fowler (1976), 136-41.
17. R. M. Bryant, 'St Mary de Lode, Gloucester', *Bull. CBA Churches Comm.* xiii (Dec. 1980), 15-18.
18. P. A. Barker *et al.*, 'Two burials under the refectory of Worcester Cathedral', *Med. Arch.* xviii (1974), 146-51; S. Bassett, 'Churches in Worcester before and after the conversion of the Anglo-Saxons', *Antiq. J.* lxix (1991), 225-56, at note 107.

Christianity, but the evidence comes not from the several archaeological excavations in the priory but from the etymology of Wenlock's name.[19]

The evidence of placenames and written sources produces further examples. A case can be made, for instance, for there having been a Christian community, and perhaps a bishop, at the Romano-British settlement of *Letocetum* – now called Wall – 2 miles south-west of Lichfield. Lichfield's name, meaning 'open land of *Letocetum*', shows a close early link between the two settlements. It has been suggested more than once that the focus of Christian organization in the area shifted from *Letocetum* to the site of Lichfield at some time in the post-Roman period.[20] If so, that would certainly explain Bishop Wilfrid's statement that Lichfield was a suitable place in which to establish the see of the Mercians.[21]

Or there is Bede's report that Æthelwealh, king of the South Saxons, was baptized at the court of King Wulfhere of Mercia, an event which the Anglo-Saxon Chronicle dates to no later than 661. Bede tells us that Æthelwealh's wife Eafe 'had been baptized in her own country, the kingdom of the Hwicce. She was the daughter of Eanfrith, Eanhere's brother, both of whom were Christians, as were their people.'[22] Bede clearly means us to understand from this that Eafe was a Christian before her husband was, as were her father, her uncle and the rest of the Hwicce. Elsewhere he tells us that the first Christian mission to the Mercians did not begin until 653, and that they were not officially converted until after Penda's death in 655.[23] There seems no reason at all why Bede should pass over in silence the conversion of the Hwicce *en masse* between then and 661, the date by which Æthelwealh of the South Saxons had been baptized. But if they were converted before 653, they were not converted by any missionaries mentioned by or known to Bede. This fits with the archaeology: as we have already seen, it is far more likely that their conversion had begun in the sixth century – or, rather, the conversion of the immigrant Anglo-Saxons who had been but one element of the doubtless hybrid society known by the seventh century as the Hwicce. Logically this means that Eanfrith, Eanhere, and Eafe's Germanic ancestors were converted by Britons.

19. H. Woods, 'Excavations at Wenlock Priory, 1981-6', *JBAA*, cxl (1987), 36-75; M. Biddle and B. Kjølbye-Biddle, 'The so-called Roman building at Much Wenlock', *JBAA*, cxli (1988), 179-83; M. Gelling, 'The early history of western Mercia', in *Origins of Anglo-Saxon Kingdoms*, ed. Bassett, 192-3.
20. M. Gelling, *Signposts to the Past* (1978), 59, 100; A. L. F. Rivet and C. Smith, *The Place-Names of Roman Britain* (1979), 387-8; J. Gould, 'Letocetum, Christianity and Lichfield', *Trans. S. Staffs. Archaeol. & Hist. Soc.* xiv (1973), 30-1; R. Studd, 'Pre-Conquest Lichfield', *ibid.* xxii (1982), 24-5.
21. '[Wilfrithus] sciebat sub Wulfario rege Merciorum ... locum donatum sibi Onlicitfelda et ad episcopalem sedem ... paratum': *Vita S. Wilfridi*, c.15. ('He knew of a place in the kingdom of Wulfhere, King of the Mercians ... which had been granted to him at Lichfield and was suitable as an episcopal see': *The Life of Bishop Wilfrid by Eddius Stephanus*, ed. B. Colgrave (1927), 33.)
22. Bede, *HE* iv. 13.
23. Bede, *HE* iii. 24; v. 24.

These, then, are the sorts of information which we get from our familiar sources about the presence of British Christians in the West Midlands in the migration period, and about the extent and efficacy of their efforts to convert the Anglo-Saxons who settled among them. Taken individually these pieces of information are not much to look at, but the whole they make is rather greater than their sum as parts. We can base on them a consistent, if largely circumstantial, case for there having been an active, well-organized British church in the West Midlands when the Anglo-Saxons arrived there, and for its having persisted, moreover, to the time when Anglo-Saxon dioceses were eventually created there.

That is the best that we can do with evidence of the accustomed sort. It reveals something of what the pagan Anglo-Saxons found in the way of Christianity and an organized church on their arrival in the West Midlands, although the picture which it allows us to draw is incomplete and unfocused. It tells us nothing, however, about how much the newly arrived Anglo-Saxon church retained of what it found already in place. For that, and for more specific information about the British church itself in the West Midlands, we must turn to topographical evidence.

This less familiar sort of historical evidence is gathered by studying the layout and organization of the human landscape in the past. Topographical evidence still exists to some extent on the ground or on reliable maps drawn in the last two centuries or so. But it is also to be found, often incidentally, in a wide range of written sources, both secular and ecclesiastical, and sometimes in placenames. If we adhere scrupulously to certain conventions, we can use this sort of evidence to throw light on a variety of problems of early medieval history. We can, for instance, discover the probable extent of the parishes served by those minster churches which were the principal centres for local religious organization in Anglo-Saxon England from the seventh to the tenth century. Sometimes we can also tease out important clues to a region's political and ecclesiastical organization *before* its assimilation by the Anglo-Saxon church.

The parishes of Anglo-Saxon minster churches were usually extensive and geographically coherent, in contrast to the much smaller or fragmented ones which typify the parochial layout of later medieval England. They were normally coterminous with an existing socio-economic land-unit (what is conventionally, if incorrectly, termed an estate).[24] In brief, for different reasons these secular land-units began to break up during the later Anglo-Saxon period and thereafter, a process which produced, for example, the numerous manors of late eleventh-century England which are recorded in Domesday Book. Meanwhile, if at a much slower rate, the minster churches saw their hold on their parishes steadily eroded by other, newer churches. Most of these were the local churches, proprietary in origin, which eventually formed the backbone

---

24. Bassett, 'Anglo-Saxon kingdoms', 20-1.

of the fully evolved parochial system of England from the thirteenth century onwards.[25]

What more, then, can we learn about the British church in the West Midlands and its legacy to the Anglo-Saxon church which supplanted it, if we add topographical evidence to our other sources? Investigations to date have revealed what look to be major British churches at some of the region's former Roman towns, together with information on their relations with the Anglo-Saxon minster churches which replaced them. The British churches to be proposed here may, moreover, in each case have been the see of a bishop, but the supporting arguments will fall far short of proof in that matter.

The western Britons certainly had bishops. Those whom Augustine met, and promptly alienated, at the end of the sixth century were said to be from the nearest British kingdoms. As the meeting was held at a spot which, in Bede's day, lay 'on the borders of the Hwicce and the West Saxons', these bishops probably included some from the West Midlands.[26] To what extent they were all diocesan, or their sees were ones which had been established in Britain in the fourth century, we do not know. The withering away of a Roman style of provincial government and of what remained of urban life need not have curtailed the role of the towns of western Britain as episcopal centres. Some of the Romano-British sees may well have disappeared. Others may have survived on their original sites or else been relocated in places more suitable to the changed conditions; and a few new sees could have been created early on.

In the fourth century there would probably have been bishops in all the cantonal capitals and some other major administrative centres of Roman Britain. If so, we could expect to find them in the West Midlands at Wroxeter, Gloucester and Cirencester, and conceivably also at such places as Wall and Kenchester.[27] The role of several of these places as Christian centres after 400 will be discussed below; but, first, Worcester is offered as an example of a settlement which is unlikely to have been a see in the fourth century but which certainly seems to have become one later on – that is to say, a British bishop's see, established long before 680.[28]

ST HELEN'S, WORCESTER

Worcester stood towards the northern end of the kingdom of the Hwicce. By 680 the Hwicce had been given their own Anglo-Saxon bishop. He

25. C. N. L. Brooke, 'Rural ecclesiastical institutions in England: the search for their origins', *Settimane di studio del Centro italiano di studi sull'alto medioevo*, xxviii (1982), 685-711; J. Blair, 'Introduction: from minster to parish church', in *Minsters and Parish Churches. The Local Church in Transition 950-1200*, ed. J. Blair (1988), 1-19.
26. Bede, *HE* ii. 2.
27. The likely whereabouts of the sees of late Roman Britain are discussed in Bassett, 'Churches in Worcester'.
28. The argument is set out fully in *ibid*.

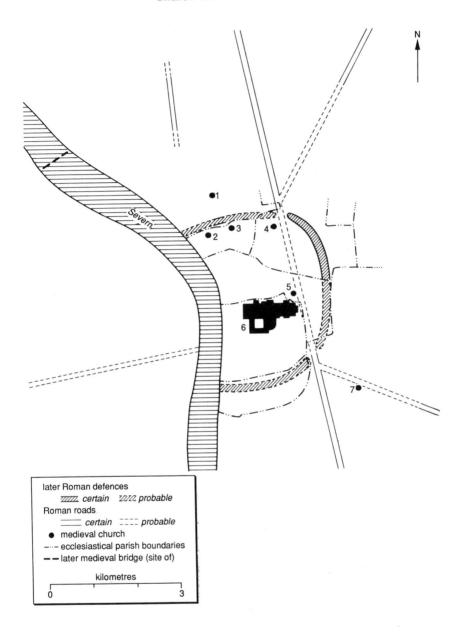

Figure 1.1 Worcester: aspects of the town in the Anglo-Saxon period,
showing the late Roman defended enclosure and relevant ecclesiastical
boundaries. Numbered sites are churches: 1. St Andrew's; 2. St Margaret's
(approximate site); 3. St Alban's; 4. St Helen's; 5. St Michael's;
6. Worcester Cathedral; 7. St Peter the Great.

established his head minster within the earthwork defences of the former Romano-British town (fig. 1.1).[29] It was dedicated to St Peter. In the later tenth century a new church, St Mary's, was built next to St Peter's as its replacement, out of which has evolved the present cathedral. Three other medieval churches also stood within Worcester's Roman defences: St Alban's, St Helen's and St Michael's. It has been suggested that St Helen's and St Alban's both originated in the pre-Anglo-Saxon period.[30] That suggestion can now be substantiated; indeed, it can be shown that St Helen's was certainly a British church and probably the seat of a British bishop.

Worcester sits on the eastern bank of the Severn at a major crossing-place. Its medieval hinterland was very extensive on both sides of the river. In the cartulary of Worcester cathedral priory there is a notification of *c.* 1113 listing twelve churches in the place's hinterland which it identifies as chapels of St Helen's (fig. 1.2).[31] Several of these were actually substantial churches in their own right, with some of the characteristics of Anglo-Saxon minster churches; but there can be no doubt that all twelve were, literally, in St Helen's parish in the early twelfth century.

It had once been even larger. Evidence derived mainly from ecclesiastical sources shows that a number of parishes which were either independent in the later medieval period or else subject to some other rural church had originally been in St Helen's parish. For example, Knightwick was a chapelry of Martley church, which was itself subject to St Helen's; and Doddenham was subject to Knightwick parish from its first appearance in our sources. Burial rights over both areas belonged to Martley until the seventeenth century at least. Knightwick and Doddenham were, therefore, both subject to Martley church and originally, through it, to St Helen's.[32] By contrast, other parishes in Worcester's hinterland were in the parish of the cathedral at their earliest appearance in the sources, or can be shown by similar means to have been in it earlier on.

So how did this pattern originate? One possibility is that St Helen's was founded in the late Anglo-Saxon period to serve as the cathedral's parish church, as may have happened in many places in England in the aftermath

29. N. Baker, 'Churches, parishes and early medieval topography', in *Medieval Worcester. An Archaeological Framework*, ed. M. O. H. Carver (*Trans. Worcs. Arch. Soc.* 3rd ser. vii, 1980), 34–5, fig. 10. It has recently been suggested that the see of Worcester had already been established by 675: P. Sims-Williams, 'St Wilfrid and two charters dated AD 676 and 680', *J. Eccles. Hist.* xxxix (1988), 168–9.
30. Baker, 'Churches', 33–4, 37.
31. *The Cartulary of Worcester Cathedral Priory (Register I)*, ed. R. R. Darlington (Pipe Roll Soc., n.s. 38, 1968), 32–3, no. 53. On its date see M. Brett, *The English Church under Henry I* (1975), 180 n.4.
32. *Taxatio Ecclesiastica Angliae et Walliae Auctoritate P. Nicholai IV circa AD 1291* [hereafter *Taxatio*] (Rec. Comm., 1802), 216; W. Thomas, 'An account of the bishops of Worcester' in his *A survey of the cathedral-church of Worcester with an account of the bishops..to..1600* (1736), 115; and 'Appendix cartarum originalium' in *ibid.* 17–18, no. 29; T. Habington, *A Survey of Worcestershire*, ed. J. Amphlett (2 vols., Worcs. Hist. Soc., 1895–9), ii, 12.

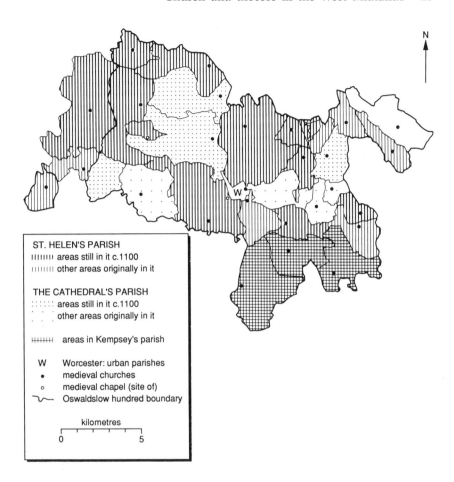

N

ST. HELEN'S PARISH
lllllll areas still in it c.1100
llllllll other areas originally in it

THE CATHEDRAL'S PARISH
:::::: areas still in it c.1100
. . . other areas originally in it

H+H+H areas in Kempsey's parish

W   Worcester: urban parishes
•   medieval churches
o   medieval chapel (site of)
ᴧᴠ— Oswaldslow hundred boundary

kilometres
0   5

Figure 1.2 Areas which lay in the parish of St Helen's, Worcester, and in that of Worcester Cathedral *c.* 1100, and other areas which had formerly been in them. Kempsey's parish is also shown.

of the Benedictine reform movement. If that was the case, fig. 1.2 merely distinguishes between the areas which the cathedral delegated to St Helen's and those which it kept in its own hands. Yet a different explanation seems to be correct: that the whole area was originally subject to St Helen's church, and that places in the cathedral's parish at the start of the twelfth century were the only ones which it had managed to take away from it.

The supporting evidence comes from two sources, one of them documentary and the other topographical. First, another notification in the cathedral priory's cartulary reports that in 1092 Bishop Wulfstan held a synod at Worcester to resolve a dispute about what the document calls 'the ancient customs and parishes of Worcester', including those of St Helen's and the cathedral.[33] After due deliberation the synod decided that there was no parish in the whole city of Worcester except the cathedral's. Christopher Brooke has rightly called this

> No doubt . . . an antique decision and [one which] represented the most conservative point of view as to the number of parishes in the city, combined with a forward-looking view as to the rights of the church, [and] of the status in canon law of bishop and parish priest.[34]

The synod's statement in support of its findings contains a remarkable admission. St Helen's, they said, had always been subordinate to the cathedral because '[it] had been a vicarage of this mother church from the days of King Æthelred [of Mercia] and Archbishop Theodore, who founded the see . . . . This institution was kept unbroken by the clerks who served in this see.'[35] These admissions – that the cathedral and St Helen's were of equal antiquity, and that the latter had always acted as the cathedral's parish church – are of the greatest significance. It was of course absurd of the synod to suggest that St Helen's had been *founded* in the late seventh century to act in that capacity (though it doubtless had been doing so for some time by 1092, as it continued to do for several centuries to come). But the circumstances surrounding the synod's statement indicate that however matters were resolved for the future, St Helen's had had good grounds for its claim to be the senior parish church of Worcester. In reality, then, St Helen's may have been the church of Worcester and its hinterland before the Anglo-Saxon cathedral was founded. If that is so, then from 680 onwards its parochial rights were steadily eroded by the newcomer, though they were not completely extinguished until the very end of the Middle Ages.

A second piece of evidence shows beyond all reasonable doubt that St Helen's was indeed a British church. The land shown in fig. 1.3 made up the core area of the bishop of Worcester's great triple hundred of Oswaldslow, with the exception of the westernmost estates. (The rest of Oswaldslow, which comprised lesser blocks of land scattered in between Worcestershire's other hundreds, does not concern us here.) The great central block can be shown to have been given to the church of Worcester by direct royal grant in its earliest years.[36] Only two peripheral areas were gained later on, at the expense of the minster churches at Hanbury and

---

33. *Cartulary of Worcester Cathedral Priory*, ed. Darlington, 31-2, no. 52; also printed, with corrections, in *Councils and Synods with other Documents Relating to the English Church*, ed. D. Whitelock, M. Brett and C. N. L. Brooke, i (1981), pt 2, 636-9. On the question of its authenticity, see Bassett, 'Churches in Worcester', n.78.
34. C. N. L. Brooke, 'The missionary at home: the church in the towns, 1000-1250', in *The Mission of the Church and the Propagation of the Faith*, ed. G. J. Cuming (Studies in Church History, 6, 1970), 64.
35. *Cartulary of Worcester Cathedral Priory*, ed. Darlington, 31.
36. Bassett, 'Churches in Worcester', 238 and n.86.

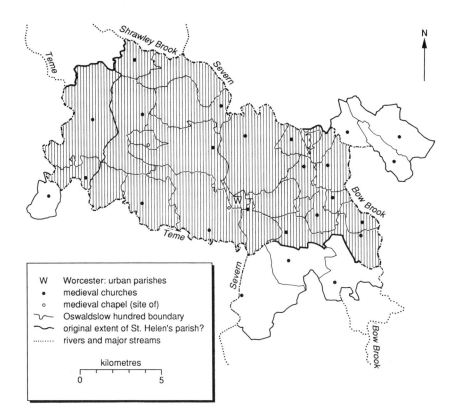

Figure 1.3 The probable extent of St Helen's parish before the creation (by 680) of the see of Worcester.

Kempsey. By 1086 the whole area was still in the church's hands, held partly by the bishop, partly by the monks of the cathedral priory.

This central block of Oswaldslow has a striking geographical unity. West of the Severn its roughly rectangular area is bounded by rivers to the north and south, though its western side mostly follows a nondescript line. East of the Severn there are sizeable streams along the eastern and much of the northern side; and if we omit the secondary acquisitions to the north-east and south, then other streams and intervening high ground complete the circuit.

This oldest block of the cathedral's lands is bounded on all sides but one by the most prominent features available. The odd one out is the western side, where the obvious natural limit is the River Teme. But the land between the Teme and the actual boundary consisted of the royal manor of Martley with its township Doddenham, lying not in Oswaldslow but in Doddingtree hundred.[37] On all available evidence it is almost

---

37. Martley: *Domesday Book seu Liber Censualis Willelmi Primi Regis Angliae*, ed. A. Farley (1783), i [hereafter DB], fos. 177a, 178a, 180c; Doddenham: *ibid.*, f.176d.

inconceivable that either place was ever held by the church of Worcester. Yet both were in St Helen's parish in the early twelfth century. From this we must conclude that the royal estate of Martley was a part of St Helen's parish *before* the cathedral gained its great block of land around Worcester, and so almost certainly before the creation of the Anglo-Saxon see by 680.

If all this is so, then St Helen's parish, at its original extent, should represent a discrete territory around the former Roman town of Worcester, which by stages passed almost entirely from royal ownership into the church's hands during the middle Saxon period. If St Helen's can be envisaged as a British church, serving a very large but geographically coherent territory, then it is not hard to imagine that that territory had an identity independent of its ecclesiastical one. At the very least we should regard it as the area under Worcester's direct control in the post-Roman period.

Worcester's position at a major Severn crossing-point probably turned a minor, defended Romano-British town into a major political centre of the post-Roman period.[38] Like Bath, Cirencester and Gloucester, Worcester probably became the focus of a British *provincia* - one of several which must eventually have been subsumed into the kingdom of the Hwicce. Worcester may well also have served as the see of a British bishop; if so, St Helen's would have been his church. It lost that role only when the first Anglo-Saxon bishop reached Worcester by 680, but its relations with the new cathedral were to echo the primacy of St Helen's church for the rest of the Middle Ages.

ST MARY-DE-LODE, GLOUCESTER

What has been suggested for Worcester may well be paralleled at Gloucester, with the role of St Helen's being played there by the church of St Mary-de-Lode. It has been tentatively proposed that it was a church of British origin;[39] but the thesis is not well substantiated as it stands. Carolyn Heighway was surely right in saying that the complex nineteenth-century geography of the parishes of St Mary-de-Lode and St Oswald's, Æthelflaed's new minster, must in origin represent the breakup of a single great parish of the middle Saxon period. She identified it as the parish of St Peter's, the minster church founded c. 679 by the Hwiccian king Osric, and gave grounds for thinking that it may have been as large as the area eventually contained by Dudstone and King's Barton hundred.[40]

There is enough circumstantial evidence to demonstrate that St Mary-de-Lode was indeed of British origin, and that it had itself served the undivided parish at all times before the foundation of St Oswald's - that is to say, both

---

38. The argument is developed in Bassett, 'Churches in Worcester', 241-3.
39. E.g. C. M. Heighway, 'Anglo-Saxon Gloucester to AD 1000', in *Studies in Late Anglo-Saxon Settlement*, ed. Faull, 46-7.
40. C. M. Heighway, 'Excavations at Gloucester. Fifth interim report: St Oswald's Priory 1977-8', *Antiq. J.* lx (1980), 217-20.

before 679 and afterwards. Establishing the original extent of that parish merely requires the use of evidence and techniques similar to those involved in the study of St Helen's, Worcester.[41] Showing that St Mary-de-Lode was of British origin, however, and that it had had an extensive extramural parish before 679 is much more difficult. Put succinctly, the case has three elements: one derived from the archaeological excavation of the church, one from its topography, and one from written sources.

The first identified structural phase of the church (period 5) is undated, and the second (period 6) is not closely datable but cannot be later than the early tenth century.[42] But the first Christian use of its site almost certainly predated the foundation of St Peter's, Gloucester's earliest Anglo-Saxon church. A timber-framed building had been erected at some time in or after the fifth century on the demolished remains of a large Romano-British courtyard house, sharing the latter's alignment. It contained three east–west aligned graves (two of them empty and the third holding an unaccompanied, headless burial), sealed below a rough mortar floor; two other orientated, unaccompanied burials to the west of it may have been contemporary depositions.[43]

The burials were apparently of pre-Anglo-Saxon date; the building itself may have stood into the middle Saxon period. It has been tentatively identified as a mausoleum or church.[44] Since its site and exact alignment were adopted by the first recognizable, if undated, structure of the present church of St Mary-de-Lode, it is a legitimate thesis that the latter was a conscious replacement of an existing, British church.

The available archaeological evidence is clearly insufficient to settle the matter. But the notion gains considerable support from St Mary-de-Lode's situation, for it lay well away from any of the several sites on which St Peter's might have been founded *c.* 679 (and from that of St Oswald's and its putative predecessor).[45] Seen in that context, its mirroring of the site and alignment of a pre-existing structure takes on a much greater significance.

Moreover, its situation not within, but well outside, the precinct of St Peter's also tells against its having originated as the latter's parish church. Wherever such an origin can be demonstrated, the subordinate church – or, as at Evesham, churches – lay within the minster's precinct, whether it was newly built for the purpose (e.g. St Michael's, Worcester) or was a church of ancient origin (e.g. St Peter's, Winchcombe).[46] The direct control, therefore, which St Peter's exercised over St Mary-de-Lode in the later

41. *ibid.*; C. M. Heighway, 'Saxon Gloucester', in *Anglo-Saxon Towns in Southern England*, ed. J. Haslam (1984), fig. 121 on 374. The writer's exploration of further sources suggests that an area even larger than that mapped by Ms Heighway can be shown to have been originally subject to St Mary's church.
42. Bryant, 'St Mary de Lode', 17; Heighway, 'Excavations at Gloucester', 219.
43. Bryant, 'St Mary de Lode', 16.
44. Heighway, 'Saxon Gloucester', 361.
45. *ibid.*, fig. 118 on 363, 366, 370-1.
46. Bassett, 'Churches in Worcester'; *idem*, 'A probable Mercian royal mausoleum at Winchcombe, Gloucestershire', *Antiq. J.* lxv (1985), 82-100.

medieval period may well not have existed until the latter had become the property of St Peter's (by the twelfth century).[47]

There is some slight evidence from a written source, too, that St Mary-de-Lode was of British origin. That source is the first three pages of the register of Abbot Frocester. Finberg argued that the account given there of the early history of Gloucester Abbey was based on a ninth-century compilation, and might, moreover, embody some much earlier, authentic material.[48] If that were so, then it is instructive to note that the text appears to allege – the Latin is execrable – that the founder of St Peter's, Osric (or possibly Eafe, by tradition its last abbess), handed over the church's endowment 'to Almighty God in heaven and the holy virgin Mary'.[49] That is, to say the least, curious, as one would have certainly expected its formal donation to be made to God and St Peter, not St Mary. As it stands, the text suggests that St Mary was thought to have a leading role in the ecclesiastical life of Gloucester in the late seventh century (or in the mid-eighth), a role which we could readily understand if the mother-church of the city and its hinterland had been dedicated to her.

The notion is reasonable, even if the evidence presented above is too fragmentary and imprecise to make for proof. The very little we know about Gloucester between the fourth century and the seventh does, however, suggest a suitable context for the origins and survival of such a pre-Anglo-Saxon mother-church. Whether or not Gloucester had been one of the sees of fourth-century Britain, its importance as a bridge-head on the Severn in the early post-Roman period would have been at least as great as Worcester's and Wroxeter's. A similar thesis can, therefore, be proposed, partly substantiated in this instance by the Anglo-Saxon Chronicle: that Gloucester became an important British political centre which controlled a substantial hinterland and was an episcopal see. As at Worcester and Wroxeter (considered below), its church would have lain quite close to the river-crossing; and as at Worcester, the eventual founding of an Anglo-Saxon minster church at Gloucester, and its endowment with much of the land in the pre-existing church's parish, would have created an anomaly on a scale likely to affect the place's parochial history throughout the medieval period.

If this model reflects historical reality it will explain the otherwise awkward discordance noted by Carolyn Heighway between the extent of St Oswald's parish (which had been carved out of St Mary-de-Lode's parish) and the manor of King's Barton at the end of the Middle Ages.[50] For if the church now known as St Mary-de-Lode had at first had Gloucester's entire

47. *Historia et Cartularium Monasterii Sancti Petri Gloucestriae*, ed. W. H. Hart (Rolls Series, 1863), I, lxxvii, no. 4.
48. H. P. R. Finberg, 'The early history of Gloucester Abbey', in *idem, Early Charters of the West Midlands*, 153–66.
49. 'et liberabat illud omnipotentis dei in celis, & sanctam Mariam uirginis': *ibid.,* 160; on the benefactor's identity: *ibid.,* 161. I am grateful to John Blair and Michael Hare for their comments on the significance of this reference to St Mary.
50. Heighway, 'Excavations at Gloucester', 219.

hinterland in its parish - the 300 *tributarii* allegedly ascribed to the city and its territory (*ciuitas cum agro suo*) in the late seventh century[51] - it would no doubt have continued to serve all royal land not granted to St Oswald's *c.* 900 and thereafter.

ST MICHAEL'S, LICHFIELD

St Michael's at Lichfield is another church which is potentially of British origin - an origin which may, moreover, have involved a migration from Roman *Letocetum* to its present site. St Michael's parish was still large in the mid-nineteenth century (fig. 1.4), containing the separate townships of Lichfield St Michael (with Freeford), Burntwood, Hammerwich, Fulfen and Streethay, as well as Fisherwick, a sizeable detached area to the east.[52] However, it may formerly have been far larger. For instance, evidence of various sorts - both topographical and written - points to its once having contained the neighbouring parishes of Whittington (including the township of Tamhorn) and Lichfield St Mary's, the church of the borough.[53]

The great Domesday manor of Lichfield held all the land discussed above. It also included the area of the parish of Lichfield St Chad. It has been suggested that St Chad's church at Stowe in Lichfield, a mile to the east of the cathedral, was the site of Bishop Chad's first cathedral, dedicated to Mary, until a new one was erected on the present site.[54] But there is no reason why this should be so; on the contrary, to judge from its isolated situation in what would then have been marshland, St Chad's is more likely to have been the 'more retired dwelling-place not far from the church' which Chad set up.[55] St Chad's parish, lying in two distinct parts

---

51. 'aliquem partem telluris, id est .CCC. tributariorum at Gleaweceasore'; Finberg, 'Early history of Gloucester Abbey', 158. See also Finberg, 'The genesis of the Gloucestershire towns', in *idem*, *Gloucestershire Studies* (1957), 55, n.2; Heighway, 'Excavations at Gloucester', 220.

52. *Inland Revenue. Tithe Maps and Apportionments (IR 29, IR 30). Part II. Nottingham to Yorkshire, Wales* (List and Index Society, vol. 83, 1972), 77, 80, 82. 84. All information about parish and township boundaries on fig. 4 is taken from the Index to the Tithe Survey map series, sheet 62 (1834), and (as appropriate) from tithe maps.

53. S. Shaw, *The History and Antiquities of Staffordshire* (2 vols., 1798-1801), i, 379; Bassett, 'Medieval Lichfield', 114-15 and refs. there.

54. Implicitly in H. P. R. Finberg, 'The Archangel Michael in Britain', in *Millenaire Monastique du Mont St-Michel*, ed. M. Baudor, iii (1971), 460; explicitly in Studd, 'Pre-Conquest Lichfield', 28. For Bede's account of the first churches there, see Bede, *HE* iv. 3.

55. 'Fecerat vero sibi mansionem non longe ab ecclesia remotiorem': Bede, *HE* iv. 3. The church of St Peter, built at an unknown date after Chad's death (but by 731), to which his bones were translated, may well have stood near to Chad's own church of St Mary. The juxtaposing of churches at major monastic sites of the middle Saxon period is a well-known tendency. For discussion of, respectively, Lichfield Cathedral's site and its early structural history: Bassett, 'Medieval Lichfield', 98; W. J. Rodwell, 'Archaeology and the standing fabric: recent studies at Lichfield Cathedral', *Antiquity*, lxiii (1989), 283-4.

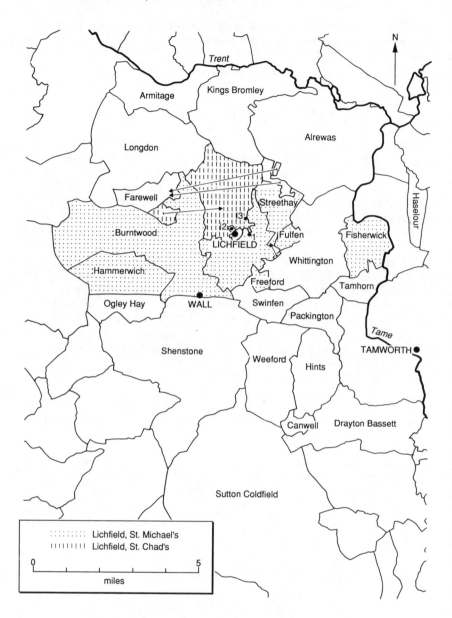

Figure 1.4 Townships in the vicinity of Lichfield in the early nineteenth century. The contemporary extents of the ecclesiastical parishes of Lichfield St Michael and Lichfield St Chad are also shown. Numbered sites are churches: 1. Lichfield St Michael; 2. Lichfield Cathedral; 3. Lichfield St Chad (at Stowe).

(together with the extra-parochial cathedral precinct), interlocks with St Michael's parish in a way which indicates that it, too, once formed part of the latter.

The same seems to be true of the small parish of Farewell. Bishop Roger de Clinton founded a Benedictine priory at Farewell *c.* 1140 on episcopal land. There was a chapel there by *c.* 1300. The core area of the parish is separated from two relatively distant detached parts by the intervention of St Chad's parish and part of St Michael's itself. Farewell, which is not separately recorded in Domesday, was apparently part of the episcopal manor of Lichfield in 1086. For these two reasons it can be assumed to have been served at first by St Michael's.[56]

In the nineteenth century St Michael's parish extended as far south as Watling Street in the vicinity of the site of the walled Roman settlement of *Letocetum* (Wall). It may at first also have included a considerable area beyond Wall, for there are very good grounds for thinking that the ecclesiastical parishes of Shenstone (including part of Ogley Hay),[57] Weeford (including Swinfen and Packington)[58] and Hints (including Canwell)[59] were

---

56. *VCH Staffs.* iii (1970), 222, 224; N. Pevsner, *The Buildings of England. Staffordshire* (1974), 131.

57. The evidence comes from the details of a dispute which arose after Shenstone church had been given by a member of the d'Oilli family to Osney Abbey (Oxon.) at, or not long after, the latter's foundation in 1129. At issue, *inter alia*, were the rights to Shenstone's spiritualities. The church of Lichfield was ultimately successful in claiming them, gaining an emphatic papal judgment *c.* 1175 that it had been unjustly deprived of the church of Shenstone and its revenues. As no claim to temporal lordship was involved, this must mean that Lichfield was Shenstone's mother-church (i.e. that Shenstone had formerly been part of St Michael's parish, for there can be no doubt that parochial responsibility for the church of Lichfield's lands lay with St Michael's, not with the cathedral itself (H. E. Savage, 'Shenstone charters', in *Collections for a History of Staffordshire*, ed. The William Salt Arch. Soc. (1923), 259, 262; *The Great Register of Lichfield Cathedral known as Magnum Album Registrum*, ed. H. E. Savage, *Collns. for a History of Staffs.* (1924), no. 170. Thereafter, Lichfield received an annual pension, latterly of 10s., from Shenstone (*ibid.* nos 24, 440; *Valor Ecclesiasticus Temp. Henr. VIII, Auctoritate Regia Institutus* [hereafter *Valor*] (Rec. Comm., 1810-34), iii, 149). Ogley Hay: Shaw, *History and Antiquities of Staffordshire*, ii, 56; DB, f.247b.

58. The church of Weeford was for a long time a perpetual curacy administered by the Dean and Chapter, since Weeford was a prebend of the church of Lichfield. Indeed it is thought to have been one of five original ones, a notion which gains some support in this instance from Domesday Book's treatment of Weeford and Packington (the latter probably including Swinfen) under the episcopal manor of Lichfield (*VCH, Staffs.* iii, 140-1; DB, f.247a). In addition Weeford's close proximity to Lichfield, and the extent to which its parish is encircled by land which was (or, in Sutton's case, which may have been) at first subject to St Michael's, make it very likely that it, too, had originally been part of the latter's parish.

59. Hints, like Weeford, was a perpetual curacy of the church of Lichfield, attached to the prebend of Handsacre. Its close link with Lichfield was certainly of Anglo-Saxon origin, for Domesday Book lists it as a member of its manor (*Valor*, iii, 510; Shaw, *History and Antiquities of Staffordshire*, i, 291-2; ii, 19; DB, f.247a). On architectural grounds it appears that there was a church at Hints by 1200 (Shaw, *ibid.*, ii, 19), but it is not recorded in Pope Nicholas's Taxation.

all once subject to St Michael's. Even the extensive royal manor of Sutton (Coldfield) could once have been in its parish, since it was presumably so named in relation to an important settlement on which it was originally dependent. To judge from Sutton's location, that should have been Shenstone, which adjoins it to the north, or else Lichfield itself.

Figure 1.4 shows that only at one point does St Michael's parish reach either of the two rivers – the River Trent and its major tributary, the Tame – by which the Lichfield region is limited to north and east. There is, however, a certain amount of evidence to suggest that it once included most, if not all, of the land up to these two rivers. To the north four places along the south bank of the Trent make up a zone of land which forms a natural adjunct to the core of St Michael's parish. The manors of Alrewas and Kings Bromley (a former chapelry of Alrewas) do not seem ever to have belonged to Lichfield; but Alrewas church looks to have been subject at first to St Michael's.[60] So more obviously do those of Longdon and Hands-acre (now known as Armitage), two of Lichfield's earliest prebends.[61]

To the east things are less clear. The ecclesiastical parish of St Edith's, Tamworth, extended westwards across the Tame into the area in question, and Drayton Bassett may also once have belonged to it. A case can be made, however (if a less well-supported one), for this whole area also having originally been subject to St Michael's.[62]

Similarly, several pieces of land beyond the Trent and the Tame which, directly or indirectly, were subject to St Michael's church may at first have belonged to other minster parishes but become attached to St Michael's as a result of their being given to the church of Lichfield at some time in the Anglo-Saxon period. Statford, allegedly one of Lichfield's earliest prebends, and Haselour, which both lie near Tamworth, are obvious candidates; another instance may be (Pipe) Ridware, one of the chapelries of Alrewas, which was a member of the manor of Lichfield in 1066.[63]

---

60. Both were royal demesne manors in 1086. On a superficial level Alrewas has the look of a superior church; but if not actually of private origin (as might be inferred from Domesday Book's record of a priest among the villeins and bordars of the manor), it was probably at first a chapel of St Michael's, since it belonged to the church of Lichfield by the mid-twelfth century and had in its parish land beyond the Trent which was in the episcopal manor in 1066 (DB, f.246a; *Magnum Registrum Album*, ed. Savage, no. 682).
61. Although Longdon does not figure in Domesday Book it was presumably in the episcopal manor by 1066, as it certainly was by the mid-twelfth century. Hands-acre was a member of that manor in 1066 (*VCH, Staffs.* iii, 141; *Magnum Registrum Album*, ed. Savage, no. 20; DB, f.247a).
62. The origins of St Edith's are hard to determine. Claimed as a royal free chapel in the fourteenth century it may have originated in the middle Saxon period as a minster church of the customary sort, or else may be a rather later foundation of the type apparently associated with a royal *burh*. In either case it could have gained royal grants of land which had until then lain in St Michael's parish (*Tithe Files. Staffs-Radnor. 1836-c.1870 (IR 18)* (List and Index Soc., vol. 226, 1987), 18; *VCH, Staffs.* iii, 311 (citing (n.32) Lich. Dioc. Regy, B/A/1/1, f.15); J. H. Denton, *English Royal Free Chapels 1100-1300* (1970), 116).
63. *VCH, Staffs.* iii, 141; Shaw, *History and Antiquities of Staffordshire*, i, 293, 389-90, 410; *Magnum Registrum Album*, ed. Savage, nos 548, 682; DB, f.247a.

There can be no doubt, then, that St Michael's parish was exceptionally large, to judge from even a conservative estimate of its original extent. If St Michael's did at first serve most or all of the region discussed above, its parish was far greater than those usually found associated with minster churches of middle Saxon foundation.

There are, however, more compelling reasons for believing that St Michael's was a church of British origin; indeed, it may in effect have been the direct successor of a late Roman or early post-Roman church – perhaps a bishop's see – at *Letocetum*. That St Michael's existed in the middle Saxon period cannot be doubted, notwithstanding the lack of any explicit written or archaeological evidence to that effect. The composition as much as the sheer size of its parish makes that plain. So too does the evident subordination to it of the church of Lichfield St Chad, whose middle Saxon origins are far more clearly indicated by its being located at a place called *stow* than by the attempts made to identify it as the site of Chad's first cathedral.[64] Moreover, had St Michael's been of later foundation than St Chad's, it surely could never have eclipsed the latter so completely.

That St Michael's existed before Chad's head minster, too, is a sustainable claim. Chiefly, it is the failure of the Anglo-Saxon cathedral to have made any discernible impact whatsoever on the parochial geography of the Lichfield region which is the most telling evidence of St Michael's primacy there. Had St Michael's been set up, as some churches were in and after the tenth century, to act as the cathedral's parish church, it is inconceivable that its parish would have been not only so large but so coherent, or indeed that it would have been situated at such a distance from its mother-church. It must, therefore, have predated it. Moreover, had it been a church of Anglo-Saxon foundation which Chad found in existence on his arrival at Lichfield, he would presumably have made it his seat. That he did not do so points to its having been of British, not Anglo-Saxon, origin. (There is a clear analogue in the case of St Helen's church at Worcester.)

But there are other pointers as well. It is very interesting to note that by the early nineteenth century, the walled area which lies astride Watling Street at the heart of Wall was bisected by the common parish boundary of St Michael's and Shenstone.[65] The walls appear to represent a mid-fourth-century or later enclosing of part of an extensive roadside settlement. It has been proposed more than once that *Letocetum* continued to be occupied well after 400, and that it may, moreover, still have controlled a large hinterland when English-speakers coined the name Lichfield.[66] The archaeological evidence, however, is extremely diffuse; and while the etymology of that name shows that *Letocetum* still had something of its

---

64. M. Gelling, 'Some meanings of *stow*', in S. M. Pearce, *The Early Church in Western Britain and Ireland* (BAR, Brit. series, 102, 1982), 187-96, at 191.
65. Index to the Tithe Survey, sheet 62 NE (1834).
66. G. Webster, *The Roman Site at Wall, Staffordshire* (HMSO, 2nd edn., 1983), 4-7; J. Crickmore, *Romano-British Urban Settlements in the West Midlands* (BAR, Brit. series, 127, 1984), *passim*; F. and N. Ball, 'Wall, Staffordshire. Roman features at SK 096 065', *West Midlands Archaeology* xxiv (1981), 118-19.

former status when Anglo-Saxons first settled in its vicinity,[67] it would be wrong to see the place as having had a role comparable to Worcester's in the migration period.

The use of Watling Street as a boundary between estates centred on Lichfield and Shenstone presumably marked the relatively early demise of *Letocetum* as an administrative focus and the consequent dismembering of its territory. By contrast, the evidence of late medieval ecclesiastical sources, by showing that an extensive area around the place was subject to a single church (St Michael's) as late as the twelfth century, invites us to surmise that in one sphere at least its role may have continued unbroken through from the early post-Roman period (if not before) into the Anglo-Saxon.

There are good grounds, then, for seeing Lichfield St Michael's as being of British origin and perhaps also the direct successor of a church at *Letocetum*. Moreover, the case has been made without recourse to the evidence (such as it is) or arguments which are customarily rehearsed in respect of St Michael's church. By introducing one such piece of evidence at this stage, however, the case is substantively reinforced.

A passage in the battle poem *Marwnad Cynddylan* tells of a raid which the Welsh under Morfael made on *Caer Lwytgoed* ('fort of the grey wood'). This can only be *Letocetum*. The raiders carried off great booty from the place, and spared neither the bishop nor 'the book-holding monks'. The passage is, admittedly, problematic, but it may well contain a genuine memory of a contemporary of Cynddylan of Powys – and, therefore, of a raid on *Letocetum* in the earlier seventh century.[68] Notwithstanding Nicholas Brooks's preference for seeing the slain churchmen as northerners installed there by Oswald rather than as Britons who had been 'permitted ... to continue at Wall to serve the needs of any British subjects' of the Mercian kings,[69] the latter interpretation of them is much more satisfactory. It is simpler, and it is wholly consistent both with the general picture of the British church's activity in the West Midlands and with the early medieval ecclesiastical topography of Wall and Lichfield discussed here.

In summary, a British bishop and monastic community may have continued to use the walled enclosure long after *Letocetum* had lost any important administrative role. The relocation of their church at the somewhat more secluded site of St Michael's at Lichfield might have been the direct result of Morfael's raid. But even if the account of that raid is invented, and the move was made for more mundane reasons, there

---

67. Gelling, *Signposts to the Past*, 59, 100; Rivet and Smith, *Place-Names of Roman Britain*, 436-7.
68. *Canu Llywarch Hen*, ed. I. Williams (1935), 50-2; D. P. Kirby, 'Welsh bards and the Border', in *Mercian Studies*, ed. A. Dornier (1977), 36-7; J. Rowland, *Early Welsh Saga Poetry: A Study and Edition of the Englynion* (1990). Dr Rowland concludes that 'The metre, vocabulary and contents [of the *Marwnad Cynddylan*] are all consistent with a seventh-century date for the poem': *ibid.*, 181.
69. N. Brooks, 'The formation of the Mercian kingdom', in *Origins of Anglo-Saxon Kingdoms*, ed. Bassett, 169.

remains the strong likelihood that the *locus* at Lichfield, which Wilfrid received from Wulfhere and then passed on to Chad, was considered 'suitable as an episcopal see',[70] not least because it had that status already.

ST ANDREW'S, WROXETER

Overall, the parochial organization of central Shropshire bears clear hallmarks of the system of minster churches set up in England in the seventh century. The church of Wroxeter, St Andrew's, was certainly an important minster church at that time. It and its neighbours kept enough of their superior status into the later medieval period for the probable original extent of their minster parishes to be discovered (fig. 1.5).[71]

Wroxeter church stands in a corner of the site of *Viroconium Cornouiorum*, which, as the fourth largest town of Roman Britain and a cantonal capital, is almost certain to have had a bishop in the fourth century. With archaeological proof of well-ordered life continuing in the town centre through into the sixth century, we can reasonably conjecture that *Viroconium*'s role as a Christian centre also continued.[72]

That it did so is most strikingly suggested by the eccentric route of the boundary between the medieval dioceses of Hereford and Lichfield,[73] which can here be taken to have followed the common border of the Magonsæte to the south, and the Wreocensæte (fig. 1.6). For most of its course the diocesan boundary was on the Severn, already a major river where it enters the region. For several miles to either side of Wroxeter, however, the boundary left the river. Two lesser deviations there are easily explained. The complex parochial geography of Shrewsbury's five or six Anglo-Saxon minster churches can be unravelled to reveal a simple middle Saxon layout, with most of the area north of the river lying in the parish of St Mary's, Shrewsbury, in Lichfield diocese, and everything south of it originally belonging to Hereford.[74] Similarly, Little Wenlock and Madeley may at first have looked to one or more central places on their own, northern, side of the river; but they were held by the church of Wenlock

---

70. See above, n.21.
71. S. Bassett, 'Medieval ecclesiastical organisation in the vicinity of Wroxeter and its British antecedents', *JBAA*, cxlv, where the argument briefly summarized below is set out in full. The church of Wroxeter was served by four priests in 1086, and remained collegiate until at least 1347: DB, f.254b; *Taxatio*, 245b, 247b; *Nonarum Inquisitiones in Curia Scaccarii temp. Regis Edwardi III* (Rec. Comm., 1807), 184; R. W. Eyton, *The Antiquities of Shropshire* (12 vols., 1854-60), vii, 314.
72. *Wroxeter Roman City. Excavations, 1966-1980*, ed. P. Barker (n.d.), 8-19; White, 'The Roman city of Wroxeter'. For the 'Wroxeter Letter', possible explicit evidence of Christianity there, see C. Thomas, *Christianity in Roman Britain to AD 500* (1981), 126-7.
73. *Taxatio*, 244-5, 247-8.
74. S. Bassett, 'Anglo-Saxon Shrewsbury and its churches', *Midland History*, xvi (1991), 1-23.

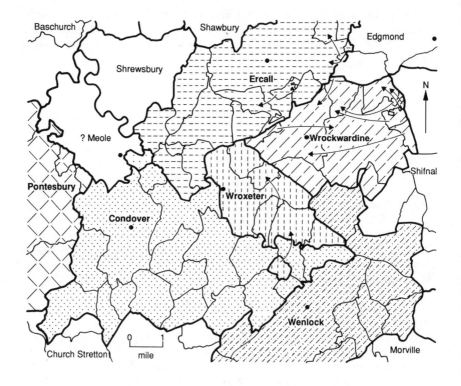

Figure 1.5 Probable Anglo-Saxon minster parishes in the vicinity of Wroxeter. Subsequent ecclesiastical parishes, including their detached parts, are also shown (except around Shrewsbury).

from well before 1066, and so were recorded *c.* 1291 as lying in the diocese of Hereford.[75]

By contrast, the diocesan boundary made one major detour from the course of the Severn which cannot be explained in such terms (fig. 1.7). This deviation takes in all the land once subject to the collegiate church of Condover.[76] The area of this former minster parish (and of Condover hundred in 1086) has a dramatic geographical unity, a semi-circle of lowland hemmed in by the northern end of the Long Mynd, Wenlock Edge, and other similarly high ground. As seen from the site of *Viroconium*, it forms the place's natural hinterland to the south; and the river-crossing and road which directly linked it to the Roman town remained intact and in use into the nineteenth century.[77]

---

75. DB, f.252b; *Taxatio*, 164a.
76. DB, fos. 253a, 254b (Berrington); *Taxatio*, 247b; Eyton, *Antiquities of Shropshire*, vi, 28–30.
77. The case for regarding this area as a British riverine land-unit, originally called Cound, which was directly controlled from *Viroconium* in the early post-Roman period is made in Bassett, 'Medieval ecclesiastical organisation'.

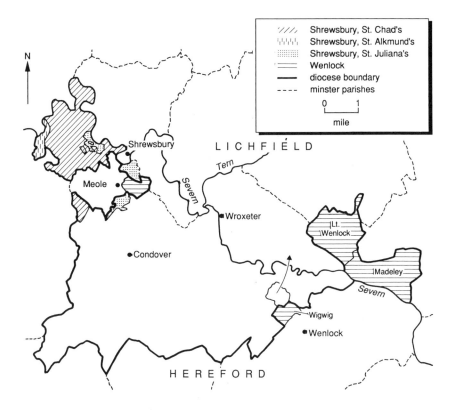

Figure 1.6 Central Shropshire: minor detours from the course of the Severn made by the common boundary of the dioceses of Lichfield and Hereford (*c.* 1291). Probable Anglo-Saxon minster parishes are shown in outline; Shrewsbury parishes are shown only to the south of the Severn.

There is nothing to suggest that the area's inclusion in the diocese of Lichfield (as opposed to Hereford) was other than the original arrangement. It should, therefore, reflect administrative links across the Severn which predate the Anglo-Saxon church's extension of its influence into the region – links which most probably originated in the control which the Britons living at *Viroconium* had maintained over the area. That is inherently likely in view of the place's continuing importance in the post-Roman period. Its southern hinterland would necessarily have been included in the region, otherwise north of the Severn, which the Wreocensæte (a people whose Old English name reflects an intimate connection with *Viroconium*)[78] came to dominate. Later on it would have become subject, together with the remainder of the territory of the Wreocensæte, to the see of Lichfield.

---

78. Gelling, *Signposts to the Past*, 59; Rivet and Smith, *Place-Names of Roman Britain*, 505–6.

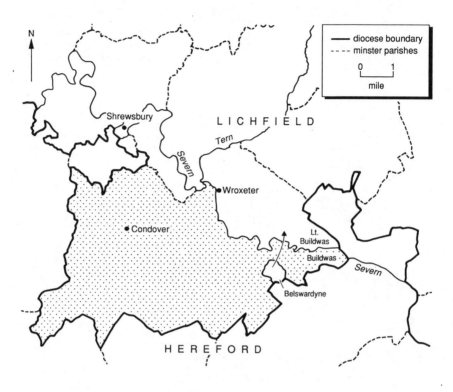

Figure 1.7 Central Shropshire: the major detour from the course of the Severn made by the common boundary of the dioceses of Lichfield and Hereford (c. 1291) in respect of the minster parish of Condover (shown stippled).

There may also be evidence of pre-Anglo-Saxon ecclesiastical links between *Viroconium* and the area in question. Two separate places south of the Severn show connections with the church of Wroxeter which are unlikely to have been formed after the region's network of Anglo-Saxon minster churches had been established - namely, the land-unit named Buildwas, which lay to either side of the Severn, and Belswardyne, a detached part of Wroxeter's minster parish which lay in the middle of Condover's.[79] These connections point directly to the possibility that the area which became Condover's minster parish had been subordinate to *Viroconium* not only in secular matters but also in ecclesiastical matters. If that were so, the church there to which it would have been subject must have been established by the Britons.[80] There is, moreover, some circumstantial evidence to the effect that the church served a district on its own

79. Bassett, 'Medieval ecclesiastical organisation' and refs. therein.
80. That church would very probably have stood on the site now occupied by St Andrew's: Bassett, 'The Roman and medieval landscape of Wroxeter'.

side of the Severn which was considerably larger than the land-unit coterminous with the Anglo-Saxon minster parish of Wroxeter. As a minimum that district seems to have comprised the future minster parishes of Wroxeter, Wrockwardine and Ercall.[81]

It must be admitted that even when all the available evidence is taken together, it is insufficient to prove that Wroxeter was an earlier, British church absorbed into the Anglo-Saxon minster system as was St Helen's, Worcester: there exists the possibility that it was newly founded in the seventh century. However, the evidence is certainly enough to support a strong supposition to this effect: and that is as much as we can reasonably hope for when searching for the British roots of the church in Anglo-Saxon England. It will be a rare occurrence indeed when it can be actually proved (as it can at Worcester) that an apparently Anglo-Saxon church was of British origin.

In conclusion, two observations are in order. The first is that the history of both British and Anglo-Saxon Christianity can be fleshed out considerably if, with due caution, we take topographical evidence into account. That appears to be true of most, perhaps all, parts of England.

Second, it has been shown here that when the Anglo-Saxons first penetrated the West Midlands – both the area of the future kingdom of Mercia and the regions further west and south-west which eventually became its satellites – they very probably encountered an active British church. It was this church which converted the immigrants. It left the missionaries from Canterbury and Iona with little to do here – and Bede with little to report, especially since he notoriously disliked the British churches and wrote them out of his *Ecclesiastical History* as much as he could.

Indeed, Canterbury's tardiness in providing so many of the peoples of the Midlands with their own bishops may not have been due simply, as Bede alleges, to a lack of suitable men. (Of course, he means suitably orthodox, and therefore not British, men.) It is likely that there were British bishops operating in the areas which Theodore eventually made into Anglo-Saxon dioceses, and this may be as true at Lincoln, for example, as at Worcester or Wroxeter. They were obviously not orthodox in the eyes of Rome (but how orthodox were the Irish bishops whom the new English church recruited?). They were probably seen as an adequate stopgap, and so were tolerated until such time as the Anglo-Saxons could at last turn out enough of their own men to take over.

It is salutary to recall that when Wine, bishop of the West Saxons, consecrated Chad to be bishop of York, he was, Bede tells us, assisted by

---

81. The evidence comprises the affiliations, both manorial and ecclesiastical, of Aston, so named in relation to Wroxeter but showing links with both Wellington (originally in the minster parish of Wrockwardine) and Wroxeter; the distribution and significance of instances of the name Ercall; and rights to the church-scot of the hundreds of Condover and Wrockwardine: Bassett, 'Medieval ecclesiastical organisation'.

two British bishops.[82] This was a wholly exceptional event (there were no other orthodox bishops in England to assist him), and so Bede pens a pithy sentence about it. However, it may very well be that what Bede does *not* tell us about British churchmen participating in the mundane affairs of the infant Anglo-Saxon church could have filled a whole book of his *Ecclesiastical History*.

---

82. Bede, *HE* iii. 28.

2   Pastoral care in early medieval Wales

HUW PRYCE

That pastoral care was provided in pre-Norman Wales is beyond doubt. Its nature and extent are, however, matters about which little can be said with certainty. Indeed the remarks of several scholars suggest that the historian approaching this topic would be well-advised to take a vow of silence. Thus, in a paper first published over a quarter a century ago, Christopher Brooke wrote that 'the true physiognomy of the Welsh Church before the Danish raids is hidden from us in impenetrable obscurity'.[1] More specifically, G. W. O. Addleshaw concluded that because the country's pastoral system had been remodelled after 1100 on the lines of the rest of Christendom, 'for most parts of Wales a reconstruction of the earlier system of pastoral care is virtually impossible'.[2] Nor did Wendy Davies, in her survey of the history of early medieval Wales, offer much encouragement, declaring that 'The occasions on which the laity came into contact with the professional Christian - monk or non-monastic cleric - seem to have been relatively limited', and also that 'we hear virtually nothing of any provision for regular ministry to the people, and nothing of parishes and parochial organization until the twelfth century.'[3]

At the root of the difficulty of ascertaining how the Christian religion was transmitted to and practised by the laity in pre-Norman Wales lies the paucity of source material. There is no body of prescriptive sources comparable with the writings of Bede or early Irish and Anglo-Saxon canon and secular law, while narrative and hagiographical evidence which might illuminate pastoral care is at a premium.[4] Nevertheless, the deficiencies of the available evidence are not so great as to render futile any consideration of the subject. After all, pastoral care must have been provided. Inscribed memorial stones show that Christianity was well established in Wales by the fifth and sixth centuries, an impression reinforced by the testimony of Gildas, writing perhaps c. 540. Admittedly his picture of British Christianity - which clearly applies to Wales, though not of course exclusively - is far from flattering.[5] Yet however much Gildas, followed later by the *Romani*

1. C. N. L. Brooke, *The Church and the Welsh Border in the Central Middle Ages* (1986), 94.
2. G. W. O. Addleshaw, 'The church between the Conway and the Dee, 400-1100', *Province* xvi (1965), 17-18.
3. W. Davies, *Wales in the Early Middle Ages* (1982), 184 [hereafter Davies, *Wales*].
4. The sources for early medieval Wales are summarized in *ibid.*, 198-218.
5. See below, p. 47.

in Ireland, Aldhelm and Bede,[6] might think that the British were bad Christians, nowhere does he or any other source accuse them of being pagans. By looking again at the contemporary sources for the church in early medieval Wales, together with those dating from the twelfth century and later, this chapter aims to highlight the problems and possibilities raised by the evidence and thereby offer some tentative conclusions about the provision of pastoral care. The bulk of the discussion will concentrate on ecclesiastical organization and what this implies about the ministry to the laity. First, however, I will summarize the evidence bearing directly on pastoral work.

Let us start with the sacrament of baptism. That baptism was administered from at least the sixth century is demonstrated by a number of sources. According to the possibly seventh-century Breton-Latin Life of St Samson, the sixth-century saint baptized and confirmed adult converts in Cornwall on his way from south Wales to Brittany,[7] and is therefore likely to have already done so in Wales after receiving episcopal status, while Bede reports that the British clergy's form of baptism was, together with their reckoning of Easter, a point in dispute with Augustine of Canterbury *c.* 600.[8] More generally, it is significant that the Welsh word for baptism, *bedydd*, was used from at least the ninth century to denote the world, in the sense of the baptized,[9] and the Welsh word *bydysawd*, first found in twelfth-century texts but presumably originating earlier, has been derived from the Latin *baptizati*.[10] In the late eleventh or early twelfth century the redactor of the vernacular prose tales, *Pedeir Keinc y Mabinogi*, assumed that baptism was synonymous with naming.[11] Since baptism was taken for granted in a number of early medieval sources, we can infer that it was administered; but if we wish to go further and find descriptions of baptisms

---

6. *Die irische Kanonensammlung*, ed. F. W. H. Wasserschleben (2nd edn., 1885), 61-2, 212-13 (*Collectio Canonum Hibernensis* xx. 6, lii. 6); *Councils and Ecclesiastical Documents Relating to Great Britain and Ireland*, ed. A. W. Haddan and W. Stubbs (1869-78), i. 202; T. M. Charles-Edwards, 'Bede, the Irish and the Britons', *Celtica* xv (1983), 42-52.

7. *La Vie de Saint Samson*, ed. R. Fawtier (1912), i. 50; Samson's own baptism in Wales is referred to in *ibid.*, i. 6. See also L. Olson, *Early Monasteries in Cornwall* (1989), 16-17; and, for different views on the Life's date of composition, H. Guillotel, 'Les origines du ressort de l'évêché de Dol', *Mémoires de la Société d'Histoire et d'Archéologie de Bretagne* liv (1977), 31-68 (early seventh century), and J.-C. Poulin, 'Hagiographie et politique. La première Vie de saint Samson de Dol', *Francia* v (1977), 1-26 (early ninth century).

8. Bede, *HE* ii. 2. See also *Venerabilis Baedae Opera Historica*, ed. C. Plummer (1896), ii. 75-6.

9. *Canu Aneirin*, ed. I. Williams (1938), line 100 and note; *Canu Taliesin*, ed. I. Williams (1960), no. 2, line 5; no. 3, lines 1, 4; *Canu Llywarch Hen*, ed. I. Williams (1935), 15 (no. 3, line 32b); I. Williams, 'Naw englyn y Juvencus', *Bull. Board of Celtic Stud.* vi (1931-3), 206, 208, 212.

10. *The Book of Taliesin*, ed. J. G. Evans (1910), 80, line 1; *Llyfr Du Caerfyrddin*, ed. A. O. H. Jarman (1982), no. 11, line 14; no. 12, line 22; *Geiriadur Prifysgol Cymru. A Dictionary of the Welsh Language* (1950-) s.v.

11. *Pedeir Keinc y Mabinogi*, ed. I. Williams (1930), 23 and note.

or discover which churches possessed baptismal rights, those sources fail us. Early Welsh poetry, possibly first written down in the ninth century, seems to take for granted a Christian world in which the laity partook of the sacraments. Thus *Y Gododdin* refers to Mynyddawg's warriors taking communion and doing penance before their attack on Catraeth.[12] Moreover two penitential texts of probable Welsh origin, first extant in a late ninth-century manuscript but assigned by Bieler to the sixth century, namely, the Synod of the Grove of Victory and Excerpts from a Book of David, lay down penances for lay persons as well as monks and other clergy.[13] Later, narrations in charters datable to the early and mid-tenth century preserved in the early twelfth-century *Liber Landauensis* relate how kings made penitential donations of land to the church following judgment in a synod.[14] More generally, the virtue of alms-giving is emphasized in a variety of sources, beginning with Gildas's *De excidio Britanniae*,[15] and continuing through the Life of St Samson[16] and the ninth- or tenth-century colloquy, *De raris fabulis*[17] to the Welsh hagiography of the late eleventh and twelfth centuries.[18] The late eleventh-century Life of St David by Rhygyfarch depicts the saint as looking after orphans, widows, the poor, weak and infirm as well as pilgrims. It also refers to his preaching before 'a vast multitude' and blessing the people at the end of mass, while Lifris in his Life of St Cadog, written at about the same time, could conceive of the people entering the saint's church on his festival to hear mass 'as usual', albeit in Scotland rather than Wales.[19]

There is also a growing amount of archaeological evidence for burial (see fig. 2.1 for the places mentioned in this chapter). This has been reviewed, together with the written evidence, by Wendy Davies and, more recently, by Heather James.[20] There is no need to go over all the ground covered by

---

12. *Canu Aneirin*, ed. Williams, lines 61, 72, 781, 917; see also *Canu Llywarch Hen*, ed. Williams, 8 (no. 2, line 1a) for a reference to confession.
13. *The Irish Penitentials*, ed. L. Bieler (1963), 3, 12-13, 68, 70-2.
14. *The Text of the Book of Llan Dâv*, ed. J. G. Evans and J. Rhys (1893; repr. 1979), 218-21, 233-4, 237-9; cf. W. Davies, *The Llandaff Charters* (1979), 120, 123-4. References in other Llandaf charters to excommunication in synods of offenders against the church, resulting in a penitential grant, appear to be late eleventh or early twelfth-century interpolations: *ibid.*, 21-4; *idem, An Early Welsh Microcosm: Studies in the Llandaff Charters* (1978), 106, 133-4.
15. *De excidio Britanniae*, cc. 27, 66, cited from *Gildas: the Ruin of Britain and Other Works*, ed. M. Winterbottom (1978) [hereafter *DEB*].
16. *Vie de Saint Samson*, ed. Fawtier, i. 2, 30.
17. *Early Scholastic Colloquies*, ed. W. H. Stevenson (1929), 6. For the date and probable Welsh origin of this colloquy see Davies, *Wales*, 213, and M. Lapidge and R. Sharpe, *A Bibliography of Celtic-Latin Literature 400-1200* (1985), 31.
18. *The Book of Llan Dâv*, ed. Evans and Rhys, 117; *Vitae Sanctorum Britanniae et Genealogiae*, ed. A. W. Wade-Evans (1944), 10, 32, 50, 122, 208, 228, 286 [hereafter *VSB*].
19. *Rhigyfarch's Life of St David*, ed. J. W. James (1967), c.31; *VSB* 100 (c.36).
20. Davies, *Wales*, 180-2, 185-91; H. James, 'Excavations at Caer, Bayvil, 1979', *Archaeologia Cambrensis* [hereafter *Arch. Camb.*] cxxxvi (1987), 51-76, esp. 64-9; *idem*, 'Early medieval cemeteries in Wales', *The Early Church in Wales and the West*, ed. N. Edwards and A. Lane (forthcoming). My discussion of burial is especially indebted to this last paper, and I am grateful to Heather James for allowing me to make use of it in advance of publication.

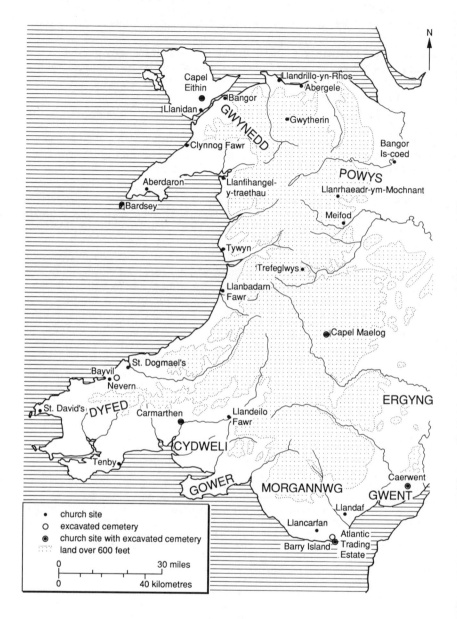

Figure 2.1 Wales: showing places mentioned in the text.

them and the excavation reports to which they refer, but the following points merit consideration in the context of the present discussion. Written sources suggest that at least high-ranking lay persons could be buried in churches or churchyards from the ninth or tenth centuries at latest. Thus a poem in praise of Tenby, *Etmic Dinbych*, refers to burial in church.[21] So too does a very small minority of the Stanzas of the Graves, also datable to that period, which describe the purported resting-places of early Welsh heroes.[22] We also have two charters, datable respectively to the eighth and the mid-tenth centuries, recording the gift of the donor's body to the recipient church for burial,[23] while in the late eleventh century the Life of St Cadog claims that the church of Llancarfan was granted the privilege of burying the kings, leaders and nobles of the kingdom of Gwynllŵg and refers to the provision of funeral vigils for laymen who bequeathed goods to the church.[24] The same Life contains a charter, datable to the late eighth century, which states that the donor made his grant for his soul and 'so that his name might be written in Cadog's book at Llancarfan';[25] a similar clause appears in the Clynnog charter, extant only in a fifteenth-century copy but clearly deriving from an earlier text, which claims that Gwithenit wished to have his name written in the Book of St Beuno, Clynnog's patron saint.[26] These statements may simply refer to the record of the donation, preserved in the saint's gospel book,[27] but they may imply some kind of liturgical commemoration of the dead, with the book functioning as a *liber memorialis*. It is also worth noting that two inscribed stones, dated by Nash-Williams to the early ninth century, call on the onlooker to bless or pray for the souls of the persons whom they commemorate.[28]

The written sources do not allow us to determine when, or indeed whether, churchyard burial became the norm for the laity as a whole prior to the twelfth century. The same is true of the archaeology. The evidence of cemeteries certainly shows that for several centuries in the post-Roman period many people in Wales were buried at sites without churches. At Caerwent, and possibly also Carmarthen, the Roman extramural cemetery continued to be used in the early Middle Ages.[29] Likewise the rural cemetery at Atlantic Trading Estate, Barry appears to have been in

---

21. I. Williams, 'Two poems from the *Book of Taliesin*', *The Beginnings of Welsh Poetry. Studies by Sir Ifor Williams*, ed. R. Bromwich (2nd edn., 1980), 158, 164-5 (lines 30-2).

22. T. Jones, 'The Black Book of Carmarthen *Stanzas of the Graves*', *Proc. Brit. Acad.* liii (1967), 100-1.

23. VSB 134 (*Vita S. Cadoci*, c.66); *The Book of Llan Dâv*, ed. Evans and Rhys, 221. Cf. Davies, *Llandaff Charters*, 118, 120.

24. VSB 90, 122 (cc. 28, 52).

25. VSB 126 (c.56). Cf. Davies, *Llandaff Charters*, 118.

26. *Registrum vulgariter nuncupatum 'The Record of Caernarvon' e codice MS. Harleiano 696 descriptum*, ed. H. Ellis (Record Commission, 1838), 258. Cf. W. Davies, 'The Latin charter-tradition in western Britain, Brittany and Ireland in the early mediaeval period', *Ireland in Early Mediaeval Europe*, ed. D. Whitelock, R. McKitterick and D. Dumville (1982), 271.

27. Cf. D. Jenkins and M. E. Owen, 'The Welsh marginalia in the Lichfield Gospels. Part I', *Cambridge Medieval Celtic Stud.* v (1983), 61-4.

28. V. E. Nash-Williams, *Early Christian Monuments of Wales* (1950), nos 125, 301.

29. *Early Medieval Settlements in Wales AD 400-1100*, ed. N. Edwards and A. Lane (1988), 37-8; James, 'Early medieval cemeteries'.

continual use from the late third to the eighth centuries, probably serving an estate of late Roman origin.[30] Admittedly in the former Roman towns the cemeteries may have acquired churches, and thus continued in use for churchyard burial. But many recently excavated sites are located on or near either Bronze Age funerary monuments or Iron Age defended enclosures. These appear to fall into Charles Thomas's category of undeveloped cemeteries, with no sign of their having been elaborated by the addition of chapels, churches or living-huts.[31] Such cemeteries were abandoned at some stage during the early Middle Ages. When this took place is difficult to determine, since dating depends on the necessarily imprecise *termini a quo* provided by a meagre number of radiocarbon dates derived from bones or wooden coffins. That undeveloped cemeteries *were* abandoned may, however, reflect an increasing tendency towards churchyard burial. This has been suggested by Heather James with regard to north-east Pembroke-shire: there she has interpreted the abandonment of undeveloped cemeteries, including Bayvil, as resulting from the emergence of powerful churches nearby at Nevern and St Dogmael's which then secured a monopoly of burial.[32] In some cases, by contrast, early medieval cemetery sites were subsequently developed with the addition of churches: there are notable examples on Barry Island and at Capel Maelog near Llandrindod Wells, where churches were built, for the first time as far as can be seen, in the twelfth century.[33] Even if these were late developers, they show that cemeteries could become the foci for religious devotion and witness to the eventual congruence of burial and church sites. Once we have more scientific excavations of cemetery sites – not one of which so far has been dug in its entirety – there is the hope that our understanding of the church's role in burial will be improved. In the meantime the most likely hypothesis is that churchyard burial became common only gradually in pre-Norman Wales, as in Anglo-Saxon England and indeed early medieval western Europe in general.[34]

We have, then, sufficient evidence to suggest that some churches and clergy ministered to the laity, or at least that they could be conceived as so doing,

---

30. See *Med. Arch.* xxxii (1988), 311.
31. James, 'Early medieval cemeteries'; C. Thomas, *The Early Christian Archaeology of North Britain* (1971), ch. 3. esp. 50-1.
32. James, 'Excavations at Caer, Bayvil', 66-8.
33. J. K. Knight, 'Excavations at St Barruc's chapel, Barry Island, Glamorgan', *Trans. Cardiff Naturalists Soc.* xcix (1976-8), 40-6; idem, 'Sources for the early history of Morgannwg', *Glamorgan County History, ii, Early Glamorgan. Pre-history and Early History*, ed. H. N. Savory (1984), 369; W. J. Britnell, 'Capel Maelog, Llandrindod Wells, Powys: Excavations 1984-87', *Med. Arch.* xxxiv (1990), 27-96. I am very grateful to Bill Britnell for allowing me to see a copy of this final report in advance of publication. On the basis of radiocarbon evidence he favours a late twelfth-/early thirteenth-century date for the first phase of the church at Capel Maelog, although stylistically it could be a century earlier. See also the brief summary in *Med. Arch.* xxxii (1988), 312-13.
34. See D. Bullough, 'Burial, community and belief in the early medieval West', *Ideal and Reality in Frankish and Anglo-Saxon Society*, ed. P. Wormald (1983), 177-201.

in pre-Norman Wales. But it is also clear that the available documentary and archaeological source material provides an inadequate basis on which to construct a general picture of how pastoral work was organized. To try and go further we need to adopt a different, more inferential approach, and explore the kinds of churches which existed in early medieval Wales. For, if we accept that pastoral care was provided, there must have been clergy to do the work. By examining aspects of ecclesiastical organization, therefore, we may be able to make some informed guesses about the structure of pastoral provision.

An obvious point of departure is the picture of the British church provided by Gildas. His *De excidio Britanniae* reveals the existence of abbots and monks,[35] but its invective was directed against the bishops and priests who were tightly enmeshed in the new political order which had emerged by the end of the fifth century in the areas under British rule: the clergy were in the pockets of tyrants like Maelgwn Gwynedd, looking to their own profit rather than the well-being of the people. Gildas clearly felt that the ecclesiastical establishment of his day neglected its pastoral duties. The eucharist was celebrated but rarely; no attempt was made to correct people's sins (indeed the clergy themselves set a sinful example, being unchaste and given to drunkenness); alms were not given as they should have been. Indeed Gildas concludes his *De excidio* by stressing the pastoral responsibilities of the *sacerdotes* and by praying that God will preserve 'the very few good pastors'.[36]

Despite this indictment, it would be rash to conclude that the British church of Gildas's day offered little by way of pastoral care. The references in the *De excidio* to bishops, priests and deacons imply some kind of ecclesiastical organization, as do four inscribed stones in north-west Wales datable to the fifth or sixth centuries, which commemorate both *sacerdotes*, probably meaning bishops, and *presbyteri*.[37] This and other evidence suggests that we are dealing with an episcopally-governed church whose origins probably lay in late Roman Britain. True, we hear of abbots and monasteries, but they are subordinate to territorial bishops.[38] It is quite conceivable that bishops ruled dioceses coterminous with the British kingdoms established during the fifth and sixth centuries. In the more Romanized, lowland areas of western Britain which continued under British rule until the late sixth century, the centres of both episcopal and royal authority may have been towns - places such as Gloucester, Wroxeter, Weston-under-Penyard (*Ariconium*) and Caerwent.[39] Thus in south-east

---

35. *DEB* cc. 28, 34-5, and see also below, pp. 51-2.
36. *DEB* cc. 66-7, 109-10.
37. Nash-Williams, *Early Christian Monuments*, 14 and nos 33, 77, 78, 83.
38. Cf. K. Hughes, 'The Celtic Church: is this a valid concept?', *Cambridge Medieval Celtic Stud.* i (1981), 1-20; C. Thomas, *Christianity in Roman Britain to AD 500* (1981), esp. 262-74; Davies, *Wales*, 169-71; *idem*, 'Charter-tradition', 278-80; R. Sharpe, 'Gildas as a father of the church', *Gildas: New Approaches*, ed. M. Lapidge and D. Dumville (1984), 200.
39. For these possibilities see K. Pretty, 'Defining the Magonsæte', *The Origins of Anglo-Saxon Kingdoms*, ed. S. Bassett (1989), 174-5, 178; Davies, *Early Welsh Microcosm*, 157-8; *idem*, *Wales*, 95; Bassett, pp. 13-40 above.

Wales, whose affinities lay with the Severn region as a whole in the Roman period, ecclesiastical organization may have evolved directly from the urban-based Christianity of Roman times. But a diocesan structure presumably also provided the model for ecclesiastical organization in those British kingdoms situated in areas which had not undergone heavy Romanization and which lacked towns: as we have seen, there were *sacerdotes* in north-west Wales. Now if, as seems to be the case, it is correct to infer the existence of a church in fifth- and sixth-century western Britain which was ruled by bishops and quite possibly organized on diocesan lines, then clearly there must also have existed Christian communities for it to serve. Admittedly, the church may have been regarded as a vehicle for furthering secular ambitions and status, and little may have been expected of the laity beyond outward conformity, especially through baptism. This was the case in Merovingian Gaul, which, as scholars have pointed out, provides suggestive resemblances with the scene depicted by Gildas.[40] Yet however short it fell of the standards demanded by Gildas, some pastoral care was surely provided.

It seems, then, that the organization of the British church in the fifth and sixth centuries resembled, and indeed continued, that which had existed in Roman Britain. Nevertheless, this was not the whole story. Organizational continuity there may have been, but it took place in a context of major economic, social and political changes resulting from the end of Roman rule in Britain. Detached from the economic and administrative structures of the Roman empire, disrupted by Irish and Anglo-Saxon raids and settlement, British society in the fifth and sixth centuries differed in fundamental respects from its Romano-British predecessor.[41] True, both secular and ecclesiastical rulers appear to have regarded themselves as the successors to Roman authority and institutions. Yet, just as commemorating the dead with titles such as *ciues* and *magistratus* could not, in reality, recreate Romano-British society,[42] neither could the continued use of Roman towns as ecclesiastical centres or the replication of an episcopally-dominated hierarchy ensure the survival of an urban-based Romano-British Christianity. The question remains, therefore, of how a church which owed much to Roman Britain in its organization and outlook adapted itself to the changed circumstances of post-Roman society in Wales. Even granted that there was a diocesan structure, what kind of ecclesiastical institutions did it comprise?

The answer usually given is that the key religious establishments in pre-Norman Wales were 'monastic'. Indeed, the history of the Welsh church from Gildas's day to the advent of the Normans has often been presented

---

40. W. H. Davies, 'The church in Wales', *Christianity in Britain, 300-700*, ed. M. W. Barley and R. P. C. Hanson (1968), 140-1, 149 n.108; J. K. Knight, 'Glamorgan AD 400-1100: archaeology and history', *Glamorgan County History, ii, Early Glamorgan*, 340. Cf. E. James, *The Franks* (1988), 127.
41. Cf. A. S. Esmonde Cleary, *The Ending of Roman Britain* (1989), esp. chs 5, 6.
42. Nash-Williams, *Early Christian Monuments*, 14, 92-3.

as consisting essentially of a falling away from a monastic golden age. Thus, for example, J. E. Lloyd related how the pristine fervour and asceticism of monastic houses founded in the sixth-century 'age of the saints' was overtaken by increasing worldliness from the eighth century onwards, due to an increase in wealth and also the attentions of the Vikings. This resulted in a transformation of what had formerly been monasteries in the strict sense of communities living by a rule into collegiate churches – known as mother-churches or *clasau* (singular, *clas*) – which had largely abandoned any regular life, including celibacy, and now consisted of hereditary corporations of canons, the head of which still used the title 'abbot'. 'The abbot was no longer an apostle, a worker of miracles, a terror to evil-doers, but simply a mighty landowner.' Indeed, by the twelfth century he might well be a layman, as at Tywyn or Llanbadarn Fawr. It was these collegiate churches, moreover (although Lloyd did not dwell long on this point), which provided the essential framework of pastoral care extending over wide *parochiae*. Such *parochiae* were sometimes apparently coterminous with secular administrative divisions, the *cantref* or commote; within them out-stations or daughter-churches, as well as estate churches, might also be established.[43]

Now, there can be no doubt that the best-evidenced ecclesiastical institutions in Wales from the sixth to the end of the eleventh century were religious establishments, each containing a group of clergy. These establishments were referred to by a variety of terms, including *ecclesia, locus, monasterium,* and *podum* in Latin,[44] *llog* (< Lat. *locus*), occasionally *mystwyr* (< Lat. *monasterium*), and especially *llan*, in Welsh.[45] To call these churches 'monasteries', however, begs questions of definition comparable to those faced by students of Anglo-Saxon *monasteria* and minsters or of ecclesiastical establishments in early medieval Ireland.

What does the ostensibly monastic vocabulary used in relation to such churches mean? Lloyd put his finger on the problem eighty years ago when, writing of ecclesiastical developments after the sixth and seventh centuries, he observed that 'it is plainly not with monasteries in the ordinary sense of the term that we have to do, but with the general framework of church organisation.'[46] The problem is best approached from two directions. First, we can inquire how far monasticism existed in pre-Norman Wales in the sense of there being communities of abbots and monks who lived a

43. J. E. Lloyd, *A History of Wales from the Earliest Times to the Edwardian Conquest* (2 vols., 3rd edn., 1939), 202-19; quotation at 214. For similar views see, for example, E. J. Newell, *A History of the Welsh Church to the Dissolution of the Monasteries* (1895), 168-9; J. W. Willis Bund, *The Celtic Church in Wales* (1897), 204-5 and *passim*; Addleshaw, 'Church between the Conway and the Dee', 17; F. G. Cowley, *The Monastic Order in South Wales 1066-1349* (1977), 2-6.
44. E.g. *Book of Llan Dâv*, ed. Evans and Rhys, 14, 72, 80; and *VSB* 10-12, 14 (*locus*); Davies, *Early Welsh Microcosm*, 121-4.
45. *Geiriadur Prifysgol Cymru* s.vv. *llan* (a), *llog*²; G. O. Pierce, 'The evidence of place-names', *Glamorgan County History, ii, Early Glamorgan*, 485-6.
46. Lloyd, *History of Wales*, 207 (this work was first published in 1911).

common life according to a rule. This is certainly a useful exercise. The trouble with it, though, is that it encourages us to look at the church as a whole through this particular pair of monastic spectacles, and thereby runs the risk of distorting our perception of ecclesiastical organization. The risk can be reduced, however, by adopting a second approach. In trying to understand what ecclesiastical communities in early medieval Wales were like, we need to keep an open mind about the significance of the monastic terminology which was applied to them and concentrate instead on the evidence for their composition and functions. Only thus are we likely to come closer to a just assessment of their pastoral role.

Evidence of a regular monastic life is by no means easy to find, even in the sixth century. It is clear that communities called *monasteria*, ruled by abbots but subject to episcopal supervision, were well established in Wales by that period. Their origins are obscure, although some seem by then to have been private aristocratic foundations.[47] Likewise, little is known about their form of life.[48] Some establishments were more austere than others. Thus, to take a well-known example, the Life of St Samson contrasts the relative comfort of Illtud's house, with its strong hereditary interests, with the more rigorous regime found at Pirus's monastery.[49] Some of the clergy in such communities had taken monastic vows; but not necessarily all.[50] How far the concept of a distinct monastic vocation continued after the sixth and seventh centuries is hard to decide. What should we make of the contrast drawn in §48 of the *Historia Brittonum*, written in early ninth-century Gwynedd, between *monks* and *laymen*?[51] Does it imply that most clergy at that time were monks in the strict sense of living according to a rule, or rather that the term had simply become synonymous with a cleric without any implication of a regular life? In addition, what weight should we give to the hints that the Irish *Céli Dé* had an impact on north-west Wales?[52] Should this be interpreted as reflecting dissatisfaction with existing forms of religious life?

In the eleventh century there were certainly signs that contemporaries

47. Hughes, 'Celtic Church', 3-5; Davies, *Wales*, 146-8. For the origins of insular monasticism, see for example, Thomas, *Christianity in Roman Britain*, 348-9 (who argues it to have been a late fifth-century innovation of Mediterranean derivation); and K. R. Dark, 'Celtic monastic archaeology: fifth to eighth centuries', *Monastic Studies* xiv (1983), 20 (who airs the possibility that some villa sites, such as Llandough and Llantwit Major in Glamorgan, became monastic sites in the sub-Roman period as some villas did in Gaul). Cf. also Knight, 'Glamorgan AD 400-1100', 328-9.
48. Davies, *Wales*, 151-5.
49. *Vie de Saint Samson*, ed. Fawtier, i. 14, 16-21. Cf. Sharpe, 'Gildas as a father of the church', 199-200.
50. *Irish Penitentials*, ed. Bieler, 60 (Gildas's Preface on Penance, cc. 1, 3).
51. *Nennius: British History and the Welsh Annals*, ed. J. Morris (1980), 73.
52. W. Reeves, *The Culdees of the British Islands* (1864), 21, 61-2; C. N. Johns, 'The Celtic monasteries of north Wales', *Trans. Caernarvonshire Hist. Soc.* xxi (1960), 30-1; T. M. Charles-Edwards, 'The seven bishop-houses of Dyfed', *Bull. Board of Celtic Stud.* xxiv (1970-2), 259. Cf. Knight, 'Sources for the early history of Morgannwg', 372.

recognized a distinct monastic vocation. We hear of the death in 1012 of Haearnddrud, a monk from Bardsey,[53] and later in the century Caradog was tonsured by Bishop Herewald of Llandaf, proceeding to lead an apparently eremitical existence at a number of different sites in south Wales.[54] Also worth considering is the account in Rhygyfarch's Life of St David of the monastic regime at St David's under its patron saint, depicting a common life of prayer, worship and physical labour and frequently referring to both *monasterium* and *monachi*.[55] Yet Rhygyfarch himself belonged to a hereditary ecclesiastical family to whom such rigours would surely have been alien,[56] and it may well be significant that he refers to St David's once as a *monastica classis*, implying that other kinds of *classis* - whence the Welsh noun *clas* - were known.[57] Moreover, the other late eleventh-century Welsh saint's Life, that of St Cadog, includes material which speaks of the *canons* of Llancarfan, each with his own prebend, who allegedly served the church *regulariter*.[58] This was probably nearer the norm at the end of our period in churches headed by abbots; possibly the monastic vocation survived primarily for individuals who wished to adopt an eremitical life.

Let us move on to consider the composition of early Welsh ecclesiastical communities, and inquire in particular whether they contained ordained clergy who could have undertaken pastoral work. Another way of putting this is to ask whether bishops, priests and deacons with pastoral responsibilities were normally based in churches which were referred to in monastic terms. That the answer to this must be in the affirmative is suggested by a variety of sources from the sixth century onwards. Thus Gildas's Preface on Penance and the Synod of North Britain, texts argued by Bieler to date from the sixth century, assume that communities will contain bishops, priests and deacons as well as abbots and monks, and the former text distinguishes priests and deacons who had taken monastic vows from those who had not.[59] Bishops were consecrated in Illtud's monastery by Bishop Dyfrig and other bishops according to the Life of St Samson,[60] while Bede condemned the priests from Bangor Is-coed who prayed King Brochfael at the battle of Chester *c.* 616, and claimed that in addition to a multitude of monks that monastery contained a holy anchorite.[61] It is worth adding in this connection that nothing in Gildas's

53. *Brut y Tywysogyon or the Chronicle of the Princes, Red Book of Hergest Version*, ed. and transl. T. Jones (2nd edn., 1973), 18-19.
54. *Nova Legenda Anglie*, ed. C. Horstmann (1901), i, 174-6; see too the discussion in Cowley, *Monastic Order in South Wales*, 6-7.
55. *Rhigyfarch's Life of St David*, ed. James, cc. 21-32.
56. N. K. Chadwick, 'Intellectual life in west Wales in the last days of the Celtic Church', *Studies in the Early British Church*, ed. *idem* (1958), 164-72. See also R. Bartlett, 'Rewriting saints' Lives: the case of Gerald of Wales', *Speculum* lviii (1983), 604.
57. *Rhigyfarch's Life of St David*, ed. James, c.20; *Geiriadur Prifysgol Cymru* s.v. *clas*.
58. *VSB* 120 (c.48); cf. Brooke, *Welsh Church and the Border*, 90-1.
59. *Irish Penitentials*, ed. Bieler, 3, 60, 62, 66.
60. *Vie de Saint Samson*, ed. Fawtier, i. 42-4.
61. Bede, *HE*, ii, 2.

De excidio rules out the possibility that the clergy whom he castigates also lived in communities. While bishops, priests and deacons occupy centre stage by comparison with monks, his text does not necessarily draw a sharp distinction between a secular and a monastic church. Even at the beginning of the Middle Ages, then, it appears that monastic communities in Wales contained what in later centuries would have been termed both secular and monastic clergy, and this may imply in turn that such communities could have provided for the pastoral needs of the laity outside them.

A similar picture of churches, described in monastic terms and containing a variety of ecclesiastical personnel, emerges from sources of the ninth century and later. Asser referred to the bishopric of St David's as a *monasterium* with a *paruchia* in the late ninth century, and *Liber Landauensis* refers to Llandaf as an *(archi)monasterium* in the early twelfth century.[62] The ninth- or early tenth-century colloquy *De raris fabulis*, which is probably of Welsh origin, lists the members of its idealized monastic *familia* as *seniores*, *sacerdotes*, and *presbiteri* together with boys and dependants, and elsewhere speaks of the abbot of the *podum*.[63] At the end of the eleventh century the community of Llancarfan was said to contain an abbot, teacher (*doctor*), and priest (*sacerdos*) as well as canons.[64] In some cases, then, a community might be headed by a bishop, as at St David's and, it seems, Llandeilo Fawr by the ninth century, Llandaf by the eleventh century, and also Bangor and possibly Llanbadarn Fawr, but the use of a common monastic terminology suggests that there was little if anything to distinguish these communities from those under abbots.[65] This is suggested too by the short passage on the seven bishop-houses of Dyfed, preserved in the Welsh lawbooks and probably deriving from a pre-Norman text, which may be interpreted as asserting the superiority of the bishop of St David's over lesser monastic communities ruled by abbots.[66] None of this is particularly remarkable: bishops were found in early Irish monasteries, Anglo-Saxon minsters (and from the tenth century in reformed Benedictine cathedral monasteries), and also in early medieval Galicia, where Martin of Braga and his successors at Dumio had their episcopal seat in a monastery.[67] The bishop-houses might also be compared with episcopal minsters in England such as Beverley, Ripon and Southwell, which were subject to the archbishop of York.[68]

62. *Asser's Life of King Alfred*, ed. W. H. Stevenson (new edn., 1959), 65-6 (c.79); *Book of Llan Dâv*, ed. Evans and Rhys, 74, 86, 129, 144, 214.
63. *Early Scholastic Colloquies*, ed. Stevenson, 2. For another example of a *senior* in a monastic community, see *Rhigyfarch's Life of St David*, ed. James, c.29.
64. VSB 120, 122 (*Vita S. Cadoci*, cc. 49, 50).
65. Davies, *Wales*, 158-60; idem, *Early Welsh Microcosm*, 149-50.
66. Charles-Edwards, 'Bishop-houses', 247-62. Cf. Davies, *Wales*, 160; and Knight, 'Glamorgan AD 400-1100', 341.
67. R. Collins, *Early Medieval Spain: Unity in Diversity, 400-1000* (1983), 83-4.
68. C. N. L. Brooke, 'Rural ecclesiastical institutions in England: the search for their origins', *Settimane di studio del Centro Italiano di studi sull'alto medioevo*, xxviii (Spoleto, 1982), 695.

Furthermore, native Welsh churches which were not in any sense Benedictine houses or communities of regular canons continued to be described in monastic terms in the twelfth and thirteenth centuries and even later. St Michael's church at Trefeglwys in Arwystli, mid-Wales, was called a *monasterium* on its foundation in the second quarter of the twelfth century, while the church of Llanidan in Anglesey was referred to as a *monasterium* in a document of 1360.[69] The testimony of the Welsh laws, whose earliest extant texts date from the late twelfth and early thirteenth centuries, together with that of Gerald of Wales and of other sources, reveals churches with communities headed by abbots in those areas of the country still under native control. Admittedly, the abbot might be a layman, as at Llanbadarn Fawr in 1188, and the community might consist of clerical and/or lay portioners, but there are strong grounds for supposing that such establishments normally included ordained priests who administered the sacraments. Thus Gerald of Wales, in condemning the way in which laymen had taken over the lands belonging to Llanbadarn Fawr, noted that the laymen's clerical kinsmen served at the altar; and other sources dating from the thirteenth century and later show that churches headed by individuals who used the title 'abbot' had one or more priests.[70] Likewise, rules in the Welsh lawbooks laying down the compensation payments to which churches were entitled for sacrilege state (in all but one version) that those churches will have priests as well as an abbot and community, almost certainly denoting portioners. Moreover, entitlement to compensation was conditional on the abbot's being educated and ordained.[71]

Obviously it is difficult to know how far native Welsh churches of the twelfth and thirteenth centuries resembled those of the pre-Norman period. There are indeed grounds for suspecting that the twin processes of lay appropriation of ecclesiastical lands and their hereditary transmission in portions resulting from partible inheritance gathered steam only in the wake of social and demographic changes beginning around 1100.[72]

---

69. 'Wynnstay MSS. - charters of Trefeglwys', ed. R. Williams, *Arch. Camb.* 3rd ser. vi (1860), 331; and see also *The Cartulary of Haughmond Abbey*, ed. U. Rees (1985), no. 1216, which calls Bleddrws, the founder of the *ecclesia* at Trefeglwys, a *monachus*; H. Rowlands, 'Antiquitates parochiales', *Arch. Camb.* iii (1848), 166 (Llanidan).
70. *Giraldi Cambrensis Opera*, ed. J. S. Brewer, J. F. Dimock and G. F. Warner (Rolls Series, 21, 1861-91), vi, 120-1 (*Itinerarium Kambriae*, ii, 4); J. C. Davies, 'Strata Marcella documents', *Montgomeryshire Collections*, li (1949-50), 181, 183; Lloyd, *History of Wales*, 206-7, n.60.
71. E.g. *Welsh Medieval Law*, ed. and transl. A. W. Wade-Evans (1909), 113-14; *The Latin Texts of the Welsh Laws*, ed. H. D. Emanuel (1967), 217, 290, 337; *Llyfr Iorwerth*, ed. A. R. Wiliam (1960), 23-4 (§43) (transl. *The Law of Hywel Dda. Law Texts from Medieval Wales*, ed. and transl. D. Jenkins (1986), 41). Cf. J. W. Evans, 'The early church in Denbighshire', *Trans. Denbighshire Hist. Soc.* xxxv (1986), 68-80; *Lawyers and Laymen. Studies in the History of Law presented to Professor Dafydd Jenkins on his seventy-fifth birthday* (1986), 340 s.v. canonwyr.
72. H. Pryce, 'Ecclesiastical wealth in early medieval Wales', *Early Church in Wales and the West*, ed. Edwards and Lane (forthcoming).

Whenever they first occurred on a wide scale, however, these processes would probably have made little difference to a church's capacity to provide pastoral care. As we have seen, the seizure by laymen of a church's property and even the title of abbot did not necessarily deprive a church of the means to provide pastoral care, since it would still, in some instances at least, be expected to possess one or more ordained clerics.[73]

The cumulative impression conveyed by the evidence, then, is that a key component of the ecclesiastical structure in Wales from the sixth century onwards were communities to which monastic vocabulary was applied, but which also contained ordained clergy who could have performed pastoral work. What should we call these communities? As we have seen, the sources have no consistent way of describing them. Modern scholarship has, on the whole, adopted an approach similar to Lloyd's: when dealing with the period up to about the eighth century, we hear of monasteries; thereafter, the preferred terms are mother-church or *clas* (plural *clasau*).[74] From the twelfth century onwards *clas* is used in a number of texts to denote a community associated with, and usually enjoying rights in, an ecclesiastical establishment under an abbot.[75] There is, however, no clear evidence that *clas* was used in this way in the pre-Norman period, though, as we have seen, the Latin noun from which it derives, *classis*, occurs in the late eleventh-century Life of St David by Rhygyfarch.[76] This does not of course prevent us from using *clas* as a convenient label. The difficulty is that it is often lumbered with pejorative connotations which tend to belittle the role of the churches to which it is applied. For, as in the case of the Anglo-Saxon minster with which it has been compared, the *clas* has in the past been regarded as a degenerate kind of religious community which had deviated from the true monastic path.[77] One solution would be to drop *clas* in favour of *monasterium* when referring to any early medieval Welsh church which contained a group of clergy. The latter term is after all used to describe such churches in both pre-Norman and later sources. In this respect it is preferable to minster, which is never used in this way in Wales, although either term has the advantage of being more neutral

---

73. Cf. H. Pryce, 'Church and society in Wales, 1150-1250: an Irish perspective', *The British Isles 1100-1500. Comparisons, Contrasts and Connections*, ed. R. R. Davies (1988), 40.
74. See above, p. 49 and n.43.
75. E.g. *Giraldi Cambrensis Opera*, ed. Brewer *et al.*, iii, 153-4; *Hen Gerddi Crefydd-ol*, ed. H. Lewis (1931), no. 16, lines 89-90; no. 35, line 159; *Llyfr Iorwerth*, ed. Wiliam, 23, 44 (§§ 43, 71) (transl. Jenkins, *The Law of Hywel Dda*, 41, 82); *Damweiniau Colan*, ed. D. Jenkins (1973), 32-3 (§ 326); *Medieval Welsh Society: Selected Essays by T. Jones Pierce*, ed. J. B. Smith (1972), 395. See also the valuable discussion in J. W. Evans, 'The survival of the clas as an institution in medieval Wales', *Early Church in Wales and the West*, ed. Edwards and Lane (forthcoming).
76. See above, p. 51, and also L. Fleuriot, 'Les évêques de la "clas Kenedyr", évêché disparu de la région de Hereford', *Études Celtiques* xv (1976-8), 225-6.
77. C. A. R. Radford, 'The Celtic monastery in Britain', *Arch. Camb.* cxi (1962), 21; cf. R. W. D. Fenn, 'The age of the saints', *A History of the Church in Wales*, ed. D. Walker (1976), 16; and Knight, 'Sources for the early history of Morgannwg', 371.

than 'monastery', with its implications of a regular life.[78]

The possibility cannot be eliminated that the ordained clergy in early Welsh *monasteria* were there solely for the purpose of serving members of the church's community and exercised no pastoral role amongst the laity outside. This is, however, extremely unlikely. The churches under discussion were the most important ecclesiastical centres in Wales, and some of them served as bishops' seats. Admittedly, as will be argued below, there must have been other churches and foci for lay devotion in early medieval Wales apart from *monasteria*. But since there is no reason to suppose that the latter were rivalled in importance by radically different kinds of churches whose primary function was to provide pastoral care, it is difficult to believe that the clergy of *monasteria* took no part in the ministry to the laity. As we have seen, we are not dealing with a society which drew sharp functional distinctions between monks and canons or between monastic and secular churches. The same was true in other parts of Europe: churches which were described in monastic language – such as the baptisteries of Lombard Italy (some of which were referred to by the terms *monasterium* or *abbatia*), early Irish monastic churches or the minsters of Anglo-Saxon England – carried out or supervised pastoral work in the areas around them.[79] Welsh *monasteria* were probably no different. Where Wales did differ from the Carolingian and post-Carolingian Continent or Anglo-Saxon England was that Benedictine monasticism began to take root there only from the late eleventh century.[80] Therefore (as in Ireland also) distinctions between regular and other kinds of religious communities appeared relatively late: as far as we can see, there had been no equivalent in Wales of Benedict of Aniane's reforms or the tenth-century Benedictine reformation in England, not least perhaps because Welsh rulers had lacked the inclination to encourage them.[81]

In what ways and to what extent did the clergy in early Welsh religious communities contribute to pastoral care? To try and answer these questions we need to turn from the composition of *monasteria* and consider their place in the church organization as a whole. Here we have to rely heavily on working back from the ecclesiastical framework revealed by twelfth and thirteenth-century sources. These show a pattern of mother and daughter-churches similar to that found over much of western Europe.

---

78. Davies, *Early Welsh Microcosm*, 122, chooses to use the term 'monastery', but adds that 'it should not be taken as implying a difference between secular and monastic religious communities which can neither be sustained nor demonstrated.'
79. C. E. Boyd, *Tithes and Parishes in Medieval Italy* (1952), ch. 3, esp. 61-4; R. Sharpe, 'Some problems concerning the organization of the church in early medieval Ireland', *Peritia*, iii (1984), 251ff.; and for Anglo-Saxon England see, for example, Thacker pp. 137-70 below and Foot, pp. 212-25 below; and also S. Foot, 'Parochial ministry in early Anglo-Saxon England: the role of monastic communities', *Studies in Church History* xxvi (1989), 43-54. See too the wide-ranging survey in G. Constable, 'Monasteries, rural churches and the *cura animarum* in the early Middle Ages', *Settimane di studio*, xxviii (1982), 349-89.
80. Cowley, *Monastic Order in South Wales*, ch. 2.
81. *ibid.*, 3; Brooke, *Welsh Church and the Border*, 3.

Thus in their rules on sacrilege the Welsh lawbooks speak of mother-churches or churches of the highest rank, consisting of an abbot, community and priests; these are explicitly contrasted with other churches or chapels in the north Welsh Iorwerth Redaction.[82] Such mother-churches are almost certainly the same as 'the greater churches to whom antiquity allows greater reverence' which Gerald of Wales tells us possessed exceptionally extensive sanctuary rights at the end of the twelfth century.[83] As in England the rights of mother-churches were defined in writing in the twelfth and thirteenth centuries. Thus it was agreed between 1165 and 1183 that the newly founded chapel of Crick should be served by the rector of Caerwent on certain specified days, but otherwise the inhabitants of Crick were to attend services at the mother-church of Caerwent, which retained the right to all their baptismal, burial and other parochial dues.[84]

Caerwent was certainly a pre-Norman foundation, known from perhaps the late ninth and certainly the mid-tenth century though possibly founded much earlier;[85] other mother-churches of the twelfth and thirteenth centuries can be shown to have pre-Norman origins. It is probably reasonable to conclude, therefore, that many mother-church *parochiae* originated prior to the twelfth century. In addition, there seems no reason to dissent from previous scholars' arguments that the *parochiae* of pre-Norman mother-churches were large, normally coinciding with the secular administrative divisions of the *cantref* or commote.[86] They would therefore have resembled early minster *parochiae* in England and Scotland, which seem to have been coterminous with *regiones* or *prouinciae*, often corresponding to secular administrative districts centred on royal vills.[87] Such generalizations of course need to be tested in local studies and it must be stressed that much remains to be done in mapping the territorial divisions and ecclesiastical geography of medieval Wales. But there is certainly evidence, particularly from the well-studied diocese of St Asaph, that thirteenth-century mother-churches not only held authority over extensive areas but that they were the only major churches within a given commote

82. See n.71 above, and cf. the list of 'highest-ranking churches' (*eglwysseu pennaduraf*) to whom Gruffudd ap Cynan made bequests before his death in 1137; *Historia Gruffud vab Kenan*, ed. Evans, 31-2.
83. *Giraldi Cambrensis Opera*, ed. Brewer *et al.*, vi, 203 (*Descriptio Kambriae*, i. 18). Cf. the high status accorded to 'old minsters' in late Anglo-Saxon law.
84. *Llandaff Episcopal Acta 1140-1287*, ed. D. Crouch (1989), no. 6. Cf. J. C. Davies, *Episcopal Acts and Cognate Documents Relating to Welsh Dioceses, 1066-1272* (1946-8), ii, 584-8.
85. S. Keynes and M. Lapidge, *Alfred the Great. Asser's 'Life of Alfred' and Other Contemporary Sources* (1983), 261; Davies, *Early Welsh Microcosm*, 136, 146; J. K. Knight, 'St Tatheus of Caerwent: an analysis of the Vespasian Life', *The Monmouthshire Antiquary*, iii (1970-8), 29-36.
86. See above, p. 49 and n.43. Cf. Lloyd, *History of Wales*, ch. 8, and R. R. Davies, *Conquest, Coexistence and Change. Wales 1063-1415* (1987), 12-13, 20-3.
87. See, for example, G. W. S. Barrow, *The Kingdom of the Scots* (1973), ch. 1, esp. 26ff.; J. Blair, 'Minster churches in the landscape', *Anglo-Saxon Settlements*, ed. D. Hooke (1988), 35-40; S. Bassett, 'In search of the origins of Anglo-Saxon kingdoms', *Origins of Anglo-Saxon Kingdoms*, ed. *idem*, 17-21; J. Blair, 'Frithuwold's kingdom and the origins of Surrey', *ibid.*, 103-5.

or group of commotes: Llandrillo-yn-Rhos (Dineirth), Abergele, Gwytherin, Llanrhaeadr-ym-Mochnant and Meifod are cases in point, and are all churches for which we have evidence suggesting pre-Norman origins – Abergele, for example, had a *princeps*, almost certainly meaning head of a religious community, who died in 858.[88] It should also be noted that with the exception of Cemais, each of the seven *cantrefi* of Dyfed seems to have been provided with a bishop-house, according to the passage in the Welsh lawbooks mentioned earlier.[89]

The question remains, however, of when the chapels and dependent churches referred to in twelfth- and thirteenth-century sources were first established. Some were clearly recent foundations, concomitants of expanding population and settlement. The earliest evidence for the consecration of new churches, to be served by single priests, comes from the second half of the eleventh century, when Bishop Herewald of Llandaf (1056–1104) is recorded as consecrating churches, most of which appear to have been new foundations by lay *heredes* – in other words, it seems, estate churches – in Ergyng (Archenfield), Gower, Cydweli and Ystrad Yw.[90] Anglo-Norman conquest and settlement gave a further impetus to this proliferation of churches in south Wales, but similar developments took place in areas of Wales outside Anglo-Norman control.[91] Thus the Welsh lawbooks contain a rule, probably dating from the twelfth or early thirteenth century, which envisages a king's giving his consent for a church to be built in a bond vill; if mass was celebrated in the church and bodies were buried there, the vill became free.[92] In addition the biography of Gruffudd ap Cynan, who died in 1137, boasts that in his time Gwynedd 'came to shine with whitewashed churches, like stars in the firmament', and even if this simply refers to rebuilding wooden churches in stone, other evidence shows that churches were founded *ab initio* too, such as Llanfihangel-y-traethau in Merioneth, founded by the Lady Gwleder during the reign of Gruffudd's son and successor, Owain Gwynedd.[93]

---

88. D. R. Thomas, *The History of the Diocese of St Asaph* (new edn., 1906-13), i, 7-8, 492-5; ii, 240, 312; iii, 188, 210; O. E. Jones, 'Llyfr Coch Asaph. A textual and historical study' (unpubl. M.A. thesis, Univ. of Wales (Aberystwyth), 1968), ii, 10-17, 41-50; Evans, 'Early church in Denbighshire', 61-81. The probable antiquity of Gwytherin, Llanrhaeadr-ym-Mochnant and Meifod is suggested by the pre-Norman inscribed stones and sculpture which survive there: Nash-Williams, *Early Christian Monuments*, nos 177, 180-1, 295. It is also worth noting that Meifod and Dineirth are named amongst the 'highest-ranking churches' which received bequests from Gruffudd ap Cynan: *Historia Gruffud vab Kenan*, ed. Evans, 32.
89. Charles-Edwards, 'Bishop-houses', 251-2, 262.
90. *Book of Llan Dâv*, ed. Evans and Rhys, 275-9.
91. F. G. Cowley, 'The church in Glamorgan from the Norman conquest to the fourteenth century', *Glamorgan County History, iii, The Middle Ages*, ed. T. B. Pugh (1971), 115-16; Davies, *Episcopal Acts*, i, 49-54; ii, 584-8; A. D. Carr, *Medieval Anglesey* (1982), 38.
92. E.g. *Welsh Medieval Law*, ed. Wade-Evans, 51; *Latin Texts of the Welsh Laws*, ed. Emanuel, 132; *Llyfr Colan*, ed. D. Jenkins (1963), 34 (§ 573).
93. *Historia Gruffud vab Kenan*, ed. Evans, 30; Nash-Williams, *Early Christian Monuments*, no. 281.

Unfortunately the dates of foundation of most chapels and dependent churches are unknown, and we therefore cannot be certain that they became numerous only from the late eleventh century onwards. If they did, it appears that in much of pre-Norman Wales what came to be termed mother-churches from the twelfth century onwards had few daughters and would thus have been directly responsible for pastoral work over wide areas in which there were few other churches. That this may well have been so in mountain areas – nearly 60 per cent of the surface of Wales is over 500 feet above sea-level – is suggested by the large size of upland parishes later in the Middle Ages: that of Llanbadarn Fawr, the largest in Wales, may have been exceptional in encompassing almost 200 square miles, but it has been asserted that it was quite usual for a parish to cover 20-30 square miles.[94] In the river valleys and lowlands, by contrast, the pattern is likely to have been different. Although evidence for early medieval Welsh settlement is meagre,[95] these were surely the areas where the bulk of the (albeit probably sparse) population lived. Here we might expect the *regiones* upon which mother-church *parochiae* were based to have had estates carved out of them to endow churches and lay proprietors at an earlier date than those in the less productive upland areas. The ecclesiastical and lay estates thus created could in turn have formed new units of ecclesiastical organization, based on tenurial relationships, thereby undermining the integrity of mother-church *parochiae*.

Such developments may have been under way from a very early date in at least one corner of early medieval Wales. The Llandaf charters show a dense concentration of almost sixty churches in the far south-east, in Gwent and Ergyng (Archenfield), some of which were in existence as early as the seventh, or possibly even the late sixth, century (fig. 2.2). Since most only appear in a single charter reference, we cannot tell how long they survived, although Diane Brook has pointed out that a significant minority re-emerge as Llandaf cathedral prebends by the mid-thirteenth century.[96] If in fact the bulk of the churches did coexist for a considerable time, this might indicate, as Wendy Davies has argued, an unusually well-developed system of rural pastoral care by the seventh and eighth centuries.[97] Of course, as Professor Davies has also observed, it may well be that the concentration of ecclesiastical provision in Gwent and Ergyng was not typical of Wales as a whole, which may have resembled rather the situation in Glamorgan, where the charters refer to only some ten churches.[98] The density of churches in Gwent and Ergyng could then be seen as reflecting the early fragmentation of territorial units – perhaps coterminous with mother-

94. G. Williams, *The Welsh Church from Conquest to Reformation* (2nd edn., 1976), 15.
95. For a recent survey see the introduction to *Early Medieval Settlements in Wales*, ed. Edwards and Lane.
96. Davies, *Early Welsh Microcosm*, 122-4, 134-8; D. Brook, 'The early Christian church in Gwent', *The Monmouthshire Antiquary* v. 3 (1985-8), 72-4.
97. W. Davies, 'The myth of the Celtic Church', *The Early Church in Wales and the West*, ed. Edwards and Lane (forthcoming).
98. Davies, *Wales*, 143-5.

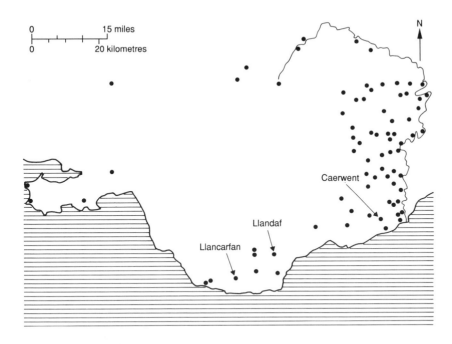

Figure 2.2 Church sites in south-east Wales. (After W. Davies, *Wales in the Early Middle Ages* (1982), fig. 50.)

church *parochiae* – in a region of low-lying, fertile and relatively well-populated land into estates which were provided, possibly with episcopal permission or encouragement, with their own places of worship.

That the south-east was different in important respects from the rest of Wales is clear enough, and the differences may have extended to the organization of pastoral care. Yet the contrast may have been less stark than the distribution of known early medieval ecclesiastical sites would seem to indicate. This is for two reasons in particular.

First, as John Lewis and Jeremy Knight have argued with respect to Dyfed and Glamorgan, it may be possible to identify early ecclesiastical sites for which we have no early written evidence from the distribution of inscribed and cross-decorated stones (Nash-Williams's Groups I and II, broadly datable to the period from the late fifth to the ninth centuries), working on the assumption that where several such stones survive together, they are likely to indicate an early Christian centre.[99]

99. Nash-Williams, *Early Christian Monuments*, 3-27; J. M. Lewis, 'A survey of early Christian monuments of Dyfed, west of the Taf', *Welsh Antiquity*, ed. G. C. Boon and J. M. Lewis (1976), 184-6; Knight, 'Glamorgan AD 400-1100', 346-7.

Second, and more importantly, both the Llandaf charters and later medieval evidence for dedications demonstrate the high proportion of local saints' cults: over a quarter of Welsh saints have only one dedication, with only five occurring twice and only six more than twice.[100] A similar picture emerges with regard to the dedications of holy wells.[101] Now, while in most cases there is no means of deciding whether a dedication is of pre-Norman origin, the pattern of dedications at least serves to alert us to the possibility of intensely localized lay devotion. Moreover, the paucity of early medieval evidence for such devotion is probably explicable by supposing that most cults were maintained by non-literate means. The earliest Lives of Welsh saints written in Wales date from the late eleventh and twelfth centuries; they promote the interests, especially the property rights, of major churches such as St David's, Llancarfan, Caerwent, Nevern and Llanbadarn Fawr.[102] But they show too that cults centred on places and relics, usually non-bodily relics such as crosiers and gospel-books associated with the saint, and these may have been the sole expressions of cults which lacked powerful promoters.[103] In the twelfth century ambitious churchmen sought to exploit these local foci of sanctity, notably Bishop Urban of Llandaf in 1120 and Robert, prior of Shrewsbury, in 1138. Urban arranged for the translation to his new cathedral church of the body of Bishop Dyfrig and the teeth of the hermit Elgar from Bardsey Island, and Robert had the body of Wenefred taken from Gwytherin to Shrewsbury.[104] Bardsey was called the 'Rome of Britain' on account of its allegedly containing the bodies of 20,000 saints – the phrase possibly echoes the early Irish use of the word *rúam* 'Rome' to denote a cemetery[105] – and Prior Robert's Life of St Wenefred relates how Wales was said to contain the bodies of many saints in various places.[106] Earlier in the Middle Ages, though, their cults may have been primarily the object of local devotion, focusing on features of the landscape, secondary relics and possibly also on shrines in graveyards such as that which may have existed on Barry Island prior to the building of the Romanesque church *c.* 1140.[107]

---

100. Davies, *Wales*, 174; W. N. Yates, 'The distribution and proportion of Celtic and non-Celtic church dedications in Wales', *J. Hist. Soc. of the Church in Wales* xxiii (1973), 1-17.
101. F. Jones, *The Holy Wells of Wales* (1954), ch. 3, esp. 31-3.
102. Davies, *Wales*, 207-8; idem, 'Property rights and property claims in Welsh *Vitae* of the eleventh century', *Hagiographie, Cultures et Sociétés IVe-XIIe siècles*, ed. E. Patlagean and P. Riché (1981), 515-33.
103. Cf. J. M. H. Smith, 'Oral and written: saints, miracles, and relics in medieval Brittany, *c.* 850-1250', *Speculum*, lxv (1990), 309-43, to which the arguments in this paragraph are much indebted. I wish to thank Julia Smith for supplying me with a copy of the article, which includes comparison with Welsh saints' cults (at 338ff.), in advance of publication. See also D. J. Corner, 'The *Vita Cadoci* and a Cotswold-Severn chambered cairn', *Bull. Board of Celtic Stud.* xxxii (1985), 50-67.
104. *Book of Llan Dâv*, ed. Evans and Rhys, 1-5; *Acta Sanctorum*, Nov., i, 708-31.
105. *Book of Llan Dâv*, 1, 83-4. Cf. Thomas, *Early Christian Archaeology of North Britain*, 89; and C. Doherty, 'The use of relics in early Ireland', *Ireland and Europe: the Early Church*, ed. P. Ní Chatháin and M. Richter (1984), 99.
106. *Acta Sanctorum*, Nov., i, 727.
107. The evidence for shrines is discussed in Knight, 'Excavations at St Barruc's chapel', 56-7, 61.

Unfortunately we can only guess the nature of the relationship between, on the one hand, undeveloped cemetery sites possessing special graves or shrines, and, on the other, churches and clergy. That Barry Island, Capel Maelog and Capel Eithin in Anglesey did eventually develop into church sites seems, however, to suggest that these cemeteries had come into ecclesiastical ownership during the early medieval period and may therefore imply some degree of ecclesiastical supervision. The same may also have been true of those cemeteries which were abandoned during the early Middle Ages, possibly as a result of the success of *monasteria* in securing a monopoly of burial.[108] Perhaps what we are seeing here is a situation comparable to that argued to have existed in seventh and eighth-century England, in which older local cult sites, particularly holy wells and cemeteries, survived within the newly established minster *parochiae*, with minster priests going to them to officiate at baptisms and burials as necessary. To quote John Blair, 'the early coherence of the *parochiae* did not preclude dispersed cult sites within them.'[109] Yet the existence of such sites in early medieval Wales and in particular the highly localized character of many saints' cults, anchored in places and secondary relics and sustained by oral tradition, also highlight the importance of the lay contribution to religious practice. For, although the sources shed little light on this point, it would surely be misguided to regard the laity as merely the passive recipients of clerical services, with their faith amounting to nothing more than what was mediated by the clergy. Indeed, in Wales as elsewhere in early medieval Europe, continuing adherence to Christianity on the part of the laity may well have owed as much, if not more, to their devotion to saints' cults as to clerical endeavour.[110]

In conclusion, pastoral care in early medieval Wales is clearly a topic about which it is much easier to ask questions than provide answers. All this survey has tried to do is present some of the evidence and possible inter-pretations from which more satisfactory answers may eventually be constructed. It has certainly not exhausted the problems and possibilities surrounding the subject. For example, more thought needs to be given to the position of bishops. These remain prominent in the sources throughout the early Middle Ages, and their role in ordaining clergy and supervising pastoral work would repay further study. They may have been more numerous than might be supposed from the known examples of episcopal seats referred to earlier. The designation in the ninth century of Elfoddw (d. 809) and Asser's kinsman Nobis as 'archbishops' of Gwynedd and St David's respectively may imply that other bishops were subordinate to them. There is also a tantalising reference to 'the bishops of the land', denoting possibly the Llŷn peninsular or else Gwynedd as a whole, who prevented Gruffudd ap Cynan

---

108. See above, p. 46, and also S. I. White, 'Excavations at Capel Eithin, Gaerwen, Anglesey, 1980: first interim report', *Trans. Anglesey Antiq. Soc. and Field Club* (1981), 15-27; Davies, *Wales*, 181-2.
109. Blair, 'Minsters in the landscape', 50-5; quotation at 55.
110. Cf. Thacker, pp. 166-9 below.

from violating the sanctuary of Aberdaron church in 1115.[111] Perhaps we should think of the *sacerdotes* in Welsh churches as possessing episcopal status throughout this period.[112] Another problem requiring clarification is the extent to which the territorial organization of the church was based on extensive multi-vill or 'multiple' estates, and the relationship of those estates to kingdoms and their subdivisions, including *cantrefi* and commotes.[113] The legal rule mentioned above on building a church in a bond vill seems to imply that such vills had not previously had churches, possibly because their religious needs were catered for by a church responsible for the whole estate of which the vill was a part. Would the latter church have merely constituted an estate church, or was it a mother-church of a *regio* which included, or was even coterminous with, the estate?

It may be doubted how far we will ever manage to answer these and other questions raised in the course of this chapter. Nevertheless, I should like to end by pointing to three directions from which there is hope of progress in attaining a greater understanding of how Christianity was mediated to Welsh people before the creation of a parochial structure in the twelfth century. First, further excavation of cemeteries should add substantially to our contemporary source material for a crucial aspect of the church's impact on lay society. Second, continuing investigation of the somewhat better documented ecclesiastical organization and religious life of the twelfth and thirteenth centuries in Wales will provide a sounder basis from which to work back to the pre-Norman period. After all, the diocesan framework established in the twelfth century was to a considerable extent based on existing churches and territorial divisions, and must therefore have implications for the ecclesiastical geography which preceded it.[114] Third, comparison with other parts of early medieval Europe, and the British Isles in particular, can suggest new ways of looking at the Welsh evidence. The ecclesiastical institutions and organization of pre-Norman Wales were not dissimilar to those found elsewhere in Europe, and a comparative approach therefore offers the prospect of overcoming, at least in some measure, the obstacles presented by the lack of Welsh sources.[115]

---

111. Charles-Edwards, 'Bishop-houses', 257-8; *Brut y Tywysogyon*, ed. Jones, 84-5.
112. See above, pp. 4, 52 and Davies, *Wales*, 158-60.
113. On the 'multiple estate' model, see for example G. R. J. Jones, 'Multiple estates and early settlement', *Medieval Settlement*, ed. P. H. Sawyer (1976), 15-40; *idem*, 'The multiple estate: a model for tracing the inter-relationships of society, economy and habitat', *Archaeological Approaches to Medieval Europe*, ed. K. Biddick (Studies in Medieval Culture, 18, 1984), 9-41; and also the cautionary remarks of Bassett, 'Origins of Anglo-Saxon Kingdoms', 20; and Blair, 'Frithuwold's kingdom', 104-5.
114. Pryce, 'Church and society in Wales', 29-30.
115. I am most grateful to Heather James and Richard Sharpe for commenting on earlier drafts of this paper; to Nancy Edwards for valuable discussion and help; and to participants at the conference at Rewley House for their questions and comments.

3 The pastoral role of the church in the early Irish laws

THOMAS CHARLES-EDWARDS

The purpose of this chapter is to discuss the pastoral role of the early Irish church in so far as that role is revealed in texts of a prescriptive character. The main texts in question are listed and very briefly described in the appendix. They are a heterogeneous but interrelated collection. I have arranged them there in sequence beginning with the more personal and ecclesiastical prescription of the penitentials in section A, moving on through more public ecclesiastical material in B and C, to texts in Irish, D and E. Section D is the crucial bridge between the ecclesiastical texts in Latin and the vernacular laws. For, whoever may have written the vernacular laws, they undoubtedly had a more secular stance than any of the other prescriptive texts.[1] Under E I have put only a very small selection from what survives, merely those texts which happen to be of particular importance for my theme.

The interrelatedness of the material will gradually become more evident in the course of my argument, but some points are best made at the outset. Much the bulkiest of all the texts on the list is the Irish Collection of Canons, the *Hibernensis* to give it its usual short name.[2] It is unlike the principal earlier canon law collections of the Western church, the *Dionysiana* and the *Hispana*; the latter are collections, first of conciliar decrees, and second of papal edicts.[3] The *Hibernensis* is not designed to perform the same task (apart from anything else, the compilers already knew the work of Dionysius Exiguus, and may not have wished to duplicate his achievement).[4] The sources of the *Hibernensis* are much more varied; while they include synodal decrees, both Irish and non-Irish, they also contain much biblical material, and also quotations from biblical commentators. The compilers evidently did their job by working their way through the Bible and other sources to find any material which had a bearing on

---

1. For arguments in favour of a clerical background for the vernacular laws, see D. Ó Corráin, L. Breatnach and A. Breen, 'The Laws of the Irish', *Peritia* iii (1984), 382-438. I have set out my own position in a chapter on the laws to appear in *The New History of Ireland*, vol. i.
2. I have used the edition by F. W. H. Wasserschleben, *Die irische Kanonensammlung*, 2nd edn. (Leipzig, 1885) [hereafter *Hib.*]; a new edition is in course of preparation by Professor M. Sheehy.
3. See J. F. Kenney, *The Sources for the Early History of Ireland: Ecclesiastical. An Introduction and Guide* (New York, 1929), 247-8 (no. 82).
4. *Hib.* xxviii. 5. *a*; 10. *a*.

how a Christian should live. The result is much more than law in the narrow sense, namely rules which are enforceable in a court. There are ecclesiastical judges and there is an array of disciplinary measures, but it is impossible that either judges or disciplinary sanctions could have been invoked to compel obedience to much of the material assembled in the *Hibernensis*.[5] Apart from anything else, the compilers' assiduous collecting of authorities disclosed contradictions which the *Hibernensis* left unresolved.[6] The collection was a reaction to a period of lively controversy carried out principally by Irish biblical exegetes; the points of controversy may often have been resolved, but not always. The *Hibernensis* may have provided an ecclesiastical judge with authorities for a judgment, but it left him with the task of deciding what, in any particular case, was the just solution. He then had to choose and interpret his authorities so as to support his verdict. Moreover, when we look at the penalties which provided the sanction for the rules stated in the *Hibernensis*, two things rapidly become obvious: usually no penalty is mentioned, and when it is, it is likely to be penitential in character.[7] The discipline set out in the penitentials underlies much of the *Hibernensis*.

The longest of these prescriptive texts, then, aims to persuade more than to command, and to worry out the solutions to difficulties as much as to persuade. These complexities are, in the long term, an advantage for the historian, for he does not have to confront evidence which presents a falsely uniform face to the inquirer, but men arguing with one another and even men uncertain of what they should think. Yet with all of them there is the possibility of defining their assumptions as well as the views they openly propagate. The latter may well be controversial; the former are more likely to betray general features of the early Irish church.

By the eighth century our texts assume a fairly dense distribution of churches. One secular legal text is discussing what should be done if someone finds a stray horse.[8] The procedure it recommends is for the horse to be tethered first of all. Then if the finder knows the person to whom the horse belongs, he should inform the owner; if he does not know who owns the horse, he should announce what he has found. There are four places within the kingdom at which such an announcement should be made: at the nearest fort of the ruler (*tigernae*), at the fort of the judge of the kingdom, at the smithy and at the chief church of the kingdom. The word for a kingdom is *túath*, literally 'people'. When used in a territorial sense it frequently refers to a small territory, about 10 or 15 miles across, closer to an English hundred than to a county. It might be a single small river valley, such as the valley of the Antrim Water near Belfast, or a coastal strip, such as that on the north side of Lough Foyle, or a peninsula such as the Ards peninsula in Co. Down. Yet, small as such a territory was, the early

---

5. E.g. *Hib.* xiv. 1.
6. Examples of contradictions in the *Hibernensis* are not confined to Book lxvii, *De contrariis causis*, e.g. xviii. 1-5; xlii. 19-21.
7. *Hib.* i. 22. *a*; ii. 25. *a*, *b*; xi. 1. *b*, 2-6; xvi. 13. *d*, xvii. 5; xxviii. 5, 10; xxix. 8.
8. *CIH* 577.31-578.9.

medieval sources assume that it was ruled by a king. We are also to understand that such a small territory might have a principal church, and presumably therefore minor churches as well.

Churches were sometimes distinguished by the status of the persons who presided over them. The *Hibernensis* records an edict of a synod of the Irish party in the seventh century about homicide within a church. Compensation had to be paid to the kinsmen, but penance had also to be undergone because of the insult to the church. The text runs as follows:

> But if they should have committed homicide in it [the church], let them do penance for seven years. The reason for this is that the bishop has seven grades and the church is septiform. If, however, they [i.e. churches] do not have bishops, but it is a small church, let them do penance for a year and a half.[9]

The bishop 'has seven grades' because that is the number of ranks within the church and he has the highest rank of all.[10] Yet a great church is not just a church ruled by a bishop, for it may be a church in which bishops lie dead.[11] The person whose status matters is not always alive.

Above the level of the *túath* the organization of the church becomes much more controversial. The controversies had a bearing on the atmosphere in which the church performed its pastoral duties, and they must, therefore, be considered briefly. The *Hibernensis* is a champion of what appears to be an Irish version of the structure of metropolitan provinces already normal on the continent. In the secular sphere the small kingdoms known as *túatha* were grouped together under overkings, who in their turn might have yet further overlords. The chain constituted by the relationship of the king and overking continued until the highest recognized status, that of a king of a *cóiced* 'fifth', a major province; such a major ruler was also known as a 'king of great kings'.[12] Similarly episcopal sees were to be grouped together into provinces under 'a greater see'[13] or a 'bishop of bishops'[14] or a metropolitan bishop.[15] A province was apparently expected to have a panel of ecclesiastical judges as well as a synod.[16] The *Hibernensis* is hostile to any reference of cases beyond the

9. *Hib.* xlii. 22 (note also the presence of an abbot implied by the phrase *ignorante abbate*).
10. On the seven grades of the church, see *Hib.* viii; and R. E. Reynolds, 'At "sixes and sevens" - and eights and nines: the sacred mathematics of sacred orders in the early Middle Ages', *Speculum* liv (1979), 669-84.
11. Cf. *Hib.* xliv. 8.
12. D. A. Binchy, *Celtic and Anglo-Saxon Kingship* (1970), 31-2.
13. *Hib.* xx. 5.
14. *Canones Hibernenses*, v. 9, ed. L. Bieler, *The Irish Penitentials*, Scriptores Latini Hiberniae, 5 (Dublin, 1963), 174.
15. *Hib.* xx. 3. *c.*
16. *Hib.* xx. 2-4.

province except for especially difficult issues which may be taken to Rome.[17]

These provisions may have provided a defence against the claims of Armagh, and to a lesser extent other churches such as Kildare, to a primacy within Ireland. They antedate, at least in part, and may be contrasted with the claims of a seventh-century text known as the Book of the Angel, preserved in the Book of Armagh.[18] In effect the *Hibernensis* is advocating a structure of episcopal government similar, allowing for different conditions, to the structure found in sixth-century Gaul (for example, in the writings of Gregory of Tours who was himself a metropolitan bishop). The Book of the Angel, however, wanted a clear primacy for Armagh over the whole island similar to that enjoyed by Canterbury in England up to 735.[19]

---

17. *Hib.* xx. 4. *a*, implies a preference for calling in judges from another province rather than taking a case to the other province. xx. 5. *a* (in the A Recension) suggests that some appeals might be made from a province to a major church within Ireland (no mention of Armagh and *ad maiorem sedem* does not suggest that there was only one greater see); this is flanked (xx. 5. *b*) by a statement of the principle that appeals might be taken to Rome (cf. also p. 61, n. (e)). The *maior sedes* may have been the principal church of a major province (= Ir. *cóiced*), such as the *Liber Angeli*, § 32, recognized Kildare to be in Leinster.

18. *Liber Angeli*, § 28, ed. L. Bieler, *The Patrician Texts in the Book of Armagh*, Scriptores Latini Hiberniae, 10 (Dublin, 1979), 184-90. For the relationship of the *Hibernensis*, Book xx, to the *Liber Angeli*, see R. Sharpe, 'Armagh to Rome in the seventh century', in *Irland und Europa: Die Kirche im Frühmittelalter*, ed. P. Ní Chatháin and M. Richter (Stuttgart, 1984), 58-72, esp. 66-8. Cf. also the note in *Cummian's Letter De Controversia Paschali and the De Ratione Conputandi*, ed. M. Walsh and D. Ó Cróinín (Toronto, 1988), line 277, pp. 92-3. Cummian, writing probably in 632-3, knew a canon corresponding to part of the B Recension of the *Hibernensis* (Book xx, p. 61 n. (e) of Wasserschleben's edn.). This shows that that canon antedated the *Liber Angeli*, composed in the middle of the seventh century. For the date of the latter, see Sharpe, 'Armagh and Rome'. On the other hand, it may well be the case that *Hib.* xx. 5. *b* (in both recensions) is derived from the *Liber Angeli*, § 29, rewritten so as to exclude all reference to Armagh, yet still ascribed to Patrick. If this is correct, *Hib.* xx. 5, contains material both earlier and later than the *Liber Angeli*, both enunciating a provincial structure and then, in the later material, defending it against the claims of Armagh.

19. Note that the *Liber Angeli*, § 28, uses the term *archiepiscopus*, as does Cogitosus in favour of Kildare (Prologue and c.32, *Acta Sanctorum*, Feb., i, 134, 141) while the *Hibernensis* (xx. 3. *c*) speaks only of a *metropolitanus episcopus* who presides over a *prouincia*. For the difference between the two in the seventh century, see W. Levison, *England and the Continent in the Eighth Century* (1946), 18-22. Similar issues were being voiced in England in a way which would have had repercussions in Ireland to judge by the claim made in the *Vita Wilfridi*, cc. 10, 16, ed. B. Colgrave (1927), that York was a metropolitan see in the time of Colmán and Wilfrid. That such claims were not entirely without effect is suggested by the language used in c. 53, that Wilfrid confessed the faith in the Roman synod 'for the northern part of Britain and Ireland and the islands which are inhabited by the peoples of the English and the Britons as well as the Irish and the Picts'. It looks as though Wilfrid had ambitions to create a great northern metropolitan province, including northern Ireland, through pursuing the paschal controversy against Iona (cf. the *aquilonaris pars* of c.10) as well as through Ecgfrith's secular power. The discussion of the issue in N. Brooks, *The Early History of the Church of Canterbury* (1984), 72, seems to me to suffer from an anachronistic assumption that Wilfrid could not simultaneously recognize Theodore's position as archbishop for the whole of Britain and claim to be a metropolitan bishop. Wilfrid was used to the church of Gaul in which the two positions were not yet combined into one.

It is sometimes assumed that the distinction between a monastic and a non-monastic church is clear-cut. Yet, in the *Hibernensis*, there is no sharp distinction between a church which is monastic and a church staffed only by *clerici*. The head of a church, usually called a *princeps* (Irish *airchinnech*, 'erenagh'), may have under his authority monks (xxxvii. 7, 37); he may also rule over *clerici* (xxxvii. 15). He may himself be a monk, but he may also be married and have sons (xxxvii. 35); moreover a *princeps* may be a bishop (xli. 3; cf. 2, 5, and xxxvii. 39). If we put all the evidence together we can see that it would be unsurprising to find the chief church of a *túath* to be both episcopal and monastic, and for the bishop to be head of the church, *princeps*, and also, in relation to the monks, *abbas* (possibly xlii. 22).

Some of those styled monks in the texts are what modern historians call 'monastic tenants'.[20] They are subject to the authority of a *princeps* and appear to live under a rule, but they are essentially peasants normally owing food-renders to the church. In particular they may be married. Their renders are interpreted as if they were the firstlings of Old Testament law.[21] It seems to be assumed that the normal economic support of a church is largely provided by its monastic tenants. When the *Hibernensis* says that one of the three things required in any church is a monk, it is quite likely that it is thinking of the monastic tenant.[22] The implications of this situation, however, require a little thought. Whether someone is a monk of the normal kind or a monastic tenant, he is called a *monachus* or, in Irish, a *manach*.[23] There is no distinction in the term used. Similarly, whether someone is a normal monk or a monastic tenant, he is subject to the authority of a *princeps*, who in his role as superior ruling 'monks' may be termed an abbot, and it is far from clear that such an abbot would always himself be a monk. A small church might have only very few monastic tenants and no monks proper; its head or *princeps* might be an ordinary priest; yet in relation to the monastic tenants he would apparently be an abbot. In general, the larger a church, the more monastic, in some sense, it was likely to be, for the simple reason that it would have more monastic tenants. For all these reasons it is extremely difficult, and perhaps wrong in principle, to try to draw a sharp line between monastic and non-monastic churches. To this extent, the debate about if, how and when the Irish church became monastic is perhaps misconceived.

The head of a church had duties towards the members of his church, including his monastic tenants, but he also had obligations towards the laity at large. An important aspect of these latter duties is the way in which

---

20. K. Hughes, *The Church in Early Irish Society* (1966), 136-7.
21. T. M. Charles-Edwards, 'The church and settlement', in *Irland und Europa*, ed. P. Ní Chatháin and M. Richter, 173-4.
22. *Hib.* xlii. 15.
23. The situation is further complicated by the possibility that a priest or deacon who is a monk may be an *operarius*, as may a monk who is of lower clerical rank than a deacon: Penitential of Cummian, ii. 2-3, derived from the Preface of Gildas, § 1, ed. Bieler, *Irish Penitentials*, 60, 112-14.

they were conceived. The laity are termed 'the people', *populus* or *plebs* in Latin, *túath* in Old Irish.[24] The one word, *túath* 'people', is both the population of a small kingdom in relation to its king and also the laity in relation to its church. A minor king is 'the king of a *túath*', but we may also have, as we have seen, a 'chief church of a *túath*'.[25] This is the basis of a general habit of drawing parallels between the church on the one side and the laity on the other, especially in the crucial area of status. Ireland in the seventh and eighth centuries was a land in which distinctions of status were numerous and pervasive. It is no accident that the scheme of the seven grades of the church appears to have been worked out in Ireland in the sixth or seventh centuries as the result of an effort to produce a consistent picture of social status which would embrace both the laity and the church.[26] The effect was that the bishop was given the same status as the king of a *túath*.

The analogy between church and laity was pursued so as to embrace yet higher ranks. The *Hibernensis*, in the course of its consideration of provinces, draws a picture of the standard province as containing one king and, under him, 'three lesser powers', and likewise one bishop and three lesser bishops: the overking corresponds to the superior bishop, the 'lesser powers' to the lesser bishops (xx. 2). It is very likely that these 'lesser powers' are kings of *túatha* and that the lesser bishops are similarly bishops of *túatha*. A further aspect of this analogy is loss of status, and with it loss of legal capacity. A king may lose his high status through shameful conduct, for example cowardice in battle.[27] The head of a church may lose his status and his legal capacity if he is a *malus princeps*, a bad head of his church.[28] A bishop is sometimes considered to be of higher status if he is a virgin, of somewhat lesser status if he is the husband of one wife, of still lesser status if he is a penitent.[29] Orthodoxy is sometimes cited as a crucial determinant of the legal capacity of the head of a church – no light matter in the seventh century when the paschal controversy and associated accusations of Pelagianism were in the air.[30] Both in the church and among the laity it was a competitive world in which rivals might be only too pleased to see someone lose status. These distinctions of status and the competition they engendered will be important when we come to consider relations between church and laity.

In Irish the relationship between the church and the laity is also the relationship between a church and a *túath*, a people. It is a relationship played out on a very restricted geographical scale. A typical *túath* might be no

---

24. Cf. *plebilis* 'a layman', *Hib.* xvii. 4, *plebeus* 'a layman', Adomnán, *Vita S. Columbae*, i. 1 etc.
25. See n.8 above.
26. *Críth Gablach*, ed. D. A. Binchy (Dublin, 1941), lines 6-9; L. Breatnach, 'The first third of *Bretha Nemed Toísech*', *Ériu*, xl (1989), §§ 13-15; and see n.10 above.
27. *Críth Gablach*, lines 538-41.
28. *Hib.* xxv. 10. c.
29. *CIH* 588. 11-14, 32-3, 39-40 (*Míadšlechta*, probably eighth century).
30. *CIH* 591. 25; *Hib.* xxix. 6, xxxvii. 35.

more than 10 miles across, and many were less. The church or churches within this small kingdom had obligations to the people, the laity. The most forthright accounts of these obligations are given in two texts, the secular legal tract, *Córus Béscnai*, and the text known as the 'Rule of Patrick'.[31] Both of them may have some connection with Armagh: the secular tract contains a version of the legend of Patrick's encounter with Irish paganism at Tara[32] and the Rule of Patrick claims the authority of a 'Testament of Patrick', a testament, moreover, to which all the souls of the men of Ireland are subject.[33] Both the appeal to Patrick's authority and the claim to enjoy a power extending over the whole of Ireland suggest an Armagh background.[34]

The obligations of a church to the people are essentially sacramental and intercessory: baptism, communion and what is called literally 'singing of what is not seen', namely singing of psalms and other prayers on behalf of the dead.[35] With communion is associated, in the Rule of Patrick, 'the offering of the Body of Christ upon the altar'.[36] So much seems to be common ground. The Rule of Patrick has, however, further concerns. It is anxious to impress on the minds of its readers the necessity of episcopal confirmation and of the spiritual direction – 'soul-friendship' in Irish – which the bishop provides for the heads of all churches and for all lords, apparently secular lords.[37] The Rule of Patrick appeals to natural sanctions in its insistence upon the importance of confirmation:

> For what causes sickness and calamities to kindreds, including both failure of crops (?) (*eltrai*) and other forms of destruction, is [for people] to go without lawful baptism and not to go 'under the hand' of a bishop at the proper time, for the fullness of the Holy Spirit does not come upon him who, however fervently he may have been baptized, does not go under the hand of a bishop after baptism.[38]

---

31. *Córus Béscnai*, CIH 520-36; the Rule of Patrick, *CIH* 2129. 6-2130. 37; and ed. and transl. by J. G. O'Keeffe, *Ériu*, i (1904), 216-24.
32. *CIH* 527. 20-529 .5, discussed by D. A. Binchy, 'The pseudo-historical prologue to the *Senchas Már*, *Studia Celtica*, x/xi (1975-6), 23-4.
33. *CIH* 2129. 6.
34. Cf. the *Liber Angeli*, §§ 8, 13, 18, 22 and 28. For discussion see Sharpe, 'Armagh and Rome in the seventh century', (as in n.18) 58-72.
35. *CIH* 2129. 32-7; 2130. 1-18, 23-31; cf. *Hib*. ii. 9, xv.
36. *CIH* 2130. 4-5, cf. 14-15, 26, 30-1. Similarly *Córus Béscnai*, *CIH* 529. 21-2.
37. *CIH* 2129. 7-8, 37-8. An interesting example is provided by the ninth-century text known as 'The Monastery of Tallaght', a collection of sayings and anecdotes modelled on earlier ascetic writings such as Cassian's *Conlationes*. 'There was a bishop of the Déisi at Finglas, named Cainchomrac: he was Duiblittir's confessor [soul-friend]', *The Monastery of Tallaght*, § 7, ed. E. J. Gwynn and W. J. Purton, *Proc. Roy. Ir. Acad.* xxix, C, no. 5 (1911). The Déisi of Brega were further west and north than Finglas (to judge by the later barony names of Upper and Lower Deece); Finglas now lies within North Dublin, and then seems to have been within one of the *túatha* known after the people of Gailenga. Yet even if Duiblittir did not have as his soul-friend the bishop of the local *túath*, he did have a bishop with local associations in that position.
38. *CIH* 2129. 21-4.

The Rule of Patrick goes on to appeal to social and political pressure, pressure both from below and from above, to ensure that each church provides the sacraments and prayer for the dead. This pressure is, in its turn, to be guaranteed by the authority of Patrick and the saints of Ireland:

> For no soul will dwell in heaven which has not been baptized with a lawful baptism before everything, so that for that reason it is an obligation incumbent on the souls of the men of Ireland together with their rulers and their nobles and the heads of churches that there should be baptism and communion and the singing of prayers for the dead in every church for proper monks (*manaig*). For an unmitigated curse and malediction will be directed from Patrick and the saints of Ireland against every ruler and against every monk who does not enforce upon his own particular church that there be within it baptism and communion and singing of prayers for the dead.[39]

Any church which does not provide these essentials 'is not entitled to tithes or a capitation cow (*bó chennaithe*) or the third share of a testament'.[40] Moreover, 'it is not entitled to the honour-price of a church of God, but it is termed by Christ a cave of robbers and thieves'.[41]

The other text, the secular law tract *Córus Béscnai*, sees the relationship between church and laity as a contract.[42] The *túath* has certain rights from the church and the church has certain rights from the laity. These rights are interdependent: if one side fails to carry out its obligations, the obligations of the other side may lapse. The church has a right that the *túath* upholds the church's rights over what are called 'its members', principally monastic tenants. From them a church is entitled to tithes and first-fruits, and also from every dying man it is entitled to a share in his bequest. More uncertainly, *Córus Béscnai* also requires lords to compel their dependants to pay tithes and first-fruits.[43] In other words, there was at least the

---

39. *CIH* 2129. 32-7. *Manach* 'monk' in this passage is normally taken to be the 'monastic tenant'. The interpretation is, however, uncertain. In my opinion there were certain kindreds subject to a church in a dependent relationship which was permanent but also perceived as contractual. They were called *manaig* 'monks'. They provided the economic support for a church and, in return, that church had a special obligation to provide for their spiritual welfare. Furthermore, because a people, *túath*, and its king endorsed such a pattern of support for a church, the people in general had a contractual right to pastoral service. Richard Sharpe, however, suggests that *manach* may have sometimes had a wide sense by which it came to be equivalent to 'lay person': see below, p. 102.
40. *CIH* 2130. 8. *Cennaithe* seems to be *cenn* 'head' + *aithe* 'payment', 'render'. Hence my literal translation, 'capitation'.
41. *CIH* 2130. 16-18.
42. *CIH* 529. 20-6 balanced by 530. 32-3; cf. the first section on the law of contract which sets the context, 520. 1-522. 19. The contractual approach is discussed by D. Ó Corráin, 'The early Irish churches: some aspects of organization', in *Irish Antiquity: Essays and Studies Presented to Professor M. J. O'Kelly*, ed, D. Ó Corráin (Cork, 1981), 334.
43. *CIH* 526. 20-1.

hope that this Old Testament taxation might be extended to the laity at large. From the church the laity, in their turn, are entitled to baptism, communion and prayer for the souls of the dead, and to the sacrifice of the Mass.[44] The laity are also entitled to have the word of God proclaimed to all who will hear, a point which is not stated in the Rule of Patrick.[45] In essence, therefore, the contract between church and *túath* provides for an exchange whereby material wealth will pass from *túath* to church, and pastoral care, principally in the form of the sacraments, will pass from the church to the *túath*. If there is no pastoral care, or inadequate pastoral care, the *túath* is fully entitled to end all payments. No doubt some such relationship between the economic support of the church and the services it provided has always obtained at least implicitly. What is unusual is the clarity with which the legal interrelationship is set out.

The background to these ideas is various. There is a concept of a contract between king and *túath*; and, moreover, this concept receives explicit and technical statement in a legal text.[46] It is commonplace to treat the relationship between lord and client and between the craftsman or the poet and his patron or customer as a contract: the poet singing the praises of one's ancestor is perhaps not so very remote from the priest singing psalms for his soul.[47] Both deserve their reward. Since the king is a lord, it is not surprising to find his authority defined in the same contractual idiom as that used for any other lord. I think, therefore, that the background of the contract between church and *túath* is native and secular. One thing which tends to confirm this view is that the same concept is not found in the *Hibernensis*.[48]

This lack of interest in the contractual approach to relations between laity and church shown by the *Hibernensis* may have other causes. One of the compilers of the A Recension in the *Hibernensis* was a monk of Iona; and neither he nor his fellow-compiler, Ruben, had any connection with Armagh.[49] The position taken on the provincial structure of the Irish church in the *Hibernensis* is flatly opposed to the primatial claims of Armagh. It has no sympathy with the referral of cases at least beyond a

---

44. *CIH* 529. 20-2.
45. *CIH* 529. 22-3.
46. *Críth Gablach*, ed. Binchy, lines 494-501 and 525-9 balanced by 502-24.
47. *CIH* 591. 27-9 alongside 591. 25-7.
48. There is *Hib*. ii. 11 (*De iure sacerdotis a populo*), but it is not balanced by a chapter entitled *De iure populi a sacerdote. Ius* here = Ir. *dliged* (cf. xxxi. 18, *ratio* = *dliged*, xxxvii. 9, *ius* = *dliged*).
49. R. Thurneysen, 'Zur irischen Kanonensammlung', *Zeitschrift für celtishce Philologie* vi (1907-8), 1-5.

level corresponding to the *cóiced* 'major province' except to Rome.[50] It dismisses in silence the claims of Armagh to an authority over the whole of Ireland. When the *Hibernensis* was compiled, the royal kindred to which the abbots of Iona generally belonged was frequently the leading dynasty among the Uí Néill – in other words it was often the leading dynasty of the northern half of Ireland.[51] It was to lose this strong position in the mid-eighth century. The situation current when Adomnán promulgated his Law of the Innocents in 697 had been peculiarly favourable to the influence of the abbot of Iona, for a close kinsman had been king of Tara.[52] The alliance between abbot and king had no doubt been a prerequisite to enable Adomnán to gather his great assembly and secure the enactment of the edict protecting the non-combatant status of women, children and clerics. The Law of Adomnán came into force through co-operation between churchmen and also kings, not through the primacy claimed by Armagh.[53] The balance of forces exemplified in 697 is consistent with the provincial structure set out in the *Hibernensis*. In terms of Irish law, both canon and secular, Adomnán was an *excelsus princeps*, an *ollam mórchathrach*, the head of a great church.[54] As such he enjoyed high status, equivalent to that of king or bishop. Yet given the attitudes of Irish canon and secular law to the status of a church and its head, both he and Iona had previously had much to fear from accusations, arising out of the Easter controversy, that they were guilty of schism. While a kinsman of the abbot of Iona remained the most powerful ruler in the northern half of Ireland, there might be little to fear from any accusations; yet the continuance of the hegemony of Cenél Conaill, and thus support from the secular power, could not be guaranteed. Such charges, if pressed home successfully, would lead

---

50. This is clearer in the B Recension: Wasserschleben, p. 61 n. (e), where the second sentence was quoted by Cummian in his letter, written probably in 632 or 633, to Ségéne abbot of Iona and the hermit Béccán, ed. M. Walsh and D. Ó Cróinín, *Cummian's Letter*, p. 92, lines 276-7, and the editors' introduction, pp. 47-9. The A Recension allows appeal to a *maior sedes*, when the disputing *clerici* within a *prouincia* cannot agree (*Hib.* xx. 5. *a.*); this I would understand, following xx. 2, to rest on a scheme corresponding to the usual lawyers' account of kings and over-kings as follows:

Ecclesiastical	Secular
(1) *plebs* or *populus*	(1) *túath*
(2) (lesser) *prouincia* with one king and three 'lesser powers' and one (leading) bishop and other 'lesser bishops'	(2) mesne kingdom of 2, 3 or 4 *túatha* and one over-king (*Críth Gablach*, lines 457-61; *CIH* 2267. 14)
(3) *maior sedes* of xx. 5. *a.*	(3) *cóiced*, e.g. Munster or Leinster

Compare the *Liber Angeli*, §§ 28-9, a version of the same canon, but including appeal to Armagh; and § 32, which implies recognition of Kildare's claim to authority within Leinster.
51. See F. J. Byrne, *Irish Kings and High-Kings* (1973), 283.
52. M. Ní Dhonnchadha, 'The guarantor list of *Cáin Adomnáin*, 697', *Peritia* i (1982), 196-7 (no. 41 and cf. no. 42).
53. Although the bishop of Armagh was placed first among the clerical guarantors of *Cáin Adomnáin*, M. Ní Dhonnchadha, 'The guarantor list', 180 and 185-6.
54. *Canones Hibernenses*, iv. 1, v. 11, ed. Bieler, *Irish Penitentials*, 170, 174; *CIH* 2282. 27 = 1618. 8 etc.

to a loss of status both for the abbot of Iona as a person, and for the monastery of which he was a head.[55] Furthermore, should that deprivation of rank come about, Iona would become vulnerable to secular pressure and even disendowment.[56] The perpetual search of any early medieval monastery for security of property required an Irish abbot to look to his reputation for orthodoxy. Yet, and this seems to be a quirk of the law, a church was relatively safe providing that its head was considered orthodox and of irreproachable spiritual life.[57] A situation when Adomnán had declared his support for the Roman party was one in which Iona was reasonably secure from potential attack, at least on this score, even though the monks may have refused to follow their abbot.[58]

There may, therefore, be two sides to the contract between church and *túath*. On the one hand, it seems a splendid way of ensuring that ecclesiastical neglect of its pastoral duties would bring retribution. On the other hand, however, it opened the door to instability in the organization of the church. It put a powerful weapon in the hand of any ruler who wished, for his own purposes, to undermine the independence of a church, and it opened the way to an alliance between a major church and a major dynasty seeking to spread their power over weaker neighbours. It may be no accident that the two texts which lay most stress on the contractual approach to relations between church and *túath* (the Rule of Patrick and *Córus Béscnai*) both have associations with Armagh; that Armagh had the most clear interest in instability, especially in undermining any acceptance of the provincial structure defended in the *Hibernensis*; and that the Cenél nÉogain, the Uí Néill dynasty which came to have particularly close links with Armagh, also had a strong interest in weakening the power of the royal kindred to which most of the abbots of Iona belonged.[59] A concern for the discharge of pastoral responsibilities may not be quite what it appears.

What the Irish laity was most anxious to demand from the church were those things which it was the duty of the priest to provide: Mass, baptism, prayers for the dead. The last of these can also be provided by any cleric, up to a point, and powerful intercession on behalf of the dead can certainly be offered by monks. Yet it remains the priest who is the central figure in the Irish church as perceived by the laws. The *Hibernensis* may open with a book devoted to the bishop, but the next book, that on the priest, is longer and contains more unconventional material. The delicate relationship between priest and bishop can be seen in a number of ways. First, the

---

55. *Hib.* xx. 6, and note how the issue of status and capacity to give judgments in ecclesiastical cases are interwoven in Book xx, esp, xx, 3. *a*, and 4. *a*.
56. Cf. *CIH* 591. 25 and 529. 20-2 (where the church should be 'iarna creitme coir' 'in accordance with the correct [pattern] of belief').
57. *Hib.* xxv. 10. *c*, assuming that the *malus princeps* is the head of the church rather than an oppressive secular ruler. The assumption is confirmed by *Hib.* xvii. 7, which states the principle very clearly.
58. For a discussion some of the problems surrounding Adomnán's stance on the Easter question see J.-M. Picard, 'The purpose of Adomnán's *Vita Columbae*', *Peritia* i (1982), 160-6, though I cannot agree with all his arguments.
59. The Cenél Conaill: see Byrne, *Irish Kings and High-Kings*, 114-15, 124-5.

Hibernensis is quite clear that they are both *sacerdotes*; both are heirs to
the Old Testament tradition begun, under the Law, by Aaron, and
prefigured by Melchisedech.[60] On the other hand, the Rule of Patrick, as
we have seen, is anxious to stress that the bishop's confirmation is
necessary for the full reception of the Holy Spirit; baptism, normally
administered by a priest, is incomplete until the person 'goes under the
hand of the bishop'.[61] What we do not know is whether it was common
for people to be baptized but not confirmed; if it was common, the pastoral
role of the bishop would have been seriously weakened.

Perhaps the most striking example of the delicacy of the relationship
between bishop and priest is spiritual direction, soul-friendship. Not only
those in orders but all those dependent on a church are expected to be
under the direction of a soul-friend.[62] Those who are in the order of
penitents - and they may include bishops[63] - are especially in need of
spiritual direction, as the penitentials by implication make clear.[64] It is
particularly important that penitents to not despair. The Penitential of
Vinnian exemplifies the point when it declares:

> If a person has sworn a false oath, great is the crime; it can hardly,
> if at all, be expiated, but none the less it is better to do penance
> and not to despair, for great is the mercy of God.[65]

It may be true that the penitentials make rather depressing reading, yet their
desire to prescribe a penance for each and every shameful deed is only a consequence of the wish to show that no sin is so terrible or so despicable that it
is beyond the mercy of God and the redemptive power of Christian penance.

The penitentials show that the priest was the normal soul-friend. The
Penitential of Cummian censures the stirrer up of novelties:

60. *Hib.* i. 3; ii. 1. *c*, and 2.
61. *CIH* 2129. 23-4.
62. *Riagail Phátraic*, §§ 1 and 6 = *CIH* 2119. 7-8, 37-8 (the bishop is soul-friend for
    nobles and heads of churches, and also for all those in orders, the *áes gráid*), leav-
    ing, by implication, the priest to provide direction for others; *CIH* 530. 2-3 (each
    manach is subject to a regime of penance, implying spiritual direction, probably
    from a priest).
63. *CIH* 588. 39.
64. Penitential of Columbanus, B, Preface (ed. Bieler, *Irish Penitentials*, 98-9); the
    Bigotian Penitential, 1-3 (ed. Bieler, 198). Bieler's arguments in favour of placing
    the composition of the Bigotian Penitential on the continent seem to me uncon-
    vincing. The main one is that it quotes the Rule of St Benedict 'of which, as far
    as I can see, there is no trace in the early Irish Church' (*Irish Penitentials*, 10).
    Yet there may be a trace in Adomnán's *Vita S. Columbae*, if the mention of
    'dura et laboriosa ... monasterialia ... imperia' of ii. 39 (in the context of a
    verbal testing of an aspirant to the monastic life) is an echo of Benedict's 'dura
    et aspera' of c.58 of the Rule (in the same context), as proposed by A. O. and M.
    O. Anderson in their edition, p. 118. It would in any case be surprising if the
    Rule had not reached Ireland *via* those 'Iro-Frankish' monasteries which followed
    the 'mixed rule'. Against Bieler is the use made of the Bigotian Penitential in the
    Old Irish Penitential. On spiritual guidance see also *Monastery of Tallaght*, ed.
    Gwynn and Purton, §§ 23 and 54.
65. Penitential of Vinnian, § 22 (ed, Bieler, *Irish Penitentials*, 80); similarly, § 12.

He who allows himself any novelty outside the Scriptures, such as might lead him to heresy, shall be sent into exile. But if he repents, he shall publicly condemn his own opinion and convert to the faith those whom he has deceived, and he shall fast at the decision of a priest.[66]

One might have expected, in such a case of the purity of the faith, that the bishop would have jurisdiction; yet it is the priest who prescribes the appropriate penance.[67]

In the ordinary secular law a lord is allowed a general disciplinary jurisdiction over his dependants, provided that he is not in breach of his contractual obligations. It is not surprising then, that the bishop should perceive the disciplinary authority of the soul-friend as a natural adjunct of his rank. In the *Hibernensis* it is the bishop who has the power of binding and loosing.[68] He, rather than the priest, is to be the principal judge in ecclesiastical cases.[69] In the Rule of Patrick, the bishop is to be the soul-friend of all heads of churches within his diocese.[70] The spiritual discipline within the *túath* is exercised principally by him. This was critical, for the offences which could make someone a penitent could also deprive them and their churches of status, expose them to economic sanctions, even to disendowment. The secular law tract called the Heptads opens with a list of ways in which a church (*cell*) may be deprived of status.[71] Churches were under pressure to live up to standards imposed, in part, by the laity (principally local rulers and the nobility) and it was important that such pressures should be directed via the bishop so that he, as ecclesiastical judge and soul-friend, could maintain control.

An area in which the Irish church made a sustained contribution was in care for those in sickness and old age, and also in care for the dead. Something of the last aspect of pastoral care has been examined already: the insistence upon prayers for the dead. They were divided, following Augustine, into those who were so good that they had no need of the prayers of the living, those who were so wicked that no prayers would help

---

66. Penitential of Cummian, viii. 1-2 (ed, Bieler, *Irish Penitentials*, 122). The Penitential of Finnian, § 12, speaks of 'the judgement of a bishop or a priest', § 9 of a *sacerdos* or a *iustus*, § 23 of an abbot or a *sacerdos*.

67. Cf. also the abbot who prescribes a penance in *Hib.* xlvii. 8. *d*, and the *seniores* who do so in *Hib.* xxix. 7. Contrast, however, the Penitential of Columbanus, B 25 (ed, Bieler, *Irish Penitentials*, 104-6), where the bishop reconciles those who have done penance for heresy. In that case the context is Burgundian (Bonosiacs).

68. *Hib.* i. 14. *a* (from Gregory the Great).

69. *Hib.* viii. 2. On the other hand there were also ecclesiastical judges, distinct from secular judges (see *Hib.* xxi. 1), pre-eminent among whom were *scribae*, apparently heads of particular ecclesiastical schools (in the annals a man is almost always a *scriba* of a named church, whereas *sapiens* is very rarely followed by any indication of a place: *sapiens* seems to be the status, *scriba* the office). *Hib.* xx. 2. *a* talks of a panel of ten *iudices* who are to judge all the cases of ten *civitates* (monastic churches or churches with rights of sanctuary?).

70. *CIH* 2129. 6-8 and 37-8.

71. *CIH* 1-3.

them, and those in between whose lot after death could be affected by not only the prayers but also the fasts and the alms of the living.[72]

There were also other issues. The place of burial was one matter of concern, partly because of the strong interest of kinsmen in the dead members of their lineage, an interest which descended from the pre-Christian period when the graves of the dead stood guard at the boundary of the kindred's land.[73] It was assumed that any individual had a church which was his, to which he belonged. This was especially true of monastic tenants, of course, but it was also true for the ordinary laity.[74] It was also assumed that such allegiance descended in the kindred and was expressed by burial.[75] A man was normally buried where his father was buried, so that the solidarity of the kindred might be expressed by burial in the same cemetery. As a result, a church would serve a set of lay kindreds; its fortunes and its continuity (wooden structures were not automatically permanent) depended upon their fortunes and their continuity. As they were, by the very nature of Irish kinship, accustomed to perceive contemporary reality and its validity as a bequest from dead ancestors, so the pressure on their church to care for those ancestors was very strong.

Such care for the ancestor began, in life, with care for the old and sick. This was a duty which lay, in the first place, on the eldest son.[76] If he cared properly for his parents, if he was, in the language of the time, a 'warm son', he may have been entitled to an extra share of the inheritance.[77] There were, however, cases in which either there were no sons or they neglected their duty – were 'cold sons'. In such cases a church might provide the 'warmth', the care of the old or the sick.[78] For such a service it too could obtain at least a temporary share of the inheritance.

The picture of the early Irish church I have attempted to give is of a church under strong pressure from the laity to provide adequate, and more than adequate, pastoral care. The sanctions were the ordinary ones of Irish society: dishonour and loss of status leading to exposure to legal and economic attack. A related theme has been that the church was exposed to serious instability. The *Hibernensis* might wish to see the consolidation of a system of metropolitan provinces; Armagh might seek a primatial

---

72. *Hib.* xv (*De cura pro mortuis*), esp. c.2.
73. *Hib.* xviii (*De iure sepulturae*); T. M. Charles-Edwards, 'Boundaries in Irish law', in *Medieval Settlement*, ed. P. H. Sawyer (1976), 83-7.
74. *Hib.* xviii. 1-7, xxxii. 22 (offering *in pretium sepulcri*). That burial in consecrated ground was not considered necessary is suggested by *Hib.* 1 (*De reliquiis in deserto humatis*). The person who 'has a church' in the special sense of *Hib.* xxxii. 13, is probably someone who is subject to an abbot or other head of a church to the extent that he lacks full legal capacity (xli. 9).
75. Cf. the *paternum sepulcrum* of *Hib.* xviii. 2, 4-5.
76. On all this see D. A. Binchy, 'Some Celtic legal terms', *Celtica* iii (1956), 228-31. The duty of the eldest son is implied by Adomnán's *Vita S. Columbae*, ii. 39.
77. M. Dillon, 'The relationship of mother and son, of father and daughter, and the law of inheritance with regard to women', in *Studies in Early Irish Law*, ed. D. A. Binchy (Dublin, 1936), 141-2.
78. *CIH* 535. 1-2; Kelly, *A Guide to Early Irish Law*, 103.

authority over the whole of Ireland. Neither system established itself securely; and, indeed, their opposition may have prevented any overall structure from putting down firm roots.

Appendix: Some types of early Irish prescriptive text

Kelly   F. Kelly, *A Guide to Early Irish Law* (Dublin, 1988),
                 Appendix 1
Kenney   J. F. Kenney, *The Sources for the Early History of
                 Ireland: Ecclesiastical. An Introduction and Guide*
                 (New York, 1929)
Lapidge and Sharpe   M. Lapidge and R. Sharpe, *A Bibliography of Celtic-
                 Latin Literature 400-1200* (Dublin, 1985)

A. PENITENTIALS (Kenney, nos 72-5; Lapidge and Sharpe, nos 598, 601, 614, 640):

The penitentials of Vinnian (sixth century) and Cummian (seventh century), and the Old Irish Penitential (eighth century), appear to have been written in Ireland. That of Columbanus (*c.* 600) and possibly the Bigotian Penitential (second half of seventh or eighth century) were written on the continent. The nationality of Vinnian is open to dispute (some scholars think that he was a Briton), but the circulation of the text within Ireland is not in doubt (it is quoted in the *Irish Collection of Canons*, for which see below, under the name of Vinnian and was used by Cummian). If the author was a Briton he may have worked in Ireland. The texts are edited and translated by L. Bieler, *The Irish Penitentials* (Scriptores Latini Hiberniae, 5; Dublin, 1963).

B. ACTS OF SYNODS

1. Synodus episcoporum or the First Synod of St Patrick (Kenney, no. 30; Lapidge and Sharpe, no. 599)

A set of canons attributed in the sole surviving manuscript (CCC Cambridge 279) to Patrick, Auxilius and Iserninus; not generally thought by modern scholars to be as early as the fifth century. They were already attributed to Patrick, but not to the other two, in the early eighth-century *Irish Collection of Canons*. Edited and translated by L. Bieler, *The Irish Penitentials*, 54-9

2. Synodus Patricii or **the Second Synod of St Patrick** (Kenney, no. 79; Lapidge and Sharpe, no. 600)

A set of canons attributed in only two of six manuscripts to Patrick. In this case the *Irish Collection of Canons* generally attributes its quotations from the text to a synod of the 'Romans', that is, almost certainly, to a synod of the Roman party within the Irish church. The date would then probably be within the seventh century. The text is edited and translated by L. Bieler, *The Irish Penitentials*, 184–97.

C. CANON LAW COLLECTIONS

The Irish Collection of Canons/Collectio Canonum Hibernensis, often abbreviated *Hibernensis* (Kenney, no. 82; Lapidge and Sharpe, nos 612–13)

Although there are complications, the text survives in two main recensions (A and B). In one manuscript of the A Recension there is a note at the very end, somewhat corrupted; it was convincingly amended to reveal the names of two compilers: 'To this point Ruben of Dairinis and Cú Chuimne of Iona [wrote the text]'. Fortunately, both of these scholars are known. Ruben of Dairinis (a monastery in the south of Ireland in what is now Co. Waterford) died in 725; Cú Chuimne died in 747. The easiest interpretation of the note is that these two scholars were responsible for the A Recension (since the note occurs in a manuscript of that recension). The A Recension must therefore be dated to the first quarter of the eighth century. F. W. H. Wasserschleben, *Die irische Kanonensammlung*, 2nd edn. (Leipzig, 1885) is mainly based on two manuscripts of the A Recension.

D. CÁNAI 'EDICTS'

These texts are an ecclesiastical offshoot of a secular tradition of law-making. As a result they are written in Irish and have more or close links with the secular laws. Although two of them, at least, were promulgated by, or at, semi-ecclesiastical assemblies, their particular mode of enforcement, as well as their language, separates them from the texts listed under B.

1. Cáin Fhuithirbe (Kelly, no. 39)

Promulgated at a Munster assembly in the 680s.

2. Cáin Adomnáin, 'The Law of Adomnán' (also known as *Lex Innocentium*, 'The Law of the Innocents'; Kenney, no. 81; Kelly, no. 74)

Promulgated at an assembly at Birr in Co. Offaly in 697, summoned by Adomnán, abbot of Iona. The present text contains a list of guarantors, probably substantially genuine, implying that the edict had the consent of a great mass of kings and leading churchmen from Ireland and also from Dál Ríata and from the land of the Picts. It also contains much prefatory matter which is evidently of a much later date.

3. Cáin Domnaig, 'The Edict about Sunday' (Kenney, no. 270; Kelly, no. 73)

Probably eighth century, designed to enforce Sunday observance.

4. Ríagail Phátraic, 'The Rule of Patrick'

A text in Irish, probably eighth century, surviving only in one late manuscript. The ascription to Patrick is, of course, false, but perhaps it indicates that it originated at Armagh or an allied church. I have placed it under this heading because of verbal resemblances to other *cánai*. It is to be distinguished from the lost *Cáin Phátraic* (Kelly, no. 5).

E. SECULAR LAWS

1. Córus Béscnai, 'The Proper Arrangement of Custom' (Kelly, no. 10)

A secular law tract, probably of the early eighth century, belonging to the great lawbook of the northern half of Ireland, the *Senchas Már*. It is secular in the sense that these law tracts were distinguished by contemporaries, in terms of the authority and of the tradition lying behind them, from the law of the church. *Córus Béscnai* may well, however, have been written by a clerical lawyer. It contains Patrician material.

2. The Heptads (Kelly, no. 3)

A tract, also belonging to the *Senchas Már*, containing a collection of items grouped in sevens; probably to be dated between *c*. 650 and *c*. 725.

4 Churches and communities in early medieval Ireland: towards a pastoral model

RICHARD SHARPE

In the previous chapter Thomas Charles-Edwards has set out what the lawyers of the Irish church in the eighth century thought should be provided by way of pastoral care. In a manner characteristic of Irish texts in this period, whether law tracts or not, they adopt a contractual attitude: the people will bring their alms to the church, and in return they expect the services of a priest. *Riagail Phátraic*, the Rule of Patrick, emphasizes baptism, communion, and prayers for the dead, and the evidence as a whole confirms that the church was expected to provide pastoral care from the cradle to beyond the grave.

A perennial problem with sources of a prescriptive type is uncertainty about how much all this was reflected in practice, and, if it was, over what period and in how much of the country. Some reassurance can be derived from the fact that much of what we learn from the legal texts is what they refer to in passing as actual circumstances or as incidentals to the prescriptive purpose. My aim here is to gather a variety of evidence, different in kind and scattered in date, which allows us to suppose that expectations of pastoral care were to a considerable degree fulfilled in the early Middle Ages. I shall go on to suggest that the pastoral organization did not remain stable right through the period, and I shall try to make historical sense of the fragmentary information we have on how this functioned.

One angle of approach is to consider what we know about the sacraments in early medieval Ireland, asking whether the evidence indicates a high level of lay participation.

Baptism is frequently mentioned and is specifically an obligation on the local priest.[1] *Confirmation* required the participation of a bishop, and it is not easy to find examples of its happening: all over Europe it is the most elusive of the sacraments, but Irish texts do refer to 'going under the hand of a bishop' after baptism in token of confirmation.[2] A Life of St Darerca mentions how, when St Patrick came to the area where her family lived,

---

1. *Paenitentiale Uinniani*, § 48, ed. L. Bieler, *The Irish Penitentials* (Dublin, 1963), 74-95; *Paenitentiale Cummeani*, ii. 33, ed. L. Bieler, *ibid.*, 108-35; *Riagail Phátraic*, §§ 1, 5, 9, ed. J. G. O'Keeffe, *Ériu*, i (1904), 215-24.
2. *Riagail Phátraic*, § 3.

'not a few [people] were brought to him by the care of religious men so that they could be dipped in the sacred spring of baptism and confirmed by the laying on of hands'.[3] *Mass* was said regularly in churches and was an obligation on the priest. An Irish synod required that a priest reside at his church; he was to do penance if he was absent on one Sunday, and to be degraded if he missed two or three.[4] It is, however, not absolutely clear that the laity attended on a regular basis nor, if they did, whether they received communion. An early Life of St Colmán Élo mentions as remarkable a layman called Ciarán, 'faithful and just, a good man, who on solemn days used to come to St Colmán in order to receive the sacrament from his hand'.[5] The earliest churches were for the most part too small to accommodate a congregation, but services could be held outside, and one story about such a celebration has the officiating priest and other clergy enter the church after the reading of the gospel.[6] This need not preclude the distribution of communion to those standing outside. We have a theological poem written around 1100 or soon after which assumes that laymen received communion but warns of the dangers of receiving it in the wrong spirit.[7] *Confession* is an area where the Irish are seen as having been innovative and influential: the first use of private penance is attributed to the Irish.[8] Most of the evidence in which we see confessions being made suggests that they were made publicly,[9] but private confession could hardly be reported and so lies beyond the scope of our evidence. Concern that laity as well as clergy should repent their sins is well attested in the Penitential texts of the sixth and later centuries. Finally, *burial* in churchyards or consecrated burial grounds was a familiar practice by the seventh century, though one should not assume that it was normal for the laity to be so buried at this date.[10] Secular burial at the traditional burying-place of the community may have been still common practice, though we learn that a cross (apparently of wood) distinguished the grave of a Christian from the pagans among whom he was buried.[11] None the less every church was expected to have a burial-ground.[12] When founding

---

3. *Vita S. Darerca*, § 1, ed. W. W. Heist, *Vitae Sanctorum Hiberniae e Codice olim Salmanticensi* (Brussels, 1965), 83-95.
4. *Hibernensis*, ii. 25, ed. F. W. H. Wasserschleben, *Die irische Kanonensammlung* (2nd edn., Leipzig, 1885).
5. *Vita S. Colmani Elo*, S. § 31, ed. Heist, *Vitae*, 209-24. The Life may well date from the late seventh or early eighth century.
6. Adomnán, *Vita S. Columbae*, iii. 17, ed. A. O. and M. O. Anderson (2nd edn., Oxford, 1991).
7. The poem 'A duine nách creit iar cóir' by Echtgus Úa Cúanáin was edited by A. G. Van Hamel, *Revue celtique*, xxxvii (1919), 345-9, and translated by G. Murphy, 'Eleventh or twelfth century Irish doctrine concerning the Real Presence', in *Medieval Studies Presented to Aubrey Gwynn S.J.*, ed. J. A. Watt et al. (Dublin, 1961), 19-28.
8. Kenney, *Sources*, 238, traces this view back to Wasserschleben and Fournier.
9. For example, Adomnán, *Vita S. Columbae*, i. 22, 30, 50.
10. E. O'Brien, 'Christian burial in Ireland: continuity and change', in *The Early Church in Wales and the West*, ed. N. Edwards and A. M. Lane (forthcoming).
11. Muirchú, *Vita S. Patricii*, ii. 2, ed. L. Bieler, *The Patrician Texts in the Book of Armagh* (Dublin, 1979), 62-123; Tírechán, § 41, ed. Bieler, *ibid.*, 124-67.
12. *Riagail Phátraic*, § 6.

a church, saints are often said to have marked out the limits of the cemetery. These newly established Christian cemeteries may initially have served only for the burial of ecclesiastical personnel. There is no direct testimony that churches took over and Christianized existing secular grave-sites, though there is both placename and archaeological evidence suggesting sites where this is likely.[13]

I know of no text which allows one to see these pastoral attentions stage by stage through the career of an individual. One might have expected that the Lives of saints would be a rich source here but they are not. Most saints' baptisms are mentioned in their Lives, but the circumstances usually involve the saint's parents seeking out a priest who was noted for his holiness and who would in many cases recognize the future sanctity of the infant. There is no case documented where the child was taken specifically to the priest under whose pastoral care the parents lived. With burials the evidence of saints' Lives is even more abnormal, because the saints whose Lives we have were the founders of churches. They were buried at their own foundations, there to rise again on the last day. In the course of a saint's career we often hear of people arriving to seek baptism for a child; to do penance for a sin committed; to bring alms to the holy man; or of their dying at his church and their burial in its graveyard. I could assemble a catalogue of such references here from different texts, but each text, each reference would need an explanation of its peculiarities. I fear that any general picture would be too hedged with qualifications to make much sense. Moreover, the focus on the holy man is likely to mean that these stories do not shed light on the norms of pastoral care in local communities. Indeed, the Lives of Irish saints to a very considerable extent ignore the church's pastoral role. They depict saints as leaders of monastic life, not as pastors for the laity. The contrast between the pastoral assumptions of the prescriptive literature and the bias of saints' Lives towards religious retreat encapsulates the great problem of early Irish Church history.

A second approach is to look for evidence of the framework within which pastoral care was given. The texts which Dr Charles-Edwards has discussed make the assumption that 'any individual had a church which was his, to which he belonged', and that churches carried pastoral responsibility for their lay people.[14] The unit with which historians associate this is primarily the *parish*, but parishes in the medieval and modern sense developed rather late in the history of the church. In England we can see their development in many areas during the tenth to twelfth centuries. In Ireland this development seems to be much later than in most parts of England. It is usually said that the organization of parishes did not begin until the 1170s and that it was not complete even at the date of the well-

---

13. O'Brien, op. cit. n.10.
14. Charles-Edwards, p. 76.

documented papal taxation of 1302 × 1307.[15] This view, however, is to a large extent a matter of assumption, as we shall see. It may be a dangerous assumption, because undiscriminatingly applied it leads to a reluctance to ask how the late medieval parochial organization was related to what existed previously.

Before the development of the parish it is now accepted, as a model at least, that in England pastoral care was organized through large 'parishes' served by teams of priests and other clergy operating from important central churches. These churches are familiarly called 'minsters' (a convenient translation for *monasterium*),[16] and their large parishes are usually termed *parochiae* or 'minster parishes'. Many of the minster churches date from the seventh and eighth centuries, but their origins are in many cases highly speculative and very often their status as minsters and the extent of their *parochiae* have to be inferred from much later topographical and documentary evidence. For the student of early medieval Ireland there is no accepted terminology, there is no accepted model, and the evidence which might allow the creation of a model is more fragmentary than that available in England.

In identifying ancient minsters and their *parochiae* historians rely heavily on the continuity with which church sites have been used in England: a medieval church very often still stands and still serves a medieval parish. In Ireland almost every church still in use dates from the eighteenth century and after (and a good many nineteenth-century churches are now Romantic ivy-covered ruins), but there is a very large number of older churches and church sites dotted about the countryside. Most of these have little or no documentation, and it can often be difficult even to know under what name they may appear in historical records. A high proportion of medieval parish churches fell into disuse during the sixteenth and seventeenth centuries, so that even for these it can take a great deal of effort using visitation records of that period to establish the connexion between a parish church named in late medieval sources and a site on the ground.

Even so, major uncertainties remain over the extent of the late medieval parish. In England parish boundaries of the eleventh and twelfth centuries have generally remained accessible, thanks both to their continuity and to their being marked on the maps in everyday use until the 1970s. For most of Ireland good large-scale maps have not been produced since 1913.[17]

---

15. The papal taxation is summarized in *Calendar of Documents Relating to Ireland*, ed. H. S. Sweetman and G. F. Handcock, 5 vols. (1875-86), v, 202-323 (nos 693-727). See also G. J. Hand, 'The dating of the early fourteenth-century ecclesiastical valuation of Ireland', *Irish Theological Quarterly*, xxiv (1957), 271-4.

16. S. Foot, p. 215 below.

17. For an account of what maps are available and which are most useful for archaeological purposes, see T. J. C. Reeves-Smyth, 'Landscapes in paper: cartographic sources for Irish archaeology', in *Landscape Archaeology in Ireland*, ed. T. J. C. Reeves-Smyth and F. W. Hamond, BAR, British Series 116 (1983), 119-77.

Civil parishes have been obsolete for 150 years; there has been very little work on the historical status of ascertainable parish bounds. In England we can relate known parish churches and bounds to the information provided for most of the country by Domesday Book. For some areas there exists even more detailed local information, and more than 1,000 pre-Conquest charters help fill in details in our understanding of land-holdings in Anglo-Saxon England. Although there is no shortage of early data from Ireland, consisting largely of names of churches and church sites, it is not comparable with the English evidence in its topographical coherence, and many of the early placenames are very hard to identify. This discontinuity between field evidence and the historical record may in part be overcome with sufficient research, but that is still a long way off.

The nature of the evidence inevitably influences the approach adopted by historians. In England there is much topographical history for this period, allowing fruitful collaboration between documentary historians and historical archaeologists. In Ireland histories of individual churches have tended to be heavily prosopographical, reflecting the richness of the annals and genealogies. A good example is Dr Herbert's study of Kells in the ninth and tenth centuries, in which she investigates the dynastic affiliation of the coarbs of St Columba and may by this means situate the church of Kells in the political history of Brega.[18] For minor churches, few of which are mentioned in the annalistic sources, the topographical approach is the only one available, and it has borne some fruit. This approach, however, demands work with late medieval and post-medieval records, even for study of the early Middle Ages, and it needs to be combined with archaeological fieldwork.

Both sides of the task are more challenging than is the case with the English evidence, but it is increasingly possible to establish and document continuity at individual sites. For example, the medieval church of Cannaway parish, Co. Cork, is first mentioned in documentary sources as *Cennmugi* in a papal privilege of 1199, and next as *Kanwy* in the early fourteenth-century papal taxation. Its site can be identified as the early medieval enclosure now called Bawnatemple, from where a cross-inscribed stone of the seventh or eighth century was recently published.[19] Kilkieran in Co. Kilkenny is an enclosed burial-ground with three impressive crosses of the eighth century.[20] Documentary references are few and insecure, but it appears that in 1350 the site was known as *capella de Lissentane* and in 1351 *Tainewyrghlan*.[21] All surface remains apart from the crosses were destroyed around 1780, but excavations in 1985 revealed the remains of a stone-walled enclosure, perhaps 80–100 metres in diameter, and signs of use

18. M. Herbert, *Iona, Kells, and Derry* (1988), pp. 68–108.
19. V. Hurley and B. D. O'Flaherty, 'A cross-inscribed stone from an early ecclesiastical enclosure at Bawnatemple near Macroom, Co. Cork', *J. Cork Hist. and Archaeol. Soc.* lxxxvi (1981), 53–62.
20. N. Edwards, 'An early group of crosses from the kingdom of Ossory', *JRSAI*, cxiii (1983), 5–46.
21. M. F. Hurley, 'Excavations at an early ecclesiastical enclosure at Kilkieran, Co. Kilkenny', *JRSAI*, cxviii (1988), 124–34 (p. 125).

from the period of the crosses into the later Middle Ages. Sites of this kind are not discussed by historians of the early Irish church, whose studies have been dominated by more or less theoretical models of how the church as an institution was organized and governed.

One of the main difficulties has been marrying together general theories and information on any particular church, even a church such as Kells, which is well documented in early sources. Dr Herbert has commented, 'There have been, perhaps, too many attempts at synthesis and too few close studies of particular aspects of the Irish ecclesiastical scene.'[22] Yet it is scarcely possible to study an individual church or a particular aspect of organization without invoking a model to supply the wider framework. Once invoked, the model influences the detailed studies in such a way as to make the two mutually supportive. Our existing models have grown up by degrees over a long period and it is often not easy to see them for what they are. The differences between our models for the earlier and later Middle Ages have been further reinforced by cautious scholarship that avoids using evidence from across the boundaries of period.

The twelfth century in particular has acted as a barrier limiting the perspective of historians and archaeologists. The church up to this period has been interpreted through a monastic model, and early medieval historians have not had regard to the work needed in late medieval sources to make sense of the minor churches lying outwith the annalistic evidence. Specialists in late medieval Ireland have often (though with notable exceptions) assumed that the twelfth century saw a new beginning in ecclesiastical arrangements. On sites where there is obvious continuity the archaeologist is likely to remark that the late medieval parish church was established on the site of an early Irish monastery. The difference in model gives rise to the different terminology and leads both sides to maintain the barrier. Yet the evidence on the ground establishes that many churches, large and small, were in continuous use throughout the Middle Ages. From the twelfth century on these churches had a pastoral function. There is ample evidence for a pastoral organization during earlier centuries, though it has generally been overshadowed by the monastic model. It seems worthwhile to see whether we can find a model which will explain better the role of the large number of minor churches attested by topographical evidence as functioning continuously throughout the medieval period.

Early in the Middle Ages we have good evidence for the widespread distribution of churches in the seventh century. There survives in the Book of Armagh a unique copy of a most unusual work. Its author Tírechán was a bishop; his family belonged to Co. Mayo on the west coast of Ireland, but he was himself associated in some way with the church of Armagh.[23] We do not know that he was actually based at Armagh, but he regarded himself, his kin, and his native church as subordinate to the bishop of

---

22. Herbert, *Iona, Kells, and Derry*, 5.
23. Ed. L. Bieler, *The Patrician Texts in the Book of Armagh* (Dublin, 1979), 124-62; my quotations and translations differ in some respects from Bieler's edition.

Armagh. He wrote his book some time between the *floruit* of Bishop Ultán of Ardbraccan (who died in 655) and the death of Bishop Áed of Sleaty in 700; more precisely he refers to the fact that many churches had been left without clergy as a result of recent plagues, referring to the serious plagues of the years 664-9 or those of 684-8.[24] Modern scholarship tends to favour the former date, and we date Tírechán's book therefore to *c.* 670.

What Tírechán does is describe St Patrick's supposed missionary journey through eastern, northern and western Ireland, recording the names of churches which he founded and of the priests and bishops he installed in them. In some parts of the narrative the listing of sites can be very dense:[25]

> Plantauit aeclessiam super uadum Segi et alteram aeclessiam Cinnena⟨e⟩ sancta⟨e⟩ super uadum Carnoi i mBoind et altera⟨m⟩ super Coirp raithe et altera⟨m⟩ super fossam Dallbronig, quam tenuit episcopus Filius Cairtin, auunculus Brigtæ sanctae. Fundauitque alteram in campo Echredd, alteram in campo Taidcni, quae dicitur Cell Bile (apud familiam Scire est), alteram in campo Echnach, in qua fuit Cassanus praespiter, alteram in Singitibus, alteram in campo Bili iuxta uadum Capitis Canis, alteram in Capite Carmelli in campo Teloch, in qua sancta Brigita pallium cepit sub manibus Filii Caille in Huisnech Midi. Mansit iuxta Petram Coithrigi, sed occissi sunt circa se alii peregrini a filio Fechach filii Ne⟨i⟩ll; cui maledixit, dicens: 'Non erit de stirpe tua rex, sed seruies semini fratrum tuorum.' Et alteram aeclessiam in Capite Aird in regionibus Roide, in qua possuit altare lapideum, et alteram hi Cuil Corræ. Et uenit per flumen Ethne in duas Thethbias et ordinauit Melum episcopum et aeclessiam Bili fundauit et ordinauit Gosactum filium Milcon maccu Booin, quem nutriuit in seruitute septem annorum, et mittens Camulacum Commiensium in campum Cumi et digito illi indicauit locum de cacumine Graneret, id est aeclessiam Raithin. Et uenit in campum Rein et ordinauit Bruscum prespiterum et aeclessiam illi fundauit; qui dixit mirabile post mortem eius altero sancto, qui fuit in insola generis Cotirbi: 'Bene est tibi dum filium tuum habes; ego autem, tedebit me mors mea, quia solus sum in aeclessia in diserto, in aeclessia relicta et uacua, et non offerent iuxta me sacerdotes.' In noctibus ⟨tribus⟩ somnium †factus est: tertio die surrexit sanctus et arripuit †anulum et trullam ferrumque et sepulcri fossam fodiuit et portauit ossa Brusci sancti secum ad insolam in qua sunt, et resticuit.

> [Patrick] founded a church at Áth Segi [*Assey, Co. Meath*], and another church for St Cinenna at Áth Carnói on the Boyne, and another on Coirp Raithe, and another on the ditch of Dal bronig,

---

24. Tírechán, § 25, quoted below, p. 92.
25. Tírechán, § 16.

which St Brigit's uncle Bishop Mac Cairthin held. And he founded another [church] in Mag nEchred, another in Mag Taidcni, which is called Cell Bile (this belongs to the community of Scire), another in Mag nEchnach where the priest Cassah was, another at Singite, another in Mag Bili near the Ford of the Dog's Head, another at the Head of Carmell in Mag Teloch, in which St Brigit took the veil at the hands of Bishop Mac Caille in Uisnech Midi. He settled at the Stone of Coithrigi, but some of his foreign companions were killed by Fiachu mac Néill, whom he cursed, saying: 'There will not be a king from your lineage, and you will serve the seed of your brothers.' And [he founded] another church at Art's Head in the territory of Roide, where he set up a stone altar, and another [church] at Cúl Corrae. And he crossed the River Ethne into the two Tethbai and consecrated Mel as bishop, and he founded the Church of Bile and ordained Gosacht mac Milchon maccu Bóin, whom he had brought up during his seven years of slavery. And sending Camelach of the *Commienses* to Mag Cumi, from the summit of Granard he pointed out a place for him, that is the church of Raithen [*Rahan, Co. Offaly*]. And he came into Mag Rein and ordained Bruscus as priest and founded a church for him. This man spoke miraculously after his death to a saint who was in the island of the race of Cothirbe: 'It is well for you because you have your son. But I – my death is a weariness to me because I am alone in a church in the desert, in a church empty and abandoned, and there are no priests celebrating mass beside me.' For <three> nights he had this dream, and on the third day the holy man arose and took a †ring and a shovel and a tool and dug up the trench of the grave and brought the bones of Bruscus with him to the island where they still are and he fell silent.

The notion of St Patrick's itinerary is no more than a literary device enabling Tírechán to catalogue the churches in which Armagh had or claimed some interest. In this way he names nearly eighty individual churches as having been founded by St Patrick. More than half of these are not mentioned in any independent sources – though many reappear in the Tripartite Life,[26] a tenth-century Irish Life which incorporates a revised translation of Tírechán – and the same is true of many of the topographical names which are our principal guide to locating these churches. This is a difficult exercise, but after a hundred years of trying a fair number can now be located, though no one has published either a list or a map.

Other sources from the seventh and eighth centuries greatly increase the number of individual churches known. No single text mentions so many minor churches, but the saints' Lives add a good number, and the annals give us the names of a considerable number of more significant churches.

26. Ed. with English transl. W. Stokes, *The Tripartite Life of Patrick with Other Documents*, Rolls Series 88 (1887); the parallels between the Irish text and Tírechán are highlighted in the edition by K. Mulchrone, *Bethu Phátraic* (Dublin, 1939).

Among the hundreds of place and tribal names known from Ireland before the year 800 I should say, at a guess, that we know the names of about 250 churches. This may well be a larger number than can be named in the whole of England from evidence of such early date, or indeed from any comparable area of France or Spain.

Evidence of the ninth and tenth centuries adds still more church names and sources with no very clear date mention uncounted numbers of churches.[27] It would be a great labour to list and map all this information. The reference tools for doing this are hardly adequate, and the location of one placename often depends on the location of another or other names – in many cases the designations of population groups which may have only a relatively short currency or which may change position. It would be a great asset to have a cumulative index or database of churches referred to in sources before 1200, and it would be even better if a significant number could be mapped. The information, however, would be defective in several ways. First of all, we know it would be incomplete because of the gaps in our evidence. Second, there is no evidence that would give us the assurance that we had a complete list for any area, however small. The earliest local lists which might be found useful in this way are found in papal privileges of the late twelfth century. The imperfect distribution in our database would reflect:

1. the geographical distribution of the source material;
2. the bias of the annals towards more important churches;
3. the imbalance caused by a few detailed sources such as Tírechán; and
4. the cumulative reckoning of churches which were never in use simultaneously: many small churches named in saints' Lives may have disappeared quite quickly.

For the most part the available evidence in written sources is unhelpful in the matter of categorizing churches. Some we know were places of religious retreat – monasteries in the modern sense – and some were major centres, churches which had grown up into small towns, and in a few cases not such small towns. However, a great many of the churches known by name were small churches where a priest attempted to deliver pastoral care to the local lay population.

The assumptions which underlie the *Hibernensis* or the Rule of Patrick, about a principal church in every petty kingdom (*túath*), about lesser churches, and about pastoral services to the laity are not easily tested against other evidence. None the less, an indication of the extent to which the church had reached out to provide care in every inhabited corner of Ireland can be gained from the few areas where a field survey has been carried out. (These have not been done for the areas where the early documentary

---

27. For example, the list of local saints associated with specific local churches in the Book of Leinster, printed in *The Book of Leinster*, ed. R. I. Best *et al.* (Dublin, 1954-83), vi, 1578-83.

evidence is rich, so the opportunities for correlating written sources and field evidence are less than one might have hoped for.)

In the Dingle peninsula, on the south-west coast of Ireland, there are nineteen parishes. The archaeological survey of this area records sixty-eight 'early ecclesiastical sites' (nos 810–77), twelve 'sites of churches' (nos 968–79), and a further nineteen 'medieval churches' (nos 980–98), a total of ninety-nine.[28] There are some sites in this number which must be discounted, and there are some quite serious problems: the Papal Taxation mentions a parish church of Minard, not located but identified in the survey as perhaps Kilmurray (no. 986) or Aglish (no. 810); the latter was an early Christian site and has yielded a cross-marked stone and a second stone bearing an inscription; out of these it is possible that we have either two or three church sites but never more than one in use at any date.

This archaeological survey contains maps of the topographical and administrative units, one showing the civil parishes (p. 363) and another showing townlands (pp. 12–13): civil parish bounds are not marked on the latter, so the user must mentally transfer them from the other map. The 1,600 monuments recorded in the survey are located by ordnance datum; the maps show no grid-squares and the monument record makes no reference to parish or townland. It is very difficult, therefore, to read the archaeological information in a topographical or administrative context.[29] It is obvious from the townland map that the townlands are much larger in the three large parishes over which Mount Brandon spreads: are there fewer church sites in this area, compatible with a lower density of settlement, or is there evidence for churches in remote districts? Questions of this kind can only be answered by putting in a good deal of work with the 6-inch maps – or by consulting the records of the survey, preserved at Ballyferriter, where all this information is marked on sheets of the 25-inch map. Good maps can be a great help in understanding data of this kind.

In an important paper Vincent Hurley provides a map of early ecclesiastical settlement in the counties of Cork and Kerry.[30] Unfortunately this map is on a very small scale and has no key to identify the sites marked. A slightly larger-scale map with a key shows fifty-one sites in these two counties: these are 'principal sites', though the definition of 'principal' is not included; five of the ninety-nine sites in Dingle are marked on this map: 6 = Ballywiheen (Survey no. 827), 23 = Gallarus (no. 839), 25 = Illauntannig (no. 843), 35 = Kilmalkedar (no. 855), 45 = Reask (no. 874). If one were to multiply 51 in the proportion 5 to 99, the total number of sites projected for these two counties would be over a thousand. The quantity of field evidence is very considerable. The recording of it was energetically begun in the 1980s, but we have not yet started to interpret

---

28. J. Cuppage *et al.*, *Archaeological Survey of the Dingle Peninsula* (Ballyferriter, 1986).
29. A more useful map appears in D. Ó Conchúir, *Corca Dhuibhne* (Dingle, 1976).
30. V. Hurley, 'The early church in the south-west of Ireland: settlement and organisation', in *The Early Church in Western Britain and Ireland*, ed. S. M. Pearce, BAR, British Series 102 (1982), 297–332.

it. The very idea of taking a close topographical look at the distribution of field evidence with or without reference to such matters as townland or parish has scarcely been put into practice.

Attempts at a typology of sites are only marginally more advanced. Vincent Hurley has recorded the diameter of ecclesiastical enclosures in the counties of Cork and Kerry. He maps them as large, medium and small. Thirteen sites in Dingle are on his map, all of them classified as 'small', but this was drawn up before the Dingle survey was begun. Ecclesiastical enclosures are being rediscovered every year, in some cases only as crop-marks. Their dimensions vary between about 30 metres and 400 metres in diameter, but most (we are told, though the evidence has not yet been systematically presented) are between 100 and 200 metres in diameter.[31] This does not help us very much.

A different approach to typology was adopted by Deirdre Flanagan. She attempted to compare the ecclesiastical nomenclature used in Latin and Irish texts with placename elements designating churches.[32] The information is treated linguistically and not topographically, with no attempt to correlate between actual churches named in written sources and the forms in their placenames. Tírechán presents a particular problem by his Latinizing of Irish names, especially the generic element. Churches are usually referred to as *aeclessia*, more rarely as *cella* or *cellola*, and there is no consistent relationship between his Latin words and the vernacular word used as the generic element in the actual placename. Often these can only be ascertained from the topographical indications in the text. Even when topographical and archaeological evidence is taken into account, it has proved impossible to establish any clear correlation between types of ecclesiastical foundation on the ground and the words used as the generic element. It is not practical, therefore, to establish a typology by bringing together the linguistic approach, the field evidence, and the prescriptive texts with their apparent terminological distinctions between different types of church.

None the less, some of the onomastic evidence appears very significant, such as the use of words emphasizing the age of a church. Tírechán, writing as we have said c. 670, mentions that St Patrick came *ad Dumecham nepotum Ailello et fundauit in illo loco aeclessiam quam sic uocatur Senella cella Dumiche usque hunc diem* 'to Dumach Úa nAilello and in that place he founded a church which is called the old church of Dumach to this day' (§ 23). The word *dumach*, gen. *dumaige* means 'mound, bank' and commonly 'grave-mound'; so the placename almost certainly means

31. D. L. Swan, 'Enclosed ecclesiastical settlements and their relevance to settlement patterns of the first millennium AD', in *Landscape Archaeology in Ireland*, ed. T. J. C. Reeves-Smyth and F. W. Hamond, BAR, British Series 116 (1983), 269-94 (pp. 270, 274).
32. 'Ecclesiastical nomenclature in Irish texts and place-names', in *Proceedings of the 10th International Congress of Onomastic Sciences*, ed. H. H. Hornung (Vienna, 1969), 379-88; 'The Christian impact on early medieval Ireland: place-name evidence', in *Ireland and Europe: The Early Church*, ed. P. Ní Chatháin and M. Richter (Stuttgart, 1984), 25-51.

'the grave-mound of Uí Ailello'. Here then is a case where the placename element may indicate that the church took over the traditional burial-ground of the community identified as Uí Ailello. The text goes on to say that someone went on *per montem filorum Ailello* 'over the mound of the sons of Ailell' (§ 24) to found a second church, Tamnach, some distance away. It seems possible that we have two designations for the same place, and the Tripartite treats both as Dumach Úa nAilello. The context, however, tends to imply that the *mons* is a major geographical feature, perhaps some Sliab macc nAilello whose name was no longer recognized by the Tripartite translator.[33] A further difficulty arises when one compares another passage, which appears to give a different location for the *mons filiorum Ailello* and apparently a different founder for Tamnach.[34] Tírechán's Latin account of these two foundations is not easily understood, and my translation differs from Bieler's at several points:

> Patricius uero uenit de fonte Alo Find ad Dumecham nepotum Ailello et fundauit in illo loco aeclessiam quae uocatur Senella Cella Dumiche usque hunc diem, in quo reliquit uiros sanctos Macet et Cetgen et Rodanum prespiterum. Et uenit apud se filia felix in peregrinationem nomine Mathona soror Benigni successoris Patricii, quae tenuit pallium apud Patricium et Rodanum; monacha fuit illis et exiit per montem filiorum Ailello et plantauit aeclessiam liberam hi Tamnuch et honorata fuerat a Deo et hominibus et ipsa fecit amicitiam ad reliquias sancti Rodani et successores illius epulabantur ad inuicem. Post haec autem posuerunt episcopos iuxta sanctam eclessiam hi Tamnuch, quos ordinauerunt episcopi Patricii, id est Bronus et Bi[e]theus; non quaerebant aliquid a familia Dumiche nissi amicitiam tantum-modo, sed quaerit familia Clono, qui per uim tenent locos Patricii multos post mortalitates nouissimas.

> Patrick went from the well of Ail Find [*Elphin, Co. Roscommon*] to Dumach Úa nAilello, and he founded there a church called Senchell Dumaige [*Shankill, Co. Roscommon*] to this day, where he left the holy men Machet and Cétgen and the priest Rúadán. And there came to them as a pilgrim a blessed girl called Mathona, the sister of Patrick's successor Benignus, and she took the veil in the presence of Patrick and Rúadán. She was their nun and she [?] went over the Mount of the Sons of Ailill [?] and founded a free church at Tamnach [*Tawnagh, Co. Sligo*], and she was honoured by God and men and made a treaty of friendship at the burial-place of St Rúadán, and his successors and hers exchange hospitality. Thereafter they set bishops in the holy church at Tamnach, whom St Patrick's bishops Brón and Bitheus ordained, and they sought nothing from the community at Dumach except friendship only,

---

33. The Curlew Mts would certainly fit the context here.
34. Tírechán, § 46.

but the community of Cluain seeks, who hold by force many churches of Patrick after the most recent plagues.

Behind this story may be the fact that Senchell Dumaige was not a Patrician foundation at all: Rúadán appears to be the local saint associated with the church, and, whether one translates *reliquiae* as 'relics' (with Bieler) or 'cemetery' (following OIr. *reilic* < Lat. *reliquiae*), it seems likely that he was buried there. Mathona's foundation of Tamnach lies about 15 miles north of Senchell Dumaige, and began its existence as a free church, though it later became an episcopal church. Its relationship with Senchell Dumaige was one of friendship, and this did not change when it became a see, apparently subordinate to Armagh. The position of Senchell Dumaige, however, had recently changed for the worse; this, I take it, is what Tírechán means in saying that the Patrician bishops 'did not seek anything from the community of Dumach except friendship only, but the community of Clonmacnoise seeks, who holds by force many of St Patrick's churches after the latest plagues' (§ 24). In this opaque way Tírechán suggests a relationship between the church at Tamnach and the community in the old church at Dumach which served the population group called Uí Ailello. This old church, *Senella cella Dumiche* can be identified as Shankill, Co. Roscommon: OIr. *sen chell* means 'old church', and it seems that it was already known as this in the seventh century. Elsewhere Tírechán calls the same place *aeclessiam senem nepotum Ailello*, again 'the old church of Uí Ailello' (§ 7). Does Tírechán suggest that this was a church which was already 'old' as an institution? Shankill is not uncommon as a placename element: may we infer that these form a class (or part of a class) of churches with a special character depending on their antiquity? I think so, though one must beware of making the further inference that these 'old churches' were necessarily ancient; a church founded only one generation before Tírechán wrote might have seniority, and consequently superiority, over little, local or private churches founded subsequently.

Another word for church which puts an emphasis on the church's age is OIr. *andóit*, deriving from *antitatem*, a contraction of Lat. *antiquitatem*. In the law-tract *Córus Béscnai* the word is used to designate a specific type of ecclesiastical foundation of high status.[35] In occurs also as a generic in placenames, but rarely, and not in cases with early documentary evidence.

In another passage Tírechán claims for St Patrick *omnes primitiuae aeclessiae Hiberniae* 'all the primary churches of Ireland' (§ 18). I have suggested elsewhere that by this he meant the first-founded churches which served the needs of local communities, the mother-churches of Ireland.[36]

---

35. The word is used only once in the surviving parts of the canonical text of the tract (*CIH*, 530.9), but it is used several times in the commentary which preserves further fragments of *Córus Béscnai* (*CIH*, 1812-21). The commentators and glossators associate the church with the patron saint of the community or kin-group, while a legal glossary is particularly apposite: '*andóit*, .i. a church which precedes another is a head, and it is earlier, .i. the first' (*CIH*, 620.34).

36. R. Sharpe, 'Some problems concerning the organization of the church in early medieval Ireland', *Peritia*, iii (1984) [1986], 230-70.

One can only regret that he did not specifically provide a catalogue of places which he counted as *primitiuus*. This passage of Tírechán is based on a more elaborate statement of claims drawn up in the interests of the church of Armagh in a short text written about 640-50 called *Liber Angeli*.[37] With one emendation in the Latin text, this reads:

> Item omnis aeclessia libera et ciuitas ⟨quae⟩ ab episcopali gradu uidetur esse fundata in tota Scotorum insola et omnis ubique locus qui dominicus appellatur iuxta clementiam almipotentis Domini sancto doctori et iuxta uerbum angueli in speciali societate Patricii pontificis atque heredis eius Aird Machæ esse debuerat, quia donauit illi Deus totam insolam, ut supra diximus.

> Every free church, and every city in all Ireland which is seen to have been founded by a bishop, and every church everywhere called *domnach* ought, in accordance with the mercy of the kind and almighty Lord and with the word of the angel to the holy teacher, to belong to the special *societas* of bishop Patrick and the heir of his see at Armagh.

'Free churches' must be a significant term. Tamnach, mentioned above, was a free church before it became an episcopal church. Such churches are mentioned in the canon-law texts, and they must have been a particular class of church within the institutional organization. The same may be true of OIr. *domnach* < LL *dominicus*. The word is an early loan in Irish, reflecting a Late Latin usage; the meaning 'church' became obsolete before the seventh century, except in the names of places, and the word continued only in the sense 'Sunday'. The names of many churches, however, preserved the older meaning. In Tírechán's Latin text we find churches called *aeclessia magna* + qualifier: such churches were probably called in Irish *Domnach mór* + qualifier. There are twenty townlands called simply Donaghmore, and the *Onomasticon* records a further eighty-odd places called *Domnach mór* + qualifier. There is also a considerable number of sites called *Domnach* + qualifier, although there is no *Domnach bec*, 'little church'. It is now generally accepted that *domnach* and particularly *domnach mór* designated a church of status, almost certainly the status of a mother-church, that is a church which was the primary centre of pastoral care within an area.[38] Some *domnach mór* names are qualified by a population group (*Domnach Sairigi*) but most are followed by a territorial qualifier (*Domnach mór Maige Itha*). The qualifier in these cases presumably indicated the people whom the church served or the territory they occupied.[39]

---

37. Ed. L. Bieler, *Patrician Texts*, 184-90. On the date, see R. Sharpe, 'Armagh and Rome in the seventh century', in *Ireland and Europe: The Early Church*, ed. P. Ní Chatháin and M. Richter (Stuttgart, 1984), 58-72.
38. S. Mac Airt, 'The churches founded by St Patrick', in *Saint Patrick*, ed. J. Ryan (Dublin, 1958), 67-80 (p. 79); D. Flanagan, 'The Christian impact', 31.
39. The connexion of people and church is explicit in the case cited, 'de genere Sai de regionibus Cenachtae a Domnach Sairigi', Tírechán, § 27.

In more than a few cases the qualifier is Patrick's name (*Domnach Pátraic*), a fact which suggests that the link which Tírechán claimed was in some cases generally acknowledged. I note a particularly striking example from the Tripartite Life:[40]

> Patrick journeyed eastwards into the Glens, where the kindred of Muinremar is today. ... Patrick's Stone is there and Patrick's Hazel, a little distance westwards from the church. He made his foundation there. Srath Pátraic is its name today, but of old its name was Domnach Pátraic. Patrick rested there on Sunday [Ir. *domnach*], and this is the only church in that area.

Here, in a late Old Irish source, we see the connexion between Patrick and the *domnach*, the early obsolescence of that name, and evidence for the primary status of the *domnach* within its area.

The fact that in Tírechán's time, indeed earlier when the *Liber Angeli* was written, these were regarded as superior churches, to be grouped with 'free churches' and episcopal foundations, suggests that already in the seventh century lesser churches were becoming widespread. The *domnach* churches were already old-established: some now appear in the placename record as *Sendomnach* (seven in the *Onomasticon*), and one is already so called by Tírechán: *fundauerunt aeclessiam in Aird Licce quae sic uocatur Sendomnach* 'they founded a church in Ard Licce which is called *Sendomnach*' (§ 27). Unfortunately Tírechán provides very little information on the relationship between 'free churches' or *domnach* churches and the lay communities they served. His interest was centred on Armagh's proprietary interest in such churches. The nature of the relationships between different churches is also very difficult to grasp. Armagh had some real interest in both the old church at Dumach (claiming it as a Patrician foundation) and in the nearby free church of Tamnach; the relationship between those two was no more than friendship, but Clonmacnoise claimed a different relationship with Dumach. There is evidently a hierarchy of control and dependency here, but there are many problems in understanding the relationship between mother-churches and superior churches. Using Tírechán alone it seems impossible to understand what lesser churches there were, spreading at a later date than the primary foundations.

Turning now, therefore, to evidence of later date, I want to note two aspects of the institutional structure.

First, let us go back to the idea of the parish or of what preceded the parish. Strong local ties between the community and its church are central to the legal texts' contractual view of pastoral care. The existence of such ties is borne out in the formation of *domnach* names, which indicates that these churches served a definite area or a definite people - the two amount

---

40. *Bethu Phátraic*, r 1683-8, ed. K. Mulchrone (Dublin, 1939), 89. W. Stokes, *The Tripartite Life*, i, 144-7, emends the last sentence to read 'this is *his* only church in that territory'.

to the same thing. At what level they served, it is not easy to say. Now there is a remarkable text preserved in the fifteenth-century Book of Lismore. This text, which is not likely to date from any earlier than the twelfth century, defines the district of Caoille and its subdivisions.[41] Caoille is situated in the north of Co. Cork where the rivers Awbeg and Funshion flow south-eastwards to join the River Blackwater above and below the garrison town of Fermoy. It is a fertile plain, about 9 miles across from north to south, bounded by the Ballyhoura and Galty mountains to the north, the Nagles mountains to the south and the Knockmealdowns to the east. The district was divided into small territories (*túatha*), according to this text, *Crichad an Chaoilli*, which as far as it goes lists the settlements and the people of each territory. By this date the word *túath* designates a very small local unit rather than the older petty kingdom. These local *túatha* seem to be the size of two or three late medieval parishes. Towards the end of each section the church of the *túath* is named, and in some cases so is the family of its coarb and its clergy:

> § 3 . . . Cell Aenamhna is the church of the Eoganacht of Glen-domain. And a third of the lands of Brí Gobhann [*Brigown, Co. Cork*] belongs to that people [*túath*], namely, Carrac Cormaic and Cell Danan, Cúl Domnann, Cluain Locha, Cluain Lena, Cluain Cairbeach, Cell Bracáin, Corrlis dá Conall craescru, Tipra Grugáin, Tulach Aedha, Ard Catha, Caim innsi, Dún Droighnén to the east of Aithlis Cinn Fhaeladh. § 4 . . . Cell Conáin is the church of this *túath*. . . . § 5 . . . Cell Cruimther [*Kilcrumper*] is the church of this *túath*. And a third of the termon of Brí Gobhann belongs to Uí Chúain, namely . . . § 6 . . . And the church of this *túath* is Áth Cros Molaga [*Ahacross*], out of which are the Uí Chorcráin [*etc*]. And a third of the termon of Brí Gobhann belongs to that *túath*. . . . § 7 . . . Cell Uird [*Kilworth*] is the church of this *túath*. . . . § 8 . . . Eidhnen Molaga with its termon is the church of this *túath*; the coarb of this church is Mac Floinn and the clerk of its staff [*bachall*] is Ó Coscráin. . . .

The text names some 163 places, 135 families. Only a small proportion of the placenames can be identified. One editor of the text, seeking a context or date for its compilation, observed: 'The character of the survey does not point to a change in the ecclesiastical organization inasmuch as church matters are only touched upon from the civil point of view.'[42] By this I suppose he means that we learn only to which church a particular area looked for pastoral care, principally burial here, and to which we may suppose tithes were paid.

I use this text mainly to reinforce the point that there were strong links

---

41. Ed. J. G. O'Keeffe, 'The ancient territory of Fermoy', *Ériu*, x (1926-8), 170-89 (cited by §); also ed. P. Power, *Crichad an Chaoilli, being the Topography of Ancient Fermoy* (Cork, 1932).
42. J. G. O'Keeffe, 'The ancient territory', 171.

between communities, that is, groups of families, and particular churches. People identified a local church as 'their church'. This was so in the eighth century and appears still to have been so in the twelfth century. It is also apparent that such churches could be attached to more important churches; in this case three local churches form the endowment of Brigown, near Mitchelstown (itself subsequently a prebend of Cloyne). Some twelfth-century remains of St Findchú's church are still visible at Brigown, and it is reported that a round tower survived until about 1720.[43]

For this second aspect of the institutional structure I turn to a text about St Mochutu, *ap* 'abbot' of Raithin, and how he was expelled from his *cathair* 'enclosure, city.'[44] This happened in 636, and the saint moved to a new church, much further south at Lismore, where he died in 637. The Irish account of this, *Indarba Mochuda*, dates from some four centuries later, and there is a passage here on which Vincent Hurley has hung an interpretation of the relationship between different churches.[45] The clergy of Meath and the king, Diarmait mac Áedo Sláine, wished to drive Mochutu away from their country:

> Lots were cast between the congregation of Finnian and Ciarán and Colum Cille to find out which of them should go with Diarmait. The lot fell on the family of Clonmacnoise. They cast lots on their *fairche* and the lot fell on the family of Cell Achid Druimfata [*Killeigh, Co. Offaly*]. They cast lots on their churches and the lot fell on the family of Cluain Congusa in Cenél Ardgair. 'I will go to expel him,' said the erenagh.

Three very important churches are referred to here by the names of their founders, St Finnian of Clonard, St Ciarán of Clonmacnoise, and St Colum Cille or Columba of Durrow. All three were churches of more than local significance. Killeigh, part of the jurisdiction of Clonmacnoise, is a fairly substantial enclosure of about 20 acres, some 30 miles east of Clonmacnoise. Cluain Congusa, one of Killeigh's churches, appears to be the principal church for the people of Cenél Ardgair. The line of authority passes through three tiers – the great church, the churches of its *fairche* (< Lat. *parochia*), and the local churches linked to these. The story of the expulsion is long and involved: the *airchindech* 'erenagh' of Cluain Congusa fails, the *secnap* 'second to the abbot' of Killeigh changes heart, the *fosairchindech* 'sub-erenagh' of Clonmacnoise fails, the *secnap* of Durrow laments the course of events, the *airchindech* of Durrow fails, the coarb of Ciarán, also referred to as *ap* 'abbot', eventually succeeds with support from the *ap* of Clonard.

---

43. S. Lewis, *A Topographical Dictionary of Ireland* (2nd edn., 1840), i, 225.
44. *Indarba Mochuda*, § 15, ed. C. Plummer, *Bethada Náem nÉrenn* (1922), i, 300-11, with translation, *ibid.*, ii, 291-302. Plummer knew (*Bethada*, i, xxxviii) but did not collate a variant copy of the story, included in one of the later medieval commentaries on the Martyrology of Oengus (*c.* 830); this text was printed by Stokes, *The Martyrology of Oengus the Culdee* (1905), 92-7. It omits the middle stage in the casting of lots.
45. Hurley, 'The early church', 323.

Within the same region there are several churches of the same important status: Clonmacnoise, Clonard and Durrow are referred to in the text. Their property dependencies form an elaborate jigsaw pattern – or so one may expect. By the early twelfth century we know that Durrow's property interests extended further afield.[46] A pattern of jurisdiction, defined by relationships and not by territorial boundaries, was not confined to Ireland. The earliest dioceses of Anglo-Norman Scotland form a very complex pattern of interlocking detached areas, reflecting the *fairche* which preceded the dioceses established under David I.[47] The same is true of some dioceses in Brittany. In countries where diocesan boundaries were well defined, it was still common for parishes to form a detached part of the jurisdiction of a different bishop from the one whose diocese lay all around: the liberties and peculiars of medieval England reflect the principle of jurisdiction based on property interests. We must be chary, however, of jumping to the conclusion that the three great churches in the story were the diocesan centres for their *fairche*, though two came to have this status in the twelfth century, when 'the *fairche* of the churches of Meath was divided between the bishop of Clonmacnoise and the bishop of Clonard'.[48] The story as told in the *Indarba* makes no mention of bishops; leaders of churches at all three levels are referred to by words signifying their position as heads of churches (erenagh, coarb) or as abbot. This terminology reflects the role of clerics as rulers and says nothing about the sacramental or pastoral responsibilities of their churches. We learn that there was an erenagh at Cluain Congusa, but not what kind of church he headed.

I am coming back to the question which has dominated all discussion of the Irish church since the 1840s, the problem of the episcopal-monastic antithesis in the development of the early Irish church. The words which the Irish church used of itself in the eighth to eleventh centuries were predominantly monastic, and 'monasticism' has been perceived as the dominant idea. Pastoral care was altogether lost sight of, as historians (many of them in holy orders) devised and refined a history of the Irish church which runs basically thus: in the beginning St Patrick established a church governed by bishops and organized in territorial dioceses. At some point – and the dating has differed quite widely – this pattern was overtaken by the spread of monasteries and monastic federations. The date for this development which has won widest acceptance is during the late sixth and seventh century.[49] In the late seventh century the surviving churches of

---

46. An agreement between Durrow and Killeshin, datable to 1103 × 1116, is translated and discussed by R. Sharpe, 'Dispute settlement in early medieval Ireland: a preliminary inquiry', in *The Settlement of Disputes in Early Medieval Europe*, ed. W. Davies and P. Fouracre (1986), 169-89 (pp. 170-1).
47. G. Donaldson, 'Scottish bishops' sees before the reign of David I', *PSAS*, lxxvii (1952-3), 106-117. See the map below, fig. 5.2.
48. *Chronicum Scotorum, s.a.* 1107, ed, W. M. Hennessy, Roll Series 46 (1866), 314.
49. This dating was most lucidly argued by K. Hughes, *The Church in Early Irish Society* (1966), 65-78.

episcopal origin busily reorganized themselves, giving up their territorial diocesan interests (and, by implication, their connexion with the *túath*) and acquiring instead dispersed proprietary interests, in some cases extending over much of Ireland. From then the church was dominated by monasticism until the twelfth century, when reformers reinvented dioceses. The formation of parishes followed on from the establishment of dioceses.

This presentation of a development from a diocesan church to a church without territorial divisions, and back again, presupposes clear-cut distinctions between episcopal and monastic but evades the question of how pastoral care was provided at any point before the twelfth century. All the terms on which the theory depends are open to question. Moreover, the evidential basis for this development is very weak, as I have shown elsewhere.[50] The one text from Ireland which really illustrates monastic life without a pastoral role is Adomnán's *Vita S. Columbae*, but there are several eighth-century *uitae* with a strong monastic emphasis.[51] The widespread use of monastic language in the annals invited the assumption that all Irish churches were monasteries. Much of the evidence was then subordinated to a monastic model, and the origins of this imagined peculiarity of Irish (or 'Celtic') churches were sought in the desert monasticism of Egypt and in southern European monasteries such as Lérins. Irish monasticism, empanelled in a century or more of historical writing, is no more than a model, and it has proved to be one which does not accommodate a major part of the evidence we have.

I should challenge almost every element in the model, but where it principally runs aground is here: there is no evidence that pastoral care in local communities depended on monks, and the monastic model contains no provision for pastoral care. The evidence in the laws, in *Riagail Phátraic*, and elsewhere gives no monastic colour to pastoral care, and it was brushed aside.[52] It was first restored to a significant position by Mgr Corish, who - largely on the strength of *Riagail Phátraic* - argued for the survival of a non-monastic church, with dioceses equated with petty kingdoms, in which bishops ensured that local churches, whether free or impropriated to lay or ecclesiastical landlords, provided for 'baptism and communion and the singing of intercession'.[53] Every line of this text is important in showing the

---

50. Sharpe, 'Some problems', 239-51.
51. Saints, for example, are credited with monastic rules in several *uitae* roughly datable to the eighth century: *Vita S. Lugidi*, § 64, ed. Heist, *Vitae*, p. 144; *Vita S. Fintani*, § 4 (p. 147); *Vita S. Finani*, § 4 (p. 153); *Vita S. Aidi*, § 3 (p. 168); *Vita S. Cannechi*, § 6 (p. 183); *Vita S. Fintani* (*Munnu*), §§ 4, 6 (p. 199); *Vita S. Colmani*, §§ 6, 26 (pp. 211, 218). For discussion of the frame within which these Lives are to be dated, see R. Sharpe, *Medieval Irish Saints' Lives. An Introduction to Vitae Sanctorum Hiberniae* (1991), 297-339.
52. Explicitly so by J. Ryan, *Irish Monasticism. Its Origins and Early Development* (Dublin, 1931), 299-301.
53. P. J. Corish, 'The pastoral mission in the early Irish church', *Léachtaí Cholm Cille*, ii (1971), 14-25; *idem*, *The Christian Mission, A History of Irish Catholicism* I.iii (Dublin, 1972), 32-41.

concern for pastoral provision, regardless of a church's proprietary status. Corish recognized that the text, referring to clergy at work 'in the small churches of the community separate from the great churches', implied an organization not covered by the monastic model.

We should note, however, that Corish did not reject the monastic model. Rather, he proposed a significantly later date for the disappearance of the non-monastic clergy – he guessed during the Viking attacks of the ninth century – as the supposed monastic organization carried all before it.[54] He makes one point in favour of the notion that the non-monastic clergy were replaced by monks: in the sixth century the Penitential of Uuinniau (or perhaps a clause added to it) prohibits monks from receiving alms from the laity because they cannot reciprocate with baptism.[55] At the beginning of the twelfth century, Corish noted, Bishop Gilbert of Limerick reiterated that monks are not qualified to baptize. He conjectured that Uuinniau was reacting to the first manifestation of the monastic take-over and that Gilbert was pronouncing that the monastic establishment of his own day was uncanonical.[56] Without any such specific background of conflict, however, canon law has repeated this prohibition at intervals. In Gilbert's case, he makes the point only as part of his summary of Amalarius of Metz, describing the two parallel structures of the secular hierarchy and the monasteries.[57] Gilbert was perhaps aware that this distinction was not drawn in the Irish church at that date, but he does not mean that baptisms were then being performed uncanonically by men not in priest's orders.

This model of a series of changes was first propounded by Todd and was last refined by Corish.[58] It has subsequently been challenged by several students, but some recent writers have not appreciated that the challenges are not further refinements: they undermine the model from start to finish. Todd and Bury assumed that fifth-century bishops administered dioceses but did not consider what happened under their jurisdiction. Evidence for *monasteria* appears in the sixth and seventh centuries, and historians supposed a conflict between two systems. In the better recorded ninth, tenth and eleventh centuries there is no tidy record of episcopal succession and therefore bishops were assumed to have lost the battle. In all the discussions historians have equated diocese with the petty kingdom or *túath*, as the early evidence surely leads one to, but they have forgotten that after the seventh or eighth century the single *túath* was of very little significance. The numerous individual bishops which the theory supposed had vanished into monasteries had, in fact, merely become too insignificant as a group to be included in the annals. Conversely the monastic element was exaggerated because, when Todd and Bury formulated the model, no one realized what we now understand about the emergence of pastoral

---

54. Corish, *The Christian Mission*, 86.
55. *Paenitentiale Uinniani*, § 49.
56. Corish, 'The pastoral mission', 25. This point was not repeated in the book.
57. Gilbert of Limerick, *De statu ecclesiae*, 998A; cited from *PL* clix, 995-1004, which reprints the edition by J. Ussher, *Veterum epistolarum Hibernicarum sylloge* (Dublin, 1632), pp. 78-87.
58. J. H. Todd, *Saint Patrick, Apostle of Ireland* (Dublin, 1864).

networks. In northern Europe there was no systematic founding of local churches by bishops: some local churches were founded as monasteries, some as private churches, and some as secular communities under episcopal control. Increasingly during the eighth and ninth centuries bishops sought to extend their control over independent churches, with varying success. In eighth-century Ireland, we are told by *Riagail Phátraic*, bishops had established an extensive control over small foundations, whatever their origins. The bishop even had the power to impose a levy on the erenagh of an independent church if he did not provide for pastoral care; this money was used by the bishop to supply such a ministry to the people whose 'proper church' (*eclais téchta*) had been neglectful.[59] Most larger churches had probably become, if they had not always been, the religious focus of a *túath* and had their own bishop, even if a lay erenagh rather than the bishop had control of the church's property. The lack of a full annalistic record of bishops in so many relatively minor churches is hardly surprising.

For the sixth, seventh and eighth centuries the evidence of the legal sources, of *Riagail Phátraic*, of Tírechán, of the terminological distinctions in the canon law and in placenames, all comes together to suggest an organization in which mother-churches served as the centres of pastoral care, and that this ministry was provided at the most local level through small churches with no more than one priest. At the same time there were, without doubt, houses of monks or nuns devoted to the religious life, and there were probably many foundations where monks and priests combined the religious life with a pastoral role.[60] This is typical of northern Europe at the appropriate parallel period. If we look for comparisons to help form a new model for the organization of the Irish church, we should do better to look at northern France and Anglo-Saxon England than at the Desert Fathers.

The use of monastic language is widespread in the early Middle Ages, but it is all too evident that *monasterium* does not necessarily mean a Benedictine monastery.[61] English historians are still not wholly resolved on the need to differentiate between the functions of the active, pastoral life and the religious contemplative life in the *monasteria* of seventh and eighth-century England, but they are getting there. The words used for churches did not define their function. In Ireland the words most frequently used for churchmen did not define their roles. If we allow that monastic language in Ireland has confused the issue here, then we may attempt some remodelling. The mother-churches were surely communities of priests and other clergy, some of whom may have been monks living under vows; the communal life may well have included the regular singing of the office, but it did not exclude priests from pastoral activity. In recognizing that such churches were communities (Lat. *familia* or *populus*, Ir. *muintir*), it is all too easy to lapse into the phrase 'monastic community' and so 'monastery',

---

59. *Riagail Phátraic*, § 7.
60. For example, Tírechán, §§ 33, 47.
61. S. Foot, pp. 212-25 below.

but we must avoid exaggerating the distinction between regular and secular communities. The small churches with only one or two clergy depended on the community of the greater churches for their staffing, training and general organizational support, though not necessarily for material support. Episcopal churches would have tended to have larger communities, including the bishop's immediate household, and perhaps also monks forming a community analogous to a cathedral priory. These are the normal structures of the church in the early Middle Ages, and they correspond to the expectations of texts such as the *Hibernensis* and *Riagail Phátraic*.

It may fairly be said that the terminology of monasticism extended more deeply (and more confusingly) in early medieval Ireland than is observable elsewhere. The extreme example of this is the semantic development of OIr. *manach* (< Lat. *monachus*) from 'monk' to designate a lay person economically tied to a particular church.[62] The conventional translation 'tenant of church lands' raises various problems, both in respect of land-tenure and settlement. In a secular context we should speak of clients rather than tenants, and we do not know nearly enough about the interaction in a rural community of secular and ecclesiastical dependants. Moreover, *Riagail Phátraic* uses the word *manach* of everyone to whom a particular church owes pastoral care and from whom the church receives tithes and other dues.[63] Since the Rule is aimed at all lords and all erenaghs, it cannot be argued that bishops were concerned only with pastoral care for a church's economic dependants, and the word therefore has extended its semantic range to something like 'parishioner'. The word for monk had come to be used of a layman in a reciprocal pastoral relationship with his local church.

At a later date, in the ninth or tenth centuries, the language of monasteries and abbots continues to be used. The church continued to be organized in communal groups, but these are collegiate churches working to provide a pastoral ministry. I should go so far as to question any general continuance of regular monastic life in Ireland at this date. The surviving 'monastic rules'[64] (so called) from this period do not attest widespread regular life, and it would be highly tendentious to argue from the several works associated with the *Céli Dé* movement and Máel Rúain of Tallaght that monastic reform in the late eighth and early ninth century led to a universal revival of a supposed 'monastic' organization. The Rule of Tallaght actually summarizes the provisions of *Riagail Phátraic* for a pastoral ministry under episcopal direction.[65] Where we can observe the

---

62. *Manaig* in the latter sense have been discussed by Hughes, *Church in Early Irish Society*, 134-42; Ó Corráin, 'Early Irish churches', 333-4; C. Doherty, 'Some aspects of hagiography as a source for Irish economic history', *Peritia*, i (1982) [1983], 300-28; T. M. Charles-Edwards, 'The church and settlement', in *Ireland and Europe: The Early Church*, ed. P. Ní Chatháin and M. Richter (Stuttgart, 1984), 167-75.
63. *Riagail Phátraic*, §§ 5-6, 8-9, 12.
64. Discussed by V. Ó Maidín, 'The Irish monastic rules', *Cistercian Studies*, xv (1980), 24-38.
65. The Rule of Tallaght, §§ 57-65, ed. E. J. Gwynn, *Hermathena*, Suppl. 2 (1927).

internal organization of particular churches, they appear to be quite secular. Kells, for example, for all its Columban origin, appears to function much like any secular cathedral of the period with its residentiary canons living off their prebendal properties. The words used are different but the structures are not. Or Armagh, as seen in the poem of Áed Úa Foirréid, could perfectly well be a cathedral church with a cathedral priory attached to it.[66] I am reminded too of the parallel again with Anglo-Saxon England, where there were numerous *monasteria* in the ninth and early tenth centuries but there was little or no regular monastic life. Monasticism was renewed in England only in the 940s and after, and this movement required a complete change in the life of the old-established *monasteria* with their secular clergy.

When we turn to the problems of understanding the twelfth-century Irish church, again we find that assumption has played a large part in current orthodoxy. Students of the twelfth century and later are liable to accept without question the commonplaces of those studying the earlier Middle Ages.[67] It has been taken as read that a monastic organization existed which it was the object of ecclesiastical reformers to displace. The reformers do not complain that the church is monastic, but they do complain about secular, often hereditary control of church property and about the fragmentation of episcopal jurisdiction. Their most obvious and lasting achievement was to rationalize the diocesan system by determining which churches should have bishops. The thirty-six new dioceses defined as a result of the synods of Rath Bresail and Kells-Mellifont were better related to prevailing political divisions and more acceptable to contemporary notions of scale. This meant that many churches which had previously had bishops were now reduced in status, and some resisted this change. Ardmore is the best documented of these, with two active bishops in the late twelfth century and a Life of its patron, St Declán, loudly proclaiming Ardmore as the see of the Déisi.

It has been assumed by some that parishes and tithes were both introduced to Ireland as part of this package. Historians tend to be divided on this point according to whether their focus is on the areas affected by Anglo-Norman colonization or not. Miss Otway-Ruthven considered that 'no more than a bare beginning' had been made in creating a parochial organization at the start of the colonization, and dates 'the real starting point of parochial organization' to 1170-1 when the Synod of Cashel decreed that every man should pay tithe to his parish church.[68] She had studied the formation of parishes in the new territorial arrangement imposed by conquest.[69] She observed:

---

66. 'A poem in praise of Aodh Úa Foirréidh, bishop of Armagh (1032-56)', in *Measgra i gcuimhne Michíl Uí Chléirigh*, ed. S. O'Brien (Dublin, 1944), 140-63.
67. Some examples are given by D. Ó Corráin, 'Nationality and kingship in pre-Norman Ireland', *Nationality and the Pursuit of National Independence*, ed. T. W. Moody, *Historical Studies*, xvi (Belfast, 1978), 1-35 (pp. 1-4).
68. A. J. Otway-Ruthven, *A History of Medieval Ireland* (1968), 118.
69. A. J. Otway-Ruthven, 'Parochial development in the rural deanery of Skreen', *JRSAI*, xciv (1964), 111-22.

Outside the area of Norman settlement, parishes seem to have been formed from the old monastic termons, from the lands of new monastic houses where these were not identical with the old termons, or from the lands of ancient family population groups.[70]

Here she is merely repeating Dr Gleeson's comments on the diocese of Killaloe, where he noted:

parochial bounds have three main origins - viz., (i) some represent the survival into the diocesan economy after Rathbreasail of the ancient monastic termons; (ii) others are coterminous with the lands of ancient family population groups; (iii) a third class are of Norman origin, or at least their institution is of later date than the Norman invasion.[71]

Even within the area of Anglo-Norman settlement Mark Hennessey presents evidence from Tipperary that the new knight's fees and 'therefore the parishes' followed the pre-existing territorial framework. He cites several examples from charters of *c.* 1200 where a church is defined as the church of such-and-such a local *túath* and one case naming the population group (*Kenel Rathonere*) which formed its parish.[72] Whether their emphasis is on novelty or antiquity in these arrangements, historians have recognized that the territorial framework existed before there were documents describing them in the parochial terms comprehensible to the ordinary medievalist. The written evidence is predominantly produced in a context where the terminology of the Anglo-French church is imposed on Irish arrangements. However, the advent of records using Latin parochial terms should not be equated with the invention and imposition of pastoral structures. The pastoral structures already existed.

Hennessey argues from a very narrow definition of how a parish was created: 'Many of the charters record the granting of the tithes of an area for the first time and therefore the initial creation of parishes.'[73] The grant of tithes created the parish and with it the responsibility for the provision of pastoral care. This formulation overlooks everything we know about the continuing existence of a large number of local churches, their association with local *túatha*, the payment of dues by the laity in return for pastoral services, and the additional funding of greater churches through property interests that came to be called 'termon lands'. Hennessey also links the provision of pastoral care directly to the creation of a parochial system:

It was not until the arrival of the Anglo-Normans in 1169-70 that

---

70. *History of Medieval Ireland*, 127.
71. D. F. Gleeson, 'The coarbs of Killaloe dioceses', *JRSAI*, lxxix (1949), 160-9 (p. 160).
72. M. Hennessey, 'Parochial organization in medieval Tipperary', in *Tipperary: History and Society*, ed. W. Nolan and T. G. McGrath (Dublin, 1985), 60-70, 437-8 (p. 63).
73. *ibid.*, 62.

> parochial organization and consequently an effective, comprehens-
> ive pastoral ministry was introduced to Ireland. The successful
> creation of a parish system was to have a radical and transforming
> effect not only on the church but on the lives of ordinary people.
> Their hitherto undirected attachment to the Christian church was
> to be replaced by a binding connection, through the payment of
> tithe, with one church and with a community contained within a
> closely defined territorial area.[74]

This not only overstates the accomplishment of an effective pastoral
ministry in late medieval Ireland; it also assumes that all older pastoral
structures had failed and disappeared long before. Yet the persistence of the
territorial units and the archaeological evidence from actual sites must
make us doubt the validity of these propositions.

It is surely true that the ideas of parochial structure introduced in the
twelfth century led to significant changes in the pastoral organization of
the country and that the irruption of Anglo-Norman principles of tenure
had its effect on this organization in a large part of Ireland. This cannot be
assessed, however, without more attention to what existed before the
1170s, which in turn will involve more study of the native pattern of
ownership of ecclesiastical property. The study of coarbs, erenaghs, and
termon lands needs to be co-ordinated with some fresh thinking about the
earlier development of the church in Ireland, and much more attention
should be given to local studies across the great temporal divide of the
twelfth century. Hitherto we have had an overactive theory of development
by drastic changes in the sixth, seventh and eighth centuries, after which
historians have tended to stop the clock. When time is set moving again
in the twelfth century, a different set of historians look back over what
they may well see as a void. The only idea which has spanned the eighth
to eleventh centuries has been the notion that the Irish church was
peculiarly 'monastic'. This label does not adequately describe how the
church functioned or how it developed.

In advance of a more thoroughly worked-out account, let me sketch a new
model, including some thoughts on how it may have developed. We should
have in mind a model in which bishops, based in and itinerating from the
senior churches, superintended the training of the clergy, their provision to
the small churches and the visitation of these churches. The laity in return
made payments to the church which provided for a priest and an assistant
(*maccléirech*). These payments included tithes, and it seems possible that a
proportion of these tithes were paid directly to the bishop. (I base this not
on contemporary evidence but on Kenneth Nicholls's demonstration that
the distribution of tithes in the Gaelic dioceses in the thirteenth and fourteenth centuries was quite different from that adopted in the Anglicized dioceses.)[75] Some of these small churches were in some sense *Eigenkirchen*,

---

74. *ibid.*, 61.
75. K. W. Nicholls, 'Rectory, vicarage, and parish in the western Irish dioceses',
    JRSAI, ci (1971), 53-82.

held in full ownership (OIr. *eclais sáindíles*) by lay patrons, and others were impropriated to the erenaghs of larger churches.[76] The significance of private control of churches has been emphasized by Professor Ó Corráin, who has drawn attention to the many churches mentioned in association with particular families by the secular genealogies.[77] This pattern too is in no way peculiar. Nor should one assume that private ownership prevented a wider pastoral ministry: the church which a lord regarded as his *eclais dúthaig* 'hereditary church'[78] may well have been perceived as the proper church of his kinsmen and all their clients; in other words, it served the local community. At present, it must be admitted, we have very little notion of the situation of churches in relation to the settlement pattern of the community.[79] It is possible that local churches, of which there may have been a very great number, were supplied with clergy from mother-churches such as those mentioned by Tírechán. These were often established at an early date, and served wide communities which looked to them as patronal churches for generations. These churches, however, were in many cases themselves held as property by greater churches. At the higher level all territorial links are likely to have broken down. In Tírechán's time, Armagh, Clonmacnoise and other great churches were claiming interests in mother-churches that in some cases were far removed in distance. In jurisdictional terms, however, the great churches were not seeking to be the episcopal church. Tírechán, setting out Armagh's claims, none the less recognized the episcopal status of other churches at a lower level than Armagh.

It seems to me likely that in Vincent Hurley's example from *Indarba Mochuda* we should imagine that the lowest rank of church mentioned, Cluain Congusa, was probably mother-church to the district of Cenél Ardgair. This was impropriated to Killeigh, which had become (perhaps at a relatively late date) subservient to Clonmacnoise. On this basis we must suppose a four-tier structure, but the number of churches at the highest level was probably quite small, and second-tier churches such as Killeigh

---

76. *Riagail Phátraic*, § 5.
77. 'The early Irish churches: some aspects of organisation', in *Irish Antiquity. Essays and Studies Presented to Professor M. J. O'Kelly*, ed. D. Ó Corráin (Cork, 1981), 327–41 (p. 337).
78. *Cáin Éimíne Bán*, § 1, ed. E. Poppe, *Celtica*, xviii (1986), 35–52, who translates, 'whether each should go to his local church to take the staff'.
79. Recently published views are not convincing. Leo Swan, 'Enclosed ecclesiastical settlements', 277–8, suggests that ecclesiastical enclosures were 'secular settlements of small communities of the early medieval period' housing 'an underlying subservient stratum, perhaps unfree or in semi-bondage', who were not settled at the ringforts of the property-owning class; some disappeared except as places of worship and burial, others developed into towns or large villages. Harold Mytum's views, based on a small sample of unrepresentative evidence, tend toward the opposite extreme. 'At this period', he writes, 'the churches did not serve the populace in the manner of the later parochial churches, and so the distribution was not related to the Christian population'; H. C. Mytum, 'The location of early churches in northern County Clare', in *The Early Church in Western Britain and Ireland*, ed. S. M. Pearce, BAR, British Series 102 (1982), 351–61 (p. 354).

may have housed a bishop. It was the constant complaint about the Irish church in the eleventh and twelfth century that it had too many bishops. Opponents including Lanfranc and St Bernard point to this as a weakness in the structure.[80] An apologist could claim it as an advantage: Jocelin of Furness, who used the Tripartite in writing his own Life of St Patrick, says that Patrick consecrated many bishops so that they should always be close to the faithful.[81] But, if we believe *Riagail Phátraic*, this is precisely what we should expect if every *túath* had its bishop and every *primthúath* its *primepscop*. In the seventh or eighth century this might give as many as 150 bishops. The *Hibernensis*, discussing the structure of the church, suggests that three bishops were enough to constitute a province.[82] This would give a figure of up to fifty or so churches with this higher status, and the bishop of such a church would have been the *primepscop*. At this level in the structure, it is not at all clear how churches were grouped. The outstanding deficiency of the Irish church (from an outside view) until the twelfth century was that it did not have metropolitans. Much of the discussion by historians of the rivalry between Armagh and Kildare or Armagh and Iona or Armagh and Clonmacnoise has treated it in terms of a conflict between two systems, a diocesan system and a so-called monastic system of organization. These conflicts could instead be seen as the outcome of an organization with many small dioceses but no archbishops with recognized metropolitan authority. Disputes between great churches at this level in the structure are about power and about property; they are not about who was responsible for the supervision of pastoral care in local communities.

When did this structure come into existence? How did it change? It is not possible to say with confidence. *Liber Angeli* and Tírechán both suggest that by the middle of the seventh century much of Ireland was already provided with mother-churches and that some at least of these were identifiably older than and superior to local small churches. At this stage the mother-churches were under the jurisdiction of a bishop whose *plebs* was probably the equivalent of a petty kingdom. This view has been widely accepted on the evidence of the early ecclesiastical legislation. During the seventh century there was some non-local rearrangement in the control or ownership of mother-churches, as Tírechán clearly says. Some great churches emerged with very extensive interests at this stage. These are the so-called 'monastic-type *paruchiae*' of the textbooks, but it is generally the case that by the late eighth or early ninth century monastic life means 'collegiate or communal life' rather than the contemplative religious life. This we are loudly told was lacking when we read the texts associated with the religious movement centred on Máel Rúain of Tallaght. Adherents of the notion that in the seventh century the church changed its character and became monastic have to explain the almost immediate shift towards

---

80. Lanfranc, Letter to Toirdelbach Úa Briain (c. 1074), ed. H. Clover and M. T. Gibson, *The Letters of Lanfranc, Archbishop of Canterbury* (1979), 70; Bernard of Clairvaux, *Vita Malachiae episcopi*, § 19, ed. J. Leclercq and A. Gwynn, *Sancti Bernardi Opera* (Rome, 1957-77), iii, 330.
81. Jocelin of Furness, *Vita S. Patricii*, § 92.
82. *Hib.* xx. 2; see also Charles-Edwards p. 68, above.

secularization. The larger ecclesiastical communities became secularized in more ways than one. Their rule, if there was one, can only have been of the simplest kind, requiring communal life but not necessarily celibacy. Their clergy, often hereditary, more nearly resemble canons than monks, whatever the words used in Latin or Irish. These communities served as a focus for large lay populations – nascent towns, such as grew up around some English minsters – and this lay population was under the jurisdiction of the notional head of the ecclesiastical community. This person, the erenagh or coarb, was very often a layman, and some of the greater churches were political units, in some respects hardly distinguishable from secular units except by their focus on a single locality.

The larger churches maintained schools where the clergy were trained. Tenth- and eleventh-century tales often involved a *maccléirech* or two, a clerical student, attached to larger churches for study and then sent out to assist priests in their pastoral role. Mother-churches, like English minster churches, probably had a staff of several clergy, though not all of them would have been priests. The smaller local churches, however, should have had one priest, but as early as the eighth century *Riagail Phátraic* recognized that it would sometimes be necessary for one priest to serve three or four local, in some cases private, churches.

These local churches must at that date have been significantly more numerous than later parochial churches, if Dingle is anything to go by. How long this density of pastoral provision lasted I hesitate to say. Professor Ó Corráin has noted that the maintenance of an active pastoral ministry in small churches under pressure from proprietary interests can only have been 'a matter of chance'.[83] Discontinuity in the nature of the written sources makes arguments from silence quite worthless, and we shall have to depend on the accumulation of archaeological evidence from church sites with continuity and those without. Already, it seems to me, there is sufficient evidence to assert continuity on a significant number of sites. Two factors, however, suggest that decline had begun before the twelfth-century reform. First, there is the large proportion of field monuments where there is only 'early' stonework or crosses, with no sign of twelfth-century use. Second, in *Crichad an Chaoilli* we find that one church is specified as the church of each territory, but the other placenames within the territory often include several which are ecclesiastical: Túath O Cuscraid, for example, had as their church Áth Cros Molaga, but their territory included Cluain Mac Cairthain, Cell Mochuille and Daire Faiblenn, all of which could have been churches and Cell Mochuille must have been. These territories, with their church, were the parishes of the pre-Norman organization. Each is the area of two or three later civil parishes here in north Cork, but elsewhere, in Connacht for example, parishes remained much larger than in the Anglicized areas. The native organization, I suggest, was focused on these territories: these with their mother-churches are Ireland's equivalent of the ordinary minsters of England. They were controlled by an organization which differed from the English in its

---

83. 'Early Irish churches', 339.

superstructure. Its infrastructure of local churches developed considerably earlier than in England, and at a more strictly local level, but was already beginning to shrink in the twelfth century.

Pending the completion of field surveys for the whole country, and the still more remote time when this evidence will have been assimilated, we can give some quantitive expression to this organization on the basis of placename evidence. Ireland has 2,428 civil parishes, but its townland names include 2,890 names in *cell*, more than 900 names in *cluain* and an uncounted number of other ecclesiastical types, including *domnach*, *sendomnach*, *senchell*, and later types such as *teampull*. These names and the unsurveyed field monuments bear witness to what in its time was one of the most comprehensive pastoral organizations in northern Europe.

5 Early Christian religious houses in Scotland: foundation and function

ALAN MACQUARRIE

How much is known of the performance of the pastoral function in the Scottish church in the period before the systematic establishment of parishes in the twelfth century? The greatest writer on Scottish church history of the present day has remarked that 'we know far too little' of ecclesiastical structure, 'the maintenance of services and the cure of souls'.[1] We know of the existence of some bishoprics, and even the names of some bishops. We know also of monasteries and their abbots, but much less than we would like of the functions they performed. We are vaguely aware of the gradual secularization of some religious houses, of the rise of *Céli Dé* communities and their coexistence alongside corporations of secularized *personae* or monks. We have some slight information about communities of *clerici* or secular clergy who may have performed a service similar to that of the English minster. But the subject has never been treated systematically, and indeed the available information has never been drawn together in a satisfactory form to enable such treatment.[2] It has seemed best, then, rather than to attempt a discussion of the pastoral work of the Scottish church before the twelfth century, to try instead to put together the prolegomena to such a discussion. This will centre on the foundation of religious houses, and the agency and motivation which lay behind their foundation. Something will be said also of their constitution and function, of the episcopate, of the development of *parochiae*, and of the relationship between religious houses and episcopate and between *parochiae* and the later dioceses.

The discussion will be limited to the kingdom of the Scots, i.e., the area north of the Forth-Clyde isthmus (see fig. 5.1). The exception to this rule will be the area of Govan and Glasgow in Strathclyde, where the Scottish kings of Fortrenn seem to have exercised some measure of authority for some of the time at least from the late ninth century onwards.

The earliest record of a grant of land by a Scottish king comes in the entry of the *Annals of Ulster* for 574: 'Mors Conaill mic Comgaill, anno

---

1. G. Donaldson, 'Bishops' sees before the reign of David I', *Proc. Soc. Antiq. Scotland*, lxxxvii (1955), 106-17; repr. in G. Donaldson, *Scottish Church History* (1985), 11-24, at 19.
2. The best discussion is I. B. Cowan, 'The post-Columban church', *Records of the Scottish Church History Soc.* xviii (1973), 245-60; the list of 'Early religious foundations' in I. B. Cowan and D. E. Easson, *Medieval Religious Houses: Scotland* (2nd edn., 1976), 46-54, has some omissions.

Figure 5.1 Scotland: showing places mentioned in the text.

regni xvi sui, qui obtulit insolam Iae Columbe Cille'.[3] The Iona provenance of these early annals has been demonstrated,[4] and we should probably accept that this represents Iona's own version of its foundation. Adomnán has nothing to say about the grant of Iona to Colum Cille or the foundation of the monastery, and the only hint of a royal grant could be taken from his statement that Colum Cille was 'coram Conallo rege conversatus' on his first arrival in Britain.[5] Bede's statement that Colum Cille received Iona from the Picts under their king Bridei son of Mailcon probably reflects information supplied to him by eighth-century Pictish sources, and the known political realities of his own day, when Pictish kings were undoubtedly exercising authority over Iona and elsewhere in the lands of the Dál Riata.[6] Despite suggestions to the contrary,[7] we must believe that Colum Cille received Iona as the gift of Conall mac Comgaill, king of the Dál Riata, for the foundation of his church.

It must remain a subject for speculation why Conall should have given Colum Cille a remote island in the lands of the Cenél Loairn, rather than lands in the territories of his own people, the Cenél nGabráin, who were centred in Kintrye, Knapdale and Cowal.[8] Colum Cille had other monasteries in the lands of the Cenél Loairn, for example on Tiree. It may have been that Colum Cille sought remoteness from the centres of power of the Dál Riata (though he was visited by kings on Iona, himself made visits to their courts and to a *caput regionis* of the Dál Riata, and even attended a conference of kings in northern Ireland).[9] It may be that Conall planted Colum Cille and his monks among the Cenél Loairn to emphasize his lordship over them. It is possible, but unlikely, that there were more uninhabited or thinly populated islands in their territories; the southern Hebrides are full of tiny islands, some of which do have early Christian remains on them.[10] The important island site of Hinba has not been satisfactorily identified.[11]

What cannot be doubted, however, is that Iona was intended to be a remote settlement, at least a day's journey from royal centres and free from

---

3. *Annals of Ulster*, ed. W. M. Hennessy and B. MacCarthy (Dublin, 1887-1901), s.a.; new edn. to AD 1131 by S. MacAirt and G. MacNiocaill (Dublin, 1983) [hereafter *AU*].
4. J. W. M. Bannerman, *Studies in the History of Dalriada* (1974), 9-26; A. P. Smyth, 'The earliest Irish annals', *Proc. Royal Irish Academy*, lxxii (1972), 1-48; K. Hughes, *Early Christian Ireland: Introduction to the Sources* (1972), 99-159.
5. Adomnán, *Life of Columba*, i. 7, ed. A. O. Anderson and M. O. Anderson (1961).
6. Bede, *HE* iii. 4.
7. See Bannerman, *Studies*, 79.
8. *ibid.*, 111-15.
9. *Life of Columba*, iii. 6; i. 8; ii. 36; ii. 34; i. 22; i. 35.
10. Many of these are described in the *RCA&HM of Scotland, Inventory of Argyll*, esp. ii (1975), iv (1980), and v (1984).
11. *ibid.*, v, 27. The identification of *Hinba* is discussed by W. D. Lamont and W. R. McKay in *Notes and Queries of the Society of West Highland and Island Historical Research*, vii (1978), 3-6; ix (1979), 8-17; xii (1980), 10-15; and xiii (1980), 19-23.

influence by kings and local rulers. Although Adomnán's account gives the impression that Iona was sometimes a very busy place with frequent visitors,[12] it was first and foremost an eremitic site where the monks lived austere contemplative lives according to the rule of their founder. In Bede's day this remained the predominant impression given by Iona: 'reliquit successores magna continentia ac divino amore regularique institutione insignes'.[13]

The same impression is given by other religious foundations of the 'Age of the Saints'. In the southern Hebrides there are a number of eremitic or monastic sites impressive for their remoteness. The best known is on Eileach an Naoimh in the Garbh Eileach group in the Firth of Lorne, where drystone beehive cells in an enclosure have been partly restored.[14] This has been identified with the monastery of Ailech founded in Britain by St Brendan of Clonfert.[15] On Nave Island off the northern coast of Islay, there are traces of an enclosure within which stands a medieval chapel; a fragment of a free-standing early Christian cross seems to confirm an early date.[16] An almost complete 'Iona school' cross at Kilnave on Islay nearby may point to a dependency run by the community at Nave Island.[17] A similar relationship may have existed between an early Christian monastery on Eilean Mór in the Sound of Jura, dedicated to the Leinster saint Abbán moccu Corbmaic, and a complete standing cross at Keills on the Knapdale mainland.[18] These two examples may show offshore churches of early date, seventh century and earlier, providing pastoral care by establishing mainland stations for preaching and other ministrations to the local populace.

In these cases, we have no information about the role of laymen in the granting of land for the foundation. Adomnán indicates that Colum Cille sought lay approval for monastic foundations; he describes how Colum Cille 'commended' the monk Cormac to Bridei son of Mailcon, so that the sub-king of the Orkneys, of whom Bridei held hostages, should not harm him when he came to the Orkneys, 'sailing over the pathless sea seeking to find a hermitage'.[19] Adomnán goes on to indicate that Colum Cille's intervention was effective, stating that his commendation saved Cormac from the hostility of the Orcadian sub-king. The fate suffered by Colum Cille's younger contemporary, St Donnan of Eigg, in 617 may indicate how

12. *Life of Columba*, esp. i. 19, 20, 21. See A. Macquarrie, *Iona through the Ages* (Inverness, 1983), 8.
13. Bede, *HE* iii. 4.
14. *Inventory of Argyll*, v, 170-82.
15. C. Plummer, *Vitae Sanctorum Hiberniae* (1910), i, pp. cxxv, 143; ii, 315-6; *Inventory of Argyll*, v, 182.
16. *Inventory of Argyll*, v, 225-8.
17. *ibid.*, 219-22.
18. D. MacLean, 'The Keills cross in Knapdale, the Iona school, and the Book of Kells', in *Early Medieval Sculpture in Britain and Ireland*, ed. J. Higgitt, BAR, British ser. 152 (1986), 175-97.
19. *Life of Columba*, ii. 43.

prudent it was to obtain an agreement with the local laity before founding a church.[20]

We know that Iona was given to Colum Cille for the building of his community; we know that he 'commended' Cormac to the Pictish king and thus made it possible for him to found a hermitage in the Orkney Isles. We suspect hostility between Donnan and the local Pictish laity, resulting in his martyrdom in 617. For the most part, we have no record of the involvement of laymen in the establishment of religious houses until a later period. We do not think of Iona or its contemporaries as 'royal monasteries' because they were founded on the saints' own initiative with royal approval or a royal grant. But from the eighth century onwards, as religious foundations became more numerous and records about them more abundant (although still sparse), we seem to find more involvement on the part of laymen in the foundation of religious houses with kings and others actually taking the initiative. The houses founded by them were often near royal centres. Some at least may have had functions other than, or additional to, a monastic purpose.

Although the foundation legends of Abernethy claim a very early date for its foundation, the earliest religious house founded by a Pictish king of which we have knowledge is that founded by Nechton son of Derilei *c.* 710.[21] It is likely, however, that there were Columban churches in Pictland before this, for Colum Cille and his monks had been active there for well over a century, and the *Annals* record the expulsion of Columban monks 'trans Dorsum Britanniae' in 717.[22] But the location of their houses on the Pictish side of Drumalban cannot be certainly determined. In a famous passage Bede describes how, a few years before the expulsion of the Columbans, King Nechton had written to Ceolfrith, abbot of Wearmouth and Jarrow, requesting information on the catholic calculation of the date of Easter and on the Roman tonsure. 'He also asked for masons to be sent to build a church of stone after the Roman fashion in his land, promising that it should be dedicated in honour of the blessed prince of the apostles.'[23] The identification of this church with an ancient tower incorporated into the later priory of St Peter at Restennet is attractive, but modern opinion does not favour so early a date for this, so it must remain doubtful.[24] Whether Restennet really is Nechton's foundation or not, we see in his action the first certain example of a religious foundation by the initiative of a Pictish king. The main purpose was to reduce the influence of Iona and its monks in Pictish affairs. The Northumbrians had already attempted to do this by the establishment of a short-lived bishopric at

---

20. *AU* 617; see the discussion in A. P. Smyth, *Warlords and Holy Men: Scotland AD 80-1000.* (1984), 108-9.
21. Bede, *HE* v. 21.
22. *AU* 717. Cf. Bede, *HE* iii. 4.
23. *ibid.*, v. 21.
24. G. Donaldson, 'Scotland's earliest church buildings', *Records of the Scottish Church History Soc.* xviii (1973), 1-9; repr. in Donaldson, *Scottish Church History*, 1-10; A. Ritchie, *Picts* (Edinburgh, 1989), 34.

Abercorn,[25] but Nechton was beginning a trend which was to have a much longer history.

The identification of Restennet as Nechton's church must be doubtful; also uncertain is the nature of the new foundation. Bede does not mention a bishop at the new church, and does not state explicitly that it was to be a *monasterium*. Yet his words, 'All ministers of the altar and monks were tonsured in the shape of a crown, and the corrected nation rejoiced to submit to the discipleship of Peter, the most blessed prince of the apostles, and under his protection, as if anew', might be taken to imply that Nechton's foundation was staffed by priests and monks and had an extensive jurisdiction throughout the Pictish kingdom.[26]

The different accounts which survive of the foundation of Abernethy cannot be readily reconciled; all that they have in common is the assertion that Abernethy was founded by a Pictish king and dedicated to St Brigit of Kildare. In one version, embedded in a Pictish king-list in a fourteenth-century manuscript, Darlugdach, abbess of Kildare, came to Britain in the third year of 'Necton Morbet filius Erip', who in the following year gave Abernethy to God and St Brigit in her presence; and Darlugdach 'sang Alleluia over that offering'.[27]

This account is followed by what purports to be the foundation charter of Abernethy, running in the name of *Nectonius Magnus filius Wirp*, which is a very rare example of such a document coming from the territories of the Picts.[28] The Pictish king-lists enter a 'Nectu nepos Uerb' with a reign of twenty years at a point which makes him possibly identifiable with the 'Nechtan mac Canonn' whose death is entered under the year 621 in the *Annals of Ulster*. Nechton, although apparently not an uncommon Pictish name, is the name of only one other king in the king-list, Nechton son of Derilei, mentioned above, who reigned *c.* 705-24.[29] It seems unlikely that he was in fact the founder of Abernethy, since a policy of co-operation with the churches of Anglian Northumbria is not easy to reconcile with a foundation in honour of St Brigit of Kildare.

A different version of the Abernethy foundation legend is interpolated by Walter Bower, abbot of Inchcolm, in his copy of John of Fordun's version of the Pictish king-list.[30] This states that 'Garnard filius Dompnach sive Makdompnach' founded and built a collegiate church at Abernethy after

---

25. Bede, *HE* iv. 26.
26. *ibid.*, v. 21.
27. M. O. Anderson, *Kings and Kingship in Early Scotland* (Edinburgh, 1973), 247; W. F. Skene, *Chronicles of the Picts, Chronicles of the Scots* (Edinburgh, 1867), 6-7.
28. W. Davies, 'The Latin charter tradition in Western Britain, Brittany, and Ireland in the early mediaeval period', in *Ireland in Early Mediaeval Europe: Studies in Memory of Kathleen Hughes*, ed. D. Whitelock *et al.* (1982), 258-80, at 273 and n.55.
29. *AU* 621; K. H. Jackson, 'The Pictish language', in *The Problem of the Picts*, ed. F. T. Wainwright (1955), 129-60, at 140-1, 145; Anderson, *Kings and Kingship*, 231-3.
30. Walter Bower, *Scotichronicon*, ed. D. E. R. Watt (Aberdeen, 1987 - in progress), iv. 12; vol. ii (1989), 302 and nn. on 458-9.

Saint Patrick had brought Brigit and her nine virgins into Scotland, and he gave Brigit and her nine virgins all the lands and teinds which the canons of Abernethy now (c. 1440) hold. The nine virgins all died within five years and were buried in the north part of the church. At this time when, Bower claimed, there was only one bishop in Scotland, three elections were held in this church; it was the principal royal and episcopal (*pontificalis*) place of the Picts for a long time. It was founded 226 years before Dunkeld, or, *in alia cronica*, 244 years. In a later revision of the *Scotichronicon* Bower adds that Dunkeld was founded by Constantine son of Fergus, king of the Picts.[31] This king is datable c. 789-820.[32] On this calculation the foundation of Abernethy would have been c. 570-90. The Pictish king Gartnait son of Domelch appears to have had a reign covering part of the 590s,[33] and he is presumably the king intended in Bower's version of the foundation legend. Other kings named Gartnait died in 635 and 663 according to the *Annals of Ulster*. At 649 the *Annals* record 'warfare between the descendants of Aedán and of Gartnait mac Accidáin', presumably between the Dál Riata and the Picts. A romantic Pictish hero called Cano mac Gartnait from Skye may have been thought to belong to the early seventh century.[34]

The foundation stories of Abernethy are irreconcilably muddled. They seem to indicate that Abernethy was founded by a Pictish king (possibly but not certainly called either Nechton or Gartnait), at or near a centre of Pictish royal power, and that it was in some way associated with the church of St Brigit of Kildare. The date of the foundation is a matter for guesswork, but it seems to have been considerably earlier than that of Dunkeld.

There is evidence at the site itself for what may have been an early ecclesiastical foundation close to a royal centre. A Class I Pictish symbol-stone bearing the Pictish 'tuning-fork' and 'crescent and V-rod' symbols flanked by a hammer and anvil has been found close to the tenth- or eleventh-century round tower. Several fragments of later sculptures have also been uncovered at Abernethy, mostly reused for building purposes. Above Abernethy stands a hill 'crowned by an iron-age fort that may have been re-used by the Picts'. There are other examples, such as Craig Phadraig near Inverness, of Iron Age forts that were reoccupied in the Pictish period.[35]

These indications, taken together with the dedication to St Brigit, suggest that an ecclesiastical foundation existed at Abernethy in the seventh century. We have seen that Columban monks were extensively settled in

---

31. *ibid.*, 459.
32. Anderson, *Kings and Kingship*, 192-4, 233.
33. *ibid.*, 169, 231; 'Annals of Tigernach', ed. W. Stokes, *Revue Celtique*, xvii (1896), 6-33, 119-263, and 337-420, at 162.
34. Bannerman, *Studies*, 92-3; F. J. Byrne, *Irish Kings and High-Kings* (1973), 105, 243.
35. Ritchie, *Picts*, 16, 44. The only other round tower is at Brechin. For Craig Phadraig, see L. Alcock, 'Pictish studies: present and future' in *The Picts: a New Look at Old Problems*, ed. A. Small (1987), 80-92, at 82. For Colum Cille's visit to Bridei's fort, see *Life of Columba*, esp. ii. 34, 35, 36.

Pictland before their expulsion in 717. The activities of St Donnan of Eigg and later of St Maelruba of Applecross (a monastery of the *familia* of St Comgall of Bangor) show the work of Irish founders outwith the *familia* of Colum Cille in Pictish territories, as the probable association of Eileach an Naoimh with St Brendan of Clonfert may show it within the lands of the Dál Riata.[36] The link between Abernethy and St Brigit of Kildare may be part of the same phenomenon, and so could well belong to the seventh century.

Both versions of the foundation legend stress royal involvement in the establishment of the church of Abernethy. It is possible that this may be an anachronistic reflection of the conditions of the eighth century and later, but one must remember the proximity of the hill-fort just to the south. One possible contender as the founder of Abernethy is Gartnait son of Domnall, whose death is recorded in the *Annals of Ulster* at 663; in the Pictish king-list he is styled Gartnait, son of Donuel.[37] It is possible, though by no means certain, that his father was Domnall Brecc, king of the Dál Riata, who died in 642.[38]

What sort of religious centre was Abernethy? Clearly it was a place of great antiquity and continuing importance, but beyond that it is not easy to say. There was a tradition of stone-carving going back probably to the seventh century, and there was an imposing Irish-style round tower of tenth- or eleventh-century date. The mention of three episcopal elections being held at Abernethy, at a time when there was only one bishop in Scotland, indicates that it may have been an episcopal centre with a succession of bishops. In the central Middle Ages Abernethy was a detached parish belonging to the diocese of Dunblane. We shall see that the episcopal centre of Dunblane was probably moved there from an earlier residence at Muthill,[39] and it may be that Abernethy was ancestral to Muthill and so ultimately to the medieval diocese of Dunblane. In the early twelfth century a community of *Céli Dé* apparently shared the house with ordinary *clerici*, but were distinct from them.[40] By the end of the twelfth century the *clerici* had disappeared, and the revenues were divided equally, with half belonging to the family of the lay abbot and half belonging to the *Céli Dé*.[41] These later became regular canons. In the twelfth century there is also mention of a *rector scholarum* at Abernethy.

So Abernethy was a royal foundation, the seat (for a time) of a bishop, close to a probable royal centre, with a community of clerks who were at one time distinct from, but probably merged with, a *Céli Dé* community. Both communities included *sacerdotes* (priests rather than bishops). Abernethy seems to have had dependent churches or chapels, including Dron, Dunbog, Abdie (?), Flisk and Coultra (now in Balmerino), forming a

---

36. Smyth, *Warlords*, 107-11; see n.16 above.
37. *AU* 663; Anderson, *Kings and Kingship*, 231, 248.
38. *AU* 642; on Pictish succession, see Anderson, *Kings and Kingship*, 165-79, 231-3; Smyth, *Warlords*, 57-73; W. D. H. Sellar, 'Warlords, holy men, and matrilinear succession, *Innes Review*, xxxvi (1985), 29-43.
39. Below, pp. 128-9.
40. A. C. Lawrie, *Early Scottish Charters prior to 1153* (Glasgow, 1905), 11-12.
41. *Liber S. Thome de Aberbrothoc* (Bannatyne Club, 1848-56), 25-6.

compact group stretching from the lower Earn in a straight line along the southern shore of the Firth of Tay.[42] Such a group of churches or chapels within easy reach of a major religious centre is a phenomenon we shall encounter again in our examination of early church organization in Scotland, as at Brechin, Muthill, St Vigeans and elsewhere; perhaps this is how we should understand the typical *parochia* of a major religious centre. One point worth stressing about Abernethy is that with its royal and episcopal connections, its *clerici*, and its dependent churches and chapels, it was not an isolated or eremitic community, but had in part at least a public function.

The role of the bishops is not easy to describe with certainty. The source of the Abernethy foundation legend is anxious to stress Abernethy's anti- quity in relation to Dunkeld; since in 864, according to the *Annals of Ulster*, the office of *primepscop Fortrenn* was held by the abbot of Dunkeld, the Abernethy writer may have been recalling a time when the chief bishop of Scotland resided at Abernethy. In 721 a certain Fergustus, *episcopus Scotiae Pictus*, attended a council in Rome held by Pope Gregory II.[43] He may have been one of the three successive bishops resident at Abernethy mentioned in Bower's source.

The sources relating to the foundation of Abernethy are so uncertain as to require a large element of guesswork; those relating to St Andrews allow for greater confidence, while still involving an element of uncertainty. There are two twelfth-century versions of the St Andrews foundation legend, to the longer of which is appended a description of the constitution of St Andrews at the time of the erection of the Augustinian priory there *c.* 1160.[44] The shorter version attributes the foundation to a Pictish king Ungus, son of Urguist, who has a vision of St Andrew while campaigning in Mercia with his seven *comites*. After his subsequent victory, he resolves to give a tenth part of his kingdom to God and St Andrew, but he and his council cannot decide where to make the principal grant. Meanwhile a monk called Regulus in Constantinople has a vision urging him to take the relics of St Andrew and set sail with them, until he should come to a place called *rígmund*, the royal mount. Here he is met by King Ungus, who bestows on him the locality, one-third of the kingdom, and the headship of all the churches in the lands of the Picts.[45]

The longer version is equally fantastic, but differs in a number of respects. The Pictish king is called Hungus son of Forso (*lege* Forguso), or Hungus son of Ferlon. He is fighting against Athelstan at the Tyne. The

42. *ibid.*; *Regesta Regum Scottorum*, ii: *The Acts of William I*, ed. G. W. S. Barrow (Edinburgh, 1971), 342-3.
43. P. Labbé, *Sacrosancta Concilia* (1671-3), vi, 1458; Donaldson, 'Bishops' sees', 14.
44. Skene, *Chronicles of the Picts*, 138-40, 183-93; M. O. Anderson, 'The Celtic church in Kinrimund', in *The Medieval Church of St Andrews*, ed. D. McRoberts (1976), 1-10, at 1, n., dates the descriptive section (pp. 188-93) 1144 × 1153. See also M. O. Anderson, 'St Andrews before Alexander I', in *The Scottish Tradition: Essays in Honour of R. G. Cant*, ed. G. W. S. Barrow (Edinburgh, 1974), 1-13, at 7-13.
45. Skene, *Chronicles of the Picts*, 138-40.

monk Regulus brings Andrew's relics to Kylrimont, which was at that time (*tunc*) called Muckros. Here Hungus meets him and gives to St Andrew a huge *parochia* from the sea called *Ishundenema* (The Firth of Forth) to the sea called *Slethenma* (the Firth of Tay), from Largo by way of Ceres to Naughton. Hungus confirms his grant by laying earth upon the altar of St Andrews before an assembly of Pictish nobles; the list of these witnesses is a credit to the ingenuity of a twelfth-century forger, who has freely quarried their names from a copy of the Pictish king-list. Regulus sings the Alleluia upon this offering, as Darlugdach had done at Abernethy.[46]

There are two Pictish kings called Unuist son of Uurguist in the king-list, with dates *c.* 729-61 and *c.* 820-34 respectively. Neither, therefore, is a contemporary of Athelstan (924-41). The king intended must be the earlier of the two, since the death of Tuathalán abbot of *Cinrighmona* is recorded in 747 in the *Annals of Ulster*. This clearly fixes the date of the foundation of St Andrews between 729 and 747. This date accords well with the carved stones at St Andrews, which appear to date from the mid-eighth century onwards.[47]

A number of indications show that St Andrews was very much a royal foundation. The name *Cennrígmonad*, 'head of the royal mound' (later *Cellrígmonad*, 'church of the royal mound'), indicates a royal centre. The names *Muckros* ('pig headland') and *Cursus Apri* applied to the area may suggest that it was a royal residence to which the king came to hunt wild boar.[48] Both versions of the legend stress the important part which Unuist son of Uurguist played in the foundation, making his donation in thanksgiving for victory in battle. Unuist fought many battles and won most of them, but his main victims were the Britons of Strathclyde and the Dál Riata, both of whom experienced periods of political decline as a result of his depredations. He may have been responsible for an attack on the Northumbrian army after the seige of Dumbarton in 756, in which he and the Northumbrians had been allies; by the time of his death Northumbrian writers have become very hostile to him, describing him as a tyrannical slaughterer and perpetrator of bloody crimes.[49] Splendid evidence of the 'royalty' of St Andrews is given by the magnificent stone sarcophagus which was carved some time in the second half of the eighth century to house relics, probably of St Andrew; this shows a Pictish king with Mediterranean hair, beard and robes portrayed as David rending the jaws of a lion.[50] If the portrait is not that of Unuist son of

---

46. Anderson, *Kings and Kingship*, 99-100; Skene, *Chronicles of the Picts*, 183-8.
47. *AU* 747; J. Anderson and J. R. Allen, *Early Christian Monuments of Scotland*, iii (Edinburgh, 1903), 350-63.
48. Anderson, 'Celtic church in Kinrimund', 1-2 and n.6.
49. *AU* 728, 729, 734, 736, 739, 741, 750, 756, 761; A. O. Anderson, *Early Sources of Scottish History* (Edinburgh, 1922), i, 239; *idem*, *Scottish Annals from English Chroniclers* (1908), 57; Bede, *HE* continuations (ed. Colgrave and Mynors, p. 576).
50. I. Henderson, *The Picts* (1967), 88. Other writers have argued for a later date, e.g. M. O. Anderson, 'Celtic church in Kinrimund', 2 and nn.; Ritchie, *Picts*, 38-40 ('later eighth century or very early ninth century'). On its serpent-bosses, see I. Henderson, 'The Book of Kells and the snake-boss motif on Pictish cross-slabs and the Iona crosses', in *Ireland and Insular Art*, ed. M. Ryan (Dublin, Royal Irish Academy, 1987), 56-65; on the David iconography, see I. Henderson, 'The David cycle in Pictish art', in *Early Medieval Sculpture in Britain and Ireland*, ed. Higgitt, 87-124.

Uurguist himself, it can hardly be too long after his time.

One of the most puzzling problems about St Andrews is the reason for the unusual dedication to St Andrew. One notion which must be abandoned is that of contact between Pictland and Constantinople in the eighth and ninth centuries; the personal name Constantine did not come into Scotland from this source, and the affinities of works like the St Andrews sarcophagus with Mediterranean ivories are insufficient to bear too much weight. An attractive suggestion, but one which cannot be proved, is Skene's conjecture that St Andrew's relics could have been brought into Pictland by Acca bishop of Hexham when he went into exile in 732.[51] A third possibility is that the king may have chosen to dedicate his church to St Andrew because of the resemblance between the saint's name, *Andreas*, and his own, *Onuist* or *Unuist*.

St Andrews was a religious community with a royal foundation; by the beginning of the tenth century, if not earlier, it was the residence of a bishop. Bishop Cellach, recorded in 906, is the first name in a late medieval list of the bishops of St Andrews,[52] but that does not make it certain that he was the first bishop resident there. It may be that the founder, Unuist son of Uurguist, transferred the episcopal residence to St Andrews from Abernethy or from Nechton son of Derilei's church of St Peter; but there can be no certainty about this.

By the middle of the tenth century, a community of *Céli Dé* has emerged at St Andrews. King Constantine mac Aedo retired into religion in the 940s, ending his life at 'the abbey-church on the brow of the wave, in the house of the holy apostle'. The Scottish regnal list states that he was 'abbot of the *Céli Dé* of St Andrew'.[53] Even in the mid-twelfth century the *Céli Dé* still preserved something of their original austerity. The description of the constitution of St Andrews appended to the longer version of the foundation legend states that there are thirteen *Keledei* by carnal succession, who live by earthly esteem rather than by saintliness; however, when they become *Céli Dé* they no longer live with their wives or with other women about whom evil suspicion could arise. They do not perform services at the altar of St Andrew, but celebrate their own office according to their own fashion in one corner (*angulus*) of the church. In addition to the portions of the celibate *Céli Dé*, there are seven portions (*personae*) or parsonages with a share of the oblations of the altar. One portion goes to the bishop, and one to the hospital; the other five are given to five parsons (*personae*). These men have wives and children who inherit their portion of the temporalities, but not of the oblations of the altar. They owe no service to the altar of St Andrew, but must provide hospitality if the hospital has more than its full complement of six guests; and if the king or bishop is present, which rarely happens, they are required to serve at mass at the

51. W. F. Skene, 'Notice of the early ecclesiastical settlements at St Andrews', *Proc. Soc. Antiq. Scotland*, iv (1860-2), 300-21.
52. Anderson, *Kings and Kingship*, 251; Bower, *Scotichronicon*, vi. 24, ed. W. Goodall (Edinburgh, 1759), i, 339 and n.
53. Anderson, *Early Sources*, i, 447-8; Anderson, *Kings and Kingship*, 267, 274-5, 283, 288, 291; Anderson, 'Celtic church in Kinrimund', 3-4.

altar of St Andrew.[54] It is left unclear who was responsible for regular services in the church of St Andrews. The hospital was presumably a hostel for pilgrims; there was a similar institution at Whithorn in the twelfth century.[55]

If St Andrews eclipsed some other religious houses to become the most important church of the Pictish kingdom by the mid-eighth century, it did not itself suffer serious eclipse when a great new royal foundation was established in the following century. This was the church of Dunkeld, which was founded according to some versions of the king-list by Constantine son of Fergus (c. 789-820), one of the last Pictish kings, but which has also been convincingly identified as the church built by Kenneth mac Alpin in the land of the Picts c. 849. We are told that in the seventh year of his reign (which began c. 842) he brought relics of Colum Cille to this church. The *Annals* record a major translation of Colum Cille's relics to Kells in 849, so it may be that Kenneth received a small share of the relics as compensation; part of this may have been the Monymusk Reliquary or *Brecbennoch Coluim Chille*, a silver and enamel reliquary which may be as early as c. 700.[56]

The translation of Colum Cille's relics into Pictland to a great church built there by Kenneth must have been a potent symbol in ecclesiastical terms of the mastery which he had also asserted in dynastic and political terms. A Pictish king had expelled the *familia* of Colum Cille across Drumalban in 717, and now the saint was making a triumphant return. The importance of Dunkeld is indicated by the record of the death of Tuathal, abbot of Dunkeld and *primepscop Fortrenn*, in 865. Professor Donaldson has pointed out that the term *primepscop*, 'chief-bishop', implies that there were other bishops;[57] although in its narrowest sense *Fortrenn* means Strathearn and Gowrie, it also has a wider meaning embracing the whole kingdom ruled by the king of Scots,[58] so we may assume that at this time the bishop of St Andrews was of lower standing than the bishop of Dunkeld.

In the tenth century and later, the abbots of Dunkeld were important secular figures. An abbot was killed in a battle between two rivals for the Scottish kingship in 965. Crinán, abbot of Dunkeld, was the son-in-law of Malcolm II (1004-34), and on Malcolm's death was able to have his son Duncan made king (1034-40). When Duncan was killed by Macbeth, mormaer of Moray, Crinán rebelled against Macbeth, and was himself

---

54. Skene, *Chronicles of the Picts*, 188-9.
55. *Liber Cartarum Sancte Crucis de Edwinesburg* (Bannatyne Club, 1840), 20.
56. *AU* 849; Donaldson, 'Bishops' sees', 15; R. B. K. Stevenson, 'Pictish Art', in *Problems of the Picts*, ed. Wainright, 97-128, at 108-10; F. Henry, *Irish Art in the Early Christian Period* (1940), 70.
57. *AU* 865; Donaldson, 'Bishops' sees', 15-17.
58. *ibid.*, 15 and n.30; Anderson, *Kings and Kingship*, 139-42. It is usually assumed that *Fortrenn* is the genitive of an n-stem, nominative *Fortriu*; this remains conjectural. Although the genitive is the most frequently occurring form (see *ibid.*, 140), in the Pictish foundation legend *Fortrenn* is used as the nominative of a personal name; *ibid.*, 245.

killed in battle in 1045.[59] Clearly such men were lay administrators of a church's temporalities, not monastic abbots; the term was used in the same sense in Ireland.

Late traditions that there had been *Céli Dé* at Dunkeld have been regarded as doubtful.[60] Yet a strong indication that there were probably *Céli Dé* at Dunkeld (which is anyway inherently likely) is provided by a cross-slab of late ninth or (more likely) tenth-century date, now kept in the chapter-house.[61] On the front there is a cross in relief with curving cusped arms; carved on the cross-head is a battle scene with horsemen, foot-soldiers, and a jumble of decapitated corpses; beneath this, on the shaft, is a scene of Daniel in the lion's den; on one side of the slab is another horseman, a large figure with a halo (an angel, or Colum Cille?), and below him three small figures, who may represent the three children in the fiery furnace; on the back is a scene of the feeding of the multitude by multiplication of loaves and fishes, beneath which stand the twelve apostles in two rows of six. The slab has had other carvings, which are now too worn to be identifiable.

Some of these scenes, notably the multiplication of loaves and fishes and the twelve apostles, are very rare on Scottish cross-slabs. They occur frequently, however, on the granite high crosses of the Barrow Valley school in Ireland, of which the best examples are at St Mullins, Castleder-mot (two), Moone and Old Kilcullen. The great pyramidal base of the cross of Moone, probably a subsequent addition to the cross itself, has the best arrangement of scenes illustrating the theme of divine aid, known also from *Céli Dé* literature: the fall of man, the sacrifice of Isaac, Daniel in the lion's den, the three children, the flight into Egypt, the multiplication of loaves and fishes, the crucifixion, the twelve apostles, St Paul and St Antony in the desert, and the temptation of St Antony.[62] The Dunkeld slab is an interesting translation of some of these images on to the typically Pictish medium of the cross-slab in high relief. In some ways its closest affinities may be with the south cross at Castledermot: the rather unsystematic arrangement of the imagery, the juxtaposition of the apostles and the miracle of loaves and fishes, the representation of the multitude, and the similar treatment of the rows of featureless standing figures, are all features which they share in common. Castledermot was an early ninth-century *Céli Dé* foundation, while Moone bears a dedication to Colum Cille.

59. Anderson, *Early Sources*, i, 472-3, 576-7, 583-4.
60. Cowan and Easson, *Medieval Religious Houses: Scotland*, 47.
61. Anderson and Allen, *Early Christian Monuments of Scotland*, iii, 317-9; J. Stuart, *The Sculptured Stones of Scotland* (1856-67), i, plates L, LI.
62. F. Henry, *Irish High Crosses* (Dublin, 1964), 25-6; Henry, *Irish Art in the Early Christian Period*, 138, 147-9; F. Henry, *Irish Art During the Viking Invasions* (new edn. 1967), 137-40; M. and L. de Paor, *Early Christian Ireland* (1958), 146-50; E. de Bhaldraithe, *The High Crosses of Moone and Castledermot* (Bolton Abbey, 1987), esp. 8-9; M. Herity, 'The context and date of the high crosses at Dísert Diarmata (Castledermot), Co. Kildare', in *Figures from the Past: Studies in Honour of Helen M. Roe*, ed. E. Rynne (Dublin, 1987), 111-30, esp. 121; Stevenson, 'Pictish Art', 128.

Thus the Dunkeld slab, with its free use of *Céli Dé* imagery related to that on the crosses of Castledermot and vicinity, may be taken as evidence of a community of *Céli Dé* at Dunkeld in the tenth century.

Because Dunkeld is mentioned in early records and became the site of a later cathedral (see fig. 5.2), we possess more than the testimony of early carved stones to show that this was an early religious site. We shall see below that the peculiar shape of the medieval diocese of Dunkeld, with its many detached parishes scattered across eastern Scotland, points in the same direction.[63] For some early Christian religious centres in Scotland, however, a collection of carved stones is all that survives to show the antiquity of the site. These include Meigle and St Vigeans in the east, and Govan in the west.

Meigle is mentioned briefly and enigmatically in the longer version of the St Andrews foundation legend. In a single sentence sandwiched between the legend itself and the description of the constitution of the church of St Andrews in the mid-twelfth century, the writer states: 'Thana filius Dudabrach hoc monumentum scripsit regi Pherath filio Bergath in villa Migdele.'[64] In the Pictish king-list there is a king called Uurad or Ferad son of Bargoit, who died *c.* 842.[65] The fine collection of late Pictish and post-Pictish stones now housed in the Meigle Museum does not include one with an inscription to this king, but it seems likely that what now survives is only part of a once greater collection. Enough survives to have drawn Mrs Ritchie to the conclusion 'that there was once a major church or even monastery nearby'.[66] The collection includes secular burial-markers as well as cross-slabs, and the words interpolated in the St Andrews source indicate that Meigle was the burial-place of at least one Pictish king. The nature of the community at Meigle is difficult to determine. One of the cross-slabs (Meigle no. 2) has a fine scene of Daniel in the lion's den, but that alone is hardly sufficient to confirm the assumption that there were *Céli Dé* at Meigle. In spite of its earlier importance, by the mid-twelfth century Meigle had become a *uilla* and a parish church; it had not retained the importance which made it the burial-place of one of the last Pictish kings and the site of a collection of imposing ninth and tenth-century tombstones. The character of an early religious centre of some importance, with a group of churches or chapels within an enclosure, is suggested in a charter of 1178 × 1185, whereby the local landowner gave the church of Meigle to St Andrews Priory *cum capella eidem ecclesie adiacente.*[67] This grant to St Andrews and the mention of Meigle in the St Andrews foundation legend are suggestive of some sort of relationship between Meigle and St Andrews. On the other hand, in 1207 the patronage of the church of Meigle was successfully claimed by the bishop of Dunkeld, and the parish of Meigle was within the medieval diocese of Dunkeld.[68] So

---

63. Below, pp. 127-9.
64. Skene, *Chronicles of the Picts*, 188.
65. Anderson, *Kings and Kingship*, 233, 249, 263, 273, 281, 287.
66. Ritchie, *Picts*, 58.
67. *Acts of William I*, 254-5.
68. I. B. Cowan, *The Parishes of Medieval Scotland* (Scottish Record Society, 1967), 145.

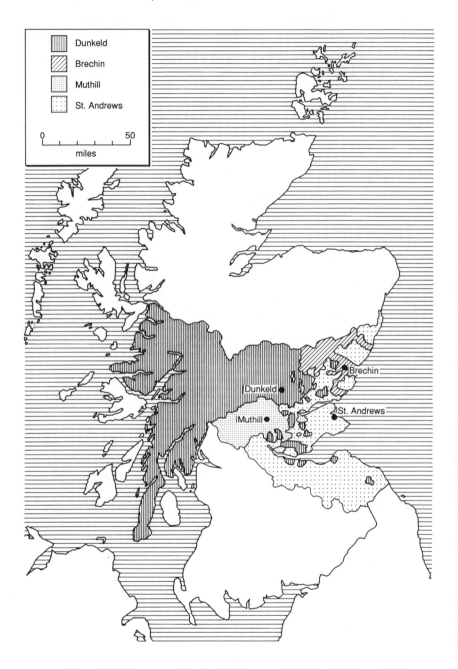

Figure 5.2 Dioceses and cathedrals in central Scotland before *c.* 1180.

some kind of relationship between Meigle and the church of Dunkeld also seems to be indicated. What these relationships were, and how they worked, cannot now be determined.

St Vigeans, now within the town of Arbroath, is equally obscure. Its fine collection of early Christian carved stones dates from the eighth century extending into the post-Pictish period. One of them bears an inscription seeming to commemorate members of the Pictish aristocracy: DROSTEN IPE UORET ETT FORCUS, followed by a blank space presumably for the addition of other names.[69] Drust son of Ferat (died c. 849) is the last name in one version of the Pictish king-list, but it cannot be certain that he is one of the persons named on this stone.[70] What is likely, however, is an important church with a school of stonecarving patronized by the Pictish aristocracy, perhaps by kings. By 1178 St Vigeans had become merely 'the church of the town of Arbroath' when King William gave it to his newly founded monastery of St Thomas the Martyr there.[71] Some of the parish churches given to Arbroath Abbey at that time may earlier have belonged to St Vigeans; they included Ethie, Dunnichen, Kingoldrum, Maryton of Old Montrose *cum terra eiusdem ecclesie que Scottice abthen vocatur,* Newtyle, Banchory-Ternan, Glamis, and Haltwhistle in Northumberland.[72] The last-named of these is unlikely to have had any previous connection with St Vigeans, and Kingoldrum was a mensal church of the bishops of Brechin within their diocese.[73] The mention of *abthen* lands at Old Montrose is of interest, however, since these were presumably part of the *abthania* of St Vigeans. It may be that Arbroath Abbey was endowed in part at least with the possessions of a former important church at St Vigeans.

Govan has a fine collection of carved stones belonging mostly to the tenth and eleventh centuries, including a sarcophagus, cross-shafts, cross-slabs, hogback tombstones and a large number of recumbent grave-slabs.[74] The stones of Govan and elsewhere in its vicinity (most notably Inchinnan) belong to a period when Gaelic influence was being felt increasingly strongly in Strathclyde. After a lengthy Viking siege in 870, Arthgal king of Dumbarton was captured, taken to Dublin and put to death 'by counsel of Constantine son of Kenneth' king of Scots; Arthgal's son Rhun was, or soon became, married to Constantine's sister. A few years later according to late and unreliable Welsh sources, there was an exodus of Strathclyde aristocrats into Gwynedd because they refused to accept a new political *status quo.* Thereafter kings of Scots exercised authority over Strathclyde

---

69. Anderson and Allen, *Early Christian Monuments of Scotland*, iii, 234-42, 267-80; Ritchie, *Picts*, 34-7.
70. Anderson, *Kings and Kingship*, 233, 266, 273, 281, 287.
71. *Acts of William I*, 251.
72. *ibid.*, 250-2.
73. Cowan, *Parishes*, 113.
74. Anderson and Allen, *Early Christian Monuments of Scotland*, iii, 462-72; Stuart, *Sculptured Stones*, i, plates CXXXVI, CXXXVII; J. Stirling Maxwell, *Sculptured Stones in the Kirkyard of Govan* (Glasgow, 1899); C. A. R. Radford, 'Early Christian monuments at Govan and Inchinnan', *Trans. Glasgow Archaeol. Soc.* n.s. xv (1966), 177-88.

for some of the time at least until their permanent annexation of the kingdom in the eleventh century.[75] The Govan stonecarving belongs to this period of Gaelic dominance, although the artistic influences involved are mixed.[76] The dedication at Govan, to St Constantine, indicates an association with the dynasty of Kenneth mac Alpin, among whom the name Constantine was frequently used; there was a major dedication to St Constantine at Kilchousland (*Cill Chostantín*) in Kintyre, and Kenneth claimed descent from the Kintyre dynasty of the Cenél nGabráin. Late medieval tradition related that Constantine had been martyred in Kintyre, but the truth behind the identification of this shadowy saint cannot now be ascertained.[77] The most important point is that the king of Scots at the time of political upheaval in Strathclyde, and to which the earliest Govan stones can be roughly assigned, was himself called Constantine.[78] Probably we should view the foundation of Govan in the same light as the foundation of Dunkeld, as a visible ecclesiastical manifestation of political dominance.

Govan stood within an eliptical enclosure on the south bank of the Clyde, probably largely surrounded by water, opposite the site of a royal residence at Partick; the site and the stonecarving school suggest that Govan was an important church. But not all the early gravestones are those of ecclesiastics; five hogback tombstones presumably marked the graves of aristocratic laymen of Scandinavian descent. One remarkable feature of the Govan school is the large number of free-standing crosses, most of them originally ring-headed, in Dunbartonshire, Renfrewshire and lower Lanarkshire. Some of them stood within later church sites (as at Inchinnan, Cambusnethan, Old Kilpatrick and elsewhere), whereas others (such as Barochan) apparently did not. It is clear that stonecarvers from Govan worked at ecclesiastical sites in the area, but the relationship between these and the important church at Govan is not clear. There may have been a number of churches or chapels within enclosed burial-grounds and there may also have been unenclosed stations marked by a cross to which clergy could come for preaching or administration of the sacraments. But the evidence does not permit us to say more than that.

One problem about Govan is its relationship to the much older episcopal site at Glasgow, some 3 miles away. Glasgow was almost certainly a church founded by bishop Kentigern in the late sixth century and the place where he was buried.[79] Sedulius, 'a bishop of Britain of Scottish race' who

---

75. A. Macquarrie, 'Early Christian Govan: the historical context', *Records of the Scottish Church History Soc.* xxiv (1990), 1-17, at 6-10; Smyth, *Warlords and Holy Men*, 215-8; D. P. Kirby, 'Strathclyde and Cumbria', *Trans. Cumberland and Westmoreland Antiq. and Archaeol. Soc.* lxii (1962), 77-94.
76. Macquarrie, 'Early Christian Govan', 3-5; Radford, 'Early Christian monuments', esp. 176-80.
77. *Breviarium Aberdonense* (Spalding and Maitland Clubs, 1854), i (Pars Hiemalis), 11 March; Macquarrie, 'Early Christian Govan', 10-12.
78. *ibid.*, 12-14.
79. A. Macquarrie, 'The career of St Kentigern of Glasgow: *Vitae, Lectiones*, and Glimpses of Fact', *Innes Review*, xxxvii (1986), 3-24.

accompanied the Pictish bishop Fergustus to a council at Rome in 721,[80] may have been a bishop of Strathclyde based at Glasgow. Evidence for devotion to St Kentigern in Gwynedd may indicate the activity of the aristocrats displaced in the late ninth century, but by the time David became prince of Strathclyde *c.* 1113 the church of Glasgow seems to have been in some decay, and the title 'bishop of Glasgow' was held sometimes by suffragans of the archbishop of York who did not reside in their diocese.[81] David, ignoring the still active church of Govan, set about the revival of Glasgow as a cathedral and cult centre between 1113 and his becoming king in 1124. Within a few decades Govan, now treated merely as a parish church with a parish straddling the river, was incorporated as a prebend of Glasgow Cathedral.[82] Presumably Govan's disadvantage was that it was not the seat of a bishop. In the tenth and eleventh centuries it seems to have been a more active church site than Glasgow, but the episcopal associations of the older site must have weighed more heavily with the 'Normanizing' reformer David.

This may present a clue to the anomalies of size and shape of the Scottish dioceses as they emerged in the twelfth century. The four northern dioceses of Aberdeen, Moray, Ross and Caithness appear to conform to secular provincial boundaries, and may have been the result of David's centralized planning (though using existing churches). South of the Mounth there were three big dioceses, St Andrews, Glasgow and Dunkeld (then still including Argyll, which was detached in the 1180s); and two very much smaller dioceses, Brechin and Dunblane. St Andrews, Dunkeld, Dunblane and Brechin all had a scattering of detached parishes within the boundaries of other dioceses; these must have been remote churches within their *parochiae* which were counted as parishes within their dioceses when diocesan boundaries were drawn up.[83] Some important religious centres, such as Meigle, St Vigeans, Lochleven, Abernethy and Govan, were swallowed up in the new diocesan structure and have left little trace except as later parish churches. The two exceptions here are the two small cathedral churches of Brechin and Dunblane, and they call for special comment.

Brechin has a round tower and a collection of early Christian carved stones. The earliest documentary reference to Brechin is a statement in the *Chronicle of the Kings of Scotland* that Kenneth II (971-95) *tribuit magnam*

---

80. Labbé, *Sacrosancta Concilia*, vi, 1458; Donaldson, 'Bishops' sees', 14 and n.27.
81. Macquarrie, 'Early Christian Govan', 8-10; Macquarrie, 'The career of St Kentigern', 14-15, 21-2; D. E. R. Watt, *Fasti Ecclesiae Scoticanae Medii Aevi* (Scottish Record Society, 1969), 143.
82. *Registrum Episcopatus Glasguensis* (Maitland Club, 1843), 9-11; J. Durkan, 'The Bishops' barony of Glasgow in pre-Reformation times', *Records of the Scottish Church History Soc.* xxii (1986), 277-301, at 281-3.
83. Donaldson, 'Bishops' sees', 18-22; I do not agree that 'we can detect ... the making of two distinct types of dioceses, the monastic and the secular' (20); R. Nicholson and P. MacNeill (eds.) *An Historical Atlas of Scotland* (1975), texts 22-6, maps 32, 34-5, 40-7. For the background to the creation of the diocese of Argyll, see A. A. M. Duncan, *Scotland: the Making of the Kingdom* (1975), 275-6.

ciuitatem Brechne Domino.[84] This is not necessarily the record of the foundation of the *magna ciuitas* of Brechin, but could mean that the king granted it freedom from certain royal exactions; this type of action is familiar from the Gaelic *notitiae* in the *Book of Deer.*[85] A hereditary family of lay abbots of Brechin is recorded in the twelfth and early thirteenth centuries,[86] and in the same period there was a community of *Céli Dé* headed by a prior, which acted as a *familia* to the bishops. Before 1250 the *Céli Dé* had been transformed into a chapter of secular canons, so that 'the brethren who have been wont to be in the church of Brechin were called Keledei and now by change of name are styled canons'.[87] The church and *Céli Dé* community must have been in existence not later than 971 × 995, but it is not certain when Brechin became the residence of a bishop. On the face of it, Brechin does not appear to have been bigger or more important than some other religious houses in east central Scotland, such as Meigle, St Vigeans or Lochleven; but it became a cathedral church with its *parochia* as its diocese, whereas they did not. The first record of a bishop at Brechin is King David's grant to the bishop and *Céli Dé* of Brechin of the right to hold a Sunday market, which cannot be dated more closely than 1124 × 1153.[88] We are left with the assumption that Brechin as the residence of a bishop and *Céli Dé* and a secularized abbacy was the *status quo* which King David found there. In this respect Brechin resembled St Andrews and Dunkeld; but whereas they became the centres of great territorial dioceses, the diocese of Brechin seems to have been restricted to the churches of its own *parochia*.

The other small diocese in central Scotland was the diocese of Dunblane. In the twelfth and early thirteenth centuries the bishops here were styled 'bishops of Strathearn', and seem to have resided as often, if not more frequently, at Muthill (which is in Strathearn; Dunblane is in the province of Menteith).[89] Both Dunblane and Muthill have tall square towers probably of eleventh century date, indicating important churches at both sites. A corporate picture is clearer at Muthill, where in the late twelfth century there were *Céli Dé* with a prior and *rex scolarum*. There is no evidence for *Céli Dé* at Dunblane, although a *rex scolarum* is mentioned in the early thirteenth century.[90] By the time the bishops of Strathearn became permanently settled at Dunblane, c. 1234, the church there was roofless and its property alienated to laymen, and it was served not by a college of clergy, but 'the divine offices were celebrated in a roofless church by a rural chaplain only.'[91] It may be that in the period prior to the

84. Anderson, *Early Sources*, i, 512.
85. K. H. Jackson, *The Gaelic Notes in the Book of Deer* (1972), 117-24.
86. *ibid.*, 61; Donaldson, 'Bishops' sees', 19-20.
87. *Liber S. Thome de Aberbrothoc*, i, nos. 78, 79, 187, 188, 192, and *passim*; *Chartulary of the Abbey of Lindores*, ed. J. Dowden (Scottish History Soc., 1903), no. xcix.
88. *Regesta Regum Scottorum*, i: *The Acts of Malcolm IV*, ed. G. W. S. Barrow (1960), 170; *Registrum Episcopatus Brechinensis* (Bannatyne Club, 1856), no. i.
89. Watt, *Fasti*, 78-90.
90. *Chartulary of Lindores*, 49-50.
91. A. Theiner, *Vetera Monumenta Hibernorum et Scotorum Historiam Illustrantia* (Rome, 1864), no. 91.

twelfth-century reform Muthill had been a church with *Céli Dé* and a bishop (like Dunkeld, Brechin and St Andrews); if so, this arrangement continued throughout most of the twelfth century and into the early thirteenth, but with the bishops sometimes residing also at Dunblane. From *c.* 1234 onwards the bishops resided permanently at Dunblane and a new chapter of secular canons was constituted, in contrast to the apparently smooth transformation of *Céli Dé* into canons which happened at Brechin. The medieval diocese of Dunblane constitutes a compact territorial body in Strathearn and Menteith, with the big parish of Muthill at its centre and the cathedral city of Dunblane on its southern edge; to the east lie the five detached parishes of Culross, Tulliallan, Exmagirdle, Abernethy, and St Madoes. Dron, between Abernethy and Exmagirdle, appears first as a chapel of Abernethy and probably did not attain parochial status until the later Middle Ages.[92] The association of the ancient church of Abernethy with the medieval diocese of Strathearn or Dunblane is suggestive of some sort of relationship, but what that was cannot now be determined; and the origins of the church of Muthill are lost beyond recovery.

The same is true of a number of other early churches. There were communities of *Céli Dé* at Lochleven, associated with the obscure St Serf, and at Monymusk and Monifieth; Turriff had an abbot and a *fer léginn* in the twelfth century.[93] Clova is described as a *monasterium* in 1157. The same word is used to describe Mortlach (now Dufftown), which appears to have had a *parochia* of churches and which by later tradition was the site from which bishops moved to Aberdeen in the twelfth century; so Mortlach may have been similar in character to St Andrews, Dunkeld, Brechin and Muthill. Evidence for a similar character for Rosemarkie is less certain.[94] St Cyrus, the ancient Ecclesgirig north of Montrose, had an *abbacia* and a *parochia* in the twelfth century, and Kinkell in Aberdeenshire had *membra*, chapels constituting a *parochia*, at a much later date.[95] 'All the churches of Strathgryfe' (west Renfrewshire), which were given to Paisley Abbey *c.* 1160, may have constituted the *parochia* of an important church at Inchinnan; this church itself, where there were a standing cross, a stone sarcophagus, and recumbent grave-slabs, became the property of the Knights Templar as an appropriated parish church.[96] Deer in Buchan had

---

92. *Historical Atlas*, map 35; Cowan, *Parishes*, under the names in question; J. H. Cockburn, *The Medieval Bishops of Dunblane* (Edinburgh, 1959), 74-5.
93. *Liber Cartarum Prioratus Sancti Andree* (Bannatyne Club, 1841), 113, 369-75; A. C. Lawrie, *Early Scottish Charters*, 4-7, 9, 11, 19; *Liber S. Thome de Aberbrothoc*, i, 82; Jackson, *Gaelic Notes*, 31-2, 34-6, 67-8, 79, 84.
94. *Registrum Episcopatus Aberdonensis* (Spalding and Maitland Clubs, 1845), i, 6, 85; Bower, *Scotichronicon*, iv. 44, ed. Watt, vol. ii, 402-4; Anderson, *Early Sources*, 205, 211, nn.; Donaldson, 'Bishops' sees', 14, 22.
95. *Liber Cartarum Sancti Andree*, 27, 138, 229-30; Cowan and Easson, *Medieval Religious Houses*, 52-3.
96. *Registrum Monasterii de Passelet* (Maitland Club, 1832), 5; Radford, 'Early Christian monuments'; Macquarrie, 'Early Christian Govan', 16.

a community of *clerici* in the twelfth century; in 1219 it became a Cistercian monastery.[97]

Of all these houses, Deer is the only one about which substantial information survives, in the form of *notitiae* copied into the margins of a gospelbook belonging to the church. From these some conclusions may be drawn about the character of the community; and although one must exercise caution in this regard, it may be possible to regard Deer as fairly typical of the religious houses of Scotland in the eleventh century. The notes begin with a foundation legend which associates the foundation of the *caithir* of Aberdour and the *caithir* of Deer with Drostán, foster-son of Colum Cille, and with a local aristocrat called *B[r]ede cruthnec*, 'Bridei the Pict', *mormaer* of Buchan. If the founder was a Pict, the foundation must have taken place no later than the late ninth century, and probably earlier. When King David confirmed their privileges *c*. 1150, the community consisted of *clerici*, presumably secular clerks. One of the possessions of the church was *achad na Cléirech*, 'the field of the clerics', which may point in the same direction. *Achad na Cléirech* was given to Deer by Cathal mac Morgainn, who is presumably the same Cathal who is said to have remitted to the house of Deer all the dues of a *toísech* in return for having their goodwill; so Cathal was presumably a local *toísech*. Deer also received grants of land and remissions of dues from *mormaer* ('great steward', later 'earl') and from *rí* ('king'); *toísech* ('leader' or 'chieftain') must be an aristocratic rank inferior to the other two. So Deer was the recipient of aristocratic generosity, among other reasons, in return for its goodwill. What form this took is not specified, but it clearly implies a close relationship between the church and local aristocracy, which the latter were anxious to perpetuate.

Cathal did not confine his generosity to Deer to a grant of land and remission of dues; he also 'gave a feast for a hundred each Christmas and each Easter to God and Drostán', i.e. to the church of Deer. Professor Jackson suggests that this should not imply a community of 100 monks or clerics, but a feast for the community and their aristocratic guests, notionally to the number of 100. This interpretation, which is probably correct, has serious implications for the view that Deer and houses like it were eremitic or claustral communities.

One of the land grants to Deer by a leading Buchan aristocrat and his wife is specifically said to be for 'the consecration of a church of Christ and of Peter the apostle, and to Colum Cille and Drostán'. The place, called Pett Meic Gobraig, cannot now be identified, though presumably it was in north-east Buchan. So it is clear that Deer had dependent churches or chapels, but unfortunately we do not have enough information to try to reconstruct its *parochia*. In a difficult and obscure passage in the *notitiae*, the *mormaer* of Buchan, his wife, and the *toísech* of Clann Morgainn remit to the house of Deer all the impositions due from various grants made to the house, in return for the payment of dues from a specified area of land

---

97. The discussion that follows is based mainly on Jackson, *Gaelic Notes*, passim; see also Cowan and Easson, *Medieval Religious Houses*, 47; D. McRoberts, *Scottish Liturgical Books and Fragments* (Glasgow, 1953), 3.

'which are liable from the chief [religious] houses of Alba in general and from its chief churches' (*don-í thíssad ar ard-mandaidib Alban cu cotchenn 7 ar [a]h-ard chellaib*). Professor Jackson suggests that *ard-mennat*, (dative plural *ard-mennaitib*, whence the form here) should mean in this context 'a chief religious house', although it is not clear what distinguishes such an institution from *ard-chell*, 'a chief-church'. It seems clear, however, that the church of Deer regarded itself as a chief church, i.e., one which had subsidiary or dependent churches, although it was a house of *clerici* rather than of cloistered monks.

The *Book of Deer* provides one fleeting glimpse of the pastoral work performed by these *clerici*. Between the fragments of St Mark's and St Luke's gospels, a different hand has added part of an office for the visitation of the sick, including a rubric in Old Irish, 'Here he gives him the sacrament'. From all of this it is possible to build up part of the picture of what the *clerici* of Deer did. They maintained close relations with the local aristocracy, whom they entertained at feasts at the two greatest festivals of the Christian year; they consecrated and maintained churches out of the generosity of these laymen; and they visited the sick. More than any other church we have examined, Deer looks like a church of 'minster' type with a college of secular clergy. But that may be only because the evidence from Deer has survived, whereas for other churches it has been lost.

Queen Margaret's hagiographer Turgot presents a picture of Scotland north of the Forth in the eleventh century as a land of hermits:

> At that time in the kingdom of the Scots there were many living, shut up in cells in places set apart (*separatis inclusi cellulis*), by a life of great strictness, in the flesh but not according to the flesh; communing, indeed, with angels upon earth.[98]

Certainly such hermitages existed. Inchaffray (Gaelic *Innis Affran*, 'island of masses', Latinized as *Insula Missarum*) had a priest and hermit and a community of *fratres c.* 1200.[99] Other island monasteries, such as Inchcolm in the Firth of Forth and Inchmahome in the Lake of Menteith, are suggestive of early eremitic sites, and there are a number of casual references to hermits and anchorites in a variety of sources.[100] At Iona itself there is evidence that a genuinely monastic life was still practised in the eleventh and twelfth centuries. While Turgot does not name any of the holy men whom Queen Margaret patronized, Orderic Vitalis identifies the monks of Iona as recipients of her generosity, and says that she helped to reconstruct the buildings there. Unfortunately, no building work from her

98. 'Vita S. Margaretae Scotorum Reginae', in *Symeonis Dunelmensis Opera et Collectanea*, ed. J. Hodgson Hynde, i (Surtees Soc., 1868), 247.
99. *Charters, Bulls and Other Documents Relating to the Abbey of Inchaffray* (Scottish History Soc., 1908), nos vii, ix.
100. Lawrie, *Early Scottish Charters*, no. ccxxiii; G. W. S. Barrow, *The Kingdom of the Scots* (1973), 191; Jackson, *Gaelic Notes*, 1-2, 6-7, 32, 36.

period (1070-93) has been identified.[101] In 1164, according to the *Annals of Ulster*, the community of Iona included a *sacart mór, fer léginn, dísertach* and head of the *Céli Dé*. Yet the picture presented by Turgot is not a complete view of the Scottish church in his time. The great churches of east central Scotland, Abernethy, St Andrews, Dunkeld, Brechin, and Nechtan son of Derilei's church, were all closely associated with the monarchy; they were founded or endowed by royal initiative. The same is true of Govan in Strathclyde. The record of an inscription to a Pictish king at Meigle may put it in the same category. Most of these, and others such as St Vigeans, have gravestones which must have marked the burials of laymen. The horsemen, battles and hunting scenes which abound on the stones of Pictland and Strathclyde must have been designed to appeal to secular tastes. Some of these great 'royal' foundations had bishops: Abernethy, St Andrews, Dunkeld and Brechin all had bishops, not necessarily all at the same time. There were also bishops at churches of uncertain origin at Glasgow, Muthill, probably Mortlach and possibly Rosemarkie (the presence of bishops at Whithorn in Galloway falls outside the scope of the present discussion). The bishops must have provided an episcopal function within the *parochia* of the church in which they resided. It is not clear why the bishops of St Andrews and Dunkeld (and others) should in the twelfth century have come to preside over big dioceses while those of Brechin and Muthill (later Dunblane) were left with small dioceses, probably corresponding only to the *parochiae* of their church; there seems to have been a haphazard element in the formation of dioceses out of *parochiae* in the twelfth century.

The way in which a head church cared for the churches of its *parochia* is another example of pastoral work in progress; but unfortunately we have virtually no evidence of how this was done. The role also of *Céli Dé* communities, their place within the community, their relationship with the bishop and their pastoral care are things about which we know very little. Their place, indeed, may have varied; if at Brechin they made up the bishop's *familia*, this was definitely not the case at St Andrews. At most centres we have insufficient evidence to make certain statements.

One point which might seem so obvious as not to require comment is that not every major church with a big *parochia* finally became a cathedral with a diocese; Meigle, St Vigeans, Abernethy, Lochleven and Govan are examples of major churches that did not. In some cases proximity to an episcopal centre may provide an explanation; Scotland's cathedral churches are few and widely spaced. But there is no simple rule of correspondence between provinces or earldoms and episcopal centres. There are some points of correspondence: Glasgow for Strathclyde, St Andrews for Fife, Muthill (and later Dunblane) for Strathearn and Menteith, Brechin for Angus and Mearns, Dunkeld for Atholl, and Rosemarkie for Ross, might seem to fit such a picture; but their diocesan boundaries, especially those

---

101. Orderic Vitalis, *Ecclesiastical History*, viii. 22, ed. M. Chibnall (1969-80), iv, 272; *Inventory of Argyll*, iv: *Iona* (1982), 245-51.

of St Andrews and Dunkeld, do not. The picture also breaks down in the area between the Mounth and the Moray Firth, for in the great northern provinces of Moray, Buchan and Mar we have only one (fairly insubstantial) trace of an episcopal centre at Mortlach (now Dufftown, Banff). It lies roughly in between the three provinces, and was later claimed as ancestral to the bishopric of Aberdeen. Although we hear of a bishop of Moray in 1120, of the origins and of the diocese of Moray we know nothing. This is surprising considering the power and prestige of the *mormaer* of Moray in the tenth and eleventh centuries.[102] There is no trace of any bishops in Argyll or the north-west at all. Clearly episcopal services were very unevenly spread.

It may be that all pastoral and other ecclesiastical functions were unevenly distributed. Nevertheless, where we have evidence of lay generosity to the church (the collections of land-grants to Deer, St Andrews and Lochleven), carved gravestones of laymen at major church sites, and scenes of secular life depicted on carved stones, we can detect traces of a relationship between church and laity; not of a pastoral care which was evenly spread (the reforms of the twelfth century did not produce that), nor one that we know very much about (the *Book of Deer* is the most concrete piece of evidence here), but one which the laity was anxious to promote and encourage.

102. Donaldson, 'Bishops' sees', 21-2.

Part 2   Anglo-Saxon England

6 Monks, preaching and pastoral care in early Anglo-Saxon England

ALAN THACKER

The outstanding qualities of Bede's greatest work, the *Historia Ecclesiastica*, have ensured that the story of the establishment of Christianity in England is one of the most familiar episodes in all Anglo-Saxon history. Yet at the heart of that story there lies a mystery. Bede's stage is peopled by kings and nobles and high ecclesiastics; he has little to say about those who were not themselves grandees or within the households and communities of grandees, and ultimately he seems to have lacked the means or the will to analyse the degree to which the church fulfilled its mission to Anglo-Saxon society as a whole.

The purpose of this chapter is to try to fill that gap. The pages which follow will look afresh at the ideals which the church set before the laity, the means it had to promote or enforce them, and the impact of its activity upon ordinary men and women. To pursue such objectives it is necessary first to investigate the institutional framework within which early pastors operated and the kinds of communities to which they belonged. That is the purpose of the first two sections of this chapter. Only then in the remaining sections will it be possible to analyse the treatment of pastoral themes in the biblical commentaries, history and hagiography of seventh- and eighth-century England, and to evaluate the attempts made to implement the prescriptions of this literature through the legislation of the councils, the workings of penance and the cult of the saints.

THE HIERARCHY

As a prelude to these large themes it is instructive to consider briefly the nature of the hierarchy as actually constituted in England, at, say, about AD 700. At the apex stood, of course, the bishop, the chief pastor, originally charged with all the functions relating to preaching and the administration of the sacraments, but by this time in England as elsewhere perforce sharing them (to a greater or lesser extent) with his priests. The bishop still retained sole control of highly important prerogatives: he alone could confirm, ordain priests and abbots, and consecrate the holy oils used in anointing the sick.[1] No priestly function could be exercised in his

---

1. E.g. Theodore, *Penitential*, ii, iii. 2, 4-5, 8; ii, iv. 5 in *Councils and Ecclesiastical Documents*, ed. A. W. Haddan and W. Stubbs (3 vols., 1869-78), iii, 173-204; Bede, *In Epistolas VII Catholicas*, ed. D. Hurst (CCSL, 121), 221-2. Cf. Bede, *HE* iii. 15.

diocese without his licence, and to him fell the judgment of those committing capital offences against monks and lower-ranking *clerici*.[2] In addition, despite the complexities created by privileges and exemptions, he still bore chief responsibility for the care of the laity in his usually vast and inaccessible diocese. Bede considered it desirable that a bishop should visit every hamlet and homestead within his care at least once a year, a view echoed in contemporary Frankish councils.[3] Lacking the focus elsewhere provided by substantial urban centres, he would have needed to be perpetually on the move to fulfil adequately this burdensome role.

Intimately associated with the bishops were the priests. Although undoubtedly subject to episcopal supervision, they were nevertheless highly important, and by no means numerous, in early Anglo-Saxon England; Bede indeed is always careful to mention priestly status in his *History*, as if it were something exceptional.[4] The close links between priests and bishops in this period are demonstrated by the fact that the word *sacerdos* was applied to both grades: Bishop Acca of Hexham, for example, could address Bede, a priest within his diocese, as *frater et consacerdos*.[5] Theodore's *Penitential* contains much on the prerogatives and duties of priests, which included not only the power to preach, baptize, say mass, and prescribe penance, but also the right to consecrate abbesses and sanctify churches that had been resited.[6] In a word, where dioceses were as large and difficult to supervise as those of early Anglo-Saxon England, the role of the priest as episcopal surrogate loomed large.

Of the third major clerical grade, the diaconate, the early sources have rather less to say. Clearly, where circumstances demanded, they could take on a major pastoral role. James the Deacon, who assisted Paulinus in his Northumbrian ministry in the good days under King Eadwine, remained behind at York when his superior fled to Kent, and continued to preach and baptize.[7] Like bishops and priests, deacons once ordained were forbidden to marry, and an oath sworn upon their hands had the same status as that sworn on relics enclosed in an altar.[8] On the other hand, their role in the administration of the sacraments was limited. They could not say mass, and were expressly forbidden to prescribe penances for the laity.[9]

---

2. Theodore, *Penitential*, i, iv. 5; Bede, *HE* iv. 5; S. Foot, 'The parochial ministry in early Anglo-Saxon England: the role of monastic communities', *Studies in Church Hist.* xxvi (1989), 51-2. Cf. Synod of Chelsea (816), c.11 (Haddan and Stubbs, *Councils*, iii, 579-86); *Admonitio Generalis*, 789, c.11, ed. A. Boretius (MGH, *Capitularia* i).

3. Bede, *Epistola ad Ecgberhtum*, c.5, ed. C. Plummer, *Baedae Opera Historica* (2 vols., 1896), i. 408-9; *Die Briefe der heiligen Bonifatius und Lullus*, ed. M. Tangl, MGH, *Epistolae Selectae* (1916), no. 78.

4. E.g. Bede, *HE* ii. 14; iii. 15, 21, 23, 25, 28-9; iv. 16, 22, 29, 32; v. 1, 10, 12, 18.

5. Acca, *Epistola ad Baedam* (ed. D. Hurst, CCSL, 120, p. 5). Cf. Theodore, *Penitential*, i, iv. 5, which reserves punishment for the murder of a priest, like that of a bishop, to the king.

6. E.g. Theodore, *Penitential*, ii, i. 1; ii, ii. 7-8, 15; ii, iii. 4. For later more restrictive attitudes, see Synod of Chelsea (816), c.11.

7. Bede, *HE* ii. 16, 20.

8. Theodore, *Penitential*, i, vi. 4; i, ix. 1-4. Marriage was also forbidden to subdeacons.

9. Theodore, *Penitential*, ii, ii. 14-16.

Besides those in major orders, early sources refer to other ecclesiastical groupings, in particular to *clerici, monachi* and *sanctimoniales*. These are terms which often cannot be defined with precision. Perhaps the least debatable is *clericus*, an expression used in several related contexts; applied generally to all in ecclesiastical grades, or at least to all who could not be described as *monachi*, it could also be used in a more restricted sense to designate the members of an episcopal *familia* or those in lesser grades below the rank of priest or deacon.[10] The terms *monachi* and *sanctimoniales* are more problematic. All that can safely be said is that they were applied to men and women in some sense vowed to the religious life and resident in communities, *monasteria*. For the sake of convenience, I shall call those so designated monks and nuns, though it has long been apparent that many lived lives far removed from the classic Benedictine ideal.

THE *MONASTERIA*

The early English *monasteria* have received much attention of late, and indeed are given extensive consideration elsewhere in this volume; nevertheless, the crucial role which has been assigned to them in the pastoral structure of the period means that in this chapter too they can hardly be ignored. It is now abundantly clear that the term *monasterium* and its English equivalent, 'minster', embraced communities of very different size and status, with very different ways of life. Undoubtedly some, such as Bede's Jarrow, were close to the strict Benedictine ideal. They, however, were the exception. Many others seem to have been loosely organized establishments ruled by an abbot and housing priests and other inmates who might be described as *monachi* or *clerici*.[11] It has become commonplace to refer to the former as 'monasteries' and to reserve for the rest the term 'minster', a distinction unknown to contemporaries. Because of these anachronistic associations, this chapter will avoid the vernacular, restricting itself, like the early texts, to the Latin *monasterium*.

Pre-eminent among the *monasteria* were the great royal foundations, many of which were established at an early period. Often ruled by royal abbots or abbesses, they were usually associated with the administrative centres of royal estates and ministered to those estates through pastoral units known to contemporaries as *parochiae*.[12] Recent research has emphasized that by the late seventh century all the early English kingdoms contained some of these major churches to which ecclesiastical dues were rendered and from which priests and other *clerici* and *monachi* travelled to

---

10. *Dialogus Ecgberhti*, cc.12, 14 (Haddan and Stubbs, *Councils*, iii, 403-12); *Poenitentiale Ecgberhti*, c.5 (*ibid.*, 416-31) (general); Bede, *HE* i. 27; iii. 25; iv. 16 (episcopal *familia*); Bede, *HE* i. 27; iii. 26; iv. 27 (lesser grades).
11. Foot, 'Parochial ministry', 44-6.
12. W. J. Blair, 'Minster churches in the landscape', in *Anglo-Saxon Settlements*, ed. D. Hooke (1988), 35-58.

preach, baptize, and visit the sick.[13] A classic example is the *monasterium* of Breedon-on-the-Hill. According to the well-known and apparently authentic account of its foundation in the late seventh century, the *princeps* Frithuric granted a substantial estate at Breedon to the monks of Medeshamstede on condition that they founded there a *monasterium* and appointed 'a priest of good repute to minister baptism and preaching to the people assigned to him'. The brethren at Medeshamstede chose one of their own number, a priest named Haedda, to be abbot and Frithuric 'when he knew Abbot Haedda to be diligent in preaching to the people committed to him' further augmented the endowment.[14]

The phenomenon of the royal *monasterium* charged with the pastoral care of widely dispersed peoples is too well known and too widespread to be fully documented in this chapter. Here it is sufficient simply to note the frequent association of identifiable early sites with extensive ancient parishes. What, however, needs to be stressed (since it will affect our understanding of the nature of pastoral activity in the period) is the fact that even communities which may be regarded as monastic in the strict sense had pastoral responsibilities. This seems even to be true of communities as strictly Benedictine as Wearmouth and Jarrow, although that has often been doubted. The ancient parish of Jarrow embraced a large area south of the Tyne including the chapelry of South Shields with its early dedication to St Hilda,[15] while around Wearmouth there seems to have been an even larger unit, originally including the territory of the two later parishes of Monkwearmouth, to the north of the river, and Bishopwearmouth, to the south.[16] Moreover, Rosemary Cramp's excavations at Wearmouth have uncovered to the south of the abbatial church of St Peter a large early Christian cemetery which included lay burials of men, women, juveniles and children. These graves, which were separated from those of the monks by a substantial building attached to the church, provide clear evidence that from its foundation the community made provision for at least one important pastoral requirement of the surrounding inhabitants.[17]

Even more suggestive is evidence that at certain periods in the church's year Bede expected to preach at Jarrow to an augmented audience. In a

---

13. *ibid.*, 36-40; Foot, 'Parochial ministry', 43-54.
14. F. M. Stenton, *Preparatory to Anglo-Saxon England* (1970), 181-2; S 1803-6.
15. R. Surtees, *History and Antiquities of the Co. Palatine of Durham* (4 vols., 1816-40), i. 224; ii. 1, 66, 94; C. E. Fell, 'Hild, Abbess of Streonaeshalch', in *Hagiography and Medieval Literature*, ed. H. Bekker-Nielsen *et al.* (1981), 81.
16. That Bishopwearmouth was originally part of a *parochia* focused on Wearmouth is suggested by the fact that in the reign of Athelstan it included Dalton, known to have belonged to the monks from the time of Abbot Ceolfrid: D. J. Hall, 'The Community of St Cuthbert' (unpubl. D.Phil. thesis, Univ. of Oxford, 1983), 80. See also E. Cambridge, 'The early church in Co. Durham: a reassessment', *JBAA*, cxxxvii (1984), 75. Note that Cambridge's maps (70, 80) show clearly that Wearmouth and Jarrow were at the centre of a region not provided with other 'minsters'.
17. R. J. Cramp, 'Monastic sites', in *Archaeology of Anglo-Saxon England*, ed. D. Wilson (1976), 231.

recent thesis on Bede's homiliary, Andreas van der Walt has noticed that in his sermon for Holy Saturday, Bede not only explained the symbolism of the baptismal rites but also distinguished those among his audience who had already received the sacrament from those who were soon to do so, either at the forthcoming ceremonies or at some future date.[18] Those who were catechumens can hardly have been monks. Similarly a reference in another sermon to the additional crowd of brethren (*adiuncta fratrum caterua*) present during Lent implies that the monastery ministered to more than its own inmates during that important season.[19]

To reach this enlarged audience Bede would probably have had to employ the vernacular rather than Latin, the language in which his homilies have come down to us. That, however, is not an insuperable problem. The homilies are written in a much simpler style than the biblical commentaries; they could easily have been used as the basis for vernacular preaching, especially if the copy the preacher used had been glossed.[20] A more difficult question is the absence of any reference to women, an indication that the catechumens and additional brethren to whom Bede referred came from a special and select group. Sarah Foot has recently suggested that the celebrated figure of 500-600 *fratres* at Wearmouth and Jarrow did not apply simply to inmates of the two communities but included those resident on the monastic estates.[21] Her view accords with evidence from Whitby, where Hadwald, described as a *frater* from the abbess's *familia*, was clearly a shepherd living some distance from the monastery *in pastoralibus habitaculis*.[22] Such extramural labourers were probably not uncommon in early communities. Their existence in Mercia is implied by King Æthelbald's impressment of monks to labour on royal buildings,[23] and in Ireland by the extension of the term *monachus* (Ir. *manach*) to embrace the clients and dependants of a church.[24] Could it be therefore that among those to whom *monasteria* such as Wearmouth and Jarrow ministered was a group of tenants, perhaps tonsured and celibate, dispersed

---

18. Bede, *Opera Homiletica* (ed. D. Hurst, CCSL, 122, pp. 220-4, esp. 222); A. van der Walt, 'The Homiliary of the Venerable Bede and Early Medieval Preaching' (unpubl. Ph.D thesis, Univ. of London, 1980), 56-7.
19. Bede, *Op. Hom.* 193. Cf. the Whitsunday sermon in which Bede alluded to the baptism of catechumens customary on that day: *ibid.*, 306; van der Walt, 'Homiliary', 58.
20. van der Walt, 'Homiliary', 73-6, 162-218. I am grateful to Prof. D. A. Bullough for the point about glossing.
21. Pers. comm.
22. *Vita S. Cuthberti*, iv. 10; Bede, *Vita S. Cuthberti*, c.34. I am grateful to Dr Blair for this point.
23. Council of *Clofesho*, AD 747, c.7 (Haddan and Stubbs, *Councils*, iii. 364-5) implies that monastic labour services (*operationes*) were useful to rulers and communities alike.
24. See the chapters by Thomas Charles-Edwards and Richard Sharpe in the present volume. Prof. N. P. Brooks has pointed out to me that the administration of the tonsure to Dunstan as a child may reflect similar arrangements at Glastonbury: *Vita S. Dunstani Auctore B*, ed. W. Stubbs in *Memorials of St Dunstan*, Rolls Series (1874), 10.

over the community's estates and attending the mother-church at least on the major festivals? Such a hypothesis would help to account for Bede's references to the presence of additional *fratres*, though it leaves unexplained the nature of the monks' provision for ordinary layfolk (including women) living on their estates and within their *parochia*.

That what might be termed 'true monasteries' were expected to participate as fully in pastoral activity as other, less strict communities emerges especially clearly from Bede's allusions to Lindisfarne. Though the community was, of course, exceptional in being the seat of a bishop, the episcopal *familia* remained an integral part of the *monasterium*; all the inmates, including the bishop, priests and members of those lesser grades which Bede groups together as *clerici*, were monks under obedience to the abbot.[25] Pastoral authority over the immediately dependent *territorium* was evidently at Lindisfarne (as at Melrose) entrusted to the prior, who was expected not only to counsel the members of the community but to minister personally to the common people of the locality or to ensure that priests were sent out on such duties as the administration of the viaticum to the sick and dying or exorcism to the possessed.[26] The effect which Bede believed those arrangements to have upon the region emerges most clearly in his revealing account of the role of Lindisfarne under Aidan and his successors.[27] In that famous passage, clearly intended to point a moral for his contemporaries, he emphasizes that the exemplary life of the pre-664 community had engendered such veneration for the monastic habit (*habitus religionis*) that the people of the region not only held itinerant *clerici* and *monachi* in high respect, but also flocked to *ecclesiae siue monasteria* or to visiting *sacerdotes* and *clerici* to hear the Word of God. The couplets should not be read as an attempt to distinguish between *monasteria* and other churches; bishop and priests, monks and *clerici* were all part of a single pastoral process, enacted within the *monasterium* or *ecclesia*.[28] The whole point of the eulogy is to stress the pastoral impact which a properly-constituted *monasterium* could make upon its environs.

That dedicated communities like Wearmouth, Jarrow and Lindisfarne made pastoral provision for the surrounding inhabitants is not perhaps surprising. It is, however, sometimes suggested that they were exceptional

---

25. Bede, *Vita S. Cuthberti*, c.16.
26. *ibid.*, cc.9, 15, 16, 41; *Vita S. Cuthberti*, ii. 8; iv. 15.
27. Bede, *HE* iii. 26.
28. *Ecclesia* is a difficult term. In some instances (as here, where it is contrasted with *monasterium*) it may mean a local church. Whether it implies the presence of a resident priest is doubtful; the latter are very difficult to trace in the early sources. The *ecclesiae* established on their estates by high-ranking personages such as royal abbesses and gesiths are likely to have been what are now regarded as proprietary *monasteria*: Bede, *HE* v. 4-5; Bede, *Vita S. Cuthberti*, c.34; W. J. Blair, 'Local churches in Domesday Book and before', in *Domesday Studies*, ed. J. C. Holt (1987), 57-8; Blair, 'Minster churches', 267-8. For a different view, see P. Sims-Williams, *Religion and Literature in Western England, 600-800* (1990), 130.

and that many, even most, *monasteria* were essentially 'private' and inward-looking.[29] Undoubtedly many communities did indeed have strong dynastic associations; in addition to preserving the family estates under the privileged conditions of ecclesiastical tenure, they made provision for the founder's kin both materially, through an hereditary abbacy, and spiritually, through an appropriate cult.[30] Nevertheless, the preoccupations of such 'proprietary' foundations generally extended beyond the purely dynastic. Perhaps the clearest indication of this is provided by the activities of the so-called 'double monasteries' housing communities of both men and women. Invariably ruled initially by abbesses drawn from the founder's kin, these establishments are most likely to have been first and foremost nunneries, in which high-status women were assisted by a group of male chaplains, carrying out the priestly functions from which the nuns were necessarily debarred. That such communities attended to the pastoral needs of the surrounding inhabitants is demonstrated by the well-known examples of the Kentish double *monasteria*, with their extensive ancient *parochiae*.[31] The complexity of their responsibilities is, however, even better demonstrated by the great Northumbrian house of Whitby, the *Eigenkloster* of the Deiran royal line.[32] There the royal abbess was clearly regarded as the pastoral head of the community. The first superior, Hild, was expressly praised by Bede for ministering to the lay world outside as well as to those who lived within her *monasterium*: to her came the ordinary people, as well as kings and princes, for help and advice in their necessities.[33] Equally active was her successor, Ælfflæd, whose importance in the Northumbrian clerical hierarchy was indicated by the decisive role which she played in episcopal appointments, especially at the crucial see of York.[34] Honoured by Bede with the weighty epithets of *magistra* and *doctrix*, she was clearly at home visiting her monastic estates and supervising personally their pastoral organization.[35]

Though contemporary sources are silent about the nature of Whitby's pastoral responsibilities in the territory immediately adjacent to the mother-house, their existence can be inferred from later evidence. The double *monasterium*, which apparently came to an end in the mid-ninth century, seems to have left a considerable mark upon the succeeding Viking enclave. Whitby continued to be the administrative centre of a major estate; valued in the 1060s at £112,[36] it still exhibited signs of its

---

29. E.g. R. K. Morris, *Churches in the Landscape* (1989), 131.
30. See e.g. A. T. Thacker, 'Kings, saints and monasteries in pre-Viking Mercia', *Midland History*, x (1985), 1-25.
31. M. Deansley, 'Early English and Gallic minsters', *Trans. Royal Hist. Soc.*, 4th ser. xxiii (1941), 25-69; N. P. Brooks, *The Early History of the Church of Canterbury* (1984), 183, 187-91; D. W. Rollason, *The Mildrith Legend* (1982), esp. 44-9.
32. There is every reason to accept the tradition, first recorded in the twelfth century, that Bede's *Streanaeshaleh* was Whitby.
33. Bede, *HE* iv. 26.
34. See below, p. 149.
35. Bede, *HE* iii. 24 (*magistra*); iv. 26 (*doctrix*).
36. *VCH Yorks.*, ii, 218.

monastic past in the form of almost forty ruined structures by then interpreted as oratories and associated with a site known, significantly, as
Prestebi, 'priests' farm'.[37] In addition, Whitby or *Prestebi* was by then the
site of two churches, one of which was regarded as the successor to the
abbatial church of St Peter, while the other, the church of St Mary, was a
major parochial centre with six dependent chapelries embracing all the
later liberty of Whitby Strand except Hackness.[38] The association of a
church dedicated to St Peter with one dedicated to St Mary is well known
in the pre-Viking period; it is documented, for example, at Wearmouth,
Lichfield and St Augustine's.[39] At Whitby too the arrangement could well
be early evidence of an extensive Anglian complex,[40] which included an
abbatial church for the nuns and a parochial or cemeterial church for the
priests.[41]

Whitby's pastoral responsibilities were fulfilled in part through a hierarchy of dependent *monasteria*. The clearest indication of this is the story
of Cuthbert's consecration of a church for *Osingadun*, termed by Bede a
possessio and by the anonymous of Lindisfarne a *parochia* of Abbess
Ælfflæd.[42] The use in this context of the term *parochia*, which has been
regarded as the earliest English occurrence of the word in its modern sense
of 'parish',[43] seems more properly to imply that *Osingadun* was the site of
a *monasterium* with pastoral responsibilities. As Eric Cambridge has
pointed out, Bede's reference to the sending of a messenger thence 'to the
greater *monasterium*' (i.e. Whitby) indicates that he regarded the term as
also applicable to the dependent community. Moreover, he describes
members of that community as *famuli Christi*, a phrase with strong
monastic overtones.[44] *Osingadun* therefore is probably to be compared
with Hackness, another possession of Whitby well within a day's journey
of the mother-house and undoubtedly a fully organized community with a

---

37. *Chartulary of Whitby Abbey*, ed. J. C. Atkinson, Surtees Soc. lxix, lxxii (1878-9),
    2; A. H. Smith, *Place-Names of the North Riding of Yorks.* (1928), 127.
38. *VCH Yorks.*, *N. Riding*, ii, 502-5, 524; *Chart. Whitby*, 1-3, 28, 31-5, 163, 273-4,
    495-6, 527-8.
39. W. Levison, *England and the Continent in the Eighth Century* (1946), 259-65.
    See also John Blair's chapter in the present volume.
40. One indication that the seventh-century enceinte was large (and so could have
    included the site of the present parish church) is Bede's story of the nuns who
    lived *in extremis monasterii locis* and had to wait until the following morning
    for information of Hild's death at the previous dawn: Bede, *HE* iv. 26;
    Cambridge, 'Early church', 74.
41. The double monasteries of Francia had multiple churches with these functions:
    Marquise de Maillé, *Les Cryptes de Jouarre* (Paris, 1971), 22-51.
42. Bede, *Vita S. Cuthberti*, c.34; *Vita S. Cuthberti*, iv. 10.
43. F. M. Stenton, review in *Review of English Studies*, xvi (1940), 462.
44. Cambridge, 'Early church', 74, 84. *Osingadun* may perhaps be identified as
    Kirkdale, where there was an important Anglian *monasterium* with a stone
    church dedicated to St Gregory, a favoured saint at Whitby: H. M. and J. Taylor,
    Anglo-Saxon Architecture (3 vols., 1965-78), i, 357-61; *VCH Yorks.*, *N. Riding*,
    i, 517-23; W. G. Collingwood, 'Anglian and Anglo-Danish sculpture in the N.
    Riding of Yorks.', *Yorks. Archaeol. J.* xix (1907), 291, 344.

church and a dormitory. Though its only named inmates are nuns, there are clear indications that it also contained brethren, like Whitby itself.[45] The site of a great Anglian cross and the focus of an extensive ancient parish, by 1086 it had three churches, two of which are known from other contemporary sources to have been (as at Whitby) dedicated to St Peter and St Mary.[46] Though only one of these now survives, it seems to incorporate eighth-century fabric and hence to have been one of the churches of the Anglian *monasterium*.[47]

The density of pastoral coverage provided by Whitby and its dependent communities is replicated elsewhere in eastern Deira. Somewhat to the west of its *parochia*, we find a group of Anglian foundations at Hovingham, Stonegrave and Coxwold, all within a few miles of each other.[48] In the earlier eighth century, Stonegrave, together with Coxwold (9 miles to the west) and the unlocated *Donaemuthe* were *monasteria* under the rule of a certain unnamed abbess and thereafter of an abbot called Forthred, until they were confiscated by King Eadberht and granted to the *patricius* Moll.[49] Both identified sites bear signs of having been ecclesiastical centres of some importance. Stonegrave has fragments of Anglian sculpture, while Coxwold became the mother-church of a large medieval parish.[50] Two miles from Stonegrave, though not apparently linked with it, there was a further early ecclesiastical centre: Hovingham. The focus of another large parish, in Anglian times it had a stone church enshrining an elaborate sarcophagus, presumably the resting-place of an unidentified saint.[51] Though clearly of high status, none of these foundations seems to have been royal, or strictly monastic. Rather they provide evidence that the initiative of local magnates could lead to a planting of proprietary *monasteria* sufficiently dense to make possible effective pastoral ministrations.

Two rulings of Archbishop Theodore, recorded in the early eighth century, throw further light on the pastoral responsibilities of *monasteria* in general. The first of these, that it was the *libertas* of a *monasterium* to adjudge penances to the laity, seems to have been made principally on the grounds that such communities would contain *clerici*, one of whose responsibilities this was expressly said to be. The second was unambiguous: anyone who wished to set his *monasterium* in another place was to do so only on the advice of the bishop and was to release a priest for the ministry

45. A. H. Thompson, 'The monastic settlement at Hackness', *Yorks. Archaeol. J.* xxvii (1924), 388-9.
46. *VCH Yorks.*, ii, 264; *Chart. Whitby*, xxxvii-xxxix, 2-3, 31-3, 155-7, 163, 223-4; J. J. Winterbotham, *Hackness in the Middle Ages* (2nd edn., 1985).
47. There is confusion about the dedication: Taylor and Taylor, *A-S Architecture*, i, 268-70; *VCH Yorks., N. Riding*, ii, 528-32; F. Rimmington, 'The three churches of Hackness', *Trans. Scarborough Archaeol. and Hist. Soc.* xxvi (1988), 3-4.
48. Morris, *Churches in Landscape*, 121-2.
49. D. Whitelock, *English Hist. Documents*, i (2nd edn., 1979), 830; M. S. Parker, 'An Anglo-Saxon monastery in the Lower Don Valley', *Northern History*, xxi (1985), 19-32.
50. *VCH Yorks., N. Riding*, i, 548, 561-2; ii, 5-8, 55-8; Collingwood, 'Anglian sculpture', 401-2.
51. Taylor and Taylor, *A-S Architecture*, 1, 326-8; *VCH Yorks., N. Riding*, i, 505-11.

of the church (*ad ministeria ecclesiae*) on the former site.[52] This requirement of a local minister in priest's orders should be seen in the context of
the frequent references to ecclesiastics as priest and abbot in such sources
as the *Ecclesiastical History* and Stephen's Life of St Wilfrid.[53] The
repeated coupling stems in part no doubt from the fact that ordained status
was exceptional and that many (perhaps most) inmates of *monasteria* were
not priests.[54] It may also, however, be an indication of a high and distinctive rank within the hierarchy, whose holders had personal charge of the
parochiae with which their community was associated. That certainly
seems to have been the case at Breedon, where pastoral care was expressly
assigned to the first priest and abbot,[55] and where one of his successors
was elevated to the see of Canterbury.[56] Close links between abbacy and
priesthood were also apparent at Ripon, where ordination quickly followed
Wilfrid's appointment as head of the community, and at Wearmouth-
Jarrow, where the unordained Biscop found it necessary from the beginning
to appoint a priestly coadjutor.[57] All these figures should be regarded as
bearing the formal designation *presbyter abbas*, a style with strong pastoral
connotations familiar in contemporary Gaul and Kent.[58]

While clearly it would be rash to make any general assumptions about
institutions as diverse as the English *monasteria*, the evidence adduced
above suggests that they were envisaged as having some kind of pastoral
responsibility for the localities in which they were planted.[59] The nature
and scope of those responsibilities, however, remain in some ways
ambiguous. Were the *monasteria* viewed as ministering informally to those
rustici who happened to live nearby or to a recognized territorial unit and
if the latter, what was the territory which constituted the *parochia*? Was
it some early unit of local government or simply the community's own

52. Theodore, *Penitential*, ii, vi. 7; ii, vi. 16.
53. E.g. Bede, *HE* i. 33; ii. 14, 16; iii. 4-5, 28; iv. 16, 22; v. 1, 2, 15; Stephanus, *Vita
S. Wilfridi*, cc.10-11, 49, 58, ed. B. Colgrave (1927).
54. This was certainly the case at Jarrow, where Bede expected the audience for his
sermons to include unordained *fratres*: van der Walt, *Homiliary*, 65, Bede, *Op.
Hom.* 84. The Lindisfarne *Liber Vitae* distinguishes 'priest-abbots', 'abbots' and
'deacon-abbots': *The Oldest English Texts*, ed. H. Sweet, Early Eng. Text Soc.,
o.s. 83 (1885), 155-6.
55. The separation of priest and monastery at Breedon has recently been strongly
stressed by Morris: *Churches in Landscape*, 132. It is incorrect, however, to see
the priest as merely an 'attachment' to the community to serve the local laity.
The king and bishop involved in the foundation clearly intended the pastoral and
abbatial roles to be combined: see above.
56. Bede, *HE* v. 23.
57. Stephanus, *Vita S. Wilfridi*, cc. 8-9; *Vita Ceolfridi*, c.6, ed. C. Plummer, *Baedae
Opera Historica* (2 vols., 1896), i, 388-404. Significantly the laws of Wihtred
(c.17), required the head of a minster (*mynstris aldor*) to clear himself with a
priest's exculpation: *Laws of the Earliest English Kings*, ed. F. Attenborough
(1922), 28-9.
58. Brooks, *Church of Canterbury*, 187; S 12, 23; Deansley, 'Early English and Gallic
minsters', 38 (citing Austregisil, priest-abbot of the basilica of St Nicetius). For
eighth and ninth-century priest-abbots in Worcester diocese, see Sims-Williams,
Religion and Literature, 156-7, 170-1.
59. Morris, *Churches in Landscape*, 130-3.

estates? These questions are not easy to answer. In some texts, such as the Breedon charters, the pastor was treated as responsible for the local *populus*, while in others, such as Canon 9 of the 747 council of *Clofesho*, it was a question of districts (*loca et regiones*). Where the duty was said to be to a *regio* it seems likely that what was meant was a major royal estate, and in such instances we may suspect that the boundaries of jurisdiction were ancient and well known. David Rollason has shown, for example, that the *parochia* of Minster on the island of Thanet was defined on its landward side by a boundary which may well date back to the original endowment of the seventh century.[60] In such circumstances, the unit of pastoral care almost certainly marched with a long-standing unit of local government. In other instances, most notably aristocratic 'proprietary' *monasteria*, the unit of pastoral care must have been limited to the founder's own estates. But whether royal or aristocratic, the community would have been, at least in theory, responsible for a definable territory likely to extend beyond its own landed endowment.[61]

It is hard to know how practice measured up to the expectations recorded in the charters of founders and the canons of councils. Undeniably the hagiographical sources give the impression that initially pastoral activity was somewhat random; preachers such as Cuthbert seem to have sought out remote places in pursuit of a personal ascetic ideal as much as a systematic plan of pastoral care. Moreover, whatever the preacher's underlying motives, the difficulty of reaching a population often dispersed over a wide area remained. The ministrations of a community such as Lindisfarne must necessarily have depended on those who could apply to them in time of need, and that is most likely to have been either the very local or the well-to-do, such as the *praefectus* Hildmaer.[62] Against this, however, we must set the fact that some provision was made in more distant localities at special holy sites or in humble oratories. Such structures, to which the sources make only fleeting and casual allusion, almost certainly had no permanent staff, but were used by itinerant priests or *clerici* journeying out from their communities. Though lacking in the early stages of the conversion (Bede notes that *oratoria uel baptisteria* had yet to be built in Eadwine's reign), they seem to have been taken for granted by the early eighth century if not before; there was clearly nothing remarkable in the *oratorium uillulae* to which Drythelm went to pray after recovering from the dire illness which occasioned his momentous vision.[63]

The local oratories were probably often the setting for the administration of one of the most important pastoral responsibilities of the *monasteria*:

---

60. D. W. Rollason, 'The date of the parish boundary of Minster-in-Thanet', *Archaeologia Cantiana*, xcv (1979), 7-17.
61. Certainly that was the case by the earlier tenth century when the *ealdan mynsters* ruled well-defined units from which tithes, burial fees and church-scot could be exacted: Attenborough, *Laws*, 124/5; A. J. Robertson, *The Laws of the Kings of England from Edmund to Henry I* (1925), 20/1-22/3.
62. *Vita S. Cuthberti*, ii. 8.
63. Bede, *HE* ii. 14; v. 12. See also Mayr-Harting, *Coming of Christianity*, 246, 319; Morris, *Churches in Landscape*, 151, 159-61.

the rite of baptism. The stress on the dispensing of the sacrament by itinerant ecclesiastics and Bede's linking of *baptisteria* with *oratoria* suggests that from the very earliest times the rite was not exclusively enacted in the mother-church itself.[64] Very probably the same was true of burial. Donald Bullough has recently emphasized the pre-Carolingian church's lack of interest in the rites of burial in both Gaul and England,[65] and certainly that seems to be reflected in the writings of Bede, for whom the essential pastoral duties were preaching, baptizing and visiting the sick.[66] Theodore too showed little interest in regulating the rite of burial, though he did envisage requiem masses for clerics and religious laymen.[67] While *monasteria* such as Wearmouth undoubtedly had cemeteries for the laity from an early period, there is little to suggest that (as later) there was any attempt to centralize burial within their precincts.[68] Doubtless provision was made for those who lived nearby, and also for the specially devout or socially grand who were anxious like the *praefectus* in the *Vita S. Cuthberti* to ensure that they or their loved ones were buried *in locis sanctis*, on ground made holy by proximity to sacred shrines and relics (and hence to a major church).[69] Even so, burial in a cemetery belonging to the mother-church was neither expected nor demanded.

The centralization of control over the administration of the sacraments, especially burial, in late Saxon times was associated with a demand for fees.[70] In the early period, however, there is little to show that the *monasteria* had any certain income beyond that from their (often extensive) landed estates. Among the West Saxons 'church-scot' (*ciricsceat*), which was linked with 'the estate (*hlaforde*) and house where a man resided at midwinter', was presumably paid to the local *monasterium*, but that is nowhere made explicit.[71] Similarly, there was no formal requirement that tithes, also apparently included by Theodore within the *tributum ecclesiae*, be rendered to the local church; first enforced by the Carolingians, that regulation was not introduced into England until the time of Eadgar.[72] In practice, many communities may have been more dependent on the support of those to whom they ministered than is sometimes suggested. Bede, for example, exhorted *auditores* to sustain preachers in their temporal needs, recommending the example of Gaius, who although he was unable to preach for himself nevertheless rejoiced to provide for those who did.[73]

64. Blair, 'Minster churches', 50-2.
65. D. A. Bullough, 'Burial, community and belief in the early medieval West', in *Ideal and Reality in Frankish and Anglo-Saxon Society*, ed. P. Wormald (1983), 185-92.
66. E.g. Bede, *HE* iii. 26. For the additional duty of burying the dead see Bede, *Op. Hom.* 64.
67. Theodore, *Penitential*, ii, v. 5-6.
68. Blair, 'Minster churches', 52-5.
69. Bede, *Vita S. Cuthberti*, c.15.
70. For 'soul-scot' see Attenborough, *Laws*, 124/5.
71. Attenborough, *Laws*, 36/7, 56/7. In his *Epistola ad Ecgberhtum*, c.7 (ed. Plummer, i, 410-11) Bede refers only to *tributum* rendered to the bishop.
72. Theodore, *Penitential*, ii, xiv, 10; Robertson, *Laws*, 20/1-22/3; G. Constable, *Monastic Tithes* (1964), 25, 35, 42.
73. *Epist. Cath.*, 332.

The very fact that Bede is so insistent that avarice and the desire for worldly gain was a besetting sin of the preacher would indicate that renders were both expected and received from the laity.[74]

The pastoral functioning of the English *monasteria* was crucially affected by one other factor: their relations with the episcopate. Across the Channel, the new foundations of Columbanus and the numerous noblemen who came under his influence seem in general to have basked in episcopal favour and to have received generous privileges.[75] In the England of the seventh and early eighth centuries, however, the situation was more complicated. Unlike many of their Gallic counterparts, the English bishops did not on the whole enjoy the assured status provided by leadership of an urban community. Although their role as sole dispenser of crucial rites and sacraments and their right to receive *tributum* from their flock was unquestioned, their authority over their own and other communities within their dioceses was less certain. At Lindisfarne, notoriously, the bishop was subject to an abbot within the confines of the *monasterium*, an arrangement which Bede may also have envisaged in the new monastically-based sees which he proposed in his letter to Archbishop Ecgberht.[76] The hierarchy was similarly ill-defined elsewhere. At Whitby, for example, Bede tells us that in 685 after Ecgfrith's defeat by the Picts Bishop Trumwine withdrew thither with a few of his clergy to live for many years 'a life useful to many'.[77] The implication of these evasive words seems to be that during Ælfflæd's abbacy Whitby had a tame bishop on the premises, who could minister to its *parochia* and who perhaps acted as the head of its *familia* of male clergy. If so, however, his presence in no way inhibited the independence of the abbess, who in the later 680s looked neither to Trumwine nor to her diocesan at York but to her personal friend Cuthbert for the dedication of her church at *Osingadun*.[78] Indeed, the more closely we look at Whitby's position in the diocese of York, the more anomalous it becomes. The community clearly played a crucial role in the career of Wilfrid: its pupils, Bosa, John of Beverley and Wilfrid II, supplanted Wilfrid at York and even for a time at Hexham, while Abbess Ælfflæd's consent was essential to the saint's return in 686/7 and 706. If we put all this beside the fact that Whitby was the scene of the crucial synod which settled the

---

74. E.g. the condemnation of those 'sacerdotes et ministri qui sumptus ... suo gradui debitos sumere a populo delectantur': *In Ezram et Neemiam* (ed. D. Hurst, CCSL, 119A, 386). Cf. *ibid.*, 248, 250; *De Tabernaculo* (ed. D. Hurst, CCSL, 119A, 115).

75. R. Kaiser, 'Royauté et pouvoir episcopal au nord de la Gaule', in *La Neustrie*, ed. H. Atsma (2 vols., 1989), i, 143-60; P. Wormald, 'Bede and Benedict Biscop', in *Famulus Christi*, ed. G. Bonner (1976), 162.

76. Bede, *Vita S. Cuthberti*, c.16. *Epistola ad Ecgberhtum*, c.10.

77. Bede, *HE* iv. 26.

78. *Vita S. Cuthberti*, iv. 10; Bede, *Vita S. Cuthberti*, c.34. The Synod of Chelsea, AD 816, c.2 (Haddan and Stubbs, *Councils*, iii, 580) expressly decreed that, 'following ancient custom', the consecration of churches was restricted to the diocesan.

Easter calculations, we might almost be forgiven for thinking that it rather than York was the mother-church of the Deiran diocese.[79]

The dominance achieved by such influential communities is further illustrated by a famous comment of Wilfrid's biographer Stephen on the dismemberment of his hero's see:

> in the absence of our bishop and in his proper episcopal place (*in sua propria loca episcopatus*), irregularly and contrary to all precedent, he [i.e. Archbishop Theodore] ordained by himself three bishops found elsewhere and not drawn from the subjects of this *parrochia*.[80]

In this instance, *parrochia* does not mean 'diocese' (as some have suggested) but rather seems to designate the immediate *familia* of, or the network of communities closely tied to, a major *monasterium*. Its use in this context shows that like Ælfflæd, the Wilfridians viewed the Deiran see as the peculiar property of a particular monastic connexion. It also highlights the strong sense of corporate identity which characterized the great *monasteria*, an attitude often reinforced by the grant of papal privileges exempting them from the authority of their diocesan.[81] Such developments undoubtedly fostered a strong independence of outlook among those so privileged. A particularly striking instance of this is Bede's aggressive and impertinent response to a charge of heresy levied by a member of his diocesan Wilfrid's *familia*; in an open letter expressly intended to be read aloud in Wilfrid's presence, he saw fit to describe his bishop's closest associates as 'boors' (*rustici*), given over to making and listening to senseless allegations while drunk in their cups.[82]

A similar confident disregard for the susceptibilities of the hierarchy informs Bede's admonitory discourse to Archbishop Ecgberht.[83] Yet that letter also manifests an awareness of the episcopate's need to strengthen its hand over communities less well regulated (and less privileged) than the author's own. Bishops were seen as having a duty to inquire into the affairs of *monasteria* within their dioceses, and to live up to their assertion that they had control of the proprietary communities.[84] Bede's words are an indication of growing tensions between the episcopate and the independent proprietary *monasteria*, tensions which are even more evident at the Council of *Clofesho* in 747, with its recommendations that *ecclesiastici* preserve peace among themselves.[85]

---

79. Stephanus, *Vita S. Wilfridi*, cc. 24, 43, 60-1.
80. *ibid.*, c.24; C. T. R. Cubitt, 'Wilfrid's usurping bishops', *Northern History*, xxv (1989), pp. 18–38.
81. Levison, *England and Continent*, 22–33; Wormald, 'Biscop', 146-8.
82. Bede, *Opera de Temporibus*, ed. C. W. Jones (1943), 313, 315.
83. Bede, *Epistola ad Ecgberhtum*, passim.
84. *ibid.*, c.14.
85. Council of *Clofesho*, AD 747, c.2. Sims-Williams notes 'the growing friction' between the bishops of Worcester and the *monasteria* 'which escaped direct episcopal control': *Religion and Literature*, 173.

Hidden divisions may also be detected in the ambiguous language about the institutions of pastoral care in the canons of the council of 747. As Sarah Foot has recently argued, the bishops, unlike writers such as Bede, treat pastoral care as primarily the work of priests, and distinguish between *monasteriales* and *sanctimoniales* on the one hand, and *clerici* and *ecclesiastici* on the other.[86] This discrepancy is, perhaps, more apparent than real; Canon 29 of the council clearly implies that all these groups, whether *clerici*, *monachi* or *sanctimoniales*, were expected to live in *monasteria*.[87] Undeniably, however, the bishops were reluctant to acknowledge explicitly the role of such communities in sustaining the priests to whom they had assigned *loca et regiones laicorum*. The consistent description of pastors simply as priests, and the confining of all discussion of the role of abbots to the regulation of their communities, looks like a deliberate attempt to ignore the link between priest and abbot so evident in the narrative sources. From the bishops' point of view it was priestly status and subordination to the diocesan which mattered most in the pastoral context.[88] Their attitude has to be seen in the light of a struggle to assert episcopal control over royal and proprietary *monasteria* which was to be pursued more fully in later councils.[89]

The arrangements which have just been described were essentially *ad hoc* expedients. Though kings may have envisaged an orderly ecclesiastical network focused on royal vills, they were in practice very much dependent upon the initiative of local prelates and grandees, the pattern of whose lordship must have been the principal factor in shaping the units of pastoral care in early Anglo-Saxon England.[90] That did not necessarily produce satisfactory results. We can be fairly sure that royal and aristocratic initiative had produced large numbers of *monasteria* at a relatively early date,[91] and in some areas, such as those around Whitby, or Stonegrave, Hovingham and Coxwold, they were undoubtedly thickly planted. Nevertheless, it is difficult to believe that this kind of coverage was achieved throughout the English kingdoms.[92] Where distribution was less regular and less intensive, the pastoral impact of the *monasteria* would have been correspondingly diminished.

The position of these institutions within the ecclesiastical hierarchy was marked by similar improvization and lack of definition. In many cases bishops could not rival the high status of the royal rulers of the great

---

86. Foot, 'Parochial ministry', 48-51.
87. Cf. the reference to *clerici in monasteriis* in Ecgberht's *Dialogus*: below, p. 161.
88. An example of a cleric who styled himself *abbas*, but was termed 'priest' by his bishop, is Abbot Balthun of Kempsey: Sims-Williams, *Religion and Literature*, 170-1.
89. See below, pp. 164-6.
90. Morris, *Churches in Landscape*, 130-8.
91. J. Campbell, *Essays in Anglo-Saxon History* (1986), 51-3.
92. For another area (Worcester diocese) with a considerable density, see Sims-Williams, *Religion and Literature*, xiv-xv, 115-76. Cf. however, the markedly irregular distribution of surviving early churches in Co. Durham: Cambridge, 'Early church', 65-85, esp. 69, 71.

monasteria, and in some instances it seems they were actually subject to them; their equivocal standing may have rendered them more susceptible to challenges from abbots with powerful lay connexions. An equally crucial imprecision characterized contemporary evaluations of these communities, and culminated in Bede's denunciation of many (perhaps most) of them as 'false' in 734. Such tensions, reflected in the ecclesiastical legislation of the period and the repeated calls for reform by the greatest theologian of the day, have perhaps disguised the true nature of the majority of the *monasteria*. To assess the quality of the reformers' judgements, it is first necessary to understand the strict monastic bias which informed their critique of the contemporary church. It is therefore to the theology which underpinned that critique – as embodied primarily in the writings of Bede – that we must now turn.

THE PASTORAL THEOLOGY OF BEDE AND THEODORE

Bede saw the care of the faithful as the sphere of a spiritual élite, whom he usually referred to as the *sancti doctores* and *praedicatores*, the holy preachers and teachers of the faithful. By preaching and teaching he did not simply mean the delivering of sermons or instructions to the faithful, but rather the setting forth in word and deed of a wide range of contemplative, missionary and pastoral activities. For Bede, the exalted status of *doctor* and *praedicator* was achieved only through the practice of both the ascetic life of contemplation (as understood by Benedict and other monastic legislators) and the active life of the pastor.[93] Such views derive most immediately from Pope Gregory the Great. In his main exegetical works, the *Moralia* on the Book of Job and the *Homilies* on Ezekiel, as well as in his more popular book on pastoral care, Gregory had largely dispensed with the normal terminology for pastors (i.e. bishop, priest, deacon) and replaced it with deliberately vague and ambiguous references to 'sacred rulers', 'teachers' and 'preachers'.[94] His aim in thus avoiding the formal usage was to stress that 'spiritual authority was not to be equated with ecclesiastical office'.[95] The guidance of souls was a skilled and demanding occupation, to be practised only by those who, through a rigorous ascetic training, had acquired deep spiritual reserves and self-knowledge.[96] Such views – essentially those of a monk-pope whose favourite audience and associates were also monks – involved Gregory in ambiguity about the role of monasteries and their inmates. On the one hand, in his correspondence with Italian

---

93. A. T. Thacker, 'Bede's ideal of reform', in *Ideal and Reality*, ed. Wormald, 130-2.
94. *ibid.*, 133-5; J. McClure, 'Gregory the Great: exegesis and audience' (unpubl. D.Phil thesis, Univ. of Oxford, 1978), 38-40, 46-50, 83-5, 106-8, 120-1, 124-31, 237-40.
95. McClure, 'Gregory', 237.
96. *ibid.*, 47-9, 121-2, 126-9, 239-40; Gregory the Great, *Cura Pastoralis* (Patrologia Latina, 77, cols. 12-128), i.1-2, i.10, iv.

bishops he was careful to insist that monks should be kept apart from the world and all its cares; on the other, he chose monks from his own monastery to lead the English mission and insisted that even when they became bishops they should continue to live according to their vows.[97] In addition, Gregory's application of monastic ideals to the pastoral office and his intrusion of monks into the English pastorate also created uncertainty about the nature of the leadership within the church; although the order of preachers and teachers overlapped with that of bishops and priests, the two were not necessarily to be regarded as identical.[98]

These ambiguities and inconsistencies are also to be found in Bede, soaked as he was in Gregory's thought and ideals. But in early eighth-century England, where ecclesiastical structures were less set and evangelical demands more urgent, he was probably far less conscious of them. Despite his emphasis on the need for personal asceticism and on the achievement of sanctity through withdrawal from the world, it seems never to have occurred to Bede to question the involvement of English *monasteria* in missionary and pastoral activity. For him it was natural and Gregorian to envisage a *monasterium* as an episcopal *familia* or to cast his hero Cuthbert as both prior and monastic *praedicator*.[99]

Bede, then, perhaps even more than Gregory, perceived the pastorate, the order of teachers and preachers, as essentially monastic, the proper activity of men schooled in a recognizably Benedictine tradition. Though (as a priest himself) he had the highest respect for the ordained ministry, in the last resort his ideal pastors were first and foremost monks in the classic sense. Essentially the episcopal office was valued as the supreme means of exemplifying and mediating the monastic *conuersatio*. Hence the recommendation that new sees be placed in reformed *monasteria*. Furthermore, strictly monastic communities were thought to have a crucial role for all involved in pastoral work: they were not simply to serve the needs of their localities but were to be training centres where contemplatives of superior education and intellect expounded the heavenly *arcana* of those of more active disposition and talent, in preparation for the latter's work in the field.[100] In short, Bede envisaged his own institution and others like it as powerhouses from which would emanate an élite pastoral force formed in the monastic *doctor*'s own image.[101]

Given this starting point, it is perhaps not surprising that like Gregory, Bede envisaged the relationship between the pastor-preacher and his flock in very monastic terms. The pastor was a ruler placed over spiritual subjects, whom it was his duty to guide and correct wherever possible through wise counsel and personal example.[102] Bede is often regarded as an

---

97. Gregory, *Registrum Epistolarum*, ed. D. Norberg (CCSL, 140, 140A), 46, 229, 266, 578.
98. McClure, 'Gregory', 124-5, 237-8.
99. Thacker, 'Bede's ideal', 136-49.
100. See Bede's treatment of Lindisfarne (above, p. 142).
101. Thacker, 'Bede's ideal', 131-3. For the comparable role assigned to minsters at the Council of *Clofesho*, see Foot, 'Parochial ministry', 52-3.
102. Thacker, 'Bede's ideal', 132.

unworldly monk, incapable of formulating practical policy, but there is no doubt that he intended his monastically trained teachers and preachers to have an impact outside the religious communities. He lays stress, for example, upon the varied nature of their audience: in a passage which clearly draws upon Gregory's *Cura Pastoralis*, he recommends that the pastor's *sancta praedicatio* be adapted to the condition of his hearers, whether they were wise or foolish, rich or poor, healthy or infirm, old or young, men or women, celibate or married, prelates or subjects.[103] He even seeks to extend his teaching on the pastorate to a purely lay environment. In a highly significant passage in his sermon for Christmas Day, he emphasized that the term pastor could be applied not only to bishops, priests, deacons and the rulers of monasteries, but to any of the faithful who exercised a right custody of his home, however humble.[104]

Obviously the first necessity was to bring the laity into the church through instruction and baptism. Despite the insistence on universal infant baptism in the laws of Ine,[105] and the assumption that baptism was primarily for infants in the council of 747,[106] Bede seems to have envisaged a world where an adult catechumenate, if not the norm, was nevertheless not unknown.[107] Certainly he thought in terms of a laity which, even if baptized, remained ignorant, uninstructed and unconfirmed. Hence his repeated emphasis on the pastor's duty to travel, to seek out the numerous remote places which had received no clerical ministrations of any kind, perhaps for many years.[108] In such circumstances elementary preaching and instruction and the administration of baptism were seen as the immediate and primary duties of the itinerant pastors. Though these activities were properly the prerogative of those in episcopal and priestly orders, they were not restricted to such (as Bede's own references to James the Deacon reveal), and could where necessary be entrusted to *clerici* sent out from *monasteria*.[109]

Once they had been received into the church, however, the needs of laymen were best furnished by the monk-priest. Bede is clear that the faithful should not only hear mass but also receive communion frequently,[110] and indeed set forth as an attainable minimum its reception every Sunday and on the major weekday feasts.[111] Such a programme,

---

103. *De Tab.* p. 26. Cf. *Super Parabolas Salomonis*, i. 8 (Patrologia Latina, 91, col. 963D), where Bede stresses that Christ's mission was to both sexes and all sorts and conditions of men.
104. Bede, *Op. Hom.* 49.
105. Attenborough, *Laws*, 36-7 (c.2.1). Wihtred, c.6, however, punishes neglect of baptism of the sick in terms which do not suggest that it was simply a question of infants: *ibid.*, 26-7.
106. Council of *Clofesho*, AD 747, c.11.
107. E.g. Bede, *Op. Hom.* 222. Cf. *ibid.*, 235, where Bede follows Jerome in emphasizing that 'modern preachers' should ensure that instruction both preceded and followed baptism: van der Walt, *Homiliary*, 121.
108. Bede, *Epistola ad Ecgberhtum*, cc. 5, 7; Bede, *Vita S. Cuthberti*, c.9.
109. E.g. the characterization of the itinerant preacher as *clericus vel presbyter*, Bede, *Vita S. Cuthberti*, c.9. Cf. Bede, *HE* iii. 26.
110. E.g. *In Marc.* ed. D. Hurst (CCSL, 120), 520; M. T. A. Carroll, *The Venerable Bede: His Spiritual Teachings* (1946), 108.
111. Bede, *Epistola ad Ecgberhtum*, c.15.

however, had considerable implications for the 'more religious laymen' (*laici . . . religiosiores*). Contemporary requirements for participation in communion were relatively strict, involving preliminary fasting, penance and abstinence from sexual relations.[112] It is significant, therefore, that when he lists those laymen sufficiently blameless to enter into this felicity, Bede turns first to the virginal young or the abstinent old, rather than to the married, who are only granted access if they practise a due standard of continence. It is essentially a monastic ideal, in which sexually active husbands and wives are only grudgingly allowed a share.[113]

Indeed, it is perhaps in the views of marriage purveyed by Bede and his fellow monks that the nature of the Christian ideal set before the laity is most clearly apparent. Bede undoubtedly took a low view of the married state. He repeatedly stresses the merits of virginity and places the married in the lowest category of the faithful; far inferior to rulers and teachers and to those vowed to celibacy are the good spouses who faithfully serve the Lord.[114] Moreover, if we examine the duties and requirements of these good spouses, the monastic bias becomes even more evident. Though Bede, in fact, devotes little attention to marriage, when he does so the effect is chilling. In his early commentary on 1 Peter, for example, he argues that for husbands to abstain from sexual intercourse is to accord honour to woman, the weaker vessel. He goes on to quote Paul's statement that the married should not refuse one another, except by agreement to provide leisure for prayer, and to argue from this that Paul views active sexuality as impeding prayer. He then points to another passage in which Paul says that mankind should pray without ceasing. The conclusion is obvious: spouses should never indulge in conjugal relations lest they be hindered from that prayer in which they should continually persevere.[115] This comes close to an outright condemnation of the married state. Given such views it is scarcely surprising that in his letter to Ecgberht Bede raged against the married clerics who polluted the 'false' *monasteria* with their lusts.[116]

During the course of a long life and much reading of Gregory the Great, Bede perhaps retreated a little from the extreme views of his youth.[117] Nevertheless, it should be borne in mind that they may well represent the conventional prejudices of the monastic world in which he was educated. Certainly, as Plummer long ago pointed out, the views of Archbishop

---

112. E.g. Theodore, *Penitential*, i, xii. 5; i, xiv. 17; ii, xii. 1; Bede, *HE* i. 27.
113. Bede, *Epistola ad Ecgberhtum*, c.15.
114. Bede, *De Tab.* 31-2.
115. Bede, *Epist. Cath.*, 243-4. Bede did not apparently derive these views from the Fathers.
116. Bede, *Epistola ad Ecgberhtum*, cc. 10-13.
117. For more emollient teaching, see Bede, *Op. Hom.* 95; *In Luc.*, 280; *In Genesim*, ed. C. W. Jones (CCSL, 118A), 24, 28-9. Significantly, in two of these passages Bede was quoting from Gregory the Great (*Homeliae in Evangeliis*, ii. 36) and Jerome (*Commentary on Galatians*, vi. 8). In a further two instances he goes on to stress that virginity is a higher calling than marriage.

Theodore, as transmitted in the *Penitential* which bears his name, amount to the notion that marriage is sinful.[118] Theodore (also, be it noted, a monk) required the married to abstain from intercourse for three nights before taking communion and to keep from each other entirely during the long weeks of Lent.[119] Like Bede, he regarded it as permissible with the assent of one's spouse to sever the marriage bond by entering a monastery.[120] Indeed, his only positive provision on the subject was that at a first marriage a priest should celebrate mass and bless the couple; even this, however, was accompanied by the requirement that the newly married should absent themselves from church for thirty days and then perform a further forty days of penance.[121]

All this, it should be said, is in marked contrast to the teaching of Gregory the Great, both in the *Moralia* and in the *Responsiones* to Augustine of Canterbury, which Bede quotes in the *Ecclesiastical History*. Gregory, of course, did not deny that sexual intercourse indulged in purely for pleasure was sinful, but nevertheless only required of a husband who took delight in the act that he wash and refrain from entering a church until his mind was free from fleshly desire.[122] Theodore certainly never expresses himself as positively as this. The gulf between his and Gregory's attitudes to sexual matters is well demonstrated by the difference in their treatment of menstruating and newly-delivered women; Theodore's view that these were not to enter church had been expressly rejected by Gregory in the *Responsiones*.[123]

Taking such a sombre view of sexuality, the monastic élite of the early English church effectively turned their backs upon the married. The many strict provisions with which marriage was hedged about, if applied in their full severity, would have made it very difficult for the average spouse to have been a frequent participant in the liturgy even where it was regularly available. Perhaps this was always recognized. Certainly Theodore's legislation on the permanence of the marriage bond shows that he envisaged a class of married people of whom little could be expected and who might be bound by long periods of penance.[124]

Marriage was not the only subject on which the church sought to intervene decisively in the daily lives of the laity. A further set of prohibitions attended practices which were regarded as pagan. In Theodore's *Penitential* harsh penalties were visited upon those who sacrificed to pagan deities or indulged in incantation, divination or the taking of auguries.[125] Bede's attitudes, expressed in his condemnation of all dalliance with

---

118. *Baedae Opera Historica*, ed. Plummer, ii, 53.
119. Theodore, *Penitential*, ii, xii. 1-2 (Haddan and Stubbs, *Councils*, iii. 199).
120. *ibid.*, i, xii. 8. Bede praised Æthelthryth's refusal to consummate her marriage with King Ecgfrith and her eventual desertion of him to become a nun: *HE* iv. 19.
121. Theodore, *Penitential*, i, xiv. 1.
122. Bede, *HE* i. 27.
123. *ibid.*, i. 27; Theodore, *Penitential*, i, xiv. 17-18.
124. Theodore, *Penitential*, i, xiv. 2-3, 5.
125. *ibid.*, i, xv. 1, 4-5.

secular culture,[126] are probably echoed in the rigorous demands of Archbishop Ecgberht and of the fathers assembled at *Clofesho* in 747. While Ecgberht included within his condemnation such practices as making offerings to or vows at trees, keeping Thursdays in honour of Thor, and celebrating the first of January, at *Clofesho* the council expressly condemned all pagan observances, singling out for special mention *diuinos, auguria, aruspicia, fylacteria, et incantationes*.[127] Since many of these practices were an important part of the fabric of social life in the period, the disruption arising from their abandonment would have been considerable.

The layman's response to these exacting demands would clearly have depended very much upon the manner in which they were set forth. He was scarcely likely to be impressed by those whose sexual conduct or cultic practice differed little from his own. Yet the sheer weight of references in Bede's work to the need for right teaching, for clergy with a proper understanding of Christian belief, and for the preacher to show forth in deed what he proclaimed in word, does not inspire confidence that such standards were generally achieved.[128] In the absence of effective exposition and example, the church was forced back to another more coercive weapon: penance.

In the early church the administration of penance was confined to the bishop, and was a solemn and indeed terrifying affair. Post-baptismal sin was viewed very gravely, and those who admitted to it were only allowed one chance. After making confession, either in public or to their bishop, they were enrolled in the order of penitents, which entailed separation from their families and the adoption of a semi-monastic mode of life for the rest of their earthly existence. This strictness, not surprisingly, led to the deferment of confession to the end of life.[129] In its place there arose, initially in monasteries, a more informal (and repeatable) mode of penance, which involved resort to a spiritual adviser, and the performance of various acts of penitence, including *compunctio* (or tearful self-abasement), almsgiving, fasting and psalm-singing.[130] Such penance, which involved no formal act of confession or public humiliation, was much stressed by Gregory the Great as a desirable form of Christian living.[131] Undoubtedly, however, it was more suited to life within a monastery than to the contemporary secular world. A more effective development was that which seems to have arisen in insular milieux in the sixth and seventh centuries, and which involved confession to, and the receipt of penance from, a priest or bishop. To guide the confessor, lists of sins, accompanied by tariffs of penance,

---

126. *In I Samuhelis*, ed. D. Hurst (CCSL, 119), 122.
127. Council of *Clofesho*, AD 747, c.3; *Poenitentiale Ecgberhti*, viii, 1-4 (Haddan and Stubbs, *Councils*, iii. 363-4, 424); Morris, *Churches in Landscape*, 60.
128. See below, pp. 162-3.
129. H. P. Forshaw, 'The pastoral ministry of the priest confessor in the early Middle Ages' (unpubl. Ph.D. thesis, Univ. of London, 1976), 39-56.
130. *ibid.*, 57-105.
131. *ibid.*, 124-34; Carroll, *Ven. Bede*, 162-3.

were circulated in handbooks known as penitentials.[132] These practices have often been regarded as the origin of later medieval auricular confession, but it needs to be remembered that the two disciplines were not the same. In the early insular system confession was followed by the imposition of a sometimes lengthy period of penance, often involving the endurance of considerable austerities. It was generally only after this had been completed that reconciliation took place.[133] In these respects insular penance was closer to ancient canonical penance than to later medieval practice.[134]

Seventh-century England, it is now universally believed, was familiar only with insular confession. Certainly, the much-quoted statement of Archbishop Theodore that public penance was unknown there seems to support that view.[135] Nevertheless, the position is more complex than is sometimes suggested, and indeed it would seem that Theodore's *Penitential* certainly envisaged use of some of the elements of public penance, in, for example, its prescriptions relating to heretics.[136] Bede, too, though he was presumably familiar with insular practice, had also absorbed through his patristic reading the procedures of ancient canonical penance, and the ideals of spiritual counselling recommended by Gregory the Great.[137] It is not surprising, therefore, that his views on penitential procedure are not always consistent. Though in his early work on the Catholic Epistles he is clear that confession was made to priests (*presbyteri*), later in his commentary, *De Tabernaculo*, he writes as if the formal reconciliation of a penitent was properly the preserve of a bishop.[138] In some passages, especially those dealing with the mortally sick, he seems to assume that 'sincere repentance, purpose of amendment, and acceptance of the acts of satisfaction brought immediate absolution',[139] but more often he adopts the older view that reconciliation should be deferred until the completion of the prescribed penance.[140] On occasion he even cites humiliating ancient rituals such as the public imposition of hands on a penitent arrayed in sackcloth and ashes.[141]

Undoubtedly Bede's views on penitential observance, especially as presented in the *Ecclesiastical History*, were remarkably austere. He clearly approved of the behaviour of Adomnàn, a monk of Coldingham, who as a

---

132. J. T. McNeill and H. M. Gamer, *Medieval Handbooks of Penance* (1938), 3-50; Forshaw, 'Pastoral Ministry', 141-63; A. J. Frantzen, *The Literature of Penance in Anglo-Saxon England* (1983), 1-93.
133. E.g. L. Bieler, *The Irish Penitentials* (1975), 60, 76, 82, 86, 98, 102-6, etc.; T. Oakley, *English Penitential Discipline and Anglo-Saxon Law* (1923), 62-3.
134. Immediate reconciliation was allowed to the seriously ill: Bede, *Epist. Cath.* 221-2.
135. Theodore, *Penitential*, i, xiii. 4.
136. *ibid.*, i, v; Oakley, *English Penitential Discipline*, 75-8.
137. Carroll, *Venerable Bede*, 145-81. esp, 162-4, 171-2.
138. Bede, *Epist. Cath.* 221-2; *De Tab.* 115. For references to penance administered by *presbyter vel clericus*, *sacerdotes*, and *episcopi et presbyteri* see Bede, *Vita S. Cuthberti*, c.9; *In Ezram*, 321; *Op. Hom.* 146.
139. Carroll, *Venerable Bede*, 168-9.
140. Bede, *De Tab.* 115.
141. Carroll, *Venerable Bede*, 171-2.

young man had been adjudged to a severe penance by an Irish priest or bishop (the word used is *sacerdos*), and who, having been abandoned without reconciliation, took satisfaction in continuing his regime of fasting for all but two days a week until his life's end.[142] The story is instructive since it shows Bede recommending one of the harshest aspects of canonical penance, its permanence. That this was an abiding concern is confirmed by the inclusion in the *Ecclesiastical History* of a second such story, that of Dryhthelm, a married man who, after an overwhelming visionary experience of the torments of hell and the delights of heaven, abandoned his family, received the tonsure, and devoted himself to a life of extreme penitential observance.[143] Here the fact that Bede's penitential ideals were strongly coloured by his monastic experience is especially evident. Ultimately the layman's best hope was to adopt the life of a *conuersus*.

This disposition to recommend the monastic *conuersatio* to the world at large emerges even more strongly in Bede's advocacy of mutual confession between two laymen as a means of atoning for minor sins not requiring sacerdotal absolution, a practice probably based upon the monastic custom of confessing slight sins publicly to one another.[144] The rigorous observance which it implies, like the penitential austerities of a life such as Dryhthelm's, can only have been possible within the environs of a strictly monastic community.

It is instructive to compare Bede's teaching on penance with the attitudes implicit in the near-contemporary compilation ascribed to Archbishop Theodore, a work clearly intended for the laity in general.[145] Like Bede, Theodore was severe. Even for relatively minor sins, such as drunkenness, a layman was to undergo fifteen days of penance.[146] For grave sins such as indulging in homosexual practices the penalty could be as much as fifteen years.[147] The repeated commission of the most serious offences such as homicide, adultery and theft, was punished as in contemporary Gaul by incarceration in a monastery to perform penance until death.[148] Of course, the severity of such sentences depended to some extent on the nature of penitential observance. On this we should be better informed if the *libellus penitentiae* which (it seems) was intended to be used with the Theodorian collection had in fact survived;[149] but even without this some conclusions may be drawn. In most instances the principal requirement was some form of abstinence. The much-married, for example, were directed to give up meat on Wednesdays and Fridays and for the three forty-day periods of Advent, Lent and the weeks after Pentecost.[150] Other penances involved abstinence

---

142. Bede, *HE* iv. 25.
143. *ibid.*, v. 12.
144. Carroll, *Venerable Bede*, 161, 173-6; A. Teetaert, *La Confession aux laiques dans l'église latine* (1926), 28-9.
145. Frantzen, *Literature of Penance*, 66-7.
146. Theodore, *Penitential*, i, i. 5 (Haddan and Stubbs, *Councils*, iii, 177-8).
147. Theodore, *Penitential*, i, ii. 4-7.
148. *ibid.*, ii, vii. 1; C. Vogel, *La Discipline Pénitentielle en Gaule des origines à la fin du VII⁰ siècle* (Paris, 1952), p. 159.
149. Frantzen, *Literature of Penance*, 68; Theodore, *Penitential*, Epilogue.
150. Mayr-Harting, *Coming of Christianity*, 259; Theodore, *Penitential*, i, xiv. 2-3.

from strong drink or from fat, or adherence to a diet of bread and water.[151] In many instances, where the nature of the penance was not specified, the main requirements were probably, as later, psalm-singing, almsgiving and fasts of varying degrees of severity.[152] In all, however, an equally important and potentially humiliating element was exclusion from communion, often for considerable periods; the rigour of what was envisaged is clear from Theodore's provision for the commutation of long sentences to terms of six months or a year, 'out of pity' for the penitents.[153]

The pastoral theology expounded by Bede, and implicit in the *Penitential* of Theodore, was austerely monastic. It was ferociously hostile to all aspects of pagan custom and culture, it placed a low value on marriage, and it commended the rigours of ascetic observance. Such a programme of Christian living, evolved by the élite inmates of strict *monasteria*, can have held little attraction for the laity. Yet undoubtedly Bede and others hoped for Christian households in which communion was received frequently, and spouses lived chastely (and largely abstinently) and adopted some at least of the penitential discipline of the strictly observant monk. It is difficult to believe that they can ever have expected to achieve all this without the use of force.

THE IMPACT OF THE CHURCH'S TEACHING

Crucial to any understanding of the impact of the church on early Anglo-Saxon society is an assessment of the effectiveness of its means of discipline. Two problems have to be faced: detection and enforcement. Obviously there were many remote areas where the long arm of the church could never reach and where (as Bede lamented) legislation such as Theodore's remained a dead letter. Equally obviously, many of the penances prescribed can often have been enforced only with a degree of co-operation from the penitents themselves, especially those relating to intimate and private acts. Nevertheless, it is worth remembering that privacy was probably rare amongst the early English, with their often closely-knit settlements and their relatively open and undivided dwellings. Theodore may well have expected his rulings to be effective. That indeed is implied by the mere existence of the collection, culled as it seems to have been from judgments made in response to specific cases.

Even in areas where the church could exert most influence such as the environs or estates of *monasteria*, the long periods of abstinence and excommunication must have encouraged offenders to conform cynically or to abandon the church altogether. To prevent such lapses would have required coercion. Though Theodore's *Penitential* is very unspecific about this delicate subject, there are hints that in the case of serious crime there

---

151. *ibid.*, i, i. 6.
152. Council of *Clofesho*, AD 747, cc. 26-7 (Haddan and Stubbs, *Councils*, iii, 371-4).
153. Theodore, *Penitential*, i, xii. 4.

was a desire 'to establish the church's disciplinary authority by linking it with the king's'.[154] Thus if a thief made restitution to the injured party or a homicide paid the blood-price to the victim's kin, the statutory penitential term of seven years could be reduced.[155] That in turn secular power might enforce ecclesiastical penalties is implicit in the requirement that those guilty of 'many evil deeds', including murder, adultery and theft, should enter a *monasterium* to do penance until death.[156]

If such attitudes were likely to prevail anywhere, it was within the archbishop's own kingdom of Kent. There indeed the laws of Wihtred, probably promulgated at a council attended by Theodore's successor Berhtwald, laid down heavy fines for a variety of ecclesiastical offences, including entering into illicit unions, offering to devils and violating the regulations governing fasting and Sunday observance.[157] Even so, the extent to which the church could rely upon the secular arm to enforce much of its moral code clearly depended largely upon the degree to which local magnates sympathized with its teachings. It is, of course, Bede's awareness of this fact which explains his much-discussed concern with the conversion of men of rank.

Ultimately, any assessment of the church's impact on early Anglo-Saxon society has to be tentative. At one end of the spectrum stand those who would have us believe that the discipline of penance became an ingrained habit for the English laity in the earlier eighth century.[158] At the other stand those who see the church of this period as primarily, if not exclusively, royal and aristocratic, indifferent to the needs of the *plebs*.[159] The best evidence for the former view is the claim in the *Dialogus* of Ecgberht, the eighth-century archbishop of York, that during the twelve days before Christmas

> not only the clergy in the minsters (*clerici in monasteriis*), but also the laity with their wives and families, would resort to their confessors, and would wash themselves of carnal concupiscence by tears, community life and alms . . .; and so purified, they would receive the Lord's communion on the Nativity.[160]

If this passage can be taken at face-value, it goes a long way towards suggesting that the full discipline promoted by Bede and Theodore had been adapted and absorbed by at least a considerable section of the English laity. But as Frantzen has recently pointed out, the *Dialogus* was written by a senior bishop for the instruction of priests, and may well reflect a

---

154. Frantzen, *Literature of Penance*, 76.
155. Theodore, *Penitential*, i, iii. 3; i, iv. 1.
156. *ibid.*, i, vii. 1.
157. Attenborough, *Laws*, 24/5-26/7.
158. Mayr-Harting, *Coming of Christianity*, 258-61.
159. E.g. D. W. Rollason, *Saints and Relics in Anglo-Saxon England* (1989), 94; Morris, *Churches in Landscape*, 131-3.
160. Haddan and Stubbs, *Councils*, iii, 412-13, transl. Mayr-Harting, *Coming of Christianity*, 260.

considerable degree of wishful thinking.[161] One piece of evidence confirming this is the lack of firm evidence for a vigorous tradition of penitential
composition or use in eighth-century England. Of the two penitentials
besides Theodore's, credited with early English authors, that ascribed to
Archbishop Ecgberht, though it probably contains genuine material, is an
inferior work, much modified by its continental transmission; the other,
credited to Bede, is almost certainly of continental provenance.[162] That the
tradition established by Theodore had more impact across the Channel
than in England itself is also suggested by the complete absence of an early
English manuscript tradition for the penitentials.[163] While it cannot be
doubted that such handbooks were composed in pre-Viking England, their
influence seems to have been relatively limited.

There is, in fact, a good deal of evidence of indifference, or even
resistance, to the monastic idealism of Bede and Theodore. In particular, it
seems likely that many of the rich and powerful cynically sought to obtain
the commutation of the irksome rigours of penance. In an interesting
passage in his work on the Tabernacle, probably written in the 720s, Bede
refers to the role of the 'prelate' (the word used is *pontifex*) in adjudging his
flock to repentance (*paenitentia*) and in subsequently dispensing the grace
of reconciliation. Though it was proper for penitents to offer gifts, 'fruits
worth of repentance', in the form of alms and good works, 'it was quite
otherwise (as was alas the case) for certain bishops to demand presents from
the faithful and not to labour at all in the chastisement or purgation of
their iniquities'.[164] Here then is more than a hint that for those who could
afford it there were ways round the harsh penitential doctrines of the
church. That this was indeed the case is confirmed by a canon of the council of 747, at which the bishops condemned the giving of alms to abate or
commute expiatory fasts and penances (by then 'grown into a custom
dangerous to many'), and also outlawed a new abuse, whereby the rich paid
(or forced) others to expiate their sins with vicarious almsgiving, fasting and
psalmody.[165]

No assessment of the state of the early eighth-century church can neglect
the complaints of Bede, increasingly sharp from about 720 onwards.[166]
Above all he expressed concern about the quality of the clergy. As early as
716 he was lamenting compromise with pagan practices by unskilled
magistri, 'tired of the long labour of catechizing',[167] and dalliance with
secular culture by teachers and preachers who 'came down from the heights
of the word of God to listen to secular tales and devilish doctrines . . . exerciz-
ing their minds in reading pagan rhetoric and poetry'.[168] Clerical ignorance

161. Frantzen, *Literature of Penance*, 82-3.
162. *ibid.*, 69-78; A. J. Frantzen, 'The penitential attributed to Bede', *Speculum*, lviii
    (1980), 573-95.
163. Frantzen, *Literature of Penance*, 68-9.
164. Bede, *De Tab.* 115.
165. Council of *Clofesho*, AD 747, c.26.
166. Thacker, 'Bede's ideal', 132-3.
167. Bede, *In I Sam.* 122.
168. *ibid.*, 112.

also caused him anxiety. Condemnations of unlearned teachers and preachers are scattered throughout the commentaries, though the most revealing passage is in the letter to Ecgberht, where he laments the existence of monks and clergy ignorant of Latin, and recommends that unlearned priests be taught at least the Creed and the Lord's Prayer in the vernacular.[169] It is, of course, in this open letter that Bede's lamentations on the state of the Northumbrian church reach their climax. These are too well known to require detailed treatment here; suffice it to say that in the letter Bede paints a grim picture of a grasping and wordly episcopate, clinging to vast dioceses in order to retain the accompanying renders but offering little in return.[170] He combines this with a denunciation of 'false' *monasteria*, often ruled by laymen and staffed by *monachi* unworthy of the name, busy as they were with their wives and the procreation of children.[171] All this, it was alleged, had issued in an ill-taught laity, deprived of the sacraments and reluctant, even when qualified, to receive communion except at the three great feasts.[172]

Doubtless there was much truth in this gloomy vision. A particularly revealing insight into contemporary ecclesiastical standards is provided by the story of Hereball, one of Bishop John's clerics, who recovered from a riding injury only after the remedying of an imperfect baptism, performed by a priest unable to pronounce the office.[173] In some places even such faulty ministrations must have been lacking - if (as seems to have been the case) some *monasteria* were entirely without priests.[174] On the other hand, allowance must be made for Bede's austere and idealistic vision; his outpourings in the letter to Ecgberht have a polemical quality which probably led both to an exaggeration of the evils within the contemporary church and an undervaluing of the contribution of the clergy whose training and *mores* he despised.[175] It is clear, for example, that the principal failing of the 'false' *monasteria* in his eyes was their refusal to adopt strict monastic continence and poverty or to promote ascetic observance among the laity. Significantly, he does not deny that the inmates of the 'false' *monasteria* were assiduous in their performance of the offices,[176] or that they were subject to some degree of episcopal supervision. Moreover, his

---

169. Bede, *Epistola ad Ecgberhtum*, c.5.
170. *ibid.*, cc. 4, 7-8.
171. *ibid.*, cc. 11-14.
172. *ibid.*, c.15.
173. Bede, *HE* v. 6. Because of his unfitness the priest had been forbidden to baptize and catechize at his ordination, an indication perhaps of a desperate shortage of properly qualified candidates for holy orders in the late seventh century.
174. This allegation in the letter to Ecgberht is apparently confirmed by c.5 of the Council of *Clofesho*, AD 747 (Haddan and Stubbs, *Councils*, iii, 364).
175. Since this was written, Sims-Williams has argued convincingly that Bede's attack on pseudo-monasteries belongs to an ancient and well-defined tradition of monastic polemic and should not necessarily be taken at face value: *Religion and Literature*, 126-33.
176. E.g. Bede, *Epistola ad Ecgberhtum*, c.13, where Bede condemns those who 'exsurgentes de cubilibus, quid intra septa monasteriorum geri debeat, sedula intentione pertractant'. Was it in such communities that the liturgy was declaimed like secular poetry?: Council of *Clofesho*, AD 747, c.12.

disclosure that many of the institutions which he criticized were founded by *praefecti* (officials of high, even royal, rank), with the assistance of the bishops, points to those communities having more than a merely private dynastic function.[177] In the eighth century bishops sought to control proprietary *monasteria* precisely because they had a pastoral role. In many cases they probably had a good deal to offer a populace unlikely to be attracted by Bede's austere ideals or coerced by monastic notions of penance.

THE COUNCILS OF THE EIGHTH AND EARLY NINTH CENTURIES

That the church was ultimately so securely established as to survive the Scandinavian invasions comparatively intact was not simply due to the good work of Archbishop Theodore and the monks of Jarrow and Lindisfarne. If the role of the proprietary *monasteria* has perhaps been underestimated, so too have the struggles of eighth-century churchmen, especially the bishops, in legislating in council and in struggling to control their diverse pastoral institutions.[178] Though this is not the place to look in detail at the work of the great eighth-century councils,[179] it is perhaps worth considering briefly those aspects of episcopal activity which throw light on their expectations of the clergy and their flocks. One notable illustration of this is the valiant effort made in 747 at the council of *Clofesho* to accommodate the criticisms of Bede and his admirer Boniface,[180] who in his letter to Archbishop Cuthbert written in the same year, had also dwelt upon abuses within English *monasteria*, singling out a fondness for fine garments, and a propensity towards sexual indulgence and drunkenness.[181]

Pastoral matters were an overriding preoccupation of the fathers in 747. Bishops were urged to attend to their pastoral responsibilities and to make annual circuits of their dioceses; they were to ensure that all ordinands (whether monks or clerics) were of good life and sound understanding of the faith; and to appoint priests who would be diligent in baptizing, teaching and visiting, and sufficiently learned to be able to celebrate the sacraments and to explain in their own tongue the Creed and the Lord's Prayer.[182] Abbots and priests were expressly required to celebrate mass on Sundays and holy days, and on those occasions to preach to the people subject to them.[183]

---

177. Bede, *Epistola ad Ecgberhtum*, c.13; A. T. Thacker, 'Some terms for noblemen in Anglo-Saxon England', in *Anglo-Saxon Studies*, ii, BAR, Brit. ser., 112 (1981), 201–36.
178. Brooks, *Church of Canterbury*, 175–206; Sims-Williams, *Religion and Literature*, 138–41, 154–76.
179. See Cubitt, pp. 193–211 below.
180. *Briefe der Bonifatius* (ed. Tangl), nos 76, 91.
181. *ibid.*, no. 78.
182. Council of *Clofesho*, AD 747, cc. 1, 3, 6, 9, 10 (Haddan and Stubbs, *Councils*, iii, 363–6).
183. Council of *Clofesho*, AD 747, c.14.

Especially interesting are the provisions relating to the laity. Like the clergy they were admonished to communicate frequently, even when married, 'provided they can refrain from sin'.[184] Penance (perhaps optimistically) was treated as part of the normal discipline of the faithful. One of the qualities expected of candidates for the priesthood was that they be able 'discreetly to enjoin penances upon others' and (as we have already seen) various attempts to commute or evade penance were condemned.[185]

The ideals enunciated in the council of *Clofesho* were then in many ways difficult to distinguish from those which so coloured Bede's letter to Ecgberht. The situation revealed is not without its strengths. The bishops assembled at the Council displayed an impressive and informed concern to reach out to the laity and to achieve uniformity by imposing Roman liturgical practice.[186] They are scarcely to be reckoned with the irresponsible and avaricious prelates who feature so prominently in Bede's letter. On the other hand, the failure to treat openly of the pastoral work of the *monasteria* suggests, as has already been noted, unresolved tensions within the hierarchy. In particular, in the matter of reforming the proprietary communities the Council seems to have accepted defeat, confining itself to seeking their integration into the diocesan organization. Canon 5 allowed that because of human greed *monasteria* which were held by seculars could not be brought *ad religionis Christianae statum*, insisting only upon episcopal visitation and the provision of a priest. While this may well have improved pastoral arrangements, it would hardly have satisfied Bede or Boniface.[187]

In fact, by the early ninth century considerable progress had been made in the attempt to incorporate the independent proprietary *monasteria* into a coherent pastoral framework. Though the issue was ignored at the legatine synod of 786, by 803 the bishops had again taken the offensive. At the council held in that year it was decreed that no *monasterium* was to presume to elect a layman or secular as lord over Christ's inheritance.[188] Even more radical was the decree of the synod of Chelsea in 816 that abbots and abbesses were to be chosen by their diocesans with the consent of their communities.[189] To a considerable extent the way had been prepared for this legislation by episcopal initiative at the local level. In the see of Worcester in the later eighth century, bishops were active in ensuring that, wherever possible, independent proprietary communities were brought under their control and put in the charge of priests from the episcopal *familia*. In particular, bishops sought to eliminate lay lordship by securing reversions to the see or by attempting to oversee abbatial elections. In Worcester at least this policy was attended by a fair degree of success, and, as Sims-Williams has recently pointed out, was eventually to create 'the

---

184. *ibid.*, c.23.
185. *ibid.*, cc. 6, 27.
186. E.g. *ibid.*, cc. 9-14, 16, 18; see Catherine Cubitt's chapter below.
187. Brooks, *Church of Canterbury*, 178.
188. Council of *Clofesho*, AD 803, c.4.
189. Synod of Chelsea, AD 816, c.4 (Haddan and Stubbs, *Councils*, iii. 580-1).

network of episcopal minsters' which was the hub of the late Saxon pastoral system.[190]

THE CULT OF THE SAINTS

Besides what may be termed the institutional framework of diocese, *monasterium* and *parochia*, there is another phenomenon, equally important in England (and elsewhere) as a vehicle for pastoral activity, and ultimately perhaps more crucial in engendering affection for the new faith. That phenomenon is the cult of the saints. Space precludes a full treatment of this extremely complex subject in this chapter. All that can be stressed here is its ubiquity: there were in England very many saints, the cults of which were often highly localized and focused on a single community. Indeed, it is difficult to overemphasize how closely cult and *monasterium* were linked in early Anglo-Saxon England. On the one hand no cult could survive without its guardians, who maintained the memory of the saint's deeds and wonders, celebrated his festival, tended his tomb and distributed his relics. On the other the cult conferred prestige, attracted pilgrims and provided a vehicle for local pastoral work. It now seems likely that a great many, perhaps most, *monasteria* housed a cult of some kind, even if it was only some highly restricted devotion to a little-known member of the founder's family.[191]

To demonstrate these themes in the brief space remaining, it is possible to examine only one, particularly successful, cult: that of Cuthbert of Lindisfarne.[192] If Bede is to be believed, Cuthbert's skill in preaching and his exemplary life had already made him a potent pastor while he was still at Melrose. When he arrived at a remote settlement on one of his pastoral journeys, he quickly elicited from its inhabitants open confession of their sins and the due performance of the penance which he commanded.[193] Paradoxically, however, his effectiveness in this role was deemed to have been increased greatly when later he renounced his itinerant pastorate and withdrew to the remote island of Farne to live as a hermit. There he gained a reputation as a holy man with power over devils, the elements and all living things.[194] Attracted by these miracles, Bede says, many came not only from the environs of Lindisfarne but also from much more distant parts to make the difficult pilgrimage to Farne and to disclose to the saint their sins and troubles in the hope of consolation.[195] Even in that intensely local world, it seems, the holy man (or his tomb) transcended

---

190. Sims-Williams, *Religion and Literature*, 131-3, 140-3, 154-76.
191. E.g. Thacker, 'Kings, saints and monasteries', 1-25. This question was the subject of a conference held in Oxford in November 1991.
192. Thacker, 'Bede's ideal', 136-45; *idem*, 'Lindisfarne and the origins of the cult of St Cuthbert', in *St Cuthbert, His Cult and His Community*, ed. G. Bonner, D. W. Rollason and C. Stancliffe (1989), 103-22.
193. Bede, *Vita S. Cuthberti*, c.9; Bede, *HE* iv. 27.
194. *Vita S. Cuthberti*, iii. 1-5; Bede, *Vita S. Cuthberti*, cc. 17-21; Bede, *HE* iv. 28.
195. Bede, *Vita S. Cuthberti*, c.22 (added by Bede).

pastoral boundaries, partly at least, it may be suspected, because he afforded a means of bypassing the demanding observances associated with ritual confession and penance.[196]

It was, however, after his death, and the discovery of his miraculously uncorrupted body, that the cult of Cuthbert reached its apogee, attracting the sick, the possessed and the afflicted from its own territory, from a neighbouring *monasterium* and even from overseas.[197] By then the community at Lindisfarne had skilfully organized the whole phenomenon. Pre-eminent among the sacred sites was the tomb itself, surrounded by lights and votives and probably covered with precious cloths. Nearby stood personal relics of the saint, such as the new shoes with which he had been shod at his interment.[198] Outside the church there was a whole cluster of subsidiary sites associated with Cuthbert both in life and death: the hermitage on Farne, the oratory in which he prayed near the monastery, the place where the water used to wash the holy corpse had been poured away. Attendance at any of these could effect healing, and - even more important - could be used to obtain personal relics and phylacteries. The hide which formed part of the covering of Cuthbert's original oratory on Farne was cut into fragments and distributed; dust from the tomb or some other sacred site could be infused in water to produce a healing drink.[199]

Lindisfarne thus became a noted place of healing. The importance attached to this may be gauged from the fact that the brethren did not rely on Cuthbert's powers alone. In a revealing passage, the author of the earliest Life tells us that a certain paralysed youth was brought to Lindisfarne expressly because it was known to have skilled physicians.[200] Doctors (*medici*) seem indeed to have been associated quite often with famous shrines and relic centres: they occur also, for example, at Nivelles, the home of the cult of the Gaulish saint Gertrude in the early eighth century.[201] Doubtless, the training of such men was made possible by the wealth which cults generated. In the last resort, however, contemporaries placed their faith not in doctors, but in dust scraped from the tombs of saints. In times of need the faithful sought out their local (or, indeed, not so local) shrine, bypassing the formal sacraments, hedged as they might be with harsh and demanding penances.

Recently, it has been stressed that a great many of the stories involving cures and wonders actually relate to the clergy and aristocracy.[202] At Lindisfarne after Cuthbert's death, for example, cures were wrought upon a brother of Lindisfarne itself, a youth from a neighbouring *monasterium*,

---

196. For the role of the Gaulish holy man or bishop in confession, see Vogel, *Discipline Pénitentielle*, 161-2.
197. *Vita S. Cuthberti*, iv. 14-18; Bede, *Vita S. Cuthberti*, cc. 41-6; Bede, *HE* iv. 30-2.
198. *Vita S. Cuthberti*, iv. 14, 17; Bede, *Vita S. Cuthberti*, c.45.
199. *Vita S. Cuthberti*, iv. 15; Bede, *Vita S. Cuthberti*, cc. 43, 46.
200. *Vita S. Cuthberti*, iv. 17; Bede, *Vita S. Cuthberti*, c.45; Rollason, *Saints and Relics*, 95-6.
201. *De Virtutibus Sancti Geretrudis*, ed. B. Krusch (MGH, *Script. Rer. Merov.*, 2), c.5.
202. Rollason, *Saints and Relics*, 83-104, esp. 97-104.

a visiting member of the clergy of the Frisian archbishop Willibrord, and the hermit who dwelt in Cuthbert's former cell on Farne.[203] Only one certainly involved a layman, a boy from the Lindisfarne estates.[204] That to some extent is only to be expected: the monks of Lindisfarne were more likely to remember and record the visits of members of their own order and of the great of the day than those of the ordinary laity. Nevertheless, there is evidence that contemporaries thought that saints' cults ministered to society as a whole. The words which Abbot Herefrith put into the mouth of the dying Cuthbert are significant in this context:

> I think it expedient for you that I rest here [i.e. on the remote island of Farne] because of the influx of fugitives and criminals of every sort, who will perhaps flee to my body, since, unworthy as I am, my reputation as a servant of Christ has gone forth among the multitude.[205]

That this *topos* was thought appropriate for English cults is confirmed by the mid-eighth-century Life of the East Anglian hermit, Guthlac, whose author Felix expressly says that all sorts and conditions of men (*multi diuersorum ordinum gradus*) visited the saint – not only the clergy, the nobles and the rich, but also the afflicted and the poor.[206] Evidence for the involvement of the common people is especially clear in the royal cults. The earliest recorded custodian of the Northumbrian king Eadwine's remains is the *maritus* (*ceorl*) Teoful, while the beneficiaries of the miraculous earth removed from his successor Oswald's cult site at *Maserfelth* evidently included several people of only modest rank.[207] Moreover, the sheer number of obscure and unrecorded local shrines needs to be remembered; unlike the great and famous communities with their courtly and clerical contacts, they may have provided especially for the humble and the poor. At all events, by the later eighth century charms and relics obtained from the shrines of the saints were common in the homes of the rustic laity. Indeed, by then they were so taken for granted as to have become the objects of abuse. On at least two occasions Alcuin found it necessary to write to English archbishops, condemning the improper use of phylacteries derived from gospel books or relics: 'People wish to have sacred things round their necks, not in their hearts, and with these holy words of God or the relics of the saints go to their filthy acts, and even do their duty by their wives.'[208]

---

203. *Vita S. Cuthberti*, iv. 16-17; Bede, *Vita S. Cuthberti*, cc. 44-6; Bede, *HE* iv. 31.
204. *Vita S. Cuthberti*, iv. 17; Bede, *Vita S. Cuthberti*, c.45.
205. Bede, *Vita S. Cuthberti*, 37. On Herefrith's authorship of the passage, see W. Berschin, 'Opus Deliberatum et Perfectum', in *St Cuthbert*, ed. Bonner *et al.*, 102.
206. Felix, *Vita Sancti Guthlaci*, c.45, ed. B. Colgrave (1956), 138, 45. For a different view, See Rollason, *Saints and Relics*, 96-7.
207. *The Earliest Life of Gregory the Great*, cc. 18-19, ed. B. Colgrave (1968); Bede, *HE* iii. 9-10.
208. *Alcuini Epistolae*, ed. E. Dümmler (MGH, *Epistolae*, 4), 448-9.

But perhaps the most vivid contemporary illustration of lay attitudes to (and abuse of) the pastoral role of holy men and their relics comes not from England but from Gaul, though it is recorded by an Englishman, Boniface, who clearly understood the phenomenon well enough. It concerns a self-styled bishop and saint, one Aldebert, whose activities were condemned at the Roman Synod of 745. Aldebert claimed to have been given marvellous relics by an angel which enabled him to obtain from God whatsoever he wished, and as a result he had come to be regarded as a holy patron and miracle-worker by the ordinary people. He produced his own *Uita*, dedicated oratories to himself, set up crosses or small oratories in fields, at springs, or wherever he pleased, and ordered public prayers to be said at or in them, so that 'multitudes of people, scorning their bishops and deserting established churches, attended worship in such places, believing "the merits of St Aldebert will help us"'. Aldebert distributed parings from his fingernails and hairs from his head as relics and finally committed what for Boniface was the ultimate blasphemy: 'I know all your hidden sins, for your secret thoughts are known to me. There is no need of confession, your past sins are forgiven you. Go back to your homes absolved in peace and safety.'[209]

This highly instructive episode gives some indication of the response of the ordinary laity to the strict doctrines of the kind preached by Bede. A man who laid claim to *uirtus* (spiritual power), and who assured people of salvation without the horrors of penance, could soon attract a following. Though Aldebert's heresies were gross and palpable, they nevertheless give us some insight into that attraction exerted by numerous saints and shrines, which rendered them arguably one of the most effective vehicles for pastoral care and for presenting the Christian faith in England in the early Middle Ages.

CONCLUSION

This chapter began with Bede and it is only fitting that in conclusion it is to him that we return. Bede's writings (above all his historical works) have dominated our interpretation of the establishment of Christianity among the Anglo-Saxons. Yet Bede, of course, was not representative. A driven idealist from a learned and genuinely monastic milieu, he wrote in the conviction that the English had a predestined role as a new Israel, a chosen people led by holy kings and apostolic pastors. That role required the adoption of an exalted discipline – the discipline of the monk – by the people at large; family life was allowed only a minor role under strict conditions. In this scheme of things the compromises practised in the average ecclesiastical community found no place; better by far that such institutions be converted into episcopal *monasteria*; better even that they be given over to the support of young warriors to defend the chosen people from the

---

209. *Briefe der Bonifatius* (ed. Tangl), no. 59; transl. E. Emerton, *Letters of St Boniface* (1940), 101.

barbarians. Bede had scant interest in dealing justly with the proprietary communities, and his strictures must be interpreted from this perspective. Doubtless their way of life did indeed leave much to be desired, but it is questionable whether it was markedly inferior to that observed by similar bodies in, say, Gaul or Italy.

Bede's success in articulating a strict monastic pastoral code, and the survival of a penitential informed by the judgments of a monk-archbishop, have caused historians either to overestimate the impact of monastic ideals on Anglo-Saxon society as a whole or to assume that a Christian faith thus presented could have made little if any headway among the common people. While it cannot be doubted that a few of the laity adopted the ascesis expounded by Bede and regulated by Theodore, the bitter tone of the letter to Ecgberht and the canons of the fathers at *Clofesho* show that (as is only to be expected) the attempt to persuade or coerce was not generally successful. Yet by the time that the Vikings arrived, the English were in some sense a Christian people, Christian enough indeed to convert the Vikings themselves to their beliefs within a generation. That transformation must have been largely effected by institutions of which Bede and his fellow monks would strongly have disapproved. Unsystematic and irregular as their distribution may have been throughout the English kingdoms as a whole, the royal and proprietary communities were far thicker on the ground than the strictly observant *monasteria*. To them, and to the local cults which they enshrined, must be ascribed much of the responsibility for the slow dissemination of the Christian faith among the Anglo-Saxons.

7 'By water in the spirit': the administration of baptism in early Anglo-Saxon England

SARAH FOOT

INTRODUCTION

The eleventh-century Anglo-Latin Life of St Rumwold contains one of the most detailed accounts of a baptismal ceremony to survive from Anglo-Saxon England.[1] The subject of the Life, Rumwold, was supposedly the son of a Christian daughter of Penda, the seventh-century king of Mercia, and of an unidentified Northumbrian king, who had been converted to the faith on his marriage. At the moment of his birth Rumwold is said to have cried aloud three times with a loud voice, 'I am a Christian', to which two priests who were present, Widerin and Eadwald, responded, 'Thanks be to God.' The child went on to confess his faith in the Trinity, and 'asked to be made a catechumen by the priest Widerin, to be held aloft for the preliminary rite of the faith by Eadwald, and to be named Rumwold.' The parents determined to ask the neighbouring kings and rulers to receive their son from the holy water of baptism, but Rumwold restated his preference for being baptized by the priest Widerin and received by Eadwald. He then ordered the servants standing around to fetch a hollow stone lying a little distance away, in which the water of holy baptism was blessed by those same two priests,

> and thus the blessed infant Rumwold was baptized by Widerin the priest and received by Eadwald. After the baptism, he demanded that a mass be celebrated for him, and that he should be given the body and blood of Christ, so that he might take up the sacrament of Him whose baptism he had received.

---

1. *Vita S. Rumwoldi* (BHL 7385) survives in five copies, of which the earliest is Cambridge, Corpus Christi College, MS 9 (s.xi[2]), pp. 53–8. The text is printed in *Acta Sanctorum*, Nov. i, 685–90. An edition and translation of the text are being prepared by Rosalind Love for her doctoral thesis, 'Eleventh-century Anglo-Latin hagiography' (University of Cambridge, in preparation). I am very grateful to her for allowing me to use this material, from which all the following quotations derive. This text has been discussed and an attempt made to identify Rumwold's parents by R. H. Hagerty, 'The Buckinghamshire saints reconsidered 3: St Rumwold (Rumbold), Buckingham', *Records of Buckinghamshire*, xxx (1988), 103–10.

Thereafter, the precocious neophyte preached a sermon about the Christian faith and expounded the value of confession to all those who were present before, on the third day after his birth, he died.

The details of the sacrament's administration remain uncertain: was Rumwold, for example, sprinkled with water, or partially or totally immersed in the makeshift font, and was he anointed with chrism after his baptism before the communion? Rumwold's maternal grandfather, King Penda, was, according to the child's hagiographer, before his marriage, 'sprinkled with the water of holy baptism and . . . received the anointing of Christ'. None the less, this text provides useful circumstantial information of a sort that is almost totally lacking from earlier Anglo-Saxon hagiographical sources.[2] While there are a number of references in pre-Viking texts to the role of individual priests and bishops in baptism and, in the prescriptive literature of church councils, to the importance of the correct administration of the sacrament, the precise form of the rite (or rites) in use in England in this period cannot be determined from these somewhat terse statements. Nor do the Anglo-Saxon liturgical books that survive from before the tenth century contain the baptismal order.[3] It is possible, however, to determine something of the attitudes of English churchmen towards the administration of baptism from the descriptions of its performance found in the early saints' Lives and in Bede's *Historia Ecclesiastica*. Equally valuable are the discussions of the baptismal rite found in the canons of church councils and in the correspondence exchanged by leading ecclesiastics. Examination of this material reveals much about the circumstances in which the sacrament was performed, notably the part it played in the regular priestly care of the lay population, and can also serve to clarify some details of the form of the rite.

Several early Anglo-Saxon texts testify to the fact that the sacraments of initiation were considered essential for all believers. Baptism constituted the means by which believers were admitted to the fellowship of the church, whereby they were cleansed of their past sins and reborn to new and eternal life. It was thus held to be the most important of the Christian sacraments, without which salvation was unobtainable. In his commentary on Luke, Bede wrote: 'no one unless he is baptized, unless he is united to the body of Christ, shall enter the church.'[4] The necessity of baptism for

---

2. There are also no English sources equivalent to the Frankish baptismal expositions written in response to the questionnaire about the administration of
baptism sent by Charlemagne to his metropolitans in 812. For a complete list of
such texts, see S. Keefe, 'Carolingian baptismal expositions: a handlist of tracts
and manuscripts', in *Carolingian Essays*, ed. U.-R. Blumenthal (1983), 169-237.
Compare also the brief descriptions of the baptismal *ordo* found in Alcuin,
Epistolae, 134 and 137, ed. E. Dümmler, MGH, *Epistolae Karolini Aevi*, ii (1895),
202-3, 214-15.
3. H. Gneuss, 'Liturgical books in Anglo-Saxon England and their Old English
terminology', in *Learning and Literature in Anglo-Saxon England*, ed. M. Lapidge
and H. Gneuss (1985), 91-141.
4. Bede, *In Lucam*, iii, ed. D. Hurst, CCSL, 120 (1960), 5-425: 'nemo nisi baptizatus
nisi corpori Christi adunatus ecclesiam intrabit.' Compare Bede, *HE* iii. 23, and
iv. 16.

salvation was also stressed by the Whitby author of the Life of Gregory the Great, who asserted that 'without baptism none will ever see God.'[5] An individual's status was changed through baptism, he or she was thereby reborn into the body of believers; as Boniface wrote, 'it is well established that by holy baptism we all become sons and daughters, brothers and sisters of Christ and the church.'[6] This rebirth also constituted a ritual cleansing from a person's past sins,[7] a washing away of evil,[8] and it brought the candidate freedom from the slavery of the devil.[9] The sacrament was only completed by anointing with oil, by means of which the baptized were endowed with the grace of the Holy Spirit.[10]

Before looking at the circumstances in which baptism was administered in early Anglo-Saxon England, I shall start by summarizing what can be determined of the nature of the initiation rituals in the pre-Viking period in England and by considering what forms of sacramental liturgy may have been available to parochial clergy. Then I investigate the physical setting of baptismal rites and consider the identity and background of those who administered the rite. Next the recipients of the sacrament themselves are examined, and the question of infant versus adult baptism is explored. In conclusion, I look at the church's success in administering the sacrament to the laity by exploring lay attitudes to baptism.

RITES OF INITIATION

In the absence of surviving liturgical texts it is difficult to determine which baptismal rite was used in England in the pre-Viking period. The Irish missionaries to Northumbria presumably brought service books with them. The form of the baptismal rite found in the earliest surviving Irish mass book, the Stowe Missal (datable to the early ninth century),[11] although basically Roman, had a number of Gallican features.[12] Sacramentaries and missals including the Gallican rite may also have been introduced into other parts of England by Merovingian ecclesiastics such as Birinus and Agilbert, bishops of the West Saxons.[13] It is generally presumed that

5. *Liber beati Gregorii papae*, c.29, ed. B. Colgrave, *The Earliest Life of Gregory the Great* (1968).
6. Boniface, *Epistola*, 33, ed. M. Tangl, *Die Briefe des heiligen Bonifatius und Lullus* (1916).
7. Bede, *HE* iii. 7. Compare Boniface, *Epistola*, 23.
8. Theodore, *Penitential*, ii, iv. 3, ed. P. W. Finsterwalder, *Die Canones Theodori Cantuariensis und ihre Überlieferungsformen* (1929), 285-334.
9. Bede, *HE* iv. 13.
10. Bede, *Liber homeliarum*, i. 16, ed. D. Hurst, CCSL, 122 (1955). See further below, pp. 178-9.
11. G. F. Warner, *The Stowe Missal*, Henry Bradshaw Society, 31-2 (1906-15), ii, xxxii-xxxvi.
12. J. Stevenson, 'Introduction', in *The Liturgy and Ritual of the Celtic Church*, ed. F. E. Warren (2nd edn., 1987), liv.
13. Bede, *HE* iii. 7. The differences between the Gallican and Gelasian initiation rites have been discussed by J. D. C. Fisher, *Christian Initiation: Baptism in the Medieval West* (1965), 47-57.

Augustine instituted the Roman rite at Canterbury and that books containing that service were brought to England by the Roman missionaries. Such books continued to be brought into England by later Anglo-Saxon ecclesiastics such as Benedict Biscop who visited Rome.[14] At the 747 Council of *Clofesho* it was directed that the baptismal rite should be performed according to the written exemplar which the English had obtained from the Roman church, but it is not possible to identify any one formulary which was being used.[15]

It does appear that the rite being administered among the Britons at the time of Augustine's arrival differed in some notable way from the Roman ritual with which the missionaries were familiar. At his second council with the British bishops, Augustine expressed his willingness to tolerate anything that the British did contrary to his own customs as long as they would keep Easter at the proper time, preach to the heathen in fellowship with the Roman mission, and complete the sacrament of baptism according to the rites of the holy Roman and apostolic church.[16] It is not known which aspect of the British baptismal ritual caused Augustine concern. It might have been that the British, together with the Irish, only immersed candidates once, not three times as in the Roman rite,[17] but this seems to be a difference in liturgical practice sufficiently insignificant to be encompassed in Gregory's recommendation to Augustine that he adopt any customs from the Gaulish or any other church of which he approved, rather than sticking rigidly to the Roman forms.[18] Alternatively, it is possible that the British failed in Augustine's eyes to complete the rite because they omitted the episcopal laying on of hands and unction with chrism, by which confirmation the Holy Spirit was conferred on the neophyte in the Roman rite.[19] As Margaret Pepperdene has argued, in the context of an evangelical mission, the correct – and full – execution of rites of Christian initiation upon the pagan was of paramount importance, and it seems more likely that it was the British failure to provide episcopal confirmation which concerned Augustine of Canterbury. He was not successful, however, in his attempt to persuade the British to participate in his mission to the Anglo-Saxons, nor is it known whether the British church conformed thereafter to the Roman initiatory rite.[20]

---

14. Bede, *HE* i. 29; Bede, *Historia Abbatum*, cc. 4, 6, ed. C. Plummer, *Venerabilis Baedae Opera Historica* (2 vols., 1896), 364-87. See Fisher, *Christian Initiation*, 78-9.
15. Council of *Clofesho*, AD 747, c.13, ed. A. W. Haddan and W. Stubbs, *Councils and Ecclesiastical Documents Relating to Great Britain and Ireland* (3 vols., 1869-78), iii, 362-76.
16. Bede, *HE* ii. 2.
17. Warren, *The Liturgy*, 216; M. Pepperdene, 'Baptism in the early British and Irish churches', *Irish Theological Quarterly*, xxii (1955), 110-23, at 117.
18. Bede, *HE* i. 27; see Meyvaert, 'Diversity within unity, a Gregorian theme', in *Benedict, Gregory, Bede and Others* (1977), vi, 157-9. Plummer pointed out (*Baedae Opera*, ii, 76) that Gregory did not in fact commit himself regarding the superiority of triple over single immersion.
19. Plummer, *Baedae Opera*, ii, 76, 382-3; Pepperdene, 'Baptism', 119.
20. Little is known about the form of the British baptismal liturgy; for one approach to the question see S. McKillop, 'A Romano-British baptismal liturgy?', in *The Early Church in Western Britain and Ireland*, ed. S. M. Pearce, BAR, Brit. series, 102 (1982), 35-48.

The attempts made in the eighth-century English councils to impose the uniform use of the Roman liturgy on all churches suggest that there was still at that time considerable diversity in liturgical practice between different English minsters, which makes it difficult to draw any broad conclusions about the form of any individual sacrament. Even where churches possessed the necessary liturgical books, they seem not always to have used them. Writing in 801, Alcuin wondered that Eanwald of York needed to ask him about the order and arrangement of the missal: 'Surely you have plenty of mass books according to the Roman rite? You have also enough of the larger sacramentaries of the old rite.'[21] Although no such sacramentary from York survives, it is possible to establish something of the nature of the ceremony administered by certain Anglo-Saxon priests in the context of the regular ministry to the laity.

The sources that are available, however, present certain problems. If a particular aspect of the initiation ritual is not mentioned, it does not necessarily mean that it was customary for that ceremony not to be performed. So, for example, the failure of any English text to mention the *pedilauium*, which the Stowe Missal placed before the communion of the newly baptized, does not necessarily mean that the practice of foot-washing was not followed by priests educated in an Irish or Gallican context. Similarly, where Stephanus reports that Wilfrid baptized 'in the name of the Lord', it need not be assumed that the bishop did not use the Trinitarian formula.[22] Nor, on the other hand, does the fact that Cuthbert's anonymous hagiographer (in a passage relating to that saint's ministry from the minster at Melrose) quoted Christ's instruction to his disciples to baptize in the name of the Father, Son and Holy Ghost from Matthew's gospel,[23] prove that Cuthbert used the same formula to initiate the population in the mountains around the River Teviot.[24]

Much of the best evidence for the nature of Anglo-Saxon baptismal rituals is to be derived not from saints' Lives but from the prescriptive literature of penitentials and from the canons of church councils, for the manner in which baptisms were performed was of considerable interest to ecclesiastical legislators in the early period.[25] These texts appear to indicate which aspects of the rite were being omitted or incorrectly executed, but it is unwise to assume that literature of this sort can provide an accurate picture of the liturgy as it was performed by individual clerics.

Various sources discuss the manner in which candidates were prepared for baptism. In the early church the catechumenate of an adult was a

---

21. Alcuin, *Epistola*, 226. Compare Ecgberht, *Dialogi*, c.14 (ed. Haddan and Stubbs, *Councils*, iii. 403-13), which appears to refer to the use of a Roman antiphonary and mass book at York, but see D. Bullough, 'Alcuin and the kingdom of heaven: Liturgy, theology and the Carolingian age', in *Carolingian Essays*, ed. U.-R. Blumenthal (1983), 1-69, at 4-10.
22. Stephanus, *Vita S. Wilfridi*, c.26, ed. B. Colgrave (1927).
23. Matthew, xxviii. 19.
24. *Vita S. Cuthberti*, ii, 5, ed. B. Colgrave, *Two Lives of Saint Cuthbert* (1940, 60-138).
25. See for example, Council of *Clofesho*, AD 747, cc. 9-10.

prolonged period of instruction, during which his desire for initiation was tested and his mode of life observed, before, once he was accepted as a fit member of the faith, he was purified by exorcism and fasting and permitted to proceed, at the appropriate season of Easter or Pentecost, to baptism itself.[26] As infant rather than adult baptism became more usual, this lengthy preparation was curtailed, but some elements of the primitive catechumenate were preserved in the early medieval rites.[27] Both Bede and the anonymous Whitby monk attested to a period of catechism undertaken by King Edwin and his followers before their baptism,[28] but no such preparation was mentioned by Bede in relation to the conversion of Æthelberht of Kent.[29] It is possible to envisage circumstances in which missionaries might have thought it more politic to proceed relatively swiftly with the rituals of initiation, and reserve the more thorough education of the neophytes to a later point, rather than risk the alienation of potentially hostile converts anxious for the outward forms of the ceremony.[30]

Bede's account of the catechism of Herebald, a member of John of Beverley's clergy injured in a riding accident, demonstrates that this preparatory instruction could be relatively prolonged; only when the young man's skull was completely healed was he baptized.[31] However, the office was performed in this instance by a bishop, and in view of what is known of the limitations of much ecclesiastical education in this period, it is more than likely that many other clerics were intellectually incapable of more than the most perfunctory of catechisms.[32] It was in fact the incompetence of the priest who had originally baptized Herebald, particularly his inability to learn the offices of catechism or baptism, that led John to decide to rebaptize him.[33]

Equally, if many baptisms were carried out by priests and bishops travelling away from their minsters to the villages of their dioceses, it is difficult to see how the preparation of candidates could have involved a prolonged period of fasting, exorcism and instruction, unless the clergy had been able to stay amongst their flock for weeks at a time. Nor can anything more than a token catechism have been given to those baptized on their deathbed or in some other emergency; the princes who escaped from Cædwalla's conquest of the Isle of Wight must, before their baptism, have been rather

---

26. J. Lynch, *Godparents and Kinship in Early Medieval Europe* (1986), 85-90.
27. Fisher, *Christian Initiation*, 5-11.
28. *Liber beati Gregorii*, c.15; Bede, *HE* ii. 14. Compare *ibid.*, iii. 7 and iv. 13.
29. Bede, *HE* i. 26.
30. For discussion of the appeal made by Christianity to the Anglo-Saxon nobility, see P. Wormald, 'Bede, "Beowulf" and the conversion of the Anglo-Saxon aristocracy', in *Bede and Anglo-Saxon England*, ed. R. T. Farrell, BAR, Brit. series, no. 46 (1978), 32-95, at 65-8; Clare Stancliffe, 'Kings and conversion: some comparisons between the Roman mission to England and Patrick's to Ireland', *Frühmittelalterliche Studien*, xiv (1980), 59-94, at 69-76.
31. Bede, *HE* v. 6.
32. Compare Bede, *Epistola ad Ecgberhtum*, § 5, ed. Plummer, *Baedae Opera*, ii, 405-23.
33. See further below, p. 189.

sketchily instructed by Abbot Cyneberht in the 'mysteries of the Christian faith', since their execution was imminent.[34]

The baptismal rite as exercised in early Anglo-Saxon England seems to have included the exorcism of the candidate; accounts of this practice in the sources echo the vocabulary of the known rituals. As John of Beverley catechized his cleric, Herebald, he blew out on his face, presumably to exorcize him;[35] in his commentary on I Samuel, Bede declared that it was right for teachers to drive out impure spirits from the hearts of their hearers, by blowing out upon them and catechizing.[36] Similarly, Guthlac's baptism of the young man tormented by devils, who was brought to him, involved blowing into the youth's face the breath of healing and so driving away the power of the evil spirit.[37]

At the font, candidates for baptism were required (or, in the case of infants, their sponsors were obliged on their behalf) to renounce the devil and all his works, and to bear witness to their intention to follow a new life by stating their belief in God and the Trinity. One of the fires which Fursa was shown in his vision of hell was supposed to represent falsehood, 'when we do not fulfil our promise to renounce Satan and all his works as we undertook to do at our baptism'.[38] The centrality of the credal declaration in the baptismal ceremony is apparent from Stephanus's account of the conversion of the pagan South Saxons, who 'deserted idolatry and made confession of faith in almighty God'.[39] Compare Pope Zacharias's complaint to Boniface about those false priests who did not even

> know the sacred words which any catechumen old enough to use his reason can learn and understand, nor do they expect them to be uttered by those whom they are to baptize, as for instance the renunciation of Satan and so forth.[40]

The form of ceremony used at the actual moment of baptism itself cannot be determined. Presumably those who were initiated in rivers (such as the Northumbrians baptized by Paulinus)[41] were totally immersed in the water, but the sources do not specify precisely where most baptisms were performed, nor do they indicate how many times candidates were immersed.[42] Phrases such as 'having been washed in the waters of the fountain of salvation',[43] or 'he washed him in the water of the sacred fountain'[44] are open to a variety of interpretations and could encompass any

---

34. Bede, *HE* iv. 16.
35. Bede, *HE* v. 6.
36. Bede, *In I Samuhelem*, iii, xvii, 53, ed. D. Hurst, CCSL, 119 (1962), 5-272; quoted by B. Colgrave and R. A. B. Mynors, *Bede's Ecclesiastical History of the English People* (1969), 468, n.1.
37. Felix, *Vita S. Guthlaci*, c.41 (ed. B. Colgrave, 1956).
38. Bede, *HE* iii. 19.
39. Stephanus, *Vita S. Wilfridi*, c.41.
40. Boniface, *Epistola*, 80.
41. Bede, *HE* ii. 14.
42. See Bullough, 'Alcuin and the kingdom of heaven', 48.
43. Bede, *HE* iii. 23.
44. Felix, *Vita S. Guthlaci*, c.41.

one of the four methods of baptism: submersion, immersion, affusion or aspersion.[45] At the 816 council of Chelsea, priests were directed not to pour water on the heads of infants, but to immerse them in the font after the example of Christ's own baptism in the Jordan,[46] but it is not known whether this instruction was obeyed. At the moment of baptism the minister uttered the sentence, 'Baptizo te in nomine patris et filii et spiritus sancti.' This was considered by many commentators to constitute the most crucial part of the entire ritual, and those who had not been baptized in the name of the Trinity were deemed to have been incorrectly initiated and to need rebaptism. A letter from Pope Zacharias to Boniface referred to a synod of the English church at which it was decreed that whoever was baptized without the invocation of the Trinity did not receive the sacrament of initiation;[47] such persons were to be reinitiated, but baptisms performed by heretics in the name of the Trinity were not to be repeated.[48] While Bede stated in his commentary on the Acts of the Apostles that it was a rule of the church that the faithful should be baptized in the name of the Holy Trinity, he argued (quoting the authority of Ambrose and of Romans vi. 3) that baptism in the name of Christ would also be valid, because in the naming of one member of the Trinity all were designated.[49]

After baptism many candidates were reclothed in white garments as a symbol of their new life, which, if they were initiated at one of the canonical seasons, they continued to wear for the octave of the feast.[50] Cædwalla, who resigned his kingdom and went to Rome to be baptized, was said to have died while still wearing white;[51] Asser, describing the baptism of the Viking king, Guthrum, after the battle of Edington in 878, referred to the formal unbinding of the chrisom on the eighth day after Guthrum's sponsor, King Alfred, had received him from the font.[52] At some point in the initiation ceremony the candidate was anointed with consecrated oil by which the Holy Spirit was conferred upon him. In the Gelasian ritual there were two anointings: one performed by the priest after the baptism on the candidate's head before he went on to make his first communion, and the other administered on the forehead by a bishop at the end of the ceremony.[53] In the ritual preserved in the Stowe Missal, however, there was only one unction, performed by the officiating priest and clearly designed to fulfil the functions of both the Gelasian unctions, rendering the ceremony complete without the presence of a bishop. In either case, the completed baptism was followed by the celebration of a mass, at which the

---

45. See below, p. 183.
46. Council of Chelsea, AD 816, c.11 (Haddan and Stubbs, *Councils*, iii. 579-84).
47. Boniface, *Epistola*, 80.
48. Boniface, *Epistola*, 68; see below, pp. 189-90.
49. *Expositio actuum apostolorum*, x, 48, ed. M. L. W. Laistner, CCSL, 121 (1983), 3-99.
50. Plummer, *Baedae Opera*, ii, 280.
51. Bede, *HE* , v. 7. Compare *ibid.*, ii, 14.
52. Asser, *Life of King Alfred*, c.56, ed. W. H. Stevenson, *Asser's Life of King Alfred* (1904).
53. Fisher, *Christian Initiation*, 21-4, 84-5.

neophytes (infants as well as adults) made their first communion.[54]

The final episcopal unction, without which initiation was not complete, seems in early Anglo-Saxon England to have been generally performed in a ceremony separate from baptism, except in circumstances when a bishop was already present. The full rite was presumably executed at the royal baptisms described by Bede on the conversion of the people of Kent, Northumbria, or the West Saxons, or on the occasion reported by Stephanus when Wilfrid was out riding fulfilling the duties of his bishopric and 'baptizing and also confirming the people by the laying on of hands.'[55] Theodore clearly saw baptism and confirmation as separate rituals, although he implied that confirmation was frequently not provided: 'we believe no one is complete in baptism without the confirmation of a bishop, yet we do not despair.'[56] In his letter to Ecgberht, Bede drew the bishop's attention to the importance of 'performing the rites of holy baptism wherever opportunity arises',[57] but he laid greater stress on the fact that there were many areas where a bishop was lacking 'to confirm the baptized by the laying on of hands.'[58] Bede emphasized this point in order to demonstrate that the spiritual health of the Northumbrian laity was in danger:

> If we believe and confess that any advantage is conferred on the faithful by the laying on of hands, by which the Holy Spirit is received, it follows on the contrary that the same advantage is absent from those who have lacked the laying on of hands.[59]

Angenendt has argued that one reason why the canons of eighth- and ninth-century Frankish councils (which influenced English synods) laid such stress on the importance of annual visitation by bishops to all parts of their diocese was that their authors hoped thereby to increase the opportunities for the baptized laity to receive confirmation.[60]

What is certain is that the baptismal ceremony involved the use of water, and that the grace of salvation which was held to be acquired by means of the sacrament was invoked upon the candidate in the name of one or more members of the Trinity. What other elements of the Roman or Gallican liturgies were also regularly included in the baptismal ceremonies performed in early Anglo-Saxon England cannot be readily determined, nor is it clear at precisely what moment candidates were deemed to receive the Holy Spirit.[61]

---

54. *ibid.*, 20.
55. Stephanus, *Vita S. Wilfridi*, c.18.
56. Theodore, *Penitential*, ii, iv. 5. Compare *ibid.*, ii, iv. 8.
57. Bede, *Epistola ad Ecgberhtum*, § 5, ed. Plummer, *Baedae Opera*, ii, 405-23.
58. *ibid.*, § 7.
59. *ibid.*, § 8.
60. A. Angenendt, 'Bonifatius und das Sacramentum initiationis', *Römische Quartalscrift*, lxxii (1977), 133-83, at 150-8.
61. See S. A. Keefe, 'An unknown response from the archiepiscopal province of Sens to Charlemagne's circulatory inquiry on baptism', *Revue Bénédictine*, xcvi (1986), 48-93, at 81-2.

THE SETTING OF BAPTISM

The early Roman baptismal rite, which ended with the episcopal laying on of hands and the anointing of the candidates with oil, was designed to be celebrated at the seasons of Easter and Pentecost by a bishop in his episcopal church;[62] priests were first given the right to baptize only in a Roman synod of AD 402.[63] But as the number of the faithful grew, and (especially in northern Europe) where dioceses were larger and access to the episcopal church more difficult, bishops allowed the establishment of baptismal fonts in the public churches of the towns and in rural churches, known as *baptisteria plebes* or *ecclesiae baptismales*.[64] These churches (which were subject to the authority of the local bishop from whom they received the chrism and to whom they owed a number of ecclesiastical renders) were served by communities of clergy, who were pastorally responsible for the surrounding villages in their diocese. These might also supply clergy to the lesser churches in their area, oratories or aristocratic proprietary chapels, while preserving for themselves the sole right to a font.[65] The parochial rights of the Italian baptismal churches were fiercely defended and received some support from the Frankish kings, whose capitularies helped to maintain the old pastoral system; Pippin's Italian Capitulary of 790 directed that baptismal churches ought in no way to be held by laymen.[66] Within the old Frankish kingdom it proved less easy to control lay domination, but attempts were made here also to restrict the rights of baptism to churches under episcopal control; the Council of Chalon of 813, for example, directed that parents were to pay tithes at the churches where their infants were baptized.[67]

In early Anglo-Saxon England, however, there do not seem to have been special baptismal churches.[68] Cuthbert, archbishop of Canterbury (740–60), was said to have built a new church to the east of Christ Church, dedicated to St John the Baptist, which was to serve as the burial-place of the archbishops as well as a baptistery.[69] The crypt at Repton where members of the Mercian royal family were buried may also have served a dual purpose as a baptistery.[70] The coincidence of baptism and burial was a

---

62. Fisher, *Christian Initiation*, 22–3, 26–8.
63. J. D. Mansi, *Sacrorum Conciliorum Nova et Amplissima Collectio*, 31 vols. (Florence, 1759–98), iii, 1137, c.7. Various Frankish councils reaffirmed the rights of priests to baptize, for example the Council of Ver, AD 755, cc. 7–8, ed. A. Boretius, MGH, *Capitularia Regum Francorum*, i (1883), 32–7; see M. Aubrun, *La Paroisse en France des origines au XVe siècle* (1986), 34.
64. C. E. Boyd, *Tithes and Parishes in Medieval Italy: the Historical Roots of a Modern Problem* (1952), 50; Aubrun, *La Paroisse*, 28–9.
65. Boyd, *Tithes and Parishes*, 50–7.
66. Capitulary, AD 790, ed. Boretius, MGH, *Capitularia*, i, 200–1; Boyd, *Tithes and Parishes*, 58; N. Brooks, *The Early History of the Church of Canterbury* (1984), 188–9.
67. Council of Chalon, AD 813, c.19, ed. A. Werminghoff, MGH, *Concilia Aevi Karolini*, i (1906), 273–85; Aubrun, *La Paroisse*, 34.
68. See John Blair's chapter below p. 250.
69. Brooks, *Church of Canterbury*, 51.
70. M. Biddle, 'Archaeology, architecture and the cult of saints', in *The Anglo-Saxon Church: Papers . . . in Honour of Dr H. M. Taylor*, ed. L. A. S. Butler and R. K. Morris (CBA Res. Rep. 60, 1986), 1–31, at 16.

common one, derived from the Pauline interpretation of baptism as not merely rebirth but resurrection.[71] Early Christian baptismal architecture thus frequently included images of death and resurrection as well as of water, and early baptisteries were often designed to resemble mausolea.[72]

There are few surviving examples of Anglo-Saxon baptisteries. Archaeology has revealed two: at Potterne in Wiltshire and at Barton-on-Humber.[73] There are also examples of minster churches built beside Roman baths, such as Bath and Leicester, where the public bath buildings could have been used for administering baptism by immersion.[74] Wells and sacred springs may also have served as suitable sites for the baptismal ritual:[75] the east end of the church at St Paul-in-the-Bail, Lincoln, pointed towards a stone well which also lay within the forum and may have had baptismal functions.[76] There are a few later Anglo-Saxon church dedications to St John the Baptist, but none of the known seventh-century dedications is to this saint,[77] and none of the later examples is associated with cathedrals. It thus appears that English bishops did not seek to control baptism as rigidly as did their Frankish and Italian counterparts (the majority of whose episcopal complexes contained either a church dedicated to St John the Baptist or a free-standing baptistery); instead the minster church played the central role in England in the administration of baptism.

This can be demonstrated from the later evidence relating to the collection of the chrism – the holy oil for baptism and extreme unction – received by the minster from the bishop in return for a payment of chrism-money each Maundy Thursday. For Kent, for example, the Domesday Monachorum provides a list of those churches entitled to collect the chrism, including Dover, Folkestone, Lyminge and St Augustine's, Canterbury, all known to be pre-Viking minsters;[78] as Nicholas Brooks suggested, 'their annual payment of chrism-money to the archbishop is best understood as a jealously maintained relic of an age when the Kentish "monasteries" were true baptismal churches, taking a dominant role in the pastoral work of the diocese.'[79] The actual provision of baptism was not necessarily centralized in these churches.[80] In the eleventh and twelfth centuries the mother-churches of Kent received payment for the distribution of the chrism to

---

71. Romans, vi. 3-4.
72. J. G. Davies, *The Architectural Setting of Baptism* (1962), 2-18; R. Krautheimer, 'Introduction to an "Iconography of medieval architecture"', in *Studies in Early Christian, Medieval, and Renaissance Art* (1971), 115-50, at 131-41.
73. R. K. Morris, *The Church in British Archaeology*, CBA Res. Rep. 47 (1983), 67; H. M. Taylor and J. Taylor, *Anglo-Saxon Architecture* (3 vols., 1965-78), ii, 734; iii, 990, 1064-5; E. Fernie, *The Architecture of the Anglo-Saxons* (1983), 141-3.
74. John Blair's chapter, below p. 245.
75. R. K. Morris, *Churches in the Landscape* (1989), 88.
76. J. Blair, 'Minster churches in the landscape', in *Anglo-Saxon Settlements*, ed. D. Hooke (1988), 35-58, at 51.
77. Morris, *The Church in British Archaeology*, 35-8.
78. David Douglas, *The Domesday Monachorum of Christ Church Canterbury* (1944), 77-8.
79. Brooks, *Church of Canterbury*, 189. See also F. Barlow, *The English Church 1000-1066* (2nd edn, 1979), 179-80.
80. Blair, 'Minster churches', 51.

their daughter-churches,[81] and there is similar evidence from Hereford-
shire, where at least one daughter-church, at Hampton Wafer, received the
chrism not from the bishop but from its mother-church at Leominster.[82]

In the absence of sites readily identifiable as baptisteries, it can be
difficult to determine where baptismal ceremonies were regularly
performed. Some of the mass baptisms of conversion described by Bede
took place in the open air, the candidates being immersed in a river.
Paulinus, for example, baptized the crowds who flocked to the royal
residence at Yeavering in the River Glen, and in Deira he baptized many
in the River Swale beside the town of Catterick, 'for they were not yet able
to build chapels or baptisteries there in the earliest days of the church.'[83]
The initiation of newly converted kings and nobles was sometimes
performed in specially built churches, however. Eadwine was baptized at
York in 'the church of St Peter the Apostle which he had hastily built of
wood while he was a catechumen and under instruction before he received
baptism.'[84] Beyond the initial conversion period, it is not clear how often
baptism was administered at minster churches, rather than being performed
by travelling priests nearer to the dwellings of lay candidates.

Some parents did apparently take their infants to their local minster
church to have them initiated into the Christian faith, as, it may be
surmised, did St Guthlac's on the eighth day after the child's birth.[85]
However, few fonts are known to have survived from the Anglo-Saxon
period, although decorated Romanesque fonts are common,[86] and there
does survive a large number of undecorated tub fonts, which could as easily
date from before as from after the Conquest. The floor of the western annex
of the early eleventh-century church at Barton-on-Humber preserved the
base of a font,[87] and their inscriptions identify the fonts at Potterne
(Wiltshire) and Little Billing (Northamptonshire) as Anglo-Saxon.[88] It has
also been argued that the medieval font at Wells, a single drum-shaped
block of stone decorated externally with eight bays of arcading, was
originally Anglo-Saxon, although it was recut and 'modernized' later in the
Middle Ages, possibly c. 1200 (from which time dates the plinth on which
the bowl stands).[89] There is more doubt about whether the font at
Deerhurst in Gloucestershire is in fact pre-Conquest, and whether the

81. T. Tatton-Brown, 'The churches of Canterbury diocese in the 11th century', in
    Minsters and Parish Churches, ed. J. Blair (1988), 105-18, at 105.
82. B. Kemp, 'Some aspects of the *parochia* of Leominster in the 12th century', *ibid.*,
    83-95, at 92-3.
83. Bede, *HE* ii. 14.
84. *ibid.* It is possible that Blæcca, the *praefectus* of Lincoln, was baptized in the
    stone church which Paulinus had built in that town: *ibid.*, ii. 16.
85. Felix, *Vita S. Guthlaci*, c.10.
86. C. J. Bond, 'Church and parish in Norman Worcestershire', in *Minsters and
    Parish Churches*, ed. Blair, 119-58, at 149-50; Blair, 'Introduction', *ibid.*, 13, 15.
87. Fernie, *The Architecture*, 141.
88. Taylor and Taylor, *Anglo-Saxon Architecture*, iii, 1064-6.
89. W. Rodwell, *Wells Cathedral: Excavations and Discoveries* (3rd edn., 1987),
    19-20.

bowl, decorated with vine-scroll and trumpet-spirals, was originally designed for baptismal use or was only later turned over and hollowed out. The two portions were not designed together; the stem was probably originally part of a cross-shaft.[90] It is equally possible that other vessels were used by the Anglo-Saxons for baptism besides stone fonts. Romano-British lead tanks from Icklingham and Walesby have, from their decoration, been associated with baptism.[91] Could the English have used stone tanks or cisterns for baptism by affusion, where the candidate stands in a large container and water is poured over the head so that it streams down the body?[92] Alternatively, if the more commonly used methods were immersion (where the head alone is dipped in the water), or aspersion (when water is sprinkled on the head as in the modern rite), relatively small, domestic containers such as bronze or silver bowls could have been reserved for baptism.

All the accounts of baptisms recorded in the narrative sources relate to ceremonies performed away from the presiding priest's minster church. Unless it was the habit in these circumstances to baptize people by total immersion, then it must be presumed either that these ministers carried vessels which could serve as fonts, in the same way that travelling priests are known to have had portable altars, or that some domestic vessel was borrowed from a lay household for the occasion. The local countryside could not always be relied upon to supply suitable hollow stones such as that commandeered by Rumwold for his own baptism.[93]

THE MINISTERS OF BAPTISM

A significant aspect of the regular pastoral duty of all active clergy was the routine administration of the sacrament of baptism, not merely to new converts or to the urban laity, but to the mass of the adult rural population and their newborn children. Churchmen responsible for the cure of souls were held to have a continuing obligation to ensure that each succeeding generation was correctly admitted to the body of the church. In the text of the foundation charter for Breedon-on-the-Hill (Leicestershire) – which admittedly survives only in the form of a record entered in the twelfth-century register of Peterborough Abbey – the administration of baptism was singled out as one of the tasks (together with teaching the people assigned to him) which were to be performed by the 'priest of good repute', whom the community of *Medeshamstede* were to appoint to Breedon on their foundation of a minster there.[94] In this instance it would seem to have

---

90. Taylor and Taylor, *Anglo-Saxon Architecture*, i, 206; iii, 1064.
91. Thomas, *Christianity*, 220-5. D. J. Watts, 'Circular lead tanks and their significance for Romano-British Christianity', *Antiq. J.* lxviii (1988), 210-22, suggests that these tanks were used in baptism for the foot-washing rite.
92. Davies, *The Architectural Setting*, 23.
93. Above, p. 171.
94. S 1803; F. M. Stenton, 'Medeshamstede and its colonies', in *Preparatory to Anglo-Saxon England*, ed. D. M. Stenton (1970), 179-92, at 182-4.

been the spiritual needs of the local population that determined the creation of a new minster and the function it was to serve.

The church could only fulfil its parochial obligations to the laity, and particularly its sacramental duties, provided that there were sufficient trained clergy competent to administer the rites correctly. In Bede's time, there was clearly a shortage of ministers to serve the lay population. Writing to Bishop Ecgberht in 734 Bede urged that priests be ordained and teachers trained who could preach in the villages, celebrate the holy sacraments 'and especially perform the rites of holy baptism'.[95] There were seen to be serious consequences if churchmen omitted to administer the sacrament regularly: Anglo-Saxon commentators did not doubt that everlasting damnation awaited those who died unbaptized. Boniface was sure that hell was crowded with the offspring of English nuns, adulterously conceived and murdered by their mothers at birth, but it is unclear whether it was their illegitimacy or their lack of baptism (or both) which would have condemned them to such a fate.[96] On the other hand, the author of the Whitby Life of St Gregory was certain that those blessed people who, having been slain at the battle of Hatfield Chase, returned later in splendour to view their earthly bodies had undoubtedly been baptized.[97]

There were pragmatic as well as theological reasons for ecclesiastical legislators to attempt to ensure that baptism be correctly and regularly administered, since the non-performance of this aspect of priestly ministry would constitute a public failure in the church's pastoral responsibilities. Once persuaded of the spiritual benefits to be obtained by their own baptism, the laity were likely to react angrily to an individual or community of clergy whose negligence permitted their new children to die unbaptized. In lay eyes, this was surely a much more serious failing than clerical neglect of other sacraments or the inadequacies of ecclesiastical education. It may have been because of a scarcity of Anglo-Saxon clergy to initiate their children that the laity proved so ready to accept the ministrations of wandering Irish clergy.[98] The validity of the ordination of such priests was scarcely of concern to parents who feared their infant might die unbaptized. If the bishops were genuinely worried about the credibility of this aspect of their ministry in the eyes of the laity, this may serve in part to explain the insistence on the correct administration of baptism in the canons of church councils. This was expressed most forcibly at the 816 Council of Chelsea, where it was directed that while priests were not to seek greater duties than those laid on them by their bishops, this should not apply to baptism. Instead priests everywhere were charged to ensure

95. Bede, *Epistola ad Ecgberhtum*, § 5. Compare Council of *Clofesho*, AD 747, c.9.
96. Boniface, *Epistola*, 73 (Tangl, *Die Briefe*, 151).
97. *Liber beati Gregorii*, c.19. Compare also Gregory, *Moralia in Iob*, ix, xxi. 32, ed. M. Adriaen, CCSL, 143 (1979), quoted by Colgrave, *The Earliest Life*, 150-2, n.76, which argued for the damnation of those who died without having first been freed from original sin through the healing sacrament of baptism.
98. Attempts were made at church councils to prevent Irish clergy from ministering to the laity and administering sacraments of baptism and communion; compare Council of Chelsea, AD 816, c.5, and Ecgberht, *Dialogi*, c.9.

that they nowhere refused to perform the ministry of baptism, and those who failed through negligence were directed to cease from their ministry until corrected by their bishop.[99] Similar sentiments may account for the inclusion in secular law codes of statements of the punishments due to priests who failed to perform the sacrament of baptism when required. The laws of King Wihtred of Kent directed that any priest who neglected the baptism of a sick person, or who was so drunk he was unable to perform it, should abstain from all ministry until reconciled to his bishop.[100] The Penitential of Archbishop Theodore also ordered the deposition of any priest who refused to baptize a weak infant or a sick adult commended to him before that person's death.[101] More seems to be at stake here than the non-performance of a priestly duty; one senses a tough public relations exercise designed to clean up this aspect of the church's image, which in Kent, at least, had royal support.

Each of these passages assumes that baptism was to be performed by priests. It was indeed specifically listed at the 747 Council of *Clofesho* among the duties pertaining to priests,[102] and a passage in Bede's *Historia Ecclesiastica* implies that the sacrament could not be administered by *any* member of a religious community. Describing the bringing of Christianity to the Isle of Wight after its conquest by Cædwalla, Bede related how Wilfrid gave that portion of the island which he had received from the king to 'one of his *clerici* named Beornwine, who was his sister's son, assigning to him a priest called Hiddila, to teach the word and administer baptism to all who sought salvation'.[103] According to Theodore, the performance of baptism was not an exclusively priestly function, for his Penitential permitted deacons to baptize,[104] but this privilege did not extend to all religious. Theodore also decreed that 'if anyone who is not ordained performs baptism through temerity, he is cut off from the church and shall never be ordained.'[105]

Whether they were priests or deacons, there is every reason to believe that those who administered baptism to the laity were members of minster communities. As I have argued elsewhere, there is no evidence that any sort of pastoral work was ever performed in the earlier Anglo-Saxon period by clerics independent of both episcopal and monastic communities.[106] The ministry of pastoral workers whose activities are described in the

---

99. Council of Chelsea, AD 816, c.11. Compare also the less explicit statements made at the Council of *Clofesho*, AD 747, c.10, and the 786 legatine Synod, c.2, ed. E. Dümmler, MGH, *Epistolae Karolini Aevi*, ii (1895), 19-29.
100. Laws of King Wihtred, c.6 (Liebermann, *Die Gesetze der Angelsachsen* (3 vols., 1903-16), i, 12-14).
101. Theodore, *Penitential*, i, ix. 7; i, xiv. 28.
102. Council of *Clofesho*, AD 747, c.9.
103. Bede, *HE* iv. 16.
104. Theodore, *Penitential*, ii, ii. 16. Compare Council of Orléans, AD 511, c.12, ed. F. Maassen, MGH, *Concilia Aevi Merovingici* (1893), 1-14; Council of Orléans, AD 533, c.16 (*ibid.*, 61-5), which both refer to the administration of baptism by deacons.
105. Theodore, *Penitential*, i, ix. 11.
106. S. Foot, 'Parochial ministry in early Anglo-Saxon England: the role of monastic communities', *Studies in Church History*, xxvi (1989), 43-54, at 48-9.

narrative sources can always be seen to have been based round a particular minster. When Cedd was proselytizing the people of the East Saxons, he 'established churches in various places' in which were placed the priests and deacons the bishop ordained to help him with preaching and the administration of baptism.[107] Similarly, it was as a member of the community at Melrose that Cuthbert was said to have been much occupied with preaching to the people in the surrounding mountain area, and also baptizing them in the name of the Trinity.[108] In fact, the right to baptize was one of the privileges, together with burial, which was jealously guarded by English mother-churches in the eleventh century, relics of their former minster status.[109]

THE RECIPIENTS OF THE SACRAMENT

By the late sixth century, it is clear that in the Roman church the subjects of initiation were normally infants, and the baptismal liturgy preserved in the Gelasian Sacramentary was patently constructed with the needs of the very young in mind.[110] A different approach was required in the mission setting of early Anglo-Saxon England.[111] Augustine's candidates were adults who could make their own professions of faith but who would also ideally need a longer and more comprehensive period of preparation than the diluted form of the catechumenate found in the *Gelasianum*.[112] In these circumstances, very different from those with which he or his followers might have been familiar in Italy, Augustine encountered a number of practical problems. Among these was the question of baptizing adults, in particular whether he were permitted to baptize a pregnant woman.[113] Similar anxieties beset Boniface in the mission field: several of his letters to the pope concerned the proper administration of the baptismal rite to adults as well as to children.[114]

Since baptism represented the outward and visible sign which marked the inward spiritual acceptance of the Christian faith by a new believer, the administration of the sacrament was always an important public ceremony. This was particularly true when the ritual was celebrated in the context of a people's renunciation of paganism. In the surviving accounts of the successful evangelization of the English kingdoms, much stress is laid on the fact that those kings who were the first objects of the missionaries' attentions made their declaration of faith in Christ not in secret but

---

107. Bede, *HE* iii. 22.
108. *Vita S. Cuthberti*, ii. 5-6.
109. Blair, 'Minster churches', 50; and J. Blair, 'Introduction', in *Minsters and Parish Churches*, ed. J. Blair, 1-19, at 19, n.84.
110. Fisher, *Christian Initiation*, 3-11.
111. Lynch, *Godparents*, 242-3.
112. Fisher, *Christian Initiation*, 5-7.
113. Bede, *HE* i. 27.
114. See, for example, Pope Gregory's letters answering Boniface's questions: Boniface, *Epistolae*, nos. 17, 18, 25, 26.

ceremonially performed in full view of their people.[115] Eadwine of Northumbria, indeed, elected to consult with his chief men whether to accept the faith, so that if they agreed they 'might all be consecrated together in the waters of life'.[116] The public baptism of a king and his household might then inspire others of the king's subjects to follow suit, although whether they were motivated by love of God or loyalty to their ruler is uncertain.[117] Wilfrid's biographer reported that after the conversion of the king of the South Saxons, Æthelwalh, 'many thousands of pagans of both sexes were baptized in one day . . . . They deserted idolatry and made confession of faith in almighty God some of them willingly and some being compelled by the king's command.'[118]

It must have proved difficult in the early stages of the introduction of Christianity to find enough priests to baptize the large crowds of converts reported in the saints' Lives. According to Bede, after Wilfrid had baptized the king of the South Saxons and his ealdormen and *gesiths*, four priests initiated the rest 'either then or later on',[119] but in some areas the baptism of the rest of the population may have been effected very much later. Certainly this proved to be the case during the Frankish evangelization of Saxony and Frisia. The canons of early ninth-century Frankish councils indicate that the extension of catholicism into these areas had greatly overstretched the resources of the church, and that outside the cities there was a real shortage of priests to administer any sacraments, among which baptism in particular was singled out.[120]

Beyond the conversion period in Anglo-Saxon England, it is impossible to determine when the performance of infant baptism may have become the norm. Its practice must have varied in different areas according to the extent and speed of their Christianization and the availability of sufficient clergy to perform the rite. Many texts, however, appear to assume that the usual candidates for initiation were children. In his commentary on Mark, Bede stated that parents were accustomed to speak the *fides* and *confessio* for their infants at the font in order to deliver them from the devil, with the implication that infant baptism was usual.[121] The compilers of the canons of the legatine council of 786 also appear to have assumed that infant baptism was the norm, directing that those who acted as sponsors

---

115. For discussion of the importance of kings as agents of conversion, see M. Richter, 'Practical aspects of the conversion of the Anglo-Saxons', in *Irland und di Christenheit: Bibelstudien und Mission*, ed. P. Ní Chatháin and M. Richter (1987), 362–76, at 363–7.
116. Bede, *HE* ii. 13. A. Angenendt, 'The conversion of the Anglo-Saxons considered against the background of the early medieval mission', *Settimane . . . di studi sull'alto medioevo*, xxxii (1986), 747–92, at 748–9.
117. Compare Bede, *HE* ii. 5. See Stancliffe, 'Kings and conversion', 71–3.
118. Stephanus, *Vita S. Wilfridi*, c.41.
119. Bede, *HE* iv. 13.
120. P. Cramer, 'Baptism and change to the twelfth century' (unpubl. Ph.D. thesis, Univ. of Sheffield, 1983), 142–3; compare Council of Paris, AD 829, c.49, ed. A. Werminghoff, MGH, *Concilia Aevi Karolini*, i, ii (1908), 605–80, and Council of Aachen, AD 836, c.16 (*ibid.*, 704–67).
121. Bede, *In Marci Evangelium Expositio*, ii, vii. 29, lines 1419–23, ed. D. Hurst, CCSL, 120 (1960), 431–648; quoted by Lynch, *Godparents*, 243.

for children (*paruuli*) at the font and spoke for them renouncing Satan and all his works, should know the Creed and be able to teach this and the Lord's prayer to their godchildren when they were older.[122]

Several of the canons of Theodore's Penitential, clearly considering infant baptism to be ideal, appointed penalties for its non-performance: if the parents were responsible for failing to have a child who died in infancy baptized, a penance of one year was imposed; but should the child have been as old as three at its death and still unbaptized, a period of three years' penance was prescribed.[123] The laws of King Ine were similarly harsh to parents who failed to have their children baptized: if a child had still to be baptized after thirty days, thirty shillings' compensation was to be paid, but should it die without baptism, 'he is to compensate for it with all that he possesses.'[124] As has already been shown, priests could as often be to blame for the omission of baptisms. Theodore directed that 'if an infant that is weak and is a pagan has been recommended to a presbyter for baptism and dies unbaptized, the presbyter shall be deposed.'[125] It was generally held that unbaptized children would suffer the eternal torments of hell, for the report of the vision of a monk preserved with the Boniface correspondence refers to the presence in the penitential pits of a great multitude of mourning children who had died without baptism under Bishop Daniel.[126] But Bede took a rather more humane attitude, arguing that there was a lesser hell reserved for unbaptized infants.[127]

If it is accepted that from the later seventh century onwards baptism was generally (if not exclusively) given either to infants or to adults *in extremis*, it is plain that the sacrament cannot have been performed solely at the canonical seasons of Easter and Pentecost, despite the fact that the legatine council of 786 urged that it be administered at other times of year only in case of need. Without taking his statement too literally, Daniel's description in a letter to Boniface of 'the daily baptism of the children of believing Christians' as the 'purification of each one from the uncleanliness and guilt in which the whole world was once involved',[128] does imply that the bishop saw baptism as a continually administered rite, not one that was specific to particular times of year.

However, whatever such churchmen may have considered to be ideal, it cannot be assumed that within a finite period after the conversion of a kingdom's ruler the majority of adults in the area had also received baptism, and that thereafter baptisms were mainly the initiation of children

122. Legatine Synod AD 786, c.2.
123. Theodore, *Penitential*, i, xiv. 29. To this last injunction, the compiler of the Penitential added the statement that Theodore had given this decision at a certain time because it happened to be referred to him, which implies that however much infant baptism was the ideal, it was often not performed.
124. Laws of Ine, c.2, 2.1 (Liebermann, *Die Gesetze*, i, 88-123).
125. Theodore, *Penitential*, i, xiv. 28.
126. Boniface, *Epistola*, 115.
127. Bede, *In cantica canticorum*, prologue, ed. D. Hurst, CCSL, 119B (1983), 167-375; quoted by Cramer, 'Baptism and change', 223.
128. Boniface, *Epistola*, 23.

born to Christian parents. There is a good deal of evidence that numerous adults, particularly those living in rural areas, continued to lack baptism well into the nominally Christian period. Theodore's Penitential addresses the possibility that many adults may not have received baptism. In a separate section from those instructions relating to unbaptized children, he ordered the deposition of any priest who refused, because of the exertion of the journey, to travel to a sick person in order to baptize him, thus leaving the individual to die without receiving that sacrament.[129]

No less of a problem than that of those who missed initiation was the question of second or multiple baptism. Theodore apparently took a strong line, not only imposing penances on those who knowingly allowed themselves to be rebaptized, but also barring the twice-baptized from ordination 'unless some great necessity compels it'.[130] Yet, in other portions of his Penitential, he ordered the rebaptism of those lay people who had been baptized by ordained priests who were themselves not baptized; the recommendations as to whether such priests should also be reordained are equally contradictory.[131] The Dialogues of Ecgberht stated that baptism ought not to be performed more than once, even should the rite have been administered by one who was not canonically ordained.[132]

Bede, however, relates a story which reveals a quite different attitude. It concerns a young man, Herebald, at the time a member of the household of Bishop John of Beverley.[133] Herebald had been injured when racing a horse along the beach and he was being cared for by the bishop when he was asked if he had been baptized. Although Herebald was certain that he had been 'washed in the fountain of salvation for the remission of sins', John considered his baptism invalid:

> If you were baptized by that priest, you were not perfectly baptized for I know that when he was ordained priest he was so slow-witted that he was unable to learn the office of catechism or baptism; and for this reason I ordered him not to presume to exercise this ministry because he could not perform it properly.[134]

The bishop therefore began immediately to catechize the sick man, who, when he was recovered, was rebaptized. It is instructive here to refer to a letter from Pope Zacharias to Boniface, which relates to an almost identical situation.[135] Boniface had ordered the rebaptism of Christians who had been initiated by a priest whose grasp of Latin was so limited that he garbled the crucial baptismal formula, saying: 'Baptizo te in nomine *patria* et *filia* et spiritus sancti.' Zacharias, however, argued that since the

---

129. Theodore, *Penitential*, i, ix. 7. A similar injunction was made in the law code of Wihtred of Kent, see above, n.100.
130. Theodore, *Penitential*, i, x. 1-2; compare *ibid.*, i, v. 6; ii, iv. 4.
131. *ibid.*, i, ix. 12; ii, ii. 13.
132. Ecgberht, *Dialogi*, c.5.
133. See above, p. 176.
134. Bede, *HE* v. 6.
135. The parallel was noted by Plummer, *Baedae Opera*, ii, 277.

minister had not made any heretical statement and had only ignorantly muddled the Latin, the baptism should not be repeated, but should only 'be absolved by the laying on of hands'.[136]

LAY ATTITUDES TO BAPTISM

It is almost impossible to determine the extent to which the Anglo-Saxon laity could be persuaded of the importance of baptism, but Wilfrid's biographer, Stephanus, relates one incident which, if the opinion of the woman concerned was accurately portrayed, appears to indicate that aspects of the church's teaching on this subject had penetrated some lay consciences. On this occasion Wilfrid was fulfilling the duties of his episcopal office by baptizing and confirming the people by the laying on of hands at a place called *On Tiddanufri*. A woman among the crowd was nursing her dead child, who was unbaptized, and she apparently hoped that if the bishop were to confirm him he would come back to life; when she realized that Wilfrid knew that the child was dead, she implored him to baptize her son and free him 'from the mouth of the lion' so that he might 'live to God and to you'.[137] It seems that the mother's distress was occasioned at least in part by her fears for her dead son because he had not been baptized, and not exclusively by her desire to have him restored to life in this world. Equally, however, her hope in Wilfrid may have rested rather in his 'magical' powers as a holy man than in any belief in or understanding of the efficacy of the sacrament of baptism.

The baptism of a child or adult, as well as conferring spiritual benefits on the candidate, could provide an opportunity for him and his relations to create new social, and often political, bonds with those who acted as his sponsors and received him from the font.[138] The pervasiveness of relationships of spiritual kinship throughout all levels of Anglo-Saxon society may be demonstrated from the references to godfathers and godsons found in Ine's law code among statements of the compensation to be paid for slain kinsmen. This text distinguishes between godsons and godfathers whose relationship is created at baptism itself,[139] and spiritual sons at confirmation.[140] Theodore's Penitential also referred to three separate rites of *catechumenus*, baptism and confirmation, stating that it was customary for different persons to undertake the obligations of godparenthood at each stage.[141] If this was commonly done (and it is clear from Theodore's text that in fact the same person did often act as spiritual father on each occasion), it would provide further opportunities for proliferating bonds of spiritual kinship.[142]

---

136. Boniface, *Epistola*, 68.
137. Stephanus, *Vita S. Wilfridi*, c.18.
138. Lynch, *Godparents*, 170-92, 242-4; Angenendt, 'The conversion', 758-64.
139. Laws of Ine, cc. 76-76.2.
140. *ibid.*, c.76.3: 'Gif hit biscepsunu sie, sie be healfum þam.'
141. Theodore, *Penitential*, ii, iv. 8; Lynch, *Godparents*, 213-14.
142. Lynch, *Godparents*, 213.

The centrality of the sacrament of baptism in the life of Christian Anglo-Saxons may be demonstrated from the fact that in two Old English texts from the late ninth century, both recording donations made by the West Saxon ealdorman, Alfred, the word *fulwiht* (baptism) is used to represent the Christian faith in general. In his will, the ealdorman bequeathed a piece of land to one of his kinsmen on condition that he and his heirs rendered alms of 100 pence to Christ Church, Canterbury, 'as long as baptism lasts and the money can be raised from that land'.[143] Alfred left another estate to a different kinsman, Eadred, to revert on Eadred's death to Alfred's maternal kindred 'as long as baptism remains on the English island'.[144] In similar vein, when Alfred and his wife Wærburh presented the *Codex Aureus* to Christ Church, they gave the book (which they had bought from the Vikings) for the use of the religious community on condition that it be read monthly for the sake of the donors' souls 'as long as God has foreseen that baptism shall continue at that place',[145] and they prayed that no one would be 'so presumptuous as to give away or remove these holy books from Christ Church, as long as baptism may endure'.[146] Other ninth-century Latin charters demonstrate equal anxiety about the survival of Christianity in England,[147] but these refer to the hoped-for continuance of *fides catholica, christiana fides*, or *christianitas*,[148] not for the preservation of baptism.[149] Did the ealdorman consider that as a person's baptism determined his entry into the body of believers, so it represented the most significant factor distinguishing him and the rest of the initiated Christians from the pagan Vikings marauding in Kent? Alternatively, was the administration of baptism the most visible pastoral function performed by a minster community such as Christ Church, and hence that whose discontinuance Alfred took to symbolize the extinction of the entire Christian religion?

---

143. S 1508 (AD 871 × 889); F. Harmer, *Select English Historical Documents of the Ninth and Tenth Centuries* (1914) [hereafter *SEHD*], 13-15: 'þe hwile þe fulwiht sio, 7 hit man on ðem londe begeotan mege.'
144. *ibid*.: 'ða hwile þe fulwihte sio on Angelcynnes ealonde.'
145. Stockholm, Royal Library, *Codex Aureus*, fo. 10r (Harmer, *SEHD*, 12-13): 'ða hwile ðe God gesegen haebbe ðæt fulwiht æt ðeosse stowe beon mote.'
146. *ibid*.: 'ða hwile ðe fulwiht stondan mote.' I have not found any other texts in which the Old English word *fulwiht* (or any of its derivatives) is used in this sense; see A. Cameron *et al.*, *Old English Word Studies: A Preliminary Author and Word Index*, Toronto Old English Series, viii (1983); *fulluht*.
147. For a list of these charters see N. Brooks, 'England in the ninth century: the crucible of defeat', *Trans. Royal Hist. Soc.* 5th series, xxix (1979), 1-20, at 13; and F. M. Stenton, 'The supremacy of the Mercian kings', in *Preparatory to Anglo-Saxon England*, ed. D. M. Stenton (1970), 48-66, at 59, n.3.
148. *BCS* 289 (S 153), compare S 1791; *BCS* 396 (S 282), compare *BCS* 272 (S 146), *BCS* 518 (S 339), *BCS* 519 (S 1204), and *BCS* 406 (S 1269); *BCS* 351 (S 171), compare *BCS* 360 (S 181).
149. With the exception of *BCS* 434 (S 193) and *BCS* 494 (S 197), two uncertain charters of privileges for the minster of Bredon in Worcestershire; see Stenton, 'The supremacy', 59, n.3.

CONCLUSION

The prominence accorded to baptism in such a diversity of texts from early Anglo-Saxon England demonstrates that it was an essential part of the pastoral ministry of all active clergy. Indeed, it was arguably the most important of all sacraments, for those who were not baptized 'by water in the Spirit' were believed to be denied salvation.[150] Concern for the proper and regular administration of baptism is evident from the gravity with which the prescriptive literature treated failures in its provision. It seems likely that at the least a high proportion of early Anglo-Saxon minsters was responsible for supplying the sacrament to the laity in the vicinity, but it is difficult to measure the church's success in fulfilling its self-appointed task of taking baptism to the people. It may be reasonable to assume that most parts of each diocese were visited by a priest at some time in any year, and that those who wanted themselves or their children to be baptized would probably have received the sacrament, although the regularity of provision must have varied considerably in different areas. In the eleventh century, penalties for priests who failed to supply baptism, particularly to new-born infants, were still specified in the secular law codes.[151] The more normal it became for baptism to be administered regularly, the more disgraceful priestly failure would appear, not only to the ecclesiastical hierarchy but also to lay people; here secular authority is protecting lay interests against clerical incompetence. Those whose infants died early may not always have had their grief assuaged by the comfort of knowing their children had been baptized, unless, like Rumwold's parents, they produced a prodigy who could at birth declare his belief in Christ and demand 'to be made a Christian'.[152] However, by the end of the Anglo-Saxon period lay society was committed to receiving baptism; parents themselves sought out priests to administer the sacrament in haste to ailing infants, so that they might not die heathen but, through baptism, be reborn to eternal life.[153]

---

150. John, iii. 5. See Fisher, *Christian Initiation*, 13–16.
151. 'Canons of Edgar', c.15 (Whitelock *et al.*, *Councils and Synods with Other Documents Relating to the English Church: I 871–1204* (2 vols., 1981), i, 315–38); Northumbrian priests' law, cc. 8–10.1 (*ibid.*, 452–68). See also Cramer, 'Baptism and change', 144.
152. *Vita S. Rumwoldi*, c.4.
153. Ælfric, Pastoral letter for Wulfsige III, Bishop of Sherborne, § 71 (ed. Whitelock *et al.*, *Councils*, i, 196–226). This article went to press before the appearance of R. Morris, 'Baptismal places: 600–800', in *People and Places in Northern Europe 500–1600: Essays in Honour of Peter Hayes Sawyer*, ed. I. Wood and N. Lund (1991), 15–24.

8 Pastoral care and conciliar canons: the provisions of the 747 council of *Clofesho*

CATHERINE CUBITT

The concept of pastoral care is not a simple one with a fixed definition, but rather a complex of ideas which have changed from age to age, and no doubt from generation to generation. The most popular work upon pastoral care in the early Middle Ages was Gregory the Great's *Cura Pastoralis*, which was generally regarded as a handbook for bishops and was largely concerned with teaching and preaching. To modern eyes, pastoral care is perhaps less narrowly delimited: Giles Constable has defined it as the 'pastoral activities of administering the sacraments, especially baptism and the eucharist, imposing penance and preaching', and he distinguishes these activities from charitable works such as almsgiving and care for the poor and indigent. Constable framed his definition with regard to the rights and duties of a medieval parish priest who had the sole right to conduct certain services within a fixed territory.[1] When such a system came into being is one of the most important questions of medieval history. In England, minster churches had by the eleventh century assumed rights of baptism and burial; tenth-century laws also record their right, apparently within a fixed territory, to receive certain church dues (tithe and church scot, for example), but such prerogatives may have developed centuries earlier.[2] I shall use the term pastoral care (or, as an alternative, the cure of souls) to encompass those activities in Constable's definition quoted above, but it is important to remember that this is a set of ideas (including the geographical dimension) retrospectively put together by the historian, and we must be aware of assuming that such a package would necessarily have been recognized by eighth-century churchmen.

Church councils or synods had a part to play in pastoral care: they provided the fora in which bishops met together - often with other members of the clergy and with abbots - to discuss theological problems, adjudicate disciplinary cases and formulate policy. In the Anglo-Saxon church, the regular convocation of church councils is not clearly recorded

---

1. G. Constable, 'Monasteries, rural churches and the *cura animarum* in the early Middle Ages', *Settimane di Studio del Centro Italiano di Studi sull'Alto Medioevo*, xxviii (1982), 353. Constable notes that caritative works and the activities of pastoral care could overlap.
2. J. Blair, 'Minster churches in the landscape', in *Anglo-Saxon Settlements*, ed. D. Hooke (1988), 50, R. K. Morris, *Churches in the Landscape* (1989), 128.

until the second half of the eighth century, but the available evidence from before this date, scanty though it is, suggests that the church did maintain a continuous conciliar tradition from the days of Archbishop Theodore. Although there is no direct evidence of synods, for example, resolving disputes over baptism or disciplining aberrant priests, it is not too fanciful to suggest that such issues may have been brought before them.[3] Four major sets of canons reflect the formulation of policy by bishops in council, those of the councils of Hertford in 672 and of *Clofesho* in 747, those promulgated by the papal legates in 786, and those of the council of Chelsea in 816. All included canons on aspects of pastoral care – the control of the clergy, questions relating to baptism, and so on. The thirty decrees of the council of *Clofesho* in 747 are however the most detailed in this respect and constitute an immensely important source on this subject. They range over every aspect of church life – the duties of bishops and priests, baptism and the preparatory instruction of infants and their sponsors, liturgical observance and life in religious communities – and they rival in their scope the great reform capitularies of Charlemagne, promulgated half a century later. Their influence may also be traced over later English councils, since they appear to have contributed to the decrees of the papal legates in 786 and to the canons of the council of Chelsea in 816.[4] In brief, they are the single most important and most detailed source on pastoral care in England before the tenth and eleventh centuries.

These canons have been neglected by modern historians, largely, it appears, for two reasons. First, it has been thought that they simply reflected the influence of St Boniface and reproduced the rulings of his Continental councils. While it is plain that a letter from Boniface to Archbishop Cuthbert of Canterbury was a spur to their formulation and that some Frankish decrees were used, the programme of the *Clofesho* decrees ranges far more widely than the suggestions of Boniface and should be seen as an original composition on the part of the English bishops.[5] Second, the most recent research on pastoral care in Anglo-Saxon England has concentrated on the wealth of new information revealed by topographical and archaeological studies. An important hypothesis has been put forward based upon this non-literary material. It has been argued that before the tenth and eleventh centuries, pastoral care was organized through *monasteria* which had responsibility for the care of the laity within territorially defined areas and that this network was established during the seventh and eighth centuries. These communities may have

---

3. Canon 25 of the Council of *Clofesho*, AD 747, *Councils and Ecclesiastical Documents Relating to Great Britain and Ireland*, ed. A. W. Haddan and W. Stubbs (3 vols., 1869–78), iii, 371 orders bishops to refer cases which they cannot resolve to the archbishop and synod for resolution, while later conciliar texts record only the settlement of land disputes; it is probable that disciplinary problems were also adjudicated. On Anglo-Saxon synods, see C. R. E. Cubitt, 'Anglo-Saxon church councils *c.* 650–*c.* 850' (unpubl. Ph.D. thesis, Univ. of Cambridge, 1990), 22–35, 75–95.
4. See *ibid.*, 205–7, 267–70, 342–3.
5. This case is argued fully in my thesis, *ibid.*, 175–81. 188.

been of various sorts: houses of priests or houses of monks who perhaps supported a priest for this ministry. Only later - in the tenth and eleventh centuries - was it normal for priests to be linked to individual churches.[6]

The neglect of English conciliar evidence for pastoral care has been remedied in an important paper by Sarah Foot. She draws attention to the discrepancy between the hypothesis of recent scholarship and the emphasis of the *Clofesho* canons and other English conciliar rulings on the role of bishops and priests, which apparently ignore the possible role of the *monasteria* and of those of the religious who were not in orders.[7] How are the two to be reconciled? Should the apparent contradiction lead us to question the value of the *Clofesho* canons for a study of pastoral care, or should it suggest an alternative way of viewing the administration of pastoral care in early Anglo-Saxon England? These are the questions which I shall address in this chapter.

THE RULINGS OF THE COUNCIL OF CLOFESHO

The thirty canons promulgated by the council of *Clofesho* can be divided into a number of sections, each dealing with different aspects of church life. The first seven canons are largely concerned with the responsibilities of bishops, the next five with the ministry of the priesthood, and these are followed by six canons regulating liturgical observance. Canons 19 to 24 are chiefly rulings on the communal life of the religious, and the canons close with six provisions (Canons 25 to 30) on miscellaneous matters which were perhaps added to the draft of the decrees after the deliberations of the council.[8]

The canons open therefore with discussion of the responsibilities of bishops, who are described in the preamble as 'set before others by God in the place of a teacher'. Bishops must be quick to defend 'the pastoral care entrusted to them' and the 'canonical dispositions' of the church. Their lives must be an example to the *populus dei* to whom they should teach healthy doctrine. Canon 3 is more concretely framed: bishops should make annual visitations of their dioceses, call together the people and teach 'those who rarely hear the word of God', forbidding pagan practices. Canons 4 to 6 exert episcopal authority over *monasteria*: bishops must admonish the abbots and abbesses of their diocese to set a good example to their *familiae* and to ensure that they live communally according to their rule. Secular *monasteria* are the subject of Canon 5 which, while deploring their

---

6. See the introduction and collection of papers in *Minsters and Parish Churches. The Local Church in Transition, 950-1200*, ed. J. Blair (1988); and J. Blair, 'Minster churches in the landscape', 35-58, 'Secular minster churches in Domesday Book', in *Domesday Book: a Reassessment*, ed. P. H. Sawyer (1985), 104-42.
7. S. Foot, 'Parochial ministry in early Anglo-Saxon England: the role of monastic communities', *Studies in Church History*, xxvi (1989), esp. 51.
8. Compare, for example, the introductory words of Canons 27 and 30 which differ from the more uniform openings of other canons.

existence, commands that bishops visit these for the sake of the spiritual health of their inmates. Episcopal examination of candidates for ordination, monks and clerks, is dealt with in Canon 6 which requires that bishops must test candidates' fitness for office. Finally Canon 7 is directed to bishops, abbots and abbesses, exhorting them to foster study within their *familiae*.[9]

Priests are the subject of the next section. Canon 8 calls upon priests to be mindful of their high calling: they must avoid secular affairs, discharge the service of the altar with 'highest attention', look after the *domus oratorii* and all that belongs to the service of the altar, and be vigilant in reading, in prayer, in the celebration of masses and in the singing of psalms. They are to offer help to abbots and abbesses where necessary. Canon 9 directs priests entrusted with care for 'places and regions of the laity' by their bishops to be diligent in the 'evangelical and apostolic office of preaching, in baptising, teaching and visiting', they must shun drunkenness, shameful avarice and unfitting talk, lest they give a bad example to the laity and to the *monasteriales*.[10]

Canons 10 and 11 form a pair: in the first, priests are informed of the knowledge necessary for their understanding of the ministry, and in the second, of that necessary for the instruction of the laity. They must know the correct rites for the performance of their office; those who are ignorant of Latin must learn to translate and to explain the Lord's prayer, the creed and the words used in the mass and baptism, so that they understand the meaning of the intercessions and services they perform. The canon does not demand that they should explain these things to the laity, but may be directed towards the periodic examination of priests by their bishops, a practice mentioned in Continental canons and which may also have been practised in England.[11]

Canon 11 begins by demanding that priests should perform their office – defined as baptizing, teaching and judging (presumably the administration of penance) – in the same way: this concern for uniformity is seen later in those canons which are concerned with the liturgy. It goes on to require that priests should have a correct understanding of the doctrine of the Trinity and teach this and the creed to those who come to them. When children are baptized, they and their sponsors should be taught the creed and how to recite the renunciation of the devil and his works from the baptismal service – perhaps a further effort to eradicate paganism. The last of the canons to deal exclusively with priests, Canon 12, commands that they should sing the services in church following liturgical melodies, not imitating the style of secular poets.

---

9. The only translation of these canons is J. Johnson, *A Collection of all the Ecclesiastical Laws, Canons, Answers or Rescripts* . . . (2 vols., 1720), unpaginated, republished as *A Collection of the Laws and Canons of the Church of England* (2 vols., 1856), i, 242–65.
10. Canons 8 and 9.
11. For Continental canons, see for example, Canon 3 of the *Concilium Germanicum* (MGH, *Leges* iii *Concilia* ii, 1906), 3.

The next six canons are concerned with liturgical observance. The feasts of the temporal and sanctoral should be performed in the same way and at the same time by all, and in accordance with the practices of the Roman church. Similarly uniformity and agreement with Roman customs are demanded with regard to the services of the daily office and in the observance of the ember fasts. The times of the Major and Minor Litanies are also prescribed and these ceremonies must be performed by the clergy and laity with great reverence, without secular entertainments such as games and horse-racing.[12]

The canons regulating community life lay down that monks and nuns should live the regular life quietly, in obedience to the head of their house and should be simply dressed in clothes appropriate to their calling (Canon 19). Bishops should ensure that the *monasteria* are truly religious houses, devoted to prayer and reading and not filled with secular entertainers and with lay visitors. Bishops and rulers of *monasteria* should examine the suitability of laity who wish to enter community life to weed out those ill-suited to it. Canon 28 rules that no one should receive a greater congregation than he or she can provide for, and that adequate food and clothing should be given to the clergy and monks. Other canons condemn drunkenness, encourage the practice of frequent communion for those of the laity who are fitted to receive it, namely lay boys, celibates and those married people who are sexually abstemious and admonishes members of religious communities to prepare themselves carefully for communion (Canons 21-3). Clerks, monks, and *sanctimoniales* are forbidden from living among the laity and are ordered to return to the house of their profession (Canon 29). The remaining canons regulate the convocation of diocesan synods and discuss almsgiving, psalmody and relations between the laity and the church.

The thirty canons passed by the 747 council of *Clofesho* constitute an extraordinarily ambitious and complex programme: it aimed to strengthen episcopal authority, reform the communal life of monks and the secular clergy, and further the Christian understanding of the laity by the teaching and ministry of carefully chosen and trained priests. Only Charlemagne's *Admonitio generalis* contains as thoroughgoing a plan for the renewal of Christian society, sharing the English council's concern for the Christian education of the laity, for the didactic role of the clergy and for their standards of behaviour and learning.[13]

Three particular concerns can be seen in the reform programme of the *Clofesho* canons. Uniformity in the content and timing of church services is urged in a number of canons, particularly those regulating the liturgy.[14] This was not simply a question of outward appearance but, as Arnold Angenendt and Hanna Vollrath have stressed, one which affected the efficacy of the sacraments celebrated. Uniformity in timing (a preoccupation reminiscent of the paschal controversy) was very important since the

---

12. Canons 13, 15, 18, 16, *ibid.*, iii, 367-8.
13. Cubitt, 'Anglo-Saxon church councils', 205-7.
14. Canons 13, 15, 16, 18.

conferral of certain sacraments, like baptism and ordination, was linked to particular church festivals.[15]

Correctness of ecclesiastical tradition was another concern of the canons: many decrees forbid secular customs. Priests and bishops are exhorted to keep free from secular affairs, lay styles of singing are forbidden in church services, and secular entertainers and dress are banned from monasteries. The litanies must be performed without games and horse-races.

A desire for the understanding of the Christian faith and for truly Christian behaviour is the third concern, which applies not only to the clergy and the religious but also to the laity. Priests must understand the meaning of the sacraments and behave in keeping with their high calling, and the laity must be instructed in the meaning of the doctrine of the Trinity, and in the creed. The laity as well as the clergy and religious should take communion frequently, and on Sundays and feastdays the laity must be called to church to hear the Scripture, and be present at the mass and when teaching is given.

STRUCTURE OF THE ADMINISTRATION OF PASTORAL CARE

Bishops are portrayed in the *Clofesho* canons as the apex of the pyramid of ecclesiastical responsibility, endowed with authority over the clergy and the *monasteria*, as well as having their own personal obligation of diocesan visitation, teaching and the presentation of a model of righteous living to others. Priests play the most active role in ministering to the laity through their sacramental office. Canon 11 defines the work of all priests as baptizing, teaching and the administration of penance, and Canon 12 gives priests a special responsibility for visiting, baptizing and teaching in lay regions. Liturgy is also seen as a vehicle for the instruction of the laity: on Sundays and feastdays the people are called to church to attend the mass.

The canons do not, on the other hand, associate community life with responsibilities to the laity, although within the *monasteria* its rulers must act as examples of the Christian life and bear responsibility for their subjects. *Monasteria* should be houses of silence and peace, of prayer, reading and the praise of God, not filled with secular entertainers. Houses of *sanctimoniales* should likewise be given over to reading and the psalter and shun worldly luxuries. The educational and scholarly role of *monasteria* is stressed, Canon 7 rules that they should be houses of study 'to the profit of souls and the praise of the eternal King'. Abbots, monks and *sanctimoniales* do not appear in a pastoral role. Does this picture, with its stress on bishops and priests with respect to pastoral care rather than on *monasteria*, represent a curiously episcopal perception of the ministry, or can it be matched by that of other sources?

---

15. H. Vollrath, *Die Synoden Englands bis 1066* (1985), 148-50, and A. Angenendt, 'Bonifatius und das sacramentum initiationis', *Römische Quartalschrift*, lxxii (1977), 133-83.

Let us start with the role of the bishop. Alcuin, a deacon and former member of a cathedral community, also makes the bishop responsible for every aspect of church life:

> It is the part of the bishops to correct the *monasteria*, to order the life of the servants of God, to preach to the people the word of God and to teach diligently the people subject to them. It is the part of the laity to obey their preaching.[16]

He admonished Archbishop Æthelheard to preach to the bishops in synod about proper ordinations, preaching, ecclesiastical offices, baptism, almsgiving and care for the poor.[17] Bede also concurs in giving bishops the first place in church life. His letter to Ecgberht, in which he advises the bishop how to organize care of the laity within his diocese, by its very nature reflects the belief that responsibility for pastoral care lay with the bishop. Moreover, Bede advises Ecgberht to surround himself with those devoted to a godly and disciplined life so that he may be supported in resisting sinful behaviour. This, he argues, is particularly important for bishops because their rank 'has not only to take care for its own salvation, but also to devote necessary attention to the welfare of the church committed to it'.[18]

Correspondences between Bede's letter to Ecgberht and the canons of the council of *Clofesho* have already been noted by Charles Plummer and Alan Thacker: both documents urge regular communion for those of the laity who are chaste, and both advocate that the creed and Lord's prayer should be known, if necessary in the vernacular.[19] In addition to these specific points, there are broader parallels. Bede urges Ecgberht to make preaching tours of his diocese, gathering together the laity to hear his words. His remark that many places have lacked this ministry calls to mind the strictures of Canon 3, which requires bishops to preach to 'those who rarely hear the word of God'; and the reference in Canon 9 to priests who have been given charge of districts among the laity by their bishop recalls Bede's suggestion that Ecgberht establish priests and teachers who can minister to remote settlements. Episcopal authority over *monasteria* is also discussed by Bede and both texts voice serious criticism of those lay *monasteria* which lack any semblance of the religious life. The canons of the council of *Clofesho* are in remarkable accord with Bede's letter in their view of the English church.

---

16. Alcuin, *Epistolae*, no. 18, ed. E. Dümmler, MGH, *Epistolae* iv *Carolini Aevi* ii (1895), 52.
17. *ibid.*, no. 128 (Dümmler, 190).
18. Bede, *Epistola ad Ecgbertum Episcopum*, ed, C. Plummer, *Venerabilis Baedae Opera Historica* (1896), i, 405-23, 407; transl. from *English Historical Documents* i, ed. D. Whitelock (1979), 800. Interestingly Bede draws a distinction between the greater responsibility of bishops in this respect and that of other *famuli dei* (including himself).
19. See the remarks by Plummer in *Baedae Opera Historica*, ii, 378-88, and A. Thacker, 'Bede's ideal of reform', in *Ideal and Reality in Frankish and Anglo-Saxon Society*, ed. P. Wormald, *et al.* (1983), 74. It is not clear whether these resemblances stem from influence of the letter on the canons or from similarities of thought.

Moreover, Bede's account of the evangelization of the Anglo-Saxon kingdoms in the *Historia Ecclesiastica* is dominated by bishops (some of whom of course were also monks). Augustine, Aidan, Paulinus, Felix, Birinus and Wilfrid were all bishops before they began their missionary work in their respective kingdoms.[20] Usually bishops were accompanied in their missionary work by priests or those in orders: James the Deacon assisted Paulinus in Northumbria and Wilfrid worked in Sussex with four. Among the East Saxons, Bishop Cedd 'ordained priests and deacons to assist him in preaching the word of faith and in the administration of baptism, especially in the *ciuitas* called Bradwell-on-Sea and also in the place called Tilbury'.[21] In some areas the work of evangelization was initiated by priests, one of whom might subsequently be consecrated bishop when the mission had been successfully established. Cedd himself had been dispatched with another priest to the East Saxons and was later consecrated bishop, and four priests were sent to the kingdom of the Middle Angles, of whom one, Diuma, became bishop.[22]

In some areas, the work of evangelization was carried out by bishops and priests; at a later date, bishops are described on their travels as accompanied by their clergy. Such trips included the bishop's work in his diocese, preaching, baptism and confirmation. Many of the miracle stories in the anonymous *Vita S. Cuthberti* were reported by priests who had accompanied Bishop Cuthbert around his diocese, and some accounts suggest that the clergy travelling with a bishop could be fairly numerous.[23]

Bishops and priests thus figure prominently in Bede's account of the conversion; other sources bear out the primary role of priests and those in orders in evangelization and in the ministry to the laity. The same emphasis upon the work of those in orders rather than on unordained monks can be seen, however, in two other episcopal texts, Theodore's Penitential and Ecgberht's Dialogues. For example, although clerks and monks are spoken of in Ecgberht's Dialogues, only priests and deacons are mentioned in relation to the ministry to the dying.[24] In Book II of Theodore's Penitential, rulings concerning those in orders on the one hand and abbots, monks and *monasteria* on the other are given in separate

---

20. Bede, *HE* i. 23, 29; iii. 3; ii. 9; ii. 15; iii. 7 and iv. 13. For Augustine's consecration as bishop see J. M. Wallace-Hadrill, *Bede's Ecclesiastical History: a Historical Commentary* (1988), 31-2; Wilfrid's missionary work in England was of course in Sussex.
21. Bede, *HE* ii. 16, iv. 13, iii. 22.
22. Bede, *HE* iii. 21, 22.
23. See Bede, *HE* iii. 5 on Aidan, *Vita S. Cuthberti*, iv. 3-8; Bede, *Vita S. Cuthberti*, cc. 28-30, 32; Stephanus, *Vita S. Wilfridi*, c.18. See my 'Wilfrid's "usurping bishops": episcopal elections in Anglo-Saxon England, *c.* 600-*c.* 800', *Northern History*, xxv (1989), 18-38, on the tendency for a bishop to be succeeded in office by a member of his clergy.
24. Ecgbert, *Dialogues*, question 2 (ed. Haddan and Stubbs, *Councils*, iii. 404). See also questions 4-6 and 9 (*ibid.*, 405-6) which consider the problems of priests debarred from the ministry by their bishops, who then work in other dioceses, which also make no reference to those without orders.

sections; one canon states that monks and clerks can bless food, and that deacons can bless food and baptize.[25]

Accounts of ministry to the laity by members of religious communities also usually refer to the work of those in orders. In his description of itinerant preachers in the diocese of Lindisfarne, Bede states that 'the priests and the clerics visited the villages for no other reason than to preach, to baptize, to visit the sick, in brief to care for their souls'.[26] Willibald's *Vita S. Bonifatii* also describes the preaching tours of priests and clerks to the laity, but this passage is derived from Bede's account in the *Vita S. Cuthberti*. However, it later stresses that Boniface did not take upon himself the work of a preacher until he had been ordained priest at the canonical age of 30.[27]

It emerges that the emphasis of the *Clofesho* canons upon the pastoral work of bishops and priests is not unusual, but the question still remains of whether its apparent neglect of the role of *monasteria* and the ministry of unordained monks is peculiar, and it is therefore important to examine the literary evidence for this. The extent of responsibility taken by those not in orders for the cure of souls is unclear. The teaching of hermits such as Guthlac and Wilgils who attracted the laity to their retreats should not be seen as part of the regular development of pastoral care. Bede mentions the teaching by unordained monks in his account of Aidan's mission but he explicitly states that only those in priest's orders baptized. He also refers to the welcome which the laity gave to the exhortations of travelling monks and clerks from Lindisfarne.[28] Others writing of Bede have been used to suggest that all those in the religious life were considered to bear pastoral responsibility for the laity.[29] In one commentary, he lamented those *monasteria* whose inmates fail to carry out a teaching office: 'who with splendid work build *monasteria*, and by no means establish within them teachers to encourage the people of God to the works of God, but rather serve there their own pleasures and desires'.[30]

Alan Thacker has argued that Bede saw preaching and teaching as work of almost sacramental significance which was not limited only to those in orders but was also the responsibility of all Christians. His writings also advocate a balance between the active and the contemplative lives, which he illustrated in the prose *Vita S. Cuthberti*, where Cuthbert is shown not only as a hermit but also as a priest, preaching the word of God to the

25. Theodore, *Penitential*, ii, sections ii and vi, and see esp. Canons II, 15, 16, ed. P. W. Finsterwalder, *Die Canones Theodori Cantuariensis und ihre Überlieferungsformen* (1929). The decrees on the role of *monasteria* in pastoral care are discussed below. See also Foot, 'Parochial ministry', 50-2 for other rulings on bishops and priests.
26. Bede, *HE* ii. 26. (ed. Colgrave and Mynors, 311).
27. *Vita S. Bonifatii*, ed. W. Levison, MGH, *Scriptores rerum Germanicarum* (1905), 5, 12.
28. Bede, *HE* iii. 4, 26.
29. Foot, 'Parochial ministry', 46-7, 50; and see Thacker, 'Bede's ideal of reform', 130-54, who first drew attention to the importance Bede attached to preaching and teaching and to this material.
30. Bede, *In Ezram et Neemiam*, ed. D. Hurst (CCSL, 119A, 1969), 302-3.

laity.[31] The inference that Bede's views upon preaching and teaching necessarily impose on all the religious a pastoral obligation towards the laity is, however, not clearly established. Some of his writings underline the role of those in orders; in one homily, Bede wrote that:

> For this purpose especially have spiritual pastors of the church been ordained, to preach the mysteries of the word of God and show their hearers, that they may also marvel, the wonders which they have learnt in the Scriptures. By pastors are understood not only bishops, priests and deacons but also the heads of *monasteria* and all the faithful who have the care of even small households. They are rightly called pastors in as much as they have charge over their households with ceaseless vigilance.[32]

That is to say, bishops, priests and deacons are generally seen as the pastors, but this role should be extended beyond them to others. Moreover, in this and other passages Bede is arguing for an enlarged view of pastoral responsibility which takes in the behaviour of all Christians. He means that all those who have responsibility for others are spiritual shepherds: the ruler of a monastery is entrusted with spiritual responsibility for its members, and the head of a secular household for those within it.[33] This passage affirms the primacy of the bishops and priests as pastors, but also expands the definition of pastoral care so that it is imposed upon a wider range of people, including the laity. So wide a definition of pastoral responsibility is not therefore necessarily useful in looking at the more formal obligations of the church towards the laity.

Nor do Bede's writings on the active and contemplative life clearly establish the use of the religious in pastoral care. Bede defines the active life as keeping clean from sin, devotion to divine service,

> and providing succour to one's neighbour by giving food to the hungry, drink to the thirsty, clothing to the cold, and shelter to the destitute and homeless, visiting the sick, providing burial for the

---

31. Thacker, 'Bede's ideal of reform', 139-43, but see M. T. A. Carroll, *The Venerable Bede and his Spiritual Teachings* (1946), esp. 242-9, who suggests that for Bede, preaching was one of the most important duties of the priest. Carroll's views have not been properly considered in this context.
32. Bede, *Opera Homiletica*, i. 7, ed. D. Hurst (CCSL, 122, 1955), 49. See also H. M. R. E. Mayr-Harting, *The Venerable Bede, the Rule of St Benedict, and Social Class* (the Jarrow Lecture, 1976), 14-16 on Bede's clericalism.
33. The parallel of secular and religious households has been pointed out by J. Campbell in 'Elements in the background to the *Life of St Cuthbert* and his early cult', in *St Cuthbert, his Cult and his Community to AD 1200*, ed. G. Bonner et al. (1989), 13. In another passage in *De Templo*, ed. D. Hurst (CCSL, 119A, 1969), 194, Bede interprets *sacerdos* to mean those who offer spiritual leadership to others; these include 'not only the ministers of the altar, bishops and priests, but all those who stand out by the eminence of their right living and healthy teaching' as examples to others.

dead, and seizing the weak from the hand of the strong and the needy and poor from violent robbers and showing the way of truth to those in error.[34]

All these fall within the category of caritative works which were traditionally associated with monasteries, and it is noticeable that neither baptism nor the administration of the eucharist features in this list.

The role of *praedicatores* and *doctores* is undoubtedly given great prominence in Bede's writings, but it is unclear whether their activities are necessarily always directed at the laity. The scholarly and educative activities of *monasteria* and of their inmates might be seen in this light. We know that Bede prepared translations into Old English of the Lord's prayer and the creed which he gave to ignorant priests, and that on his deathbed he was preparing a vernacular version of part of St John's Gospel 'to the great profit of the church'.[35] His exegetical and didactic works would also fulfil his obligation to teach. Furthermore, the value of teaching, preaching and setting a good example was not limited to its impact upon the laity; the model which members of the community presented to one another was also of great importance to Bede. This is indicated not only by his words quoted earlier upon the pastoral office of the heads of *monasteria*, but also by his descriptions of the example which Cuthbert gave to his fellow inmates of Melrose and Lindisfarne. In his *Vita S. Cuthberti*, Bede states that Cuthbert gave 'the monastery itself counsels concerning life under the rule and an example of it' and also preached to the laity outside the house.[36] Alcuin makes this responsibility explicit in his letter to the community at Wearmouth/Jarrow:

> You, who are the fathers and shepherds of the holy congregation, most diligently teach with brotherly love the *familia* that you have accepted for ruling; and show the complete pattern of goodness in yourselves. Admonish with honour the elders as fathers, chastise with all love the young as sons, and instruct everyone in the spirit of gentleness and with honesty of speech.[37]

---

34. Bede, *Opera Homiletica*, 64, where he also states that these virtues can be carried out by the laity as well as by monks in *monasteria*, which also suggests that we are not dealing with pastoral care. It is interesting that the burial of the dead was seen as charitable work of monasteries. E. Lesne, *Historie propriétaire ecclésiastique en France* (1936), iii, 133-4 gives examples of Frankish monasteries performing this office.
35. Bede, *Epistola ad Ecgbertum*, c.5, and Cuthbert, *Epistola de obitu Bedae*, 583.
36. Bede, *Vita S. Cuthberti*, c.9 (ed. Colgrave, 185) and see also cc. 6 and 16. For Hild's example at Whitby, see Bede, *HE* iv. 23.
37. Alcuin, *Epistolae*, no. 19 (ed. Dümmler, 54), and see also nos 282, 284, 286, 280. Æthelwulf's poem, *De abbatibus*, ed. A. Campbell (1967), describes the senior members of his community as pastors and some others as *doctores* (the abbots Eanmund, Aldwine and Sigbald, and the smith Cwicwine in cc. 3, 10, 12, 13 and 14 are described as pastors; as *doctores* are the priest sent by Ecgbert to instruct the brothers in the rule c.5, and Eadfrith and Hyglac c.22).

While the writings of Bede do show members of *monasteria* involved in ministering to the laity, they do not establish that all religious, including those not in orders, bore pastoral responsibility.[38]

The emphasis in the canons on *monasteria* as places of study and prayer can also be matched in other sources. For example, Bede's portrayal of the lax community at Coldingham - written, no doubt, as an object lesson to other houses - castigates its members for their lack of religious devotion in failing to keep vigils and for their worldly occupations. Failure in its ministry to the laity is not mentioned, possibly, of course, because in this respect it was exemplary. Bede was here concerned with community life and not with pastoral care, but even when that was his main preoccupation, *monasteria* are not portrayed as the primary vehicles for the cure of souls. In writing to Bishop Ecgberht, Bede remarked that his diocese was too large to enable Ecgberht to make regular annual visitations of the whole of it. His solution was that Ecgberht should ordain more priests and train teachers to assist him in this work, and that ultimately he should himself create more dioceses to share the great responsibility which Ecgberht bore. In this letter, Bede's concern was entirely a practical one and it is therefore particularly interesting that he does not mention monastic *parochiae* with reference to the reorganization of pastoral care. *Monasteria* are mentioned but in relation to the endowment of the new sees, not as sources of manpower.[39]

What literary evidence is there for the role of *monasteria* in pastoral care? The clearest evidence is found in the writings of Bede (the *Historia Ecclesiastica* and his *Vita S. Cuthberti*) and the anonymous *Vita S. Cuthberti*. In the latter, Cuthbert is portrayed as prior of Melrose making pastoral visits to the laity in the countryside, preaching and baptizing, a picture largely repeated by Bede in his *Vita*. The laity also come to the *monasterium*: in the miracle-story of the *comes* Hildmaer's demon-possessed wife, Hildmaer comes to Cuthbert at Melrose, requests a

---

38. Thacker emphasizes that Bede, in his letter to Ecgberht, appears to distinguish between bishops and priests who were ordained and *doctores* who were instituted. However, this passage cannot bear the weight of Thacker's interpretation. Bede uses the word *doctor* simply to mean 'teacher' and thus it can describe both ordained and unordained people (see, for example, Bede, *HE* ii. 14, 15, iii. 4, 22, v. 22) there is no necessary distinction here between two mutually exclusive categories. Nor is the word 'instituit' significant: it can mean to 'train or educate' (see, for example, Bede, *HE* iv. 27, iii. 5) which could be its meaning in this passage. The other passages cited by Thacker do not seem to me to indicate a distinction between the ordination of priests and others and the institution of teachers.

39. Bede, *HE* iv. 25 and *Epistola ad Ecgbertum*, cc. 5, 9, 10 (ed. Plummer, i. 408-9, 412-4). My interpretation of this passage differs from that of Alan Thacker who suggests that Bede wished the *monasteria* to be 'fully integrated into the diocesan system' ('Bede's ideal of reform', 133). Bede refers to two types of *monasteria*, the second of which he goes on to describe as false communities, lacking any semblance of true monasticism. The new bishoprics are to be based in the first (from which bishops may be chosen, on this point see my 'Wilfrid's "usurping" bishops', pp. 21-4), and the second he explicitly states should be used to provide further lands for the new sees.

priest to provide the last rites for his wife, and asks that she should be given burial in sacred ground.[40] In the *Historia Ecclesiastica*, Bede underlines the importance of the work of the Lindisfarne community by describing how gladly the pastoral attentions of itinerant priests and clerks were received by the laity. And he records the ministry of Fursa from his monastic base in East Anglia and the failure in Sussex of the Irish house at Bosham to persuade the laity to listen to its preaching.[41] The Northumbrian (and largely Bedan) evidence is supported by some canons from Theodore's Penitential, which states that if a *monasterium* is moved a priest must be left for the ministry of the altar, and allows *monasteria* to administer penance to the laity because it is the responsibility of the clergy.[42] The foundation charter of the *monasterium* at Breedon stipulates that a priest should be provided for the work of baptism and evangelization, but the text itself is not wholly reliable and is therefore uncertain evidence.[43] More telling perhaps than these occasional references is the implication of Ecgberht's Dialogues that community life may have been the norm in eighth-century Northumbria. One ruling suggests that the consent of a 'prior' is necessary before a priest or deacon can travel, which seems to indicate that individual clerks did not live alone.[44]

The canons of the council of *Clofesho* do not give an anomalous picture of the religious life. The importance assigned to the bishop in pastoral provision is seen in other accounts. The literary sources do not clearly show an obligation for the cure of souls upon all those practising the religious life within *monasteria*, while they do depict the pastoral involvement of priests and other members of the clergy. The focus in the canons upon the devotional and scholarly life of *monasteria* agrees with other descriptions of the monastic life. But on the other hand, the two prose *Vitae S. Cuthberti* and other sources show a pastoral ministry carried out by members of *monasteria* and the evidence of Ecgberht's Dialogues is a significant indication that all monks, nuns and clergy lived communally in *monasteria*. Canon 29 of the council of *Clofesho*, requiring clerks, monks and nuns to return to the houses of their profession, may also suggest that all the religious lived in *monasteria*.

If the priests of the *Clofesho* canons were envisaged as living in *monasteria*, why then do the canons neglect the role of such houses? It is surely because the emphasis of the canons with regard to pastoral care is on priestly duties rather than on accommodation. Thus Canon 14 commands that 'all abbots and priests should remain in their *monasteria* and churches' on the sabbath, without making it clear whether both normally dwell in

40. Bede, *Vita S. Cuthberti*, cc. 12, 13, 15; *Vita S. Cuthberti*, ii. 5, 6, 8.
41. Bede, *HE* iii. 19, 26, iv. 13.
42. See Canons II, vi, 7, 14-16. Canon II.ii.15 of Theodore's Penitential restricts the administration of penance to bishops and priests. *Monasteria* may also receive the sick, and wash the feet of the laity, a traditional aspect of monastic hospitality (see also Bede, *Vita S. Cuthberti*, c.7).
43. *BCS* 841 (S 1803) - the text is part of a later composite charter *BCS* 843/842 (S 1804 and S 1805).
44. Question 6 (Haddan and Stubbs, *Councils*, iii. 406).

the *monasteria*. The canons are concerned not with institutions but with office. Pastoral duties are not portrayed as devolving upon organizations and communities, but upon individuals by virtue of their ordination. The cure of souls was seen in a spiritual rather than an institutional or geographical dimension. Priests may indeed have lived in communities, but *monasteria* are not viewed as the organizing structure for pastoral care. When the canons do display an interest in regulations concerning where clergy and monks should live, it is to prevent them from living in lay households.

Moreover, episcopal initiatives and supervision are not incompatible with pastoral activity by members of communities.[45] The rulings of Ecgberht's Dialogues show the responsibility of the abbot for the regulation of community life and that of bishops for ministry within the diocese. One decree implies that the community superior must be consulted if a priest or deacon wishes to travel, but another ruling shows that permission to minister in a diocese is a matter for episcopal authority.[46] Moreover, some of the evidence for monastic involvement in pastoral activities can be associated with bishops: Cuthbert carried out his preaching tours from Melrose, the daughter-house of Lindisfarne, and those passages describing the work of itinerant preachers in the *Historia Ecclesiastica* and in the *Vita S. Cuthberti* were written with reference to that see. The pastoral centres at Bradwell-on-Sea and Tilbury in Essex were founded by Bishop Cedd.

In Gaul, Francia and Italy, the parish system partly developed from the establishment of communities of episcopal clergy in the countryside. In the early days of the church all clergy had lived with their bishops, but with the evangelization of rural areas, houses of clergy grew up to minister to these. These communities lived under the authority of an archpriest or abbot, but were still dependent upon their bishops for ordination, the consecration of churches, baptismal chrism and the confirmation of the baptized, and their priests were called to attend the bishop's synod.[47] Was such a development possible in Anglo-Saxon England? The houses of priests which Bishop Cedd founded at Tilbury and Bradwell-on-Sea would accord with such a development. After his conversion of Sussex, Bishop Wilfrid was given a fourth part of the Isle of Wight by Cædwalla in thanksgiving for its conquest, and he made this over to one of his clergy, Beornwine, assigning him a priest for the work of preaching and baptizing in the island.[48]

---

45. For a discussion of monastic exemptions and privileges in Anglo-Saxon England, see P. Wormald, 'Bede and Benedict Biscop', *Famulus Christi*, ed. G. Bonner (1976), 146-50, and N. P. Brooks, *The Early History of the Church of Canterbury* (1984), 177-9.
46. Questions 6, 9, pp. 406-7.
47. G. W. O. Addleshaw, *The Beginnings of the Parochial System* (1952); C. E. Boyd, *Tithes and Parishes in Medieval Italy* (1952), 47-55. Imbart de la Tour, *Les origines religeuses de la France: les paroisses rurales du IVᵉ siècle* (1900), 74-87.
48. Bede, *HE* iv. 16.

The discrepancy between the office-centred view of the canons and the institution-based theory of the topographers is not a trivial one, and should alert us to some of the problems of the topographical model. It has been suggested that a network of *monasteria* was rapidly and deliberately established within every kingdom, with pastoral responsibility for territorial *parochiae*: but does the evidence of the literary sources really bear the full weight of this hypothesis? The failure of the literary sources to portray *monasteria* as the primary vehicles of pastoral care surely raises questions over whether they were seen as such in the seventh and eighth centuries. The regional provision of pastoral care does not seem to have been a driving motive in the minds of monastic founders, but rather personal salvation and the spiritual and earthly benefits of communal prayer, and indeed more worldly concerns, recently stressed by Patrick Sims-Williams. Bede also implied that the reason for the numerous lay foundations of the seventh and eighth centuries was proprietorial rather than spiritual. He condemned many lay houses as lacking any semblance of the religious life but he has been criticized as a 'purist' for doing so, and it has been argued that these communities were also part of the pastoral system.[49] Yet Bede was not alone in voicing anxiety over certain lay establishments: the bishops at *Clofesho* also saw some houses as spiritually worthless, and these clerics (in view of Bede's evaluation of the Northumbrian episcopate) may have been less unworldly than Bede.[50] Moreover, Canon 5 states that these houses lacked the ministry of a priest and it is therefore difficult to see what part they could have played in the administration of the sacraments to the laity.

Can we really generalize about the activities of all *monasteria*? Were communities of monks as committed to the cure of souls as were those of clerks? There is evidence to suggest that contact with the laity on the part of at least one house of monks was limited to the works of charity: in the poem, *De abbatibus*, Æthelwulf was keen to promote the achievements of his house and the virtues of its inmates. A number of monks are praised for their almsgiving and care for the poor, others for their devotion to prayer, the office and the psalter, and much is said of the beauty of their liturgical services, but no mention is made of any pastoral involvement with the laity. If the community had carried responsibility for pastoral care, it would be odd that Æthelwulf did not find anything worthy of note in its performance of this duty.[51]

---

49. For example, Oswiu's endowment of twelve *monasteria* after the battle of *Winwaed* was made as a thankoffering for the victory and freed from military service so that the monks might be able to 'wage heavenly warfare and to pray with unceasing devotion that the race might win eternal peace' (Bede, *HE* iii. 24). Blair, 'Minster churches', 38, suggests that these were founded as part of a network to provide pastoral care but Bede's words do not necessarily support this interpretation. On the corrupt motives of lay founders see Bede, *Epistola ad Ecgbertum*, c.12; P. Sims-Williams, *Religion and Literature in Western England 600-800* (1990), 121-2.
50. Canon 5.
51. Æthelwulf, *De abbatibus*: almsgiving, cc. 7, 15; liturgy, cc. 14, 15, 20; prayer and psalter, c.18.

One particularly valuable contribution of the debate over the pastoral role of *monasteria* has been to focus attention on the existence of houses of clerks and to question the assumption that all early Anglo-Saxon houses consisted of monks. The work of pastoral care would more naturally devolve upon houses of clerks, whose members could bear such duties by virtue of their orders.[52] There is certainly strong evidence that clerks could live in community. Archbishop Ecgberht referred in his Dialogues to the practice of confession by 'clerici in monasteriis', and Boniface, writing to the Anglo-Saxons to request their prayers, included in his address 'canonicis clericis', presumably clerks living under a rule.[53] When Guthlac entered the community of Repton, he is recorded as becoming a clerk, so possibly Repton was entirely or chiefly a house of clerks.[54] The canons of *Clofesho* also plainly refer to clerks living in community,[55] but in these canonical references as in the others, it is unclear whether there were separate communities of monks and clerks, or mixed communities. Peter Sawyer has shown how the community of Worcester cathedral in the tenth century appears to have been predominately made up of priests, deacons and clerks, with a small number of monks.[56] It is difficult to probe beneath the surface of Anglo-Saxon *monasteria*, to discern their composition, but this does not mean that this question is an irrelevant one. The sources clearly do distinguish between monks and clerks, if not between different sorts of

---

52. Constable, 'Monasteries, rural churches and the *cura animarum*', 352-3. The emphasis in the *Clofesho* canons upon the duties of office may suggest that priests in any community bore responsibilities towards the laity (although the evidence of *De abbatibus* does not suggest that priests within that house of monks carried out such duties).
53. Question 16 (Haddan and Stubbs, *Councils*, iii. 413). Boniface, *Epistolae*, no. 46, ed. M. Tangl, MGH, *Epistolae Selectae*, i (1916), 74. See also the remarks on the Kentish minsters by Brooks, *Church of Canterbury*, 187-8.
54. Guthlac's clerical status was pointed out to me by Sarah Foot: Felix, *Vita S. Guthlaci*, c.20, ed. B. Colgrave (1956). One of the intriguing features of the *Vita S. Guthlaci* is the fact that, apart from references to the example of the Egyptian monks, it mentions only clerks.
55. See Canons 28 and 29 of the Council of *Clofesho* which mention monks, clerks and *sanctimoniales* living in community.
56. P. H. Sawyer, 'Charters of the reform movement: the Worcester Archive', in *Tenth-Century Studies*, ed. D. Parsons (1975), 84-93. Susan Kelly has pointed out to me that ninth-century Worcester leases record a similarly clerical composition for the house - see BCS 304, 490, 570 (S 1262, 1273, 1416) for example - and that the only change in Oswald's time was the appearance of monks. Worcester was a cathedral community which one would expect to be made up of clergy; other houses may have included monks earlier. In BCS 380 (S 1268) Archbishop Wulfred makes reference to a monk, Dodda, perhaps a member of the Christ Church community in the early ninth century. BCS 379 (S 1433) records the testimony of 'very many monks' but does not record their house of origin. Monks may be rare in witness-lists because the value of their testimony was not as great as that of priests and deacons; see Ecgbert's *Dialogues*, Question 1 (Haddan and Stubbs, *Councils*, iii. 404).

community. It may be that by the eighth century, houses of monks were few, and that monks tended to be members of predominantly clerical communities.[57]

The monastic *parochiae* are not mentioned in the literary sources and, apart from the *Clofesho* canons, the only unit of pastoral care spoken of is the diocese.[58] The reference in *Clofesho* Canon 9 to 'places and regions of the laity' assigned to priests by their bishops is therefore particularly important. It implies that by the mid-eighth century some sort of territorial organization within the diocese had begun to develop through episcopal authority and based upon priestly office. Since these priests may have lived in *monasteria*, there may have been some association between their houses and their allotted regions. However, much of the evidence for monastic territories used by topographers is late and, as Richard Morris has pointed out, property boundaries were not fixed and could change as estates changed hands.[59] We should therefore be wary of giving too early a date to features first recorded in the tenth century and later.

There is also evidence for the involvement of institutions other than *monasteria* in pastoral care.[60] In Bede's *Historia Ecclesiastica* the missionary work of bishops is frequently associated with the foundation of churches. For example, Paulinus's career in Northumbria was cut short before he could build 'oratories and baptisteries', but he was able to establish a church on the royal estate at *Campodunum*. In Wessex, Bishop Birinus 'built and dedicated churches' in his evangelization of the people. The success of Aidan's mission led not only to the endowment of *monasteria* but also to the foundation of churches. Aidan was accustomed to go about his work of preaching from bases on royal estates where he would have 'a church and a cell', and it was at one of these that he died.[61] It is unclear whether any individual priests were appointed so early to

---

57. See, for example, Bede, *Retractatio in Actus Apostolorum* (CCSL, 121, 1983), 126, lines 104-8. See also the valuable comments of P. Wormald in 'Æthelwold and his continental counterparts: Contact, comparison, contrast', in *Bishop Æthelwold, His Career and Influence*, ed. B. Yorke (1988), 40-1 on the distorting influence of Bede's monkish interests, which have obscured the clerical element in early Anglo-Saxon monasticism. For an interesting argument attempting to distinguish between pastoral and more purely monastic communities on the basis of topographical and archaeological evidence, see E. Cambridge, 'The early church in County Durham: a reassessment', *JBAA* cxxxvii (1984), 65-85.

58. The canons of the Council of *Clofesho* use the word *parochia* for diocese (see, for example, Canons 3 and 4). The terms *diocesis* and *ecclesia*, are also employed in other texts (Ecgbert's *Dialogues*, Questions 6 and 9, for example).

59. R. Morris, *Churches in the Landscape*, 128-33. Morris also argues that the use of the term 'old minster' in the tenth and eleventh centuries (which has been influential in suggesting that their prerogatives and territories were long-established) is more likely to distinguish them from recent foundations than to imply ancient origin.

60. This material has also been stressed by R. Morris, *The Church in British Archaeology* (CBA Research Report 47, 1983), 63-6; *idem, Churches in the Landscape*, 131-2; Cambridge, 'The early church in County Durham', 65-85.

61. Bede, *HE* ii. 14, iii. 7, 3, 17 (ed. Colgrave and Mynors, 189, 233, 263); other references to churches are in Bede, *HE* i. 26, ii. 20, iii. 30, and Bede, *Vita S. Cuthberti*, c.32.

particular churches, but there is evidence of the association of individuals with churches. When Bishop Putta retired from his see at Rochester, Bede says he was given 'a church and a small estate' by the Mercian bishop Seax-wulf.[62] Oratories are also mentioned, although without reference to clergy staffing them: John of Beverley used an oratory near Hexham as a place of retreat, Dryhthelm went to pray in an oratory in his village after his vision, and one eighth-century Kentish charter provides evidence of an oratory dedicated to St Martin.[63]

The establishment of churches may have been an important early stage in diocesan organization, at a time when, as Bede tells us, few *monasteria* had been founded.[64] Some *monasteria* may have developed from these churches: the evidence of Paulinus's aspirations in Northumbria is particularly suggestive since Bede's account implies that he would have wished to found not only a major church on a royal estate but also some subsidiary chapels. Aidan's churches on royal estates were clearly originally intended for one priest but could later have perhaps supported communities. Did churches continue to be founded? The two accounts in the *Historia Ecclesiastica* of churches established on the estates of lay *comites* suggests that they were.[65] But these also could have been staffed by communities, albeit very small ones, perhaps consisting of a priest and some clerks to assist with liturgical duties. Felix's *Vita S. Guthlaci* shows the hermit saint living at Crowland with his servant, a clerk.[66] If even dedicated solitaries did not live alone, perhaps it is wrong to expect such a state on the part of other priests. Community living may have been usual for both lay and religious life.

The origins of Christianity in the Anglo-Saxon kingdoms can be found in many traditions; Italians, Franks and Irish all made their contribution. The pattern of head church and subordinate chapels which it is suggested that Paulinus may have wished to establish would have been typical of the organization of pastoral care in his native Italy. Such a pattern may have been predominant in Kent, the missionary field of the Gregorian mission.[67] Similarly, Franks like Felix may have modelled their diocesan organization upon the Frankish model, where the cure of souls was under-taken by community churches and other establishments.[68] The multifarious origins of Christianity in England should encourage us to

---

62. Bede, *HE* iv. 12 (ed. Colgrave and Mynors, 368). It is noteworthy that in their accounts of the communities of clergy established in Francia and Italy to minister to the laity, neither Boyd nor Imbart de la Tour excludes the role of small parish churches, proprietary churches or monasteries: see *Tithes and Parishes*, 55-7 and *Les origines religeuses*, 74-87.
63. Bede, *HE* v. 2, 12 and *BCS* 160 (S24).
64. Bede, *HE* iii. 8.
65. Bede, *HE* v. 4, 5.
66. Felix, *Vita S. Guthlaci*, c.35.
67. It is interesting to note that Brooks compares the Kentish minsters (which were all royal foundations) to Italian baptismal churches: see *Church of Canterbury*, 183, 187-91.
68. In Wessex, Birinus was eventually succeeded by the Franks Agilbert and Leuthere (Bede, *HE* iii. 7).

think in terms of diversity rather than uniformity when seeking the roots of some of its oldest institutions.

The canons of the council of *Clofesho* are a major source for the history of pastoral care in Anglo-Saxon England. They record the concern of the Southumbrian bishops in the mid-eighth century for the ministry to the laity and represent an important endeavour to fulfil the church's obligations in this respect. They serve too to remind us of the vital part which bishops and priests played in the cure of souls and to provide an important contemporary perspective on the organization of pastoral care.[69]

---

69. I am grateful to Geoffrey Cubitt, Susan Kelly, Patrick Wormald, Richard Sharpe and John Blair for their comments and advice.

9 Anglo-Saxon minsters: a review of terminology

SARAH FOOT

The religious house provided a focus for the expression of early Anglo-Saxon piety; it satisfied both the devotional aspirations of individual men and women and the religious needs of its lay neighbours as a group. The spiritual functions which a *monasterium* performed for the laity might include the administration of the sacraments of baptism, communion and burial, the provision of teaching and preaching to the laity, or the guardianship of holy relics.[1] Such an institution could also, however, serve a useful social role by supplying education and literary services to those of the landowning class who had need of them, as well as relief to the traveller and pilgrim, to the destitute and the sick. In these ways religious houses fulfilled a dual role in the community, serving both as the vehicle for the expression of lay devotion and as the source of a number of valued intellectual and charitable services.

The dominant role that conventual establishments, as opposed to solitary religious, were to play throughout Anglo-Saxon society during the first centuries of English Christianity was determined in the conversion period, when in each kingdom groups of clerics living in communities undertook the evangelization of the populace. The links that these congregations forged with their lay neighbours persisted beyond the latter's nominal conversion, since, as is argued elsewhere in this volume, the same religious houses took responsibility for their continuing spiritual care.[2] It was thus common for priests, monks and other clerics to leave their parent-houses and travel around their locality, teaching the laity and bringing the sacraments of baptism and communion to them. As Bede said in relation to the habits of the Irish community at Lindisfarne:

> If by chance a priest came to a village, the villagers crowded together, eager to hear from him the word of life; for the priests and the clerics visited the villages for no other reason than to preach, to baptize, and to visit the sick, in brief to care for their souls.[3]

---

1. See Thacker, pp. 137-70 above and Foot, pp. 171-92 below.
2. See Thacker, pp. 000 above. See further my 'Anglo-Saxon minsters AD 597-c. 900: the religious house in England before the Benedictine reform' (unpubl. Ph.D. thesis, Univ. of Cambridge, 1990), ch. 7. A fuller version of the arguments presented in this article may be found in *ibid.*, ch. 2. For an alternative interpretation, see Cubitt, pp. 193-211 above.
3. Bede, *HE* iii. 26.

However, some of the populace appear as often to have visited their local church either on Sundays or at festivals to attend mass, to visit a notable shrine of proven thaumaturgic powers, or in hope of receiving other benefits, such as alms or succour and shelter if in need. Each of these services might also be sought by pilgrims or others travelling further afield.

Most ecclesiastics in the early period, whether contemplative religious or active pastoral workers, were attached to some kind of communal institution. Although it can be seen that some individual ecclesiastics regularly worked for long periods away from their houses of origin, and a few left the community altogether for lives of solitary asceticism, the corporate establishment was the norm. The legislators at church councils did not indeed envisage the possibility of parochial ministers working independently of any community; the canons they drafted repeatedly stressed the importance of priests' and monks' ties to their houses of origin.[4] Equally, everyone who came to the solitary life did so only after completing some period of time within a communal establishment.[5] While the conventual life was thus central to the expression of Christianity in early Anglo-Saxon England, a good deal of confusion still seems to surround not just the nature of these religious houses, but also the language most appropriately to be employed to describe them.

It seems that the habits of different religious communities in England before the Benedictine reform were even more diverse than has hitherto been recognized, and that it is almost impossible, and indeed extremely unwise, to generalize about the practices of religious communities before the tenth century. There is no such thing as 'a typical Anglo-Saxon monastery', no single standard against which individual houses may be matched; every establishment was organized on idiosyncratic lines, according to the particular interests of its founders and subsequent inmates. While similarities can inevitably be traced between many aspects of the lives of several different institutions, there are no norms governing the practice of monasticism in England before the tenth-century reformers imposed the standards of the Benedictine rule on all monastic houses.[6] It must also be recognized that there is no evidence from the early period to indicate that such diversity of practice was in any way deplored by English ecclesiastics, other than by Bede, whose views were arguably quite untypical of his age. It is worth drawing attention to this point at the

---

4. Compare Council of Hertford, AD 672/3, c.4, in Bede, *HE* iv. 5; Council of *Clofesho*, AD 747, c.29 in *Councils and Ecclesiastical Documents Relating to Great Britain and Ireland*, ed. A. W. Haddan and W. Stubbs (3 vols., 1869-78), iii, 374-5; legatine synods, AD. 786, c.6 (E. Dümmler, MGH, *Epistolae Karolini Aevi*, ii, 19-29, at 22); and Council of Chelsea, AD 816, c.5 (Haddan and Stubbs, *Councils*, iii, 581).
5. Cuthbert, for example, was a monk at Melrose and at Lindisfarne before he adopted the solitary life on Farne: *Vita S. Cuthberti*, iii. 1, ed. B. Colgrave (1940), 96. Similarly, Guthlac spent two years at Repton before choosing the life of a hermit: Felix, *Vita S. Guthlaci*, c.24, ed. B. Colgrave (1956), 26.
6. Not all religious houses were reformed at this time; similar diversity continued to characterize the practices of those that did not adopt the Benedictine Rule.

outset, for Bede's writings provide the most comprehensive evidence for the early history of the church in England and for eighth-century perceptions of English religious houses. They have thus done much to shape the ideas of subsequent generations of historians from the tenth century onwards. Bede's abhorrence of diversity and stress on uniformity can be shown to have had considerable impact on the way in which he depicted Anglo-Saxon religious institutions, and so indirectly to have affected the way in which almost everyone else has viewed the same establishments.[7]

I should like in this chapter to explore whether the diversity of religious observance and of the practice of monasticism visible in the early period are in any way reflected in the language used of the religious life in contemporary sources, and then to consider further whether the words used by the authors of those texts ought to affect the language employed by modern historians. There has been surprisingly little interest in this issue among modern scholars. Although Eric Cambridge, in his study of the early church in Co. Durham, drew attention to the value of a systematic analysis of the semantic range of the term *monasterium* and its Old English equivalent *mynster*,[8] neither he, nor anyone else to my knowledge, has undertaken a thorough investigation of the vocabulary used to describe religious houses in early Anglo-Saxon sources.

There are two related issues here. First, which are the words used by contemporary writers, and second, which term (or terms) should we be using to describe these institutions in modern English? Of the various Latin words available, the one most employed throughout western Europe was *monasterium*. As Christopher Brooke has written, 'there is no kind of religious community, or church bereft of a religious community, which was not at one time or another called a *monasterium*.'[9] The modern English 'monastery' obviously derives from the Latin *monasterium*, and many historians have thus elected to use 'monastery' to depict a communal religious establishment, in the sense of a place of residence of a community of persons living secluded from the world under religious vows. However, in the context of the texts from early Anglo-Saxon England in which it appears, the word *monasterium* is not easily defined; Richard Morris has even argued that the word 'is not susceptible to exact or exclusive definition'.[10] In modern usage, 'monastery' has acquired certain connotations of contemplative regularity, and particularly of Benedictinism; the word is often employed in a restricted sense to distinguish communities of regular monks from secular clerks. This distinction is, however, inappropriate to

---

7. Foot, 'Anglo-Saxon minsters', 20-8.
8. E. Cambridge, 'The early church in County Durham: a reassessment', *JBAA*, cxxxvii (1984), 65-85.
9. C. N. L. Brooke, 'Rural ecclesiastical institutions in England: the search for their origins', *Settimane ... di studi sull'alto medioevo*, xxviii (1982), 685-711, at 697.
10. R. Morris, 'Alcuin, York, and the *alma sophia*', in *The Anglo-Saxon Church: Papers ... in Honour of Dr H. M. Taylor*, ed. L. A. S. Butler and R. K. Morris (CBA Res. Rep. 60, 1987), 80-9, at 81.

the early Anglo-Saxon period, when differences between contemplative monks and active secular clergy were blurred.[11] There are other words that could be used instead.

The Latin *coenobium*, meaning a community of religious, is found in contemporary texts but is much less commonly used than *monasterium*. The neutrality of the word *coenobium* would have much to commend it, for although the adjective coenobitic tends to be used of the desert fathers, it carries no implications of any particular communal religious lifestyle known in early medieval England. Nevertheless, it cannot serve as the basis for a new terminology for historians, since the noun *coenobium* has no satisfactory modern English equivalent. The word *ecclesia* is often used by early Anglo-Saxon authors with reference not just to the religious buildings on a site but to the community dwelling within them; again adoption of the term 'church' in modern usage presents problems, since its use would normally be restricted either to the whole body of Christian people, or to ecclesiastical buildings containing altars. These three - *monasterium*, *coenobium* and *ecclesia* - are the words most often used in Latin texts, but others occur occasionally, notably *cella* and *domus*, and rarely, *locus*.

Because these Latin words do not allow one to distinguish institutions of different character, and because their conventional English equivalents can further mislead, some historians have preferred to adopt the term 'minster' from the Old English *mynster*.[12] This is a loan word from the Latin *monasterium*, of which it is used as a direct equivalent in vernacular texts throughout the Anglo-Saxon period.[13] In some ways the word 'minster' seems more neutral and hence more appropriate to the diversity of early Anglo-Saxon practice. In recent years, however, 'minster' has been used in a specialized sense by some scholars to refer to those Anglo-Saxon institutions that lay behind the mother-churches of Domesday Book. These collegiate churches were distinguishable from other communal religious establishments by virtue of their primarily pastoral function in serving the spiritual needs of a number of villages in their *parochia*. In being restricted to such establishments the term minster has thus acquired exclusively parochial terms of reference, which may not always be relevant to conditions in the earlier Anglo-Saxon church. Michael Franklin, for example, defined a minster as a 'a church originally, or vestigially, with pastoral responsibilities for an area larger than a single village'.[14] An earlier student of the same institutions, Patrick Hase, preferred 'mother-church' to 'minster' precisely because of the latter's 'connotations of communal life', and restricted his use of 'minster' to translating the Latin *monasterium*.[15]

---

11. N. Brooks, *The Early History of the Church of Canterbury* (1984), 187.
12. For example Margaret Deanesly, 'Early English and Gallic minsters', *Trans. Roy. Hist. Soc.* 4th series, xxiii (1941), 25-69.
13. A. Campbell, *Old English Grammar* (1959), 204-5.
14. M. J. Franklin, 'The identification of minsters in the Midlands', *Anglo-Norman Studies*, vii (1984), 69-87, at 69.
15. P. Hase, 'The development of the parish in Hampshire, particularly in the eleventh and twelfth centuries' (unpubl. Ph.D. thesis, Univ. of Cambridge, 1975), 13.

The lack of a generally accepted terminology for religious houses causes considerable confusion. It is becoming increasingly difficult to reconcile the wide variety of terms that are currently employed by modern historians, with the result that it is often very difficult to make comparison between the studies of the same sorts of ecclesiastical establishments and personnel if they are made by different individuals.[16] Similar problems arise in the translation of Anglo-Saxon texts. To take just one example: in Dorothy Whitelock's translation of King Alfred's law code in *English Historical Documents*, there are various inconsistencies. The phrase *of ðam mynstre* in chapter 21 is translated 'out of the minster', but *mynsterham* in chapter 2 is rendered as 'monastic house', and 'if anyone takes a nun out of a nunnery' is given for *gif hwa nunnan of mynstere ut alaede* (chapter 8).[17]

It is clear that investigation of the language used of the religious life is inseparable from consideration of the parallel question of the function exercised by religious communities. One of the long-running debates in Anglo-Saxon (and indeed early medieval) ecclesiastical history has been whether distinctions should be drawn between houses pursuing an active pastoral role and those institutions devoted exclusively to contemplation. Eric Cambridge has argued that

> however blurred it became in practice there is an important functional difference in principle between a church whose raison d'être is to provide for the pastoral needs of a lay population . . . and one whose prime purpose is to accommodate the liturgical requirements of a community that has come into being as a result of a desire to live according to a monastic rule.[18]

Some historians have indeed tried to differentiate between contemplative monasteries and pastorally active minsters in the early Anglo-Saxon period. For example, G. W. O. Addleshaw distinguished between 'monasteries in the Benedictine or Celtic sense', 'monastic families' (by which he meant groups of seculars leading pseudo-monastic lives of the type denounced by Bede) and 'non-monastic churches, staffed by a group of clergy living a semi-community life'; the last type he also described as 'minsters'.[19] It is, however, questionable whether the English at least saw this issue in such clear-cut terms.[20]

16. This issue was not resolved in the collection of papers edited by J. Blair, *Minsters and Parish Churches: The Local Church in Transition 900-1200* (1988).
17. D. Whitelock in *English Historical Documents I* c. *500-1042* (2nd edn., 1979), 410-11, no. 33.
18. Cambridge, 'The early church', 66.
19. G. W. O. Addleshaw, *The Pastoral Organisation of the Modern Dioceses of Durham and Newcastle in the Time of Bede* (Jarrow Lecture, 1963), 8-9.
20. Compare G. Constable, 'Monasteries, rural churches, and the *cura animarum* in the early Middle Ages', *Settimane . . . di studi sull'alto medioevo*, xxviii (1982), 349-89, at 358-9, who showed that from the sixth century monks were increasingly involved in pastoral work.

One of the paradoxes of early Anglo-Saxon monasticism was that however much individual monks might aspire to forsake the things of the world and live apart in contemplation and devotion, in practice no religious institutions of which record survives were completely isolated from the lay society of their locality.[21] Indeed, even some of those who tried to live as solitaries were thwarted in their ambitions. Wilgils, the father of the missionary Willibrord, built himself a chapel dedicated to St Andrew on the Humber estuary where he intended to live the austere life of a solitary, but he became celebrated for his miracles, his name was in everyone's mouth, and people flocked to him in great numbers to hear the Word of God and his advice.[22] Moreover, I can find no evidence to suggest that the early English clergy perceived any fundamental incompatibility between being a monk and performing sacramental functions for the laity, or indeed that they saw any incongruity in the participation of monks in any sort of activity outside their own community. Yet, even if the boundary between the active and contemplative lives was not so clearly defined in the early period as it was to be in later centuries, such a distinction may still have been appreciated by early English ecclesiastics. Perceptible differences between individual Anglo-Saxon religious houses are visible in the sources: were these related to the functions houses were designed to perform, and were such differences reflected in the words used of them?

To investigate this question, I examined the words used for religious houses in contemporary texts written before *c.* 900. The ecclesiastical works investigated included the decrees of church councils,[23] penitential literature,[24] the letters and writings of clerics such as Aldhelm, Boniface and Alcuin, and above all, saints' lives.[25] Among works of a less overtly ecclesiastical nature the most valuable were charters (at least those that have survived as originals or early copies), law codes, and the annalistic sources collected into the Anglo-Saxon Chronicle, even though the earliest of the surviving forms date only from the late ninth century and may not necessarily reflect accurately the vocabulary of the period in which they were originally composed.

For the earliest period of England's ecclesiastical history little contemporary

---

21. This is not a peculiarity of English circumstances, but was true of Carolingian Frankia also: R. McKitterick, *The Carolingians and the Written Word* (1989), 78-9.
22. Alcuin, *Vita S. Willibrordi*, c.1 (ed. W. Levison, MGH, *Scriptores rerum Merovingicarum*, vii, 81-141, at 116).
23. In addition to the two councils whose canons are recorded by Bede in the *Historia Ecclesiastica* (at Hertford in 672/3, and Hatfield in 679) there survive also the canons of the *Clofesho* councils of 747 and 803 (Haddan and Stubbs, *Councils*, iii. 362-85 and 541-8), of the legatine synods of 786 (Dümmler, MGH, *Epistolae Karolini Aevi*, ii, 19-29) and the Council of Chelsea in 816 (Haddan and Stubbs, *Councils*, iii. 579-84).
24. Of particular interest is the Penitential of Theodore, *Die Canones Theodori und ihre Überlieferungsformen*, ed. P. W. Finsterwalder (1929), 285-334.
25. For example the *Vitae* of Ceolfrith, Cuthbert, Guthlac and Wilfrid (and of Boniface and Leoba, for information about their early lives in English houses). There is also Æthelwulf's account of the lives of the abbots of a Northumbrian house: *De abbatibus*.

material survives. Those later sources that refer to the evangelization of the different kingdoms and the creation of the first religious houses do not necessarily reflect the vocabulary used by their first inmates. Although it might be surmised that the form of the institutions founded during the missionary phase would have had some influence on the nature of the houses established later in the same areas, and hence that similar words might have been used to describe establishments from each period, considerable caution must be exercised in attempting to draw conclusions about these words on the basis of non-contemporary materials. The particular problems of using Bede's *Historia Ecclesiastica* as a source for the early Anglo-Saxon church are well known and do not need elaboration here. It should, however, be stressed that Bede's experience of the monastic life as practised at Jarrow does not seem to be at all typical of the sorts of monasticism found elsewhere even in Northumbria let alone in the rest of England. Although the influence of Bede's own spiritual milieu on the development of his ideas has never been doubted, that this would be unparalleled elsewhere must not be forgotten.

It is striking how little variation there is in the language Bede employed for religious houses. This is not typical of Bede's Latin style. On other occasions his use of language could frequently be varied: for example, when he had to describe repeatedly the same occurrences – deaths, baptisms, the assumption or exercise of royal power – he used a range of different expressions.[26] Other than episcopal sees, Bede described every English establishment housing a community of religious as a *monasterium*. There are only two exceptions in the *Historia Ecclesiastica*. Iona he described at one point as the chief and head of many monasteries, *plurima coenobia*,[27] and the house established by Dicuill at Bosham in Sussex he called a *monasteriolum*.[28]

The same word was therefore used by Bede of all-female houses such as Hackness,[29] male communities as at Gilling,[30] and double houses, for example Barking.[31] The way of life pursued by such communities included communal liturgical obligations and private devotion, but both sexes were frequently also shown as engaged in active works: spiritual, educational and charitable. Indeed, the similarities between these double houses and single-sex houses, particularly in the ideals by which their lives were governed, are more notable than any differences. This can be observed throughout Bede's *Historia Ecclesiastica*. Not only did Bede frequently make direct comparison between the habits of different houses (between Hartlepool and

---

26. J. McClure, 'Bede's Old Testament kings', in *Ideal and Reality in Frankish and Anglo-Saxon Society*, ed. P. Wormald *et al.* (1983), 76-98. It has been argued that Bede did on other occasions use a restricted vocabulary very precisely: J. Campbell, 'Bede's words for places', in *Essays in Anglo-Saxon History* (1986), 99-119.
27. Bede, *HE* iii. 21.
28. Bede, *HE* iv. 13.
29. Bede, *HE* iv. 23.
30. Bede, *HE* iii. 14.
31. Bede, *HE* iv. 6.

Whitby, connected through the person of Hild, or between Melrose and Lindisfarne, linked by Cuthbert), but he implied that all early Anglo-Saxon *monasteria* led essentially the same way of life, that they were all governed by similar principles and followed the same basic kind of rule. For Bede, all monastic communities, congregations of 'those who live having everything in common in the Lord' were following identical ideals, and modelled their conduct on the practices of the earliest apostles in Jerusalem, this representing the nearest mankind could come to imitating the lives of the saints in heaven.[32] For him there was thus no difference between a house set aside for contemplative devotion and a church with active responsibilities. All Christians had a duty to perform good works, which, indeed, he saw as an essential preparation for the ultimate perfection of contemplation.[33] While it is possible to find houses in the *Historia Ecclesiastica* to whose congregations Bede attributed no external ministry, this distinction was clearly irrelevant to Bede.

Bede did, however, draw a clear terminological distinction between *monasteria* and *sedes episcopales*. All bishop's seats he termed thus or merely as *ecclesiae*. James Campbell argued that Bede seemed to have used the term *sedes episcopalis* to describe an estate sufficient to sustain a bishop; many appropriate sites were thus royal vills.[34] It is possible that it was the primary pastoral responsibilities of bishops' communities that led Bede to distinguish them from other *monasteria*, but in fact Bede went to some lengths to stress the devotional activities of episcopal *familiae*. He stressed this point particularly in relation to the first cathedral community established at Canterbury under Augustine and to the community at Lindisfarne which he argued was modelled on that of Canterbury.[35] It may rather have been that Bede considered cathedrals differed from *monasteria* in being subject to bishops, but he was careful to demonstrate that in their religious habits episcopal and abbatial *familiae* were essentially the same.

It can thus be seen that Bede did not attempt to differentiate between alternative kinds of religious community on the grounds of the sex or occupations of their inmates, other than in distinguishing communities ruled by abbots and abbesses from those governed by bishops.

The authors of other Latin texts from the seventh and eighth centuries appear to have employed basically the same language in the same fashion

---

32. Bede, *Retractatio in actus apostolorum*, iv. 32, ed. M. L. W. Laistner (CCSL, 121, 1983), 101-63, at 126-7.
33. Bede, *Homelia*, i. 9, ed. D. Hurst (CCSL, 122, 1960), 60-7, at 64. Compare *ibid.*, i. 2 (ed. Hurst, 7-13, at 9), where Bede also recommended the advantages of performing good works.
34. James Campbell, 'The church in Anglo-Saxon towns', in *Essays in Anglo-Saxon History* (1986), 139-54, at 140; P. Sawyer, 'The royal *tūn* in pre-Conquest England', in *Ideal and Reality in Frankish and Anglo-Saxon Society*, ed. P. Wormald *et al.* (1983), 272-99, at 277-8.
35. See J. A. Robinson, 'The early community at Christ Church', *J. Theol. Stud.* xxvii (1926), 225-40; Margaret Deanesly, 'The *familia* at Christchurch, Canterbury', in *Essays in Medieval History Presented to T. F. Tout*, ed. A. G. Little and F. M. Powicke (1923), 1-13; Brooks, *Church of Canterbury*, 87-91; Foot, 'Anglo-Saxon minsters', 91-3.

as did Bede; there is in fact remarkable consistency in the vocabulary used of the religious life in all sorts of early texts. The two words most commonly employed are *monasterium* and *coenobium*, the latter being used more frequently by other authors than it was by Bede, but without the separate words apparently representing different sorts of establishment.

The writers of the early Lives of Anglo-Saxon saints all used the words *coenobium* and *monasterium* interchangeably to describe a variety of religious houses.[36] That both words could be used by one writer of the same establishment (as, for example, by Cuthbert's anonymous hagiographer when speaking of the house at Ripon)[37] demonstrates that the two were considered to be synonymous. Variation in vocabulary seems to have been introduced by authors mainly for stylistic reasons. Wilfrid's hagiographer, Stephanus, in the chapters relating to the bishop's death at Oundle, described the house there first as a *monasterium*, then as *domus*, *cella* and finally as *coenobium*.[38] If this use of *cella* as a synonym for *monasterium* was a common one, it appears that the meaning of the word was not, as its modern equivalent usually is, restricted to apply solely to the subordinate cells of other *monasteria*. In this case it would not be necessary to assume that the establishment called a *cella* by Æthelwulf in his poem *De abbatibus* was subject to Lindisfarne, although it clearly had some connection with that house; there may have been other reasons (perhaps the constraints of writing hexameter verse) that led Æthelwulf to refer to the house whose abbots he described in this manner.[39] The language employed in early texts cannot be used to determine the relationships between different houses, whether those such as Hackness directly dependent on a larger *monasterium* (in this case, Whitby),[40] or those bound into some sort of confederation by a common founder such as Wilfrid's houses,[41] the Peterborough 'colonies',[42] and the *monasteria* reputedly founded by Aldhelm in Wiltshire.[43] No writer used different words to denote 'daughter' or subject houses; they were all described as *monasteria*.

Neither was language used by the authors of saints' Lives and penitentials or by the draftsmen of church councils as a means of distinguishing between houses on grounds of the functions exercised by their inmates. Willibald, Boniface's hagiographer, used the word *monasterium* to describe

---

36. This is true of the anonymous Lives of St Cuthbert and of Gregory the Great, of Felix's Life of St Guthlac, and Stephanus's Life of St Wilfrid, and of the Lives of the Anglo-Saxon missionaries to the Continent: Boniface, Willibald and Leoba. See further, Foot, 'Anglo-Saxon minsters', 58-61. Compare also Asser, Life of King Alfred, cc. 92 and 98, *Asser's Life of King Alfred*, ed. W. H. Stevenson (1904), 79 and 85.
37. *Vita S. Cuthberti*, ii. 2.
38. Stephanus, *Vita S. Wilfridi*, cc. 65-7, ed. B. Colgrave (1927), 140-4.
39. Æthelwulf, *De abbatibus*, c.4, line 78, and *passim*, ed. A. Campbell (1967), 9.
40. Bede, *HE* iv. 23.
41. Stephanus, *Vita S. Wilfridi*, c.62 (ed. Colgrave, 134).
42. F. M. Stenton, 'Medeshamstede and its colonies', in *Preparatory to Anglo-Saxon England*, ed. D. M. Stenton (1970), 179-92.
43. *BCS* 114.

both the house at Exeter and that at Nursling, although the former community included priests responsible for preaching to the laity in their neighbourhood, while the occupants of the latter apparently devoted their time primarily to contemplation and were notable for the quality of their learning.[44] The references to *monasteria* found in Archbishop Theodore's Penitential indicate clearly the dual role undertaken by many of these houses. For example, Theodore stipulated that when a *monachus* was ordained to the rank of *presbyter*, he was 'not to give up his former habit of life',[45] in other words he should maintain his devotional activities: a clear reference to the contemplative nature of the monk's life. Yet, while permitting someone to move their *monasterium* to another place, Theodore insisted that a *presbyter* should be left behind for the ministry of the church in that place.[46] It is interesting that while several of the eighth-century texts addressed the problems caused by the lay domination of religious houses, and the issue of irregular monastic practices, such corrupt establishments were not terminologically distinguished from more regular ones. Bede in his letter to Ecgberht, Ecgberht in his own Dialogues, and the compilers of conciliar legislation all still referred to these as *monasteria*, although the 747 *Clofesho* council did add the caveat, 'if indeed it is right so to call them'.[47]

Generally the language used in early Anglo-Saxon charters is as consistent as that employed in other early texts. The word *monasterium* is used, for example, in a late seventh-century document recording a grant to the double house at Barking in Essex,[48] and in a tenth-century grant of privileges to Winchester for a house at Taunton.[49] In one charter of King Æthelstan, the nunnery at Wilton was described as a *collegium Christicolarum*,[50] but communal religious houses were most frequently called *monasteria* in charters. It is, however, not uncommon to find the word *ecclesia* used in charters with reference to the whole community living in a house, not just to the church buildings.[51] The word *locus* was

---

44. Willibald, *Vita S. Bonifatii*, cc. 1-2, *Briefe des Bonifatius, Willibald's Leben des Bonifatius*, ed. R. Rau (1968), 454-524, at 462 and 466.
45. Theodore, *Penitential*, ii, vi. 12 (ed. Finsterwalder, *Die Canones Theodori*, 321): 'si quis monachus, quem elegerit congregatio ut ordinetur eis in gradum presbiterii, non debet dimitterre priorem conuersationem suam'.
46. *ibid.*, ii, vi. 7 (ed. Finsterwalder, 320): 'si quis uult monasterium suum in alium locum ponere, ... dimittat in priori loco presbiterum ad ministeria aecclesiae'.
47. Council of *Clofesho*, AD 747, c.5 (Haddan and Stubbs, *Councils*, iii. 364): 'si tamen ea fas est ita nominare'.
48. BCS 81 (S 1171). Compare Bede's account of the *monasterium* of Barking: Bede, *HE* iv. 6-10.
49. BCS 612, 611 (S 373 and 1286). The first of these charters is probably not authentic in the form in which it survives, since it appears, contrary to the implied sense of the document, that it was in fact only on this occasion that Winchester first acquired Taunton: H. R. P. Finberg, *The Early Christian Charters of Wessex* (1964), 128, no. 424 and 221-3. Compare also BCS 841 (S 1803), the foundation charter for Breedon-on-the-Hill in Leicestershire; see further, Foot, pp. 183-4 above.
50. BCS 714 (S 438).
51. This same usage is also found, for instance in Ecgberht, *Dialogi*, c.12 (Haddan and Stubbs, *Councils*, iii. 408), where it is specified that a layman who killed a bishop, priest, deacon or monk ought to do penance and pay the man's price to his church: 'et reddat precium aecclesiae suae'.

also occasionally used to denote a religious house; in his will, Æthelric, son of Æthelmund, listed the lands that he intended to bequeath to the *locus* at Deerhurst should his body be buried there.[52]

In the period before the mid-tenth-century reform of religious houses, *monasterium*, and to a lesser extent *coenobium*, were the standard words used in Latin texts to describe religious houses, male or female, active or contemplative. These words conveyed nothing about the regularity of observance of the resident community, for the eighth-century literature lamenting the irregularity of religious houses still called them *monasteria*. However, as I have already suggested, for historians writing about the Anglo-Saxon church, 'monastery' is not necessarily the best translation of *monasterium*, because of the implications of regular Benedictinism it has acquired in modern usage. There is an urgent need for another word that might convey the diversity of early Anglo-Saxon practice more accurately. In this context it is helpful to look at the vernacular terminology for the religious life in Anglo-Saxon England.

In Old English the Latin words *monasterium* and *coenobium* are both translated as *mynster*. This is the word used throughout the late ninth-century translation of Bede's *Ecclesiastical History*, rendering Bede's *monasterium* and *coenobium*,[53] in the ninth-century Old English Life of St Chad, also based on Bede's *Historia Ecclesiastica*,[54] as well as in the Anglo-Saxon Chronicle for all types of religious house.[55] The word *mynster* was also used consistently throughout the Old English Martyrology with reference to religious houses in Britain and in other places,[56] although communities of women were distinguished from all male houses in this text in a way not paralleled in other sources: the female houses at Ely and Barking, for example, were each described as *fæmnena mynster*.[57]

Similarly, charters and wills in Old English also usually referred to religious houses as minsters. Ealdorman Alfred made bequests to 'the religious houses (*mynsterhamas*) attached to God's churches in Kent',[58] and there is a grant by King Eadwig to Abingdon in which the house is

52. *BCS* 313 (S 1187) AD 804. For similar use in the vernacular see below p. 223, and n.63.
53. *The Old English Version of Bede's Ecclesiastical History of the English People*, ed. T. Miller (Early English Text Society, o.s. 95-6 and 110-1, 1890-8). This translation invariably rendered *monasterium* as *mynster*. Bede's description of Dicuill's house at Bosham as a *monasteriolum* (iv. 13), was translated as *medmicel mynster* (iv. 17; Miller, 302), and the sole use of *coenobium* in the Latin text (iii. 21) was translated simply as *mynster* (iii. 15; Miller, 224).
54. *The Life of St Chad: An Old English Homily*, ed. R. Vleeskuyer (1953).
55. For example, *Anglo-Saxon Chronicle MS A*, ed. J. Bateley, s.a. 673, 688, 962, *The AS Chronicle: a Collaborative Edition*, ed. D. Dumville and S. Keynes, iv (1985).
56. See Old English Martyrology, 12 Jan., *Das altenglische Martyrologium*, ed. G. Kotzer, Bayerische Akademie der Wissenschaften, Philosophisch-Historische Klasse, neue folge 88 (2 vols., Munich, 1981), ii, 15.
57. *ibid.*, 23 June, 11 October (ed. Kotzer, 128, 228).
58. F. Harmer, *Select English Historical Documents of the Ninth and Tenth Centuries* (1914) [hereafter Harmer, *SEHD*], no. 10 (S 1508); compare Harmer, *SEHD* 2 (S 1482).

described first in the Latin text as a *monasterium*, and then, after the bounds, in Old English as the *mynster*.[59] Occasionally the word *stow* could denote a minster; it was used to represent Christ Church, Canterbury, in the Old English record of the donation by the Kentish ealdorman, Alfred, of the *Codex Aureus* to the cathedral church.[60] *Mynster* was the standard word used of religious houses in law codes throughout the Anglo-Saxon period,[61] although from King Eadgar's reign onwards the situation is confused by the fact that the 'old minsters' which were entitled to receive tithes and other dues, were distinguished from other churches.[62] *Minster* occurs as an element in several English placenames, particularly in the south-west.[63] It is usually presumed that these names indicate the previous existence of a church with a community on the site,[64] but the earliest examples are attested only from the late ninth century, and it is not clear whether *minster* was an element of earlier Anglo-Saxon placenames.

Although I have looked mostly at texts and documents from the earlier Anglo-Saxon period, as far as I can see the word *mynster* continued to be used in the same way in the later tenth and eleventh centuries, as a direct translation of *monasterium* and with reference to any kind of religious establishment with a church.[65] It was used of communal religious establishments in the vernacular literature relating to the reform,[66] and in charters in the tenth and eleventh centuries. The early eleventh-century text, *Secgan*,[67] listing the resting-places of saints' relics in Anglo-Saxon England, referred to some of the houses it mentioned as minsters, for example Ripon[68] and Wimborne.[69]

It is thus clear that while certain authors may have varied their vocabulary for stylistic reasons, on the whole there was substantial consistency in the language used to depict religious houses in vernacular and Latin texts written in the pre-Viking period. The word *monasterium*

---

59. *BCS* 924 (S 605); compare *BCS* 551 (S 218).
60. Stockholm Royal Library, *Codex Aureus*, fo. 10r; (Harmer, *SEHD*, no. 9).
61. Compare the law code of Wihtred, c.17, *Die Gesetze der Angelsachsen*, ed. F. Liebermann (3 vols., 1903-16), i, 13; Ine, c.6.1 (*ibid.*, 90); V Æthelstan, c.3 (*ibid.*, 168).
62. See for example, II Eadgar., cc. 1-3 (*ibid.*, 196).
63. Places such as Axminster, Beaminster, Charminster etc.; see E. Ekwall, *The Concise Oxford Dictionary of English Place-Names* (4th edn., 1960). *Stow* meaning holy place, hermitage, or religious house is also recorded as an element of a number of place-names: *ibid.*, 448.
64. K. Cameron, *English Place-Names* (1961), 127.
65. See J. Blair, 'Introduction: from minster to parish church', in *Minsters and Parish Churches: The Local Church in Transition 950-1200* (1988), 1-19, at 1.
66. Æthelwold, 'Old English account of King Eadgar's establishment of minsters', *Councils and Synods, with Other Documents Relating to the English Church: I 871-1204*, ed. D. Whitelock *et al.* (2 vols., 1981, i, 142-54, no. 33). The same text also used the word *stow* on one occasion to describe the minster at Glastonbury: *ibid.*, 148-9.
67. See D. Rollason, 'Lists of saints' resting-places in Anglo-Saxon England', *Anglo-Saxon England*, vii (1978), 61-93.
68. *Secgan*, ii. 5, F. Liebermann, *Die Heiligen Englands* (Hanover, 1889), 9.
69. *ibid.*, ii. 45 (Liebermann, 17).

and its Old English equivalent *mynster* were used interchangeably to denote any establishment housing a community of religious other than an episcopal see. Bishops' seats were distinguished terminologically from congregations of persons living under the control of an abbot, but houses were not differentiated in any other way, for example, according to the sex or clerical status of their inmates, or to the functions they performed.

There is therefore no good reason to restrict the usage of 'minster' in modern English to those communities which the sources proved to have exercised pastoral care, nor is it appropriate to use the word 'monastery' to denote an institution whose members were apparently engaged primarily in individual acts of devotion within the enclosure. All Anglo-Saxon ecclesiastics, including the members of episcopal *familiae*, appear to have spent some part of their time in personal contemplative prayer and in communal worship. Each religious house also had a prominent intercessory role, for its members were expected to say prayers and masses regularly for the sake of the king and his whole people, as well as for individuals who had made particular petitions.[70] Equally a substantial number of ecclesiastical communities may clearly be seen to have undertaken certain parochial duties for the spiritual benefit of their lay neighbours. If pastoral care is understood to consist solely of the provision of sacraments – baptism, communion and burial – then it is likely that there were *monasteria* unable to supply sufficient ordained clergy to provide such ministry on a regular basis to the laity. If, on the other hand, other sorts of pastoral activity (teaching, preaching, caring for the sick and visiting pilgrims, and the giving of alms) are also to be seen as forms of pastoral ministry, then a much greater proportion of ecclesiastical communities is likely to have been involved in such work. The latter presumption is supported by the fact that writers from the early Anglo-Saxon period saw no apparent contradiction in the expression of religious devotion through the dual roles of action and contemplation; if the *cura animarum* were solely the responsibility of those ordained to clerical orders, this would surely have been stated explicitly.[71] After the monastic reform of the tenth century, attitudes to these issues may well have changed: the Rule of St Benedict specifically prohibits monks from engaging in external ministry,[72] and houses that followed its precepts became distinct from those 'minsters' which continued to follow their former, in Benedictine eyes more irregular, lifestyle.

If it is generally agreed that the word 'monastery' cannot encompass all the aspects of the early Anglo-Saxon religious life, and particularly the

70. See Council of *Clofesho*, AD 747, cc. 10 and 27 (Haddan and Stubbs, *Councils*, iii. 366 and 373).
71. Compare Bede's statements laying the obligations of preaching on other members of religious communities than just priests: *Homelia*, i, 7 (ed. Hurst, CCSL, 122, 49). See further, Foot, 'Parochial ministry in early Anglo-Saxon England: the role of monastic communities', *Studies in Church History*, xxvi (1989), 43-54, at 47-8.
72. Rule of St Benedict, c.60 (ed. A. de Vogüé, Sources chrétiennes, 182, 634-6). See also U. Berlière, 'L'exercice du ministère paroissal par les moines dans le haut moyen âge', *Revue Bénédictine*, xxxix (1927), 227-50, at 230-3.

involvement of many communal houses in active and pastoral work, then what word should be used instead by students of these institutions? Since it is not possible to use the language current in the period before the mid-tenth century as a means of differentiating between alternative styles of conventual life, why should such distinctions be attempted by the modern historian? I can offer no good reason why all communal establishments should not be called 'minsters' in modern English. To restrict the use of this word to represent only those houses which in the tenth and eleventh centuries took pastoral responsibility for wide geographical areas,[73] is to lose the much more diverse sense that 'minster' carried in the earlier Anglo-Saxon period. Similarly, to insist on 'monastery' as a translation for *monasterium* is to apply inappropriate standards of monastic observance to early Anglo-Saxon communities, and to deny the possibility that their members were engaged in the cure of souls. Although concepts of regularity were not unknown or unimportant in the early English church (and are indeed particularly apparent in the conciliar literature), neither the quality nor nature of a minster's religious observance was indicated in the language by which it was described in contemporary sources, and modern historians should not attempt to enforce such subjective values by their own use of language. After the tenth-century reform such issues do become more relevant, when Benedictine monks drew sharp contrast between regular monasteries and houses of seculars not living by monastic rule. In that period those institutions which maintained communities of clergy assuming pastoral responsibility for their neighbours might reasonably be called mother-churches rather than minsters.[74]

The sole feature common to every early Anglo-Saxon religious house, and the one which was clearly recognized by all contemporary writers, was the corporate nature of its inmates' lives. All religious houses were distinguished from congregations of lay people, at least in theory, by the fact that as groups of brothers and sisters in Christ they shared their earthly and spiritual lives as one territorially coherent family, ostensibly devoted to some aspect of the service of God.[75] Beyond this essential communality there were wide differences in functions for which houses were created, in the status of their inmates,[76] and in the activities in which they engaged, and no further broad generalizations are possible. The very nature of the word 'minster' thus has much to commend it, for it was used contemporaneously to encompass a very wide diversity of houses: I therefore commend it as the most appropriate word for describing pre-reform religious houses in England.

---

73. Franklin, 'The identification of minsters'.
74. P. Hase, 'The mother churches of Hampshire', in *Minsters and Parish Churches*, ed. J. Blair (1988), 45–66.
75. It cannot be coincidence that in Anglo-Saxon England the words for family, Latin *familia* and Old English *hiwisc*, also denote a measurement of land, the hide, nominally the amount of land required to support one household.
76. I hope in a future article to investigate the occupants of minsters and the language by which they were described in Anglo-Saxon texts; see further, Foot, 'Anglo-Saxon minsters', pp. 68–80.

10 Anglo-Saxon minsters: a topographical review[1]

JOHN BLAIR

In a volume devoted to the pastoral functions of minsters, a survey of their forms may seem out of place. For two reasons, it is not. First, a central message of this book is that late medieval definitions of the religious life are inapplicable to early medieval religious communities, and it is important to extend this conclusion to the precincts and buildings which the communities occupied. By the twelfth century one old minster might be a great abbey with Romanesque claustral buildings, another a mere parish church, but in terms of their Anglo-Saxon origins the distinction is irrelevant.[2] Second, the topography of sites reflects their functions. Just as the enclosed and specialized character of a later medieval abbey was obvious from its layout, so an Anglo-Saxon minster often resembled, in the density and relative informality of its buildings, a very large and populous lay settlement. Monastic sites add a physical and spatial dimension to the contacts between ecclesiastics and laity upon which pastoral care depended.

Rejecting another set of received contrasts – between Celtic and English and between insular and Roman – I shall suggest a common thread of development through the various societies of north-west Europe in which religious communities were founded between the fifth and ninth centuries. When the physical and topographical data, amplified by contemporary written sources, are left to speak for themselves, remarkably few real distinctions can be sustained between the ecclesiastical planning of the British, Irish, Merovingian and Anglo-Saxon worlds.

I shall look only in passing at religious sites which did not house communities, such as chapels, cemeteries, hermitages and holy wells. This singling-out of minsters imposes a boundary which will seem arbitrary to specialists in certain periods and places, and which is never completely

1. For their comments on an earlier draft, for much additional information and for permission to reproduce figures, I am extremely grateful to Steven Bassett, Martin Biddle, Sarah Blair, Nicholas Brooks, Catherine Cubitt, Sarah Foot, Simon Loseby, Elizabeth O'Brien, David Parsons, Warwick Rodwell, Richard Sharpe, Tim Tatton-Brown, Charles Thomas and Patrick Wormald. As always, Pat Lloyd's typing skills have proved an enormous help.
2. This broad approach, and the validity of treating minsters as a distinct category, are justified at greater length in J. Blair, 'Secular minster churches in Domesday Book', in *Domesday Book: a Reassessment*, ed. P. H. Sawyer (1985), 104–42; *idem*, 'Minster churches in the landscape', in *Anglo-Saxon Settlements*, ed. D. Hooke (1988), 35–58. Cf. Sarah Foot's chapter on terminology in the present volume.

satisfactory. The smaller sites share characteristics of the large ones (notably the reuse of older enclosures and structures), and in areas of strong Christian continuity such as south-west Britain, they were often the precursors of monastic communities.[3] None the less, the political and economic importance of minsters, and the scale and complexity of their planning, provide compelling reasons for considering them as a group.

LOCATIONS

A well-worn contrast is that between the 'urban' monasteries of Romanized England and the hills and islands beloved by 'Celtic' monks. An obvious but perhaps necessary point is that in the absence of towns (other than a few coastal *wics*), no seventh-century English minster could be urban in the later medieval sense. In fact, the sites most characteristic of early religious communities in Gaul, Ireland, Britain and the English kingdoms can be defined, very simply, as prominent but not remote.

The summits or shoulders of low hills and promontories, islands in marshy floodplains and headlands in the bends of rivers or on the sea-coast, are favoured locations in Ireland, western Scotland and Wales.[4] But they are also numerous in Gaul, as at Nivelles (fig. 10.1), Manglieu (fig. 10.2), Lérins or Noirmoutier, among the sites of the Anglo-Saxon missions to Germany, as at Fulda (fig. 10.2), and in England itself.[5] In Æthelwulf's poem *De abbatibus* the instruction to build the first church on 'a small hill with a bending downward path', overgrown by thorn-bushes and the haunt of evil men, comes from the holy Ecgberht in Ireland,[6] and such early cases as Coldingham on the coast (fig. 10.1), Lastingham among its 'steep and remote hills', and Old Melrose in its bend of the Tweed,[7] may reflect direct Irish influence. Yet the pattern is widespread in areas as far apart as Northumbria (as at Jarrow, Monkwearmouth, Hartlepool, Bywell (fig. 10.1)

---

3. Cf. C. Thomas, 'Christians, chapels, churches and charters', *Landscape Hist.* xi (1989), 19-26. Other surveys which prefer not to make the distinction between minsters and lesser sites so strongly are R. Morris, *The Church in British Archaeology* (CBA, Research Rep. 47, 1983); R. Morris, *Churches in the Landscape* (1989); V. Hurley, 'The early church in the south-west of Ireland: settlement and organisation' in *The Early Church in Western Britain and Ireland: Studies Presented to C. A. Raleigh Radford*, ed. S. M. Pearce (BAR, Brit. ser. 102, 1982), 297-332.

4. Hurley, 'Early church in S.W. Ireland', 307-11; E. G. Bowen, *The Settlements of the Celtic Saints in Wales* (1954), 118-39; C. Thomas, *The Early Christian Archaeology of North Britain* (1971), 32-8.

5. D. Parsons, 'Sites and monuments of the Anglo-Saxon mission in central Germany', *Archaeol. J.* cxl (1983), 291-4; idem, 'The siting of early monasteries in Europe north of the Alps', *Actes du XIᵉ congrès de l'union internationale des sciences préhistoriques et protohistoriques* (Mainz, August-September 1987) (forthcoming); Morris, *Churches in the Landscape*, 111-12.

6. Æthelwulf, *De abbatibus*, lines 125-39, ed. A Campbell (1967), pp. 12-13.

7. Bede, *HE* iii. 23 and v. 12 (ed. Colgrave and Mynors, 286, 488).

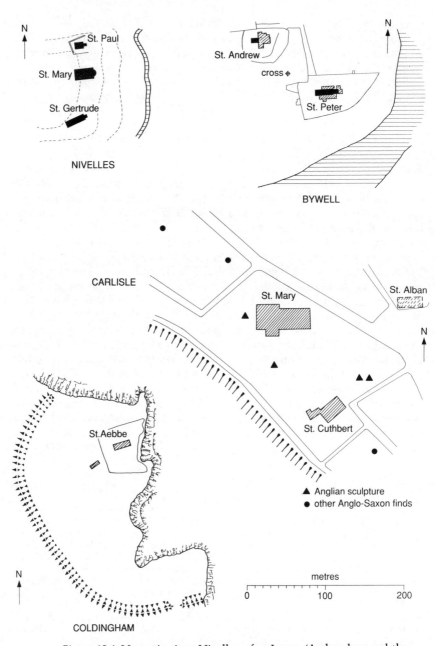

Figure 10.1 Monastic sites. Nivelles: after James, 'Archaeology and the Merovingian monastery', fig. 2.3. Bywell: after O.S. 25″ map. Coldingham: after Alcock, 'Early historic fortifications in Scotland', Fig. 38, with church from OS 25 inch map. Carlisle: after McCarthy, 'Thomas, Chadwick and post-Roman Carlisle', fig. 15.3.

Conventions: Merovingian and Anglo-Saxon churches in solid block; later medieval churches in outline.

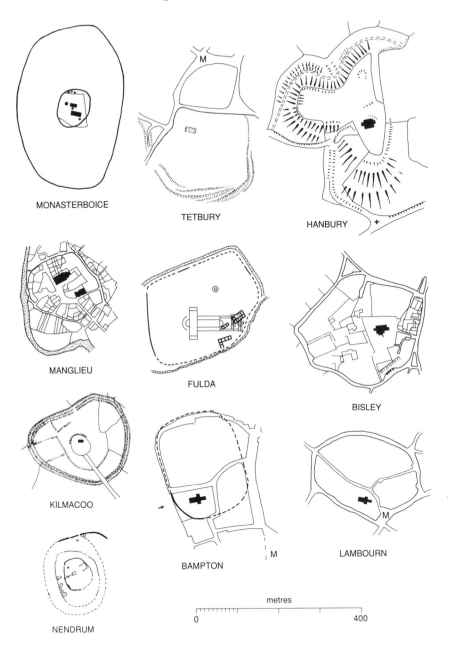

MONASTERBOICE

TETBURY

HANBURY

MANGLIEU

FULDA

BISLEY

KILMACOO

BAMPTON

LAMBOURN

NENDRUM

metres

0   400

Figure 10.2 Curvilinear monastic enclosures. Monasterboice: after Swan, 'Monastic proto-towns', fig. 4.16. Tetbury: after *VCH Glos.* xi, 260. Hanbury: after Hooke, *Anglo-Saxon Landscapes of the West Midlands*, fig. 2.6(iii). Manglieu: after Fournier, *Peuplement Rural en Basse Auvergne*, fig. 36. Fulda: after unpublished plan reproduced by kind

Pastoral Care before the Parish*

permission of David Parsons. Bisley: after OS 25 inch map. Kilmacoo:
after Hurley, 'Early church in S.W. of Ireland', fig. 18.7. Bampton: based
on survey by John Blair, in progress. Lambourn: after OS 25 inch map.
Nendrum: after Herity, 'Buildings and layout', fig. 2.
Conventions: earthworks hachured; water stippled; roads in outline; walls
and ditches in heavy line; existing medieval churches in solid black. M =
market.

or Seaham), the Midlands (as at Repton[8] or Chesterfield[9]), the Thames
Valley (as at Eynsham, Oxford,[10] Abingdon, Cookham, Staines or Chert-
sey), the coasts of Essex and East Anglia (as at Tilbury, Bradwell-on-Sea or
Iken),[11] and the south coast (as at Bosham founded by an Irishman, Selsey
founded by St Wilfrid,[12] Wareham[13] or Christchurch[14]). It must be regarded
as general practice among the builders of late seventh- and eighth-century
minsters in all the English kingdoms, preferred except when other
considerations (such as the existence of a reusable fort) dictated otherwise.[15]
Far from being remote, sites of this kind in Ireland were usually in the
prime geographical zones for farming and settlement.[16] In England, the
nucleation of settlement into lowland villages from the ninth century
onwards has left many minsters isolated, disguising a pattern which would
originally have been much closer to that still visible in Ireland. A recent
analysis of minsters in the West Midlands shows that they were often sited
amid the best agricultural land, in the kinds of places that might equally

---

8. M. Biddle, 'Archaeology, architecture and the cult of saints in Anglo-Saxon
   England', in *The Anglo-Saxon Church: Papers . . . in Honour of Dr H. M. Taylor*,
   ed. L. A. S. Butler and R. K. Morris (CBA, Research Rep. 60, 1986), 22, compares
   Repton minster and its royal mausolea, on a bluff overlooking the Trent, with
   the Sutton Hoo barrows overlooking the Deben and Beowulf's barrow on its
   coastal promontory.
9. Blair, 'Minster churches in the landscape', fig. 2.1.
10. J. Blair, 'St Frideswide's monastery: problems and possibilities', *Oxoniensia*, liii
    (1988), 228-31.
11. Bede, *HE* iii. 22; S. E. West, N. Scarfe and R. Cramp, 'Iken, St Botolph, and the
    coming of East Anglian Christianity', *Proc. Suffolk Inst. of Archaeol. and Hist.*
    xxxv (1984), 279-301.
12. Bede, *HE* iv. 13: Bosham is 'monasteriolum permodicum . . . silvis et mari
    circumdatum'; Selsey is 'locus undique mari circumdatus praeter ab occidente'.
    For the site of Selsey, see J. T. Munby, 'Saxon Chichester and its predecessors',
    in *Anglo-Saxon Towns in Southern England*, ed. J. Haslam (1984), 317-20.
13. Asser, *De Rebus Gestis Ælfredi*, c.49, ed. W. H. Stevenson (new edn., 1959), 36-
    7: Wareham, 'quod monasterium sanctimonialium inter duo flumina . . .
    tutissimo terrarum situ situm est, nisi ab occidentali parte tantummodo, ubi
    contigua terra est'.
14. P. H. Hase, 'The mother churches of Hampshire', in *Minsters and Parish Chur-
    ches*, ed. J. Blair (1988), 51.
15. The possibility that artificial mounds were sometimes raised for this purpose
    needs to be investigated archaeologically; Willibald describes the building of a
    mound for a church on the site of St Boniface's martyrdom: *The Anglo-Saxon
    Missionaries in Germany*, ed. C. H. Talbot (2nd edn., 1981), 61.
16. Hurley, 'Early church in S.W. Ireland', 310.

well have attracted royal vills.[17] Among the dispersed farmsteads of the seventh- and eighth-century countryside they would often have provided a focus, even if one set somewhat apart, dominating lesser habitations just as the hill-forts which they sometimes reoccupied had done in the late Iron Age.[18]

Although choices of site were often influenced by political circumstances, the normal relationship between royal minster and royal power-centre seems to have been one of proximity rather than absolute contiguity.[19] Churches which were integral components of royal palaces are indeed recorded in early seventh-century Northumbria: the *basilica* built by Paulinus in the royal vill of *Campodunum*; Aidan's *ecclesiae* and *cubicula* at Bamburgh and other royal vills; the apparent Christianization of the pagan cult focus at the east end of the Yeavering palace complex;[20] and the seventh-century minster buildings at Repton (Derbyshire), which seem to have reused a large timber hall.[21] Yet these cases are hard to parallel later. The communities born in the spate of minster-building from the 660s onwards were probably richer and more self-sufficient than their predecessors, and they show a different topographical pattern. Though often apparently 'twinned' with a royal centre no more than 2 or 3 miles away,[22] a minster was normally set amid its own lands and housed within its own enclosure.

CURVILINEAR ENCLOSURES

In early medieval north-western Europe, a religious community was usually contained within a stone or earthwork enclosure. Rarely strong enough to be defensive, the boundary divided sacred from secular and defined zones of jurisdiction. Except where Roman structures were reused, the typical enclosure was round or oval: such sites were merely the largest and most complex in a broad range of curvilinear religious enclosures, extending

---

17. P. Sims-Williams, *Religion and Literature in Western England, 600–800* (1990), 368–71, 394–5. Cf. the rather similar implications of R. Hill, 'Christianity and geography in early Northumbria', *Studies in Church History*, iii (1966), 126–39.
18. Such minsters, close to lay settlement if set somewhat apart from it, must of course be distinguished from genuinely secluded sites such as rest-houses and hermitages. Parsons, 'Siting of early monasteries', aptly contrasts Lindisfarne, closely linked to royal government and secular life, with Cuthbert's hermitage on Inner Farne.
19. It follows that a similar relationship between minsters founded by lay aristocrats and aristocratic centres might be expected; but at present no information is available.
20. Bede, *HE* ii. 14 and iii. 17; B. Hope-Taylor, *Yeavering: An Anglo-British Centre of Early Northumbria* (1977), 70–85.
21. Information from Martin Biddle and Birthe Kjølbye-Biddle.
22. As argued by R. Cramp. 'Anglo-Saxon settlement', in *Settlement in North Britain 1000 BC – AD 1000*, ed. J. C. Chapman and H. C. Mytum (BAR, British Ser. 118, 1983), 278–9, and by Blair, 'Minster churches in the landscape', 40–8.

down to the small circular churchyards common in south-west Britain, Ireland and Gaul.[23]

These generalizations are familiar to historians of Ireland, where the early topography has been least obscured and the most systematic fieldwork has been done. Surviving enclosures at the more important Irish monastic sites are typically between 400 and 200 metres across (e.g. Monasterboice, fig. 10.2). There is normally an inner enclosure, sometimes with stone crosses at its cardinal points, and there are often complex internal subdivisions. The boundary (described in Adomnán's Life of St Columba as the *uallum monasterii* or *cenubii septa*) is marked by an earth bank and ditch, a dry-stone wall, or both,[24]

Elsewhere remains are more fragmentary, and have been recognized more slowly. In Merovingian and Carolingian Gaul, literary sources suggest that a monastery normally had its *septa* or *uallum*. Around the huge circular enclosure at Solignac (Limousin), some 1,800 metres in circumference, was a hedge-topped earth bank, and a thorn hedge bounded the precinct of Clermont.[25] Urban growth has usually destroyed the earthworks, but an encircling road often reflects the precinct boundary. The phenomenon has been observed at several Merovingian and Carolingian monastic sites in the Auvergne (e.g. Manglieu, fig. 10.2), and a systematic search would probably reveal counterparts to the Irish enclosures at the core of many French towns.[26]

In northern Britain, enclosures of comparable shape and size have been examined archaeologically at minsters of Irish or Hiberno-Northumbrian

23. For these smaller sites, often the size of an average ring-fort or rath, see the works cited in notes 24, 26 and 32, and D. O'Sullivan, 'Curvilinear churchyards in Cumbria', *Bull. CBA Churches Committee*, xiii (1980), 3-5. There is a useful summary of recent French work in M. Fixot and E. Zadora-Rio, *L'église, la campagne, le terroir* (Paris, 1990). W. Rodwell, *The Fisherman's Chapel, Saint Brelade, Jersey* (1990), 123-38, discusses, with parallels, an example on Jersey.
24. These remarks are based on L. Swan, 'Monastic proto-towns in early Ireland: the evidence of aerial photography, plan analysis and survey', in *The Comparative History of Urban Origins in Non-Roman Europe*, ed. H. B. Clarke and A. Simms (BAR, Internat. Ser. 255, 1985), i, 77-102; Hurley, 'Early church in S.W. Ireland', 311-26; E. R. Norman and J. K. St Joseph, *The Early Development of Irish Society: the Evidence of Aerial Photography* (1969), ch. 5; Thomas, *Early Christian Archaeology*, 29-32; M. Herity, 'The buildings and layout of early Irish monasteries before the year 1000', *Monastic Studies*, xiv (1983), 247-84; A. D. S. Macdonald, 'Aspects of the monastery and monastic life in Adomnán's Life of St Columba', *Peritia*, iii (1984), 273-4, 281.
25. E. James, 'Archaeology and the Merovingian monastery', in *Columbanus and Merovingian Monasticism*, ed. H. B. Clarke and M. Brennan (BAR, Internat. Ser. 113, 1981), 40-1.
26. G. Fournier, *Le peuplement rural en Basse Auvergne durant le haut moyen age* (Publications de la Faculté des Lettres et Sciences Humaines de Clermont-Ferrand, 2nd ser. xii, 1962), 539-76, esp. Cournon (fig. 35), Manglieu (fig. 36) and Moissat (fig. 34). The air photograph of Manglieu in A. G. Manry, *Histoire de l'Auvergne* (1974), opp.97, makes a striking comparison with the photograph of Armagh in Norman and St Joseph, *Early Development of Irish Society*, fig. 69. Fixot and Zadora-Rio, *L'église, la campagne, le terroir*, 15-16, lists several examples, and for another in the Limousin see [Anon.] *Saint Léonard-de-Noblat* (Conaissance et Sauvegarde de Saint-Léonard, n.d., c. 1989).

origin (Iona, Coldingham (fig. 10.1) and Dacre).[27] They have been recognized topographically in Wales, and in other parts of Britain where minsters with pre-English origins are particularly likely to be found.[28] Disconcertingly for conventional wisdom, they are now turning up in the southern English kingdoms, and on sites where no British religious activity need be suspected. Hardly any have so far been dated by excavation, but morphologically they are extremely similar to the Irish, Gallic and northern British enclosures (see fig. 10.2). Thame, Charlbury and Bampton (Oxfordshire), Lambourn (Berkshire) and Bisley (Gloucestershire) all have the characteristic perimeter roads;[29] in the case of Bampton, excavation across the line of the road confirms that it follows a ditch, 4 metres wide, which was back-filled around the late eleventh century.[30] St Wilfrid's minster at Oundle (Northamptonshire), surrounded by its thorn hedge, may well have been similar.[31]

This fashion for curvilinear enclosures embodies older practices which were themselves common to all the insular peoples: the enclosure of cemeteries by circular boundaries,[32] and the reuse of high-status enclosures (whether originally ceremonial or defensive) for religious purposes. Grants of enclosed sites by kings to monastic founders often occur in Irish saints' lives, and there are several cases where identifiably secular cashels and raths of Iron Age date came to contain monastic churches, as at Nendrum (fig. 10.2), Dundesert and Cashel.[33] The practice may have been commoner in Britain than we know: several hill-forts have produced evidence for occupation between the fifth and eighth centuries,

27. Iona: J. W. Barber, 'Excavations on Iona, 1979', *Proc. Soc. Antiquaries of Scotland*, cxi (1981), 352-64. Coldingham: L. Alcock, 'Early historic fortifications in Scotland', in *Hill-Fort Studies: Essays for A. H. A. Hogg*, ed. G. Guilbert (1981), 162-5; *idem* in *Current Archaeology*, 79 (October 1981), 234-5. (The first phase of the Coldingham *uallum* is a double palisade of oak beams with wicker infill, dated by a radiocarbon determination to AD 630 × 770, which is interpreted as secular but could surely just as well be monastic.) Dacre: N. Higham, *The Northern Counties to AD 1000* (1986), 283.
28. There are published aerial photographs of big round enclosures at Eglwys Gymyn, Wales (W. Davies, *Wales in the Early Middle Ages* (1982), 26), and Eccleston (Cheshire) (*VCH, Cheshire*, i, Pl.19); cf. that of Bardney (Lincs.), in D. Knowles and J. K. St Joseph, *Monastic Sites from the Air* (1952), 23, which seems to show a perfectly circular boundary around the twelfth-century church and cloister.
29. Blair, 'Minster churches in the landscape', figs 2.3 and 2.5. K. Barker, 'The early history of Sherborne', in *Early Church in W. Britain and Ireland*, ed. Pearce, 104-8 and fig. 17.15, also illustrates Lambourn, Charlbury and Thame, together with examples at Sherborne, Wimborne, Beaminster, Ramsbury, Westbury and Amesbury.
30. J. Blair, 'The Bampton research project', *South Midlands Archaeology*, xviii (1988), 89-90.
31. Stephanus, *Vita S. Wilfridi*, c.67, ed. B. Colgrave (1927).
32. Cf. Thomas, *Early Christian Archaeology*, 50-68, for the prehistoric and pagan antecedents of the circular enclosed cemetery.
33. Thomas, *Early Christian Archaeology*, 32-4; Thomas, 'Christians, chapels, churches and charters', 21.

which in most cases could as well have been religious as secular.[34] The Cornish minster of St Buryan, an undoubted early Christian site, is built within a native Roman-period 'round', and several Welsh church sites within older enclosures have recently been identified.[35] A handful at least of mid-Saxon English minsters, such as Hanbury (Worcestershire), Tetbury (Gloucestershire) (both fig. 10.2), Breedon-on-the-Hill (Leicestershire) and Aylesbury (Buckinghamshire), are within Iron Age forts,[36] and the practice was echoed by the eighth-century missionaries to Germany in their foundations at Fulda (fig. 10.2), Würzburg, Büraburg and Erfurt.[37]

It seems possible that old enclosures were considered the natural and normal sites for minsters, newly-formed earthwork enclosures being imitative substitutes. Old English *burh*, 'enclosed place', seems to have acquired a secondary sense of 'minster'. The minster of St Paul's in London was called *Paulesbiri* in the eighth century; Tetbury (*Tettan byrig*) occurs as *Tettan monasterium* in the late seventh century, Westbury-on-Trym (*Uuestburg*) as *Westmynster* in 804. Other *burh* names (especially perhaps those compounded with female personal names) may denote minsters: Bibury (Gloucestershire) was leased to the thegn Leppa and his daughter Beage in 718 × 45, and its name is more likely to mean 'Beage's minster' than 'Beage's fortress'.[38]

---

34. I. Burrow, *Hillfort and Hill-Top Settlement in Somerset in the First to Eighth Centuries AD* (BAR, British Ser. 91, 1981), 163-5.
35. A. Preston-Jones, 'Road widening in St Buryan and Pelynt churchyards', *Cornish Archaeology*, xxvi (1987), 153-60; Thomas, 'Christians, chapels, churches and charters', 21-2; T. James, 'The early origins of churchyard enclosures in south-west Wales', *Bull. CBA Churches Committee*, xxvi (1989), 9-16.
36. Hanbury: D. Hooke, *Anglo-Saxon Landscapes of the West Midlands: the Charter Evidence* (BAR, British Ser. 95, 1981), fig. 2.6 (iii); Tetbury: *VCH, Glos.*, xi, 260; Breedon: D. Parsons, 'Breedon-on-the-Hill', *The Nottingham Area: Supplement to Archaeol. J.* cxlvi (1989), 14-18; Aylesbury: P. A. Yeoman in *South Midlands Archaeology*, xvi (1986), 37-8. Sims-Williams, *Religion and Literature*, 107-8, points out the likely Irish influence on the foundation at Hanbury.
37. Parsons, 'Sites and monuments', 291-4; Parsons, 'Siting of early monasteries'; D. Parsons, *Books and Buildings: Architectural Description Before and After Bede* (The Jarrow Lecture, 1987), 16-18. St Boniface described Büraburg as *oppidum* and Erfurt as *olim urbs paganorum*. As Dr Parsons points out (pers. comm.), the character of the German sites remains ambiguous:

> it seems to me still reasonable to talk about the re-use of hill-top enclosures and in most cases to talk in terms of fortified sites, but how old these were is not at all clear: one or more of them could have been of very recent date.

38. In lost charters attributed to Coenred and Offa (S 1786, S 1790), the *ecclesia sancta . . . in Londonia* or *monasterium* was said to have been popularly called *Paulesbiri*. For the other cases see F. M. Stenton, 'The place of women in Anglo-Saxon society', in *Preparatory to Anglo-Saxon England*, ed. D. M. Stenton (1970), 320-1; J. Blair, 'Thornbury, Binsey: a probable defensive enclosure associated with St Frideswide', *Oxoniensia*, liii (1988), 18-20. Adderbury (Oxon.) is another likely case (David Parsons, pers. comm.). The interpretation of *burh* as 'minster' in such contexts is supported by Sims-Williams, *Religion and Literature*, 92-3, 108-9.

There is nothing specifically British or Irish about the subcircular precinct, whether reused or new: it belonged to the common stock-in-trade of monastic founders and patrons. The features which are distinctive of Irish sites are incidental rather than fundamental: they are rounder than English sites because fifth- to eighth-century Ireland had a vernacular tradition of round houses and enclosures, and their earthwork boundaries and internal divisions have been preserved because the modern countryside of Ireland is less developed than that of England and France. Enclosures such as those at Bampton and Lambourn are direct parallels from the Anglo-Saxon world for the sites that have long been known outside it.

THE REUSE OF ROMAN STRUCTURES

Though broadly equivalent to the reuse of hill-forts, the reuse of Romano-British forts, villas, towns and public buildings raises wider issues, at the heart of controversies concerning the emergence of civilized English society and its debt to the Roman or Christian past. The differences in scale and durability between these various kinds of structure are great, and would have dictated different patterns of reuse, but to early medieval eyes their masonry would have made all of them startlingly different from any non-Roman work.

My inevitably brief review of a thorny question tries to set this aspect of Anglo-Saxon planning in a wider context, which may cut some of the problems down to size. For the question 'Was there or was there not continuity?' is often posed too starkly. The sixth-century British, the seventh-century English, the Franks, and the Irish who operated among all of them, were recipients of the same late Roman tradition by channels which did not always flow at the same speed, but which often crossed and converged. Irrespective of institutional survival, the military and public monuments of Roman Britain were numerous and prominent in the land-scape.[39] The educated knew what they were; the well-travelled had seen their counterparts put to new uses, mainly religious, in the re-emergent towns of Gaul; and missionaries sought to reaffirm Rome's stamp on the lost province.[40]

Roman forts and very small towns seem to have been appropriated in exactly the same way as prehistoric enclosures: through royal patronage, and in large numbers. The practice began on the Continent before the English were converted. This is clear from the gifts of the fort at Amboise (Indre-et-Loire) to a group of monks as early as *c*. 400, of the deserted fort

---

39. J. C. Higgitt, 'The Roman background to medieval England', *JBAA*, 3rd ser. xxxvi (1973), 1-15.
40. P. Wormald, 'Bede, Beowulf and the conversion of the Anglo-Saxon aristocracy', in *Bede and Anglo-Saxon England*, ed. R. T. Farrell (BAR, British Ser. 46, 1978), 68, remarks on 'the determination of the barbarian peoples to identify with the works of Rome (whether Augustan or Petrine)' and 'the commitment of the Anglo-Saxon educated classes to the values of the Mediterranean'.

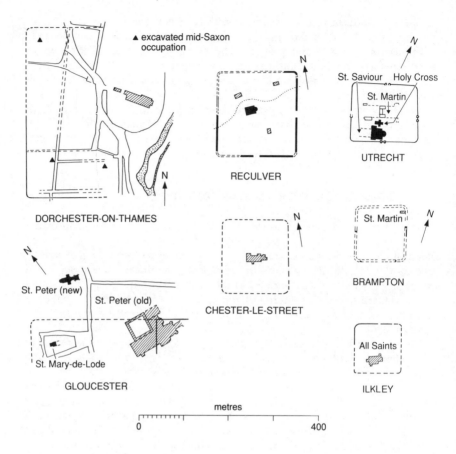

Figure 10.3 Churches in Roman towns and forts. Dorchester-on-Thames: after G. Briggs, J. Cook and T. Rowley (eds.), *The Archaeology of the Oxford Region* (1986), fig. 7. Reculver: after J. Nichols, *Bibliotheca Topographica Britannica*, i (1780–90), facing p. 170. Utrecht: after Hoekstra, 'Early topography of Utrecht', Fig. 2. Chester-le-Street: after *Archaeologia Aeliana*, xlix (1971), facing p. 104. Brampton Old Church: after *Trans. Cumberland and Westmorland AeA Soc.* n.s. xxxvi (1936), facing p. 173. Ilkley: after *Yorks. Arch. J.* xxviii (1924–6), facing p. 198. Gloucester: see below, p. 242.

Conventions: Roman walls in heavy line; Anglo-Saxon churches in solid black; later medieval churches hatched.

at Annegray (Haute-Saône) to St Columbanus by King Guntram of Burgundy, and (traditionally) of the fort at Holyhead (Anglesey) to St Cybi by the British ruler Maelgwn.[41] The phenomenon is also widespread in Switzerland and Germany.[42] In England, evidence from the early seventh century onwards suggests a spate of ecclesiastical reuse of small towns and forts as part of the process of conversion. Bede and others mention Romano-British enclosures which kings gave away so that saints could build cathedrals or minsters in them. Dorchester-on-Thames (Oxfordshire) (fig. 10.3) was given by Cynegils of Wessex to St Birinus in 634;[43] *Dommoc* by Sigeberht of East Anglia to St Felix, and *Cnobheresburg* (?Burgh Castle) by the same king to St Fursa, both in the 630s;[44] Bradwell-on-Sea (fig. 10.6) by Sigeberht of Essex to St Cedd;[45] Ebchester (perhaps) by Osuiu of Northumbria to St Æbbe;[46] Reculver (fig. 10.3) by Ecgberht of Kent to the priest Bassa in 669;[47] and, during the English mission to Frisia, Utrecht (fig. 10.3) by Pippin II to Willibrord in 690.[48] Other historical and hagiographical sources mention the adoption of Roman forts for monastic use, for instance Jumièges by St Philibert, *Kaelcacaestir* by Heiu, *Tunnacaestir* by the priest Tunna, and Chester-le-Street (fig. 10.3) by the community of St Cuthbert.[49]

---

41. Amboise: Sulpicius Severus, *Dialogus Tertius*, 3.4, ed. C. Halm, *Corpus Script. Eccles. Lat.* i (1866), 206: 'In vico Ambatiensi, id est castello veteri, quod nunc frequens habitatur a fratribus ...'. Annegray: Jonas, *Vita S. Columbani*, i. 6, ed. B. Krusch (MGH, *Script. Rerum Meroving.* iv, 1902), 72: 'Erat enim tunc vasta heremus ... in qua castrum dirutum olim ... Ad quem vir sanctus cum venisset, licet aspera vastitate solitudinis et scopulorum interpositione loca, ibi cum suis resedit ...'. Holyhead: *An Inventory of the Ancient Monuments in Anglesey* (RCA&HM Wales and Monmouthshire, 1937), xci, 31-4, and N. Edwards, 'Anglesey in the early Middle Ages: the archaeological evidence', *Trans. Anglesey Antiquarian Soc. and Field Club* (1986) 24-5. These cases are discussed by Thomas, *Early Christian Archaeology*, 32-4, and by Parsons, 'Siting of early monasteries'. The Roman fort at Caerwent contains a church and associated early medieval burials: *Early Medieval Settlements in Wales AD 400-1100*, ed. N. Edwards and A. Lane (1988), 35-8.
42. See, for instance, M. Hartmann in *Ur- und frühgeschichtliche Archäologie der Schweiz: v: Die römische Epoche* (Basel, 1975), 20-9.
43. Bede, *HE* iii. 7: 'Donaverunt autem ambo reges eidem episcopo civitatem quae vocatur Dorcic ad faciendam inibi sedem episcopalem'.
44. Bede, *HE* ii. 15: 'acceptique sedem episcopatus in civitate Dommoc'. *ibid.*, iii. 19 (ed. Colgrave and Mynors, 270): '*monasterium silvarum et maris vicinitate amoenum, constructum in castro quodam*, quod lingua Anglorum Cnobheresburg ... *vocatur* (italicized words from the *Vita* of St Fursa). On the Roman identity of *Dommoc*, see Campbell, *Essays in Anglo-Saxon History*, 99.
45. Bede, *HE* iii. 22: Cedd baptizes 'maxime in civitate quae lingua Saxonum Ythancæstir appellatur, ... in ripa Pentae amnis'.
46. Note by Colgrave in *Two Lives of St Cuthbert*, ed. B. Colgrave (1940), 318.
47. *Anglo-Saxon Chronicle MS A*, s.a. 669: 'Her Ecgbryht cyning salde Basse maessepreoste Reculf mynster on to timbranne' (ed. J. Bately, 1989).
48. Bede, *HE* v. 11: 'Donavit autem ei Pippin locum cathedrae episcopalis in castello sui inlustri quod antiquo gentium illarum verbo Uiltaburg ... vocatur'. See also T. K. Hoekstra, 'The early topography of the city of Utrecht and its cross of churches', *JBAA*, cxli (1988), 1-5.
49. James, 'Archaeology and the Merovingian monastery', 39 (for argument that Jumièges was a Roman shore-fort); Bede, *HE* iv. 23 and iv. 22; E. Cambridge, 'Why did the community of St Cuthbert settle at Chester-le-Street?', in *St Cuthbert, his Cult and Community to AD 1200*, ed. G. Bonner, D. Rollason and C. Stancliffe (1989), 367-86.

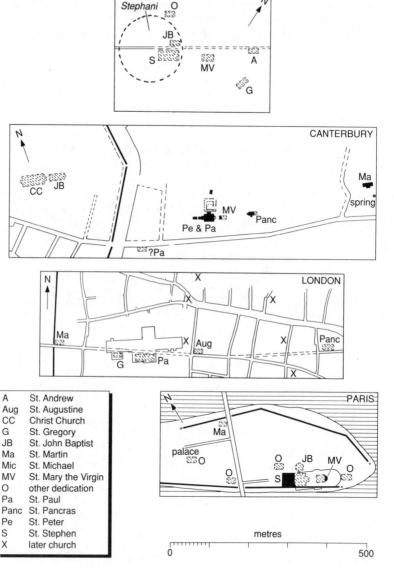

A   St. Andrew
Aug   St. Augustine
CC   Christ Church
G   St. Gregory
JB   St. John Baptist
Ma   St. Martin
Mic   St. Michael
MV   St. Mary the Virgin
O   other dedication
Pa   St. Paul
Panc   St. Pancras
Pe   St. Peter
S   St. Stephen
X   later church

Figure 10.4 Church groups. Limoges: after Barral I Altet, *Paysage Monumental*, 503. Canterbury: after Brooks, *Early History*, fig. 1, with some detail from Taylor and Taylor, *Anglo-Saxon Architecture*, fig. 61. Paris: after *Collections Mérovingiennes*, fig. 6. London: based on Tatton-Brown, 'Topography of Anglo-Saxon London', opp. p. 28; and Rodwell, 'Role of the Church in . . . London'.

'Æbbe's *ceaster*' and 'Tunna's *ceaster*' even suggest a usage in which *ceaster*, like *burh* (above, p. 234) has come to mean 'minster', underlining the distinctively monastic nature of these appropriations.

A much larger number of extant Roman forts, probably running to some dozens, lack such explicit written evidence but still contain churches. Many are recorded as minsters, or have produced sculpture fragments, coins or other finds of the seventh to ninth centuries.[50] These churches occupy a variety of positions in relation to the forts (see figs. 10.3 and 10.6). Some are roughly central (e.g. Reculver, Chester-le-Street), others set to one side (e.g. Ilkley) or squeezed tightly into a corner (e.g. Brampton). Sometimes the church overlies the *principium* or some other major structure, recalling the use (discussed below) of public buildings in larger Roman places. The church at Dorchester-on-Thames may be outside the defended circuit,[51] while St Peter's at Bradwell-on-Sea occupies the west gateway of the fort. These variations may have some chronological significance,[52] but it should be remembered that a minster normally comprised several buildings, including at least two churches, only one of which usually remains. The surviving church may sometimes be the main one, sometimes a lesser, peripheral one.[53] The latter was surely the case at Bradwell (where only the west side of the fort has survived sea erosion): St Peter's could even be interpreted as a gate-church, giving access to a precinct centred on another church or churches further to the east.[54]

It is sometimes suggested that churches were built in Roman forts because they shared them with seats of secular power. Yet the repeated references to the outright gift of forts by rulers to saints, and the virtual absence of evidence for Anglo-Saxon *uillae regales* in Roman walled places

---

50. For lists and discussions see M. Biddle, 'A widening horizon', in *The Archaeological Study of Churches*, ed. P. Addyman and R. Morris (CBA, Research Rep. 13, 1976), 65-8; *idem*, 'Towns', in *The Archaeology of Anglo-Saxon England*, ed. D. M. Wilson (1976), 111 and 143-4 note 100; S. E. Rigold, 'Litus Romanum: the shore forts as mission stations', in *The Saxon Shore*, ed. D. E. Johnston (CBA, Research Rep. 18, 1977), 70-5; Morris, *Church in British Archaeology*, 41-5.

51. A Roman cremation has been found nearby, and N. Doggett ('The Anglo-Saxon see and cathedral of Dorchester-on-Thames: the evidence reconsidered', *Oxoniensia*, li (1986), 50-7) argues that Birinus's church succeeded a late Roman *martyrium* in an extra-mural cemetery. On the other hand, the walled area could have been extended in the late Roman period (cf. Gloucester, note 69 below).

52. Rigold, '*Litus Romanum*', 74, compares the 'corner-sited' churches with the locations of some late Roman churches (e.g. Richborough) and suggests that this position is characteristic of the earliest reuses. Cf. Biddle 'Widening horizon', 67.

53. For instance, Reculver had, in addition to the main church, a chapel towards the north-west corner of the fort: Rigold, '*Litus Romanum*', 73-4. In some non-Roman monastic enclosures the main church stood near the boundary (see fig. 10.2), and at Barking the *oratorium* was on south side of the complex (Bede, *HE* iv. 7).

54. Cf. Rigold, '*Litus Romanum*', 71-3. Parsons, *Books and Buildings*, 19, gives some Merovingian instances of chapels over town gates (though these are rather different from Bradwell, where the church fills the gateway).

before the tenth century,[55] convey a different message. In 679, it is true, Hlothere of Kent issued a charter in the *ciuitas* of Reculver.[56] But this exception proves the rule: Reculver had become a minster ten years earlier (above, p. 237), so the ceremony took place in a monastic rather than a royal 'city'.[57] Whatever the reason, it does seem that old forts were of little interest to early medieval rulers, who put them to the best possible use, and into loyal hands, by founding minsters in them. Indications that they were valued in any other way are hard to find.[58]

An insular practice still closer to the mainstream of late- and sub-Roman developments in Europe is the establishment of graveyards and churches within the ruins of villas. This phenomenon was widespread in Gaul during the fifth and sixth centuries, and the adaptation of courtyard villas has been suggested as one source for the monastic cloister. Significantly in the present context, Gallic cases often represent a pragmatic reuse for monastic purposes of originally secular structures.[59] English appropriations of villas, which include a remarkable number in the south-west,[60] can be interpreted as functionally equivalent to appropriations of forts – a conclusion reinforced by the fact that three of the four known villas with *-ceaster*

55. Only a few of the places listed in P. H. Sawyer, 'The Royal *tūn* in pre-Conquest England', in *Ideal and Reality in Frankish and Anglo-Saxon Society*, ed. P. Wormald *et al.* (1983), 290-9, are known to have had Roman walls. Of those that did, the early seventh-century Northumbrian royal vills in *Campodunum* and *Ad Murum* (Bede, *HE* ii. 14 and iii. 21-2) are anomalous for the reason suggested on p. 231 above. The only other pre-900 references are: assemblies at Bath in 796 and 864; Dorchester, Dorset (or somewhere near it) as a *cyninges tūn* in 789, and assemblies there in 833 and 864; and an assembly at Gloucester in 896. Given the number of recorded charter attestations, and the number of Roman walled places, this is an extraordinarily low correlation.

56. *BCS* 45 (S 8).

57. On uses of *ciuitas*, *castrum* and *castellum*, see Rigold, '*Litus Romanum*', 70-1; Campbell, *Essays in Anglo-Saxon History*, 99-108.

58. Cf. Parsons, 'Siting of early monasteries'. Thomas, 'Christians, chapels, churches and charters', 21, takes the same view. Biddle ('Towns' and 'Widening horizon') is readier to accept the possibility of continuous use in some form.

59. J. Percival, *The Roman Villa* (1976), 183-99; James 'Archaeology and the Merovingian monastery', 34, 46-7.

60. R. Morris and J. Roxan, 'Churches on Roman buildings', in *Temples, Churches and Religion: Recent Research in Roman Britain*, ed. W. Rodwell, i, BAR, British Ser. 77(i), 1980, 175-209; cf. Morris, *Churches in the Landscape*, 100-4. What seemed a very striking case at Much Wenlock, Salop. (Blair, 'Minster churches in the landscape', 44-6) has in fact been misunderstood – see M. Biddle and B. Kjølbye-Biddle, 'The so-called Roman building at Much Wenlock', *JBAA*, cxli (1988), 179-81 – though the possibility that this minster occupies a Roman site still remains open. Roman villa walls were apparently still in use in the thirteenth-century monastic complex at Llandough: Davies, *Wales in the Early Middle Ages*, 25 and fig. 64. However, not all churches on Roman villas were minsters: for an 'ordinary' church in such a setting see W. J. Rodwell and K. A. Rodwell, *Rivenhall: Investigations of a Villa, Church and Village* (CBA, Research Rep. 55, 1986).

names have superimposed churches.[61] Although some minsters built on or in Roman buildings are apparently pre-English, the practice was too generalized to constitute in itself a means of distinguishing between British and Anglo-Saxon origins.[62] Any concerted campaign of minster-building is likely to have pressed into service such Roman structures as were available, and the earlier it occurred the more numerous these would have been. The walls of villas would have decayed more quickly than those of forts, so the large number of minsters on villas in Dorset and Gloucestershire implies an early origin for the practice there, perhaps under sixth-century British control.[63] The presence of churches in all the forts on the western half of Hadrian's Wall but none of those on the eastern half suggests a system established under the Strathclyde Britons,[64] whereas the directly comparable reuse of Saxon Shore forts along the coasts of south-east England occurred in the seventh century under Anglo-Gallic patronage.[65]

Minsters inside large towns are a different and more complex matter. The area enclosed by the walls of a city would have been far bigger than any religious community could have needed for its own buildings. There would have been great empty spaces, dotted with ruinous structures but otherwise capable of the same sorts of development as open-ground sites. In the late seventh century a few Romano-British towns seem to have resembled, if only as a pale reflection, the sub-Roman towns of Gaul.[66] There was the same tendency to regroup around nuclei; occasionally there may have been the same sharing of the walled area between religious and secular seats of

61. Morris and Roxan, 'Churches on Roman buildings', 184–5. Bicester (Oxon.) could be a fourth case: Blair, 'Minster churches in the landscape', 47. For the possibility that *ceaster* in these contexts means 'minster' see above, pp. 237–9.
62. For instance, the name of Eccles (Kent) derives from British *ecles, 'church', but the burials found on the site of the villa there were seventh-century and typically Anglo-Saxon: A. P. Detsicas, 'Excavations at Eccles', *Arch. Cant.* lxxxviii (1973), 78; lxxxix (1974), 129–30; xci (1975), 44; A. P. Detsicas and S. C. Hawkes, 'Finds from the Anglo-Saxon cemetery at Eccles, Kent', *Antiq. J.* liii (1973), 281–6.
63. S. M. Pearce, 'Estates and church sites in Dorset and Gloucestershire: the emergence of a Christian society', in *Early Church in W. Britain and Ireland*, ed. Pearce, 117–38. The first religious use of some villas seems to have been as fifth- and sixth-century burial-grounds: *ibid.*, 134–5, and C. Heighway, *Anglo-Saxon Gloucestershire* (1987), 122–6. However, C. Thomas, *Christianity in Roman Britain to AD 500* (1981), 180–4, points out how little hard evidence there is for the continuity of cults at Romano-British estate churches.
64. As pointed out by Biddle, 'Widening horizon', 67.
65. As argued forcefully by Rigold, '*Litus Romanum*', esp. 74: 'The whole usage, not a barbarous "squatter occupation" nor a case of barbarous imitation, is a reclamation of Roman sites in a fairly confident, contemporary Mediterranean mood.'
66. Among the huge literature on the post-Roman development of Gallic towns, there are convenient summaries in P. A. Février *et al.*, *Histoire de la France urbaine, i: La ville antique, des origines au IXe siècle* (Paris, 1980), 423–40; *Topographie chrétienne des cités de la Gaule*, ed. N. Gauthier and J.-Ch. Picard, i (1986) et seq.; *Le Paysage monumental de la France autour de l'an mil*, ed. X. Barral I Altet (Paris, 1987) (e.g. Tours, 293, and Limoges, 503); C. Pietri, 'Remarques sur la topographie chrétienne des cités de la Gaule entre Loire et Rhin', *Revue d'histoire de l'église de France*, lxii (1976), 189–204.

power;[67] but there was nothing that can properly be called urban life.

The continuous survival of some genuine fourth-century Christian cult sites, both in towns and around martyrs' graves outside them, is not in doubt.[68] The influence of a pre-English framework is suggested by cases such as Gloucester (fig. 10.3), where the late seventh-century minster of St Peter may have been sited with regard to the probable British church of St Mary-de-Lode.[69] But we must be cautious: contemporaries, like ourselves, were capable of making deductions (right or wrong) from physical evidence; real shades into fictitious continuity, and both into deliberate imitation. To take the most obvious case, Canterbury in 597 had a continuing Christian tradition,[70] and St Augustine's new foundations there were bi-polar on the classic late Roman pattern: a cathedral within the walls, and a minster outside them amid the late Roman cemeteries (fig. 10.4). Yet it is not at all clear that this perpetuated arrangements surviving at Canterbury, as distinct from replicating arrangements widely familiar in Europe. Near the extra-mural minster was a church already used by Queen Bertha, which she and Bede believed to have been a Roman church; but Bertha and Bede were probably wrong.[71] Augustine used for his cathedral another old building which was also interpreted as a Roman church,[72] but was this necessarily

67. Notably London, as argued vigorously and persuasively by Martin Biddle in *The City of London from prehistoric times to c. 1520: The British Atlas of Historic Towns*, ed. M. D. Lobel, iii (1989), 23-4, 28. Seventh-century Lincoln and Carlisle were controlled by royal reeves and contained royal minsters: Bede, *HE* ii. 16; *Vita S. Cuthberti*, iv. 8; Bede, *Vita S. Cuthberti*, cc. 27, 28; M. R. McCarthy, 'Thomas, Chadwick, and post-Roman Carlisle', in *Early Church in W. Britain*, ed. Pearce, 241-56. But royal power-bases in former Roman towns are otherwise hardly ever mentioned before *c.* 900 (note 55 above), and should not necessarily be inferred from tenth- and eleventh-century evidence which post-dates the era of urban renewal. Cf. the debate on the status of seventh-century Winchester: M. Biddle, 'Winchester: the development of an early capital', in *Vor- und Frühformen der europäischen Stadt im Mittelalter*, ed. H. Jankuhn et al., i (Göttingen, 1973), 239-41; B. A. E. Yorke, 'The foundation of the Old Minster and the status of Winchester in the seventh and eighth centuries', *Proc. Hants. Field Club and Arch. Soc.* xxxviii (1982), 75-83; M. Biddle, 'The study of Winchester: archaeology and history in a British town', *Proc. Brit. Acad.* lxix (1983), 116-17.
68. See especially Thomas, *Christianity in Roman Britain*, 166-80; Biddle, 'Archaeology, architecture and the cult of saints'; Biddle 'Widening horizon', 65-7; Morris, *Churches in the Landscape*, 6-45; Blair, 'Minster churches in the landscape', 46-7; Steven Bassett's chapter, above, 13-40.
69. See Bassett, 26-9 above. St Peter's is in the north-west corner of the original Roman town, St Mary's just outside it; whether or not they should be regarded as a group depends on the existence (still uncertain) of a late Roman westwards enlargement of the walled area to include the site of St Mary's.
70. See N. Brooks, *The Early History of the Church of Canterbury* (1984), 16-22.
71. Bede, *HE* i. 26. For recent analysis of the archaeological problems of St Martin's, see Morris, *Churches in the Landscape*, 20-5 (and, for a radically different hypothesis, Thomas, *Christianity in Roman Britain*, 170-4).
72. Bede, *HE* i. 33.

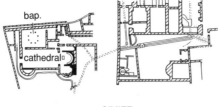

CIMIEZ

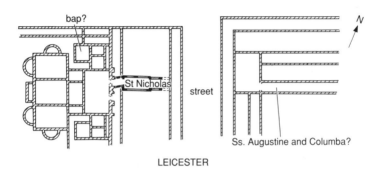

LEICESTER

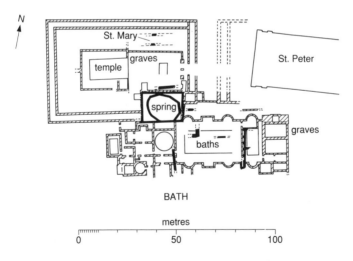

BATH

metres

0   50   100

Figure 10.5 Church groups inserted into Roman bath complexes. Cimiez: baths from Benoit, *Cimiez, La Ville Antique*, Pl. XXXIII, with detail of cathedral and baptistery from Gauthier and Picard (eds.), *Top. Chrétienne*, II, 86-8. Leicester: after Rodwell, 'Churches in landscape', fig. 3; detail of church from *VCH Leics.* iv, 385 (and evidence for eastern chapels in *ibid.* 384-5). Bath: after Rodwell, 'Churches in the landscape', fig. 4.
Conventions: Roman secular structures, shown schematically, hatched; Christian structures (known) in solid black; Christian structures (inferred) in fine stipple.

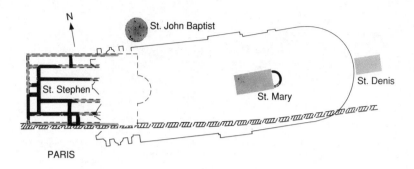

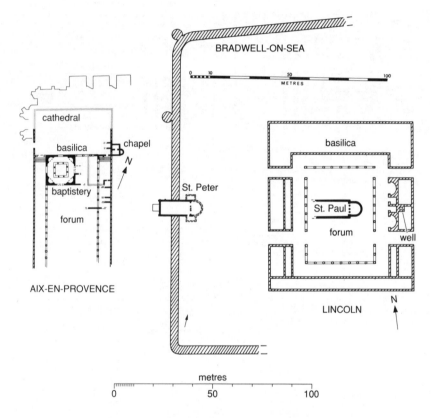

Figure 10.6 Church groups inserted into Roman military and public buildings. Paris: after *Collections Mérovingiennes*, figs. 6 and 8; and Hubert, 'Origines de Nôtre Dame'. Aix-en-Provence: after Fixot *et al.*, *Fouilles de la Cour de l'Archevêché*. Bradwell-on-Sea: Roman wall after T. Lewin, 'On the castra of the Littus Saxonicum', *Archaeologia*, xli (1867), facing p. 441; church after Taylor and Taylor, *Anglo-Saxon Architecture*, fig. 40. Lincoln: after Rodwell, 'Churches in the landscape', fig. 2. *Conventions:* as Fig. 5.

right either? One is reminded of St Senoch's hopeful diggings among the rubble for traces of St Martin.[73]

Some English minster-builders followed (albeit on a much smaller scale) the Gallic practice of annexing monumental public buildings. Major Anglo-Saxon churches were often set in the fora, basilicas or baths of large Romano-British towns,[74] using in at least some cases the grand architectural framework provided by standing Roman walls (figs. 10.5 and 10.6). This is dramatically clear at Leicester, where the *palaestra* of the public baths contains a church, and its original entrance serves as the west front.[75] The attraction of apsidal rooms and ready-made plumbing, both appropriate for baptismal rituals, may explain the frequent choice of baths, as at Bath itself where the churches of St Mary and St Peter were aligned on the north side of the temple courtyard with the spring and bathing complex immediately to their south. At Lincoln, St Paul's church (the date of which remains problematic within the range fifth to seventh century) was placed centrally in the forum, its apse pointing towards a pre-existing well in the east range.[76]

These usages are Romanizing, perhaps even learned, and suggest appreciation of the ancient structures as architecture rather than merely as rubble. But they need not show 'continuity', either political or religious:[77] they reflect the standard practice of the Christian West from the fourth century onwards, assimilated possibly by the sixth-century British and certainly by the seventh-century English. The obvious models are the Italian and Gallic cities, where the expanding church of the fifth and early sixth centuries was ready to appropriate whatever domestic, public or military buildings were available. Cimiez (fig. 10.5), where the cathedral and baptistry were fitted neatly into one of two bath-suites, and Aix-en-Provence, where they occupied the forum-basilica and part of the

---

73. Gregory of Tours, *Vita Patrum*, xv. 1, quoted Percival, *Roman Villa*, 197-9, and James, 'Archaeology and the Merovingian monastery', 34. The story of 'St Sixtus' (Brooks, *Church of Canterbury*, 20) is revealing of the cavalier attitude that Augustine and his companions might have taken to genuine cult survivals. R. Bradley, 'Time regained: the creation of continuity', *JBAA*, cxl (1987), 1-17, makes some apposite general comments on the manipulation of 'continuity' by past societies.
74. The pioneer study here is W. Rodwell, 'Churches in the landscape: aspects of topography and planning', in *Studies in Late Anglo-Saxon Settlement*, ed. M. L. Faull (1984), 3-9, and I am much indebted to it for what follows. Cf. Morris, *Churches in the Landscape*, 37.
75. Rodwell, 'Churches in the landscape', 6-7.
76. *ibid.*, 4; Morris, *Churches in the Landscape*, 37; P. Stafford, *The East Midlands in the Early Middle Ages* (1985), 87-8. The stratigraphical problems await resolution, but it is arguable that a seventh-century date remains more likely on general grounds.
77. Rodwell, 'Churches in the landscape', 4-5, argues that such churches were 'founded as adjuncts, physically and administratively, to the contemporary centres of authority in the towns'. This begs a big question: in no case can we be certain that a centre of secular power existed near the church until long after its foundation (notes 55 and 67 above).

forum itself, are analogies (in form if not in scale) for Bath, Leicester and Lincoln.[78]

For monastic founders in seventh-century England, the reuse of Roman structures was both convenient and the attested good practice of their mentors. Like the building of new stone churches 'in the Roman manner', it affirmed a civilized orthodoxy.[79] The Christian topography of re-emergent Romano-British towns came almost inevitably to resemble that of Italian and Gallo-Roman towns, for the people who moulded its development had been trained in Italy and Gaul. Thus the characteristic sprawl of churches, spreading outwards from episcopal and monastic groups across the semi-abandoned town or its cemeteries, became nearly as marked a feature of Canterbury or London as it was of Paris or Limoges (fig. 10.4).[80]

THE PLANNING OF CHURCH GROUPS

Multiplicity of churches was not confined to former Roman towns. There is overwhelming evidence that in Gaul, England and probably Ireland, a religious community of any importance would have had at least two and perhaps more churches. It is here that later architectural changes have most seriously distorted our perceptions, for the usual consequence of Romanesque rebuildings was either the abandonment of subsidiary churches, their functions transferred to the enlarged main church, or the obliteration of two or three small churches to make way for a single vast structure. Discussions of Anglo-Saxon monastic sites usually refer to 'the church', which is off the point: even when we happen to have one church surviving, there would often, perhaps nearly always, have been others. This preconception has prevented archaeologists and historians from observing

---

78. S. Loseby, 'Bishops and cathedrals: order and diversity in the fifth-century urban landscape of southern Gaul', in *Fifth-Century Gaul: a Crisis of Identity*, ed. J. F. Drinkwater and H. W. Elton (forthcoming) stimulated the thoughts in this paragraph, and I am very grateful to the author for showing it to me. Cf. Parsons, *Books and Buildings*, 18-19, 33-4. For Aix and Cimiez see *Topographie chrétienne, ii: Provinces ecclésiastiques d'Aix et d'Embrun*, ed. Gauthier and Picard (1986), 17-28, 86-8; M. Fixot *et al.*, *Les fouilles de la cour de l'archevêché* (Aix-en-Provence, 1985); F. Benoit, *Cimiez, La ville antique* (*Fouilles de Cemenelum*, i, Paris, 1977), Pl. XXXIII. For some strikingly similar reuses in post-Roman Germany see M. Martin in *Ur- und frühgeschichtliche Archäologie der Schweiz: vi: das Frühmittelalter* (Basel, 1979), 97-132, esp. 118-26.
79. Clearest, of course, in Bede's reference to the work built *iuxta Romanorum quem semper amabat morem* by Biscop's Gallic masons: *Historia abbatum*, c.5 (*Baedae Opera Historica*, ed. C. Plummer (1896), i, 368). For the symbolic significance of *Romanitas* in Anglo-Saxon architecture, see R. D. H. Gem, 'Towards an iconography of Anglo-Saxon architecture', *J. Warburg and Courtauld Inst.* xlvi (1983), 2-4. Cf. Blair, 'Minster churches in the landscape', 44-7.
80. The case for a line of early churches in the walled area of London is argued by T. Tatton-Brown, 'The topography of Anglo-Saxon London', *Antiquity* lx (1986), 21-9, and by W. Rodwell, 'The role of the church in the development of Roman and early Anglo-Saxon London' (*Festschrift* for P. A. Rahtz, forthcoming). For extra-mural London, see Biddle, 'Widening horizon', 66.

the very clear norms which emerge from contemporary evidence, both literary and physical.

Ultimately, the phenomenon goes back to the 'late antique architectural thought which . . . readily manifested itself in building complexes, not single buildings in isolation', and which, from the beginning of state-supported Christianity, generated complex groups of subordinate structures such as atria, baptisteries, mausolea and martyria around important churches.[81] Even the axiality that was to be so marked a feature of Anglo-Saxon planning is foreshadowed in groups as remote as the cathedrals at Milan, the massive complex at Gerasa (Jordan), and the Constantinian buildings around the Holy Sepulchre itself (fig. 10.7).[82] The arrangement that became characteristic of cathedrals in north Italy and adjoining areas was a pair of churches set side by side rather than end to end, often with a baptistery between them.[83]

Common though they are, the purpose of these groups is still not fully understood. Paulinus of Nola described the twin basilica and baptistery built by Sulpicius Severus at Prémillac in symbolic terms: there were three roofs for the persons of the Trinity, covering a double church which stood for the New and Old Laws.[84] In north Italy by the late fifth century a more functional definition had emerged: the southern church (the 'winter' or main church), dedicated to the Virgin Mary, was open to all, whereas only the baptized had access to the northern (or 'summer') church, which was usually under a martyr's patronage.[85]

From Italy the church group was introduced into Merovingian Gaul, though with some differences.[86] Complexes developed by accretion, over considerable periods extending through the sixth and seventh centuries and beyond. In contrast to Italian groups the churches are often laid out haphazardly (e.g. Nivelles, fig. 10.1, and Manglieu, fig. 10.2), though the side-by-side arrangement does occur, for instance in the upper Rhône

81. R. Krautheimer, 'The twin cathedral at Pavia', in his *Studies in Early Christian, Medieval and Renaissance Art* (1971), 164-5.
82. R. Krautheimer, *Early Christian and Byzantine Architecture* (1965), 169-70.
83. Krautheimer, 'Twin cathedral', 165, 170-1; J. Hubert, 'Les "cathédrales doubles" et l'histoire de la liturgie', in his *Arts et vie sociale de la fin du monde antique au moyen age* (Soc. de l'école des chartes, Geneva, 1977), 88-90. Trier is the grandest example of the type, as well as among the earliest.
84. S. Paulinus of Nola, *Epistulae*, xxxii, 5, ed. G. De Hartel (Corpus Script. Eccles. Lat., 29, 1894), 279-80; Hubert, '"Cathédrales doubles" et liturgie', 90.
85. Krautheimer, 'Twin cathedral', 170-1; Hubert, '"Cathédrales doubles" et liturgie', 91-5. These arrangements parallel those at the Holy Sepulchre, where the mass of the catechumens was celebrated in the *Ecclesia* but the mass of the faithful in the *Anastasis*.
86. The following remarks on Gallic multiple churches are based on J. Hubert, 'Les "cathédrales doubles" de la Gaule', in *Arts et vie sociale*, 97-117; Février *et al.*, *Histoire de la France urbaine*, i, 424-31; J. Hubert, *L'art pré-roman* (Paris, 1938), 38-44; J. Hubert, J. Porcher and W. Vollbach, *Europe in the Dark Ages* (1969), 294-307; James, 'Archaeology and the Merovingian monastery', 41-4. For church groups in early medieval Switzerland, see H. R. Sennhauser in *Ur- und frühgeschichtliche Archäologie der Schweiz*: vi, 133-5.

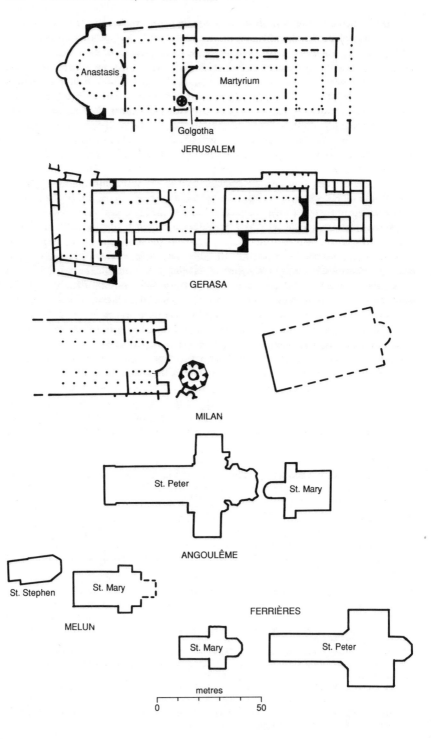

JERUSALEM

GERASA

MILAN

ANGOULÊME

St. Peter

St. Mary

St. Stephen

St. Mary

MELUN

FERRIÈRES

St. Mary

St. Peter

metres

0   50

Figure 10.7 Some prototypes for axially-planned church groups. Jerusalem: after J. Wilkinson, *Egeria's Travels* (1971), 45. Ferrières: after Hubert, 'Notes sur l'histoire de Ferrières', fig. 1. The rest from Hubert, '"Cathédrales doubles" de la Gaule', figs. 3, 5, 6, except that the W. church at Milan is after Fevrier *et al,. Hist. de la France Urbaine*, fig. 353.

valley.[87] In northern France, however, the linear, west–east layout seems to have prevailed. Some groups were extremely elaborate: Saint-Denis, with its two rows of aligned churches and its outlying chapels, has been justly described as 'une véritable cité monastique',[88] Nivelles and Jouarre included specialized burial churches, while Centula-Saint-Riquier (if the rather dubious sources can be trusted) had three churches set in a triangle linked by corridors.[89] Episcopal groups normally included a baptismal church of St John Baptist. As in Italy, there are usually two main churches, one dedicated to an apostle or martyr and the other to St Mary, though in Gaul the apostolic church is usually the principal and older one.[90] A particularly splendid case was the ecclesiastical group at Paris (figs. 10.4

---

87. J-F. Reynaud, *Lyon (Rhône) aux premiers temps chrétiens: basiliques et nécropoles* (Guides archéologiques de la France, 1986), 89-107; M. Jannet-Vallat *et al., Vienne (Isère) aux premiers temps chrétiens* (Guides archéologiques de la France, 1986), 38-42.

88. Février *et al., Histoire de la France urbaine*, i, 552. North of the main church, with its eastern crypt-chapel, is a line of no less than nine close-spaced churches built progressively from the seventh century onwards. The recent excavations are reported briefly in *Une village au temps de Charlemagne* (cat. of exhibition, Musée national des arts et traditions populaires, 1988-9) (Paris, 1988), 60-9; there is a more detailed plan in *Ville de Saint-Denis unite d'archéologie*, Fiche 3 (Sept. 1989).

89. James, 'Archaeology and the Merovingian monastery', 41-4; Hubert, Porcher and Vollbach, *Europe in the Dark Ages*, 304; Hariulf, *Chronique de l'abbaye de Saint-Riquier*, ed. F. Lot (Paris, 1894), 56, 58 (but see D. Parsons, 'The pre-Romanesque church of Saint-Riquier: the documentary evidence, *JBAA*, cxxx (1977), 21-51, which casts serious doubts on the reliability of this evidence for the eighth century). The Saint-Riquier corridors seem analogous to the corridor excavated at Monkwearmouth: R. Cramp, 'Monastic sites', in *Archaeology of Anglo-Saxon England*, ed. Wilson, 233-4. Cf. discussions of the word *porticus* by James, 'Archaeology and the Merovingian monastery', 46, and by Parsons, *Books and Buildings*, 24-6.

90. Hubert, *L'art pré-roman*, 43, n.2; *idem,* '"Cathédrales doubles" de la Gaule', 106-17; *idem,* 'Notes sur l'histoire de l'abbaye de Ferrières', in his *Nouveau recueil d'études d'archéologie et d'histoire* (Soc. de l'École des chartes, Geneva, 1985), 287-91 (which stresses the possible Columbanian influence on church groups). For this arrangement in Provence, see P.-A. Février, *Le développement urbaine en Provence* (Paris, 1964), 55-60. Another clear case is Manglieu (fig. 10.2 and cf. note 26 above), where the two churches, respectively of the Apostles and of St Mary, are described in the early eighth-century *Vita S. Boniti*: 'Splendent sanctorum martyrum aulae. Insignis micat sanctae semper Virginis Deique genitricis Mariae, atque celsior eminet turris pentacona ... Apostolorum aula non minus interea fulget, quasi nota trigona, sanctorum altaria nitent'. See J. Hubert, 'Les églises et bâtiments monastiques de l'abbaye de Manglieu', in *Nouveau Recueil*, 186-91.

and 10.6), centred on the huge Merovingian basilica of St Stephen and its eastern church of St Mary.[91]

These patterns appear in England with a consistency which leaves no doubt that the seventh- and eighth-century English were following the conventions and traditions of the sixth- and seventh-century Franks.[92] The only clear contrast is the lack (except at Canterbury, for obvious reasons exceptional, and perhaps at Repton) of special baptismal churches, a striking omission which suggests important differences in the organization of baptism.[93] The layout is sometimes irregular (as at Bywell, fig. 10.1, which is interesting to compare with Nivelles and Manglieu), and there is one probable case of a pair of timber churches side by side on the Italian pattern.[94] In most identifiable groups, however, the churches are aligned from west to east (figs. 10.8 to 10.10). St Augustine's at Canterbury is the best-known line of Anglo-Saxon churches absorbed within a great Romanesque one, but there are several others. This linearity conforms to French practice, but it may also reflect native traditions (most clearly displayed at early seventh-century Yeavering) in the planning of secular palace complexes.[95] The linear arrangement often survived the rebuilding of both churches, and later medieval parish churches which have chapels (or monastic churches) to their west or east are usually of early origin.[96]

The formation of groups was again accretive, new churches being added by successive bishops or heads. In a few cases St Mary's is both the earlier and the more westerly of two churches, and a striking number of these are very early foundations, sometimes pre-English in origin. At Glastonbury (fig. 10.10) St Mary's is traditionally the primary church, older than the main church of SS Peter and Paul set axially to its east,[97] while at

91. J. Hubert, 'Les origines de Notre-Dame de Paris', in *Arts et vie sociale*, 325-46; P. Périn in *Collections Mérovingiennes* (Catalogues d'art et d'histoire du Musée Carnavalet, Paris, 1985), 34-53, 600.
92. The Gallic influences are, of course, repeatedly obvious in Bede: see his comments on Faremoutier-en-Brie (Bede, *HE* iii. 8), where the English abbess Æthelburh began a church dedicated to all the apostles but left it incomplete at her death; seven years later the brethren decided to abandon it, and translated her body into another church dedicated to St Stephen.
93. Cf. Blair, 'Minster churches in the landscape', 51-2, and Sarah Foot's chapter in the present volume. The problem is also discussed by R. Morris, 'Baptismal places: 600-800', in *People and Places in Northern Europe 500-1600*, ed. I. Wood and N. Lund (1991), 15-24. For the eighth-century church of St John Baptist at Christ Church Canterbury, see Brooks, *Church of Canterbury*, 40, 51. For the interpretation of Phase 1 of the Repton crypt as a baptistery, see Biddle, 'Archaeology, architecture and the cult of saints', 16-22.
94. P. J. Huggins, 'Excavation of Belgic and Romano-British farm with middle Saxon cemetery and churches at Nazeingbury, Essex, 1975-6', *Essex Archaeol. and Hist.* x (1978), 29-117, at 47-76.
95. Note 20 above; it is interesting that some eleventh- and twelfth-century palace complexes (e.g. Westminster and Clarendon) are linear, in contrast to the courtyard plan which became normal in bishops' palaces.
96. As shown for instance by S. Bassett, 'A probable Mercian royal mausoleum at Winchcombe, Gloucestershire', *Antiq. J.* lxv (1985), 87. For the comparable case of Oxford, discussed in relation to some others, see Blair, 'St Frideswide's monastery', 257-8.
97. Rodwell, 'Churches in the landscape', 18-21; C. A. R. Radford, 'Glastonbury Abbey before 1884', in *Medieval Art and Architecture at Wells and Glastonbury* (British Archaeol. Assoc. Conference Trans. for 1978, 1981), 110-34.

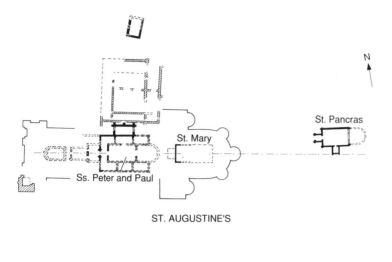

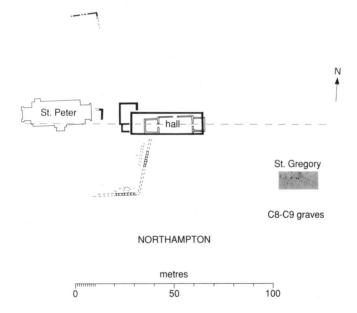

Figure 10.8 Axially-planned church groups (i). St Augustine's, Canterbury: after Taylor and Taylor, *Anglo-Saxon Architecture*, fig. 61. Northampton: after Williams *et al., Middle Saxon Palaces at Northampton.*
Conventions: seventh- to ninth-century structures (known) in solid black; later Anglo-Saxon structures (known) hatched; Anglo-Saxon structures (inferred) in fine stipple; post-Conquest structures in outline.

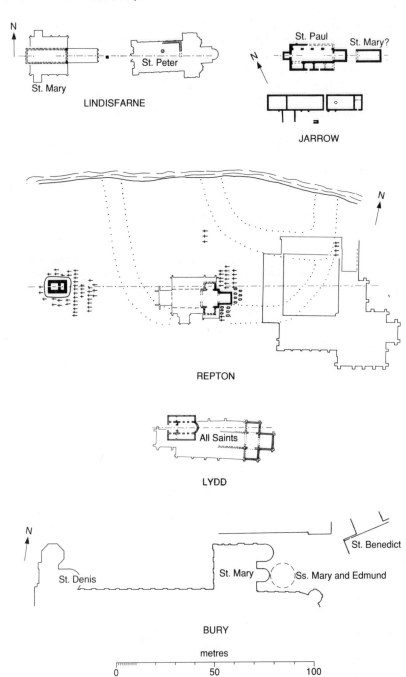

LINDISFARNE

JARROW

REPTON

LYDD

BURY

metres

Figure 10.9 Axially-planned church groups (ii). Lindisfarne: after Blair, 'Early churches at Lindisfarne'. Jarrow: after Cramp, 'Monastic sites', fig. 5.14, with some interpretation informed by other evidence. Repton: after unpublished plan reproduced by kind permission of Martin Biddle and Birthe Kjølbye-Biddle, with plan of main church after Taylor and Taylor, *Anglo-Saxon Architecture*, fig. 249. Lydd: after G.M. Livett, 'Lydd church', *Arch. Cant.* xlii (1930), facing p. 61, with plan of early church after E.D.C. Jackson and E. Fletcher, 'Excavations at the Lydd basilica, 1966', *JBAA* 3rd ser. xxxi (1968), 20. Bury St Edmunds: approximate positions of lost chapels plotted on outline plan of the Romanesque church after information in Gem and Keen, 'Late Anglo-Saxon finds from St. Edmund's Abbey', 1-2.
Conventions: as fig. 8.

Gloucester (fig. 10.3) St Mary-de-Lode seems again to predate St Peter's.[98] Bath (fig. 10.5) may be comparable, if we allow that the bath complex could have been appropriated in the fifth or sixth century rather than the seventh.[99] Bede says of Lichfield that St Chad was buried first in St Mary's but subsequently moved into St Peter's, which was built later; and of Lindisfarne that St Aidan was initially buried in the cemetery but translated after the building of the *basilica maior* and its dedication to St Peter.[100] At Lindisfarne the arrangement of two axial churches, with St Mary's to the west, can still be recovered (fig. 10.9).[101] At Wells (fig. 10.10) St Mary's chapel, in this case to the east of the main church of St Andrew, perpetuates a late Roman mortuary building.[102] Either the oldest churches of early Christian England were often dedicated to the Virgin (which on chronological grounds is unlikely),[103] or existing churches were rededicated to the Virgin and supplemented by new (and bigger) churches under apostolic patronage. It may be relevant that the groups in which St Mary's was the earlier church are in areas where Anglo-Saxon penetration was relatively late. There is a pattern here which needs further study.

More often, a main church dedicated to an apostolic saint acquired in due course a subsidiary church for the Virgin,[104] usually eastwards and sometimes (as at Canterbury, Jarrow and Wells) so close as to be almost touching.[105] Aldhelm built two churches at Malmesbury, one for SS Peter

98. Above, p. 242.
99. Rodwell, 'Churches in the landscape', 7-8. For the possibility of another church at Bath, axially to the west of St Mary's and in an area called 'Bimberg' (Beonna's *burh*?), see E. Holland and M. Chapman, *The Story of the White Hart Inn: i: the Site from the Saxon to the Tudor Age* (1990).
100. Bede, *HE* iv. 3 and iii. 17 (ed. Colgrave and Mynors, 344, 264).
101. J. Blair, 'The early churches at Lindisfarne', *Archaeologia Aeliana* 5th ser. xix (1991), 47-51.
102. W. Rodwell, *Wells Cathedral: Excavations and Discoveries* (3rd edn., 1987).
103. M. Clayton, *The Cult of the Virgin Mary in Anglo-Saxon England* (1990) traces the gradual rise of the cult through the seventh and eighth centuries.
104. As Hubert comments ('"Cathédrales doubles" de la Gaule', 117), this seems to be the normal sequence in Gaul from the mid-seventh century onwards.
105. In Aldhelm's poem for the abbess Bugga the eastern apse of her church is said to be dedicated to the Virgin: Aldhelm, *Carmina Ecclesiastica*, iii, ed. R. Ehwald (MGH, *Auct. Ant.* xv, Berlin, 1919), and *Aldhelm: The Poetic Works*, transl. M. Lapidge and J. L. Rosier (1985), 40-1. This is oddly reminiscent of post-Conquest 'Lady Chapels'; did this late twelfth-century fashion owe something to much older precedents?

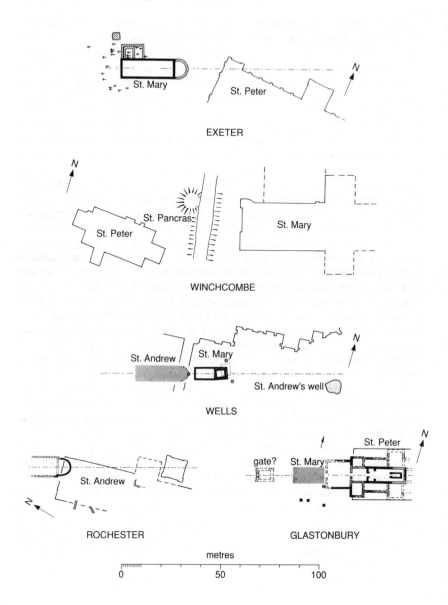

EXETER

WINCHCOMBE

WELLS

ROCHESTER

GLASTONBURY

metres

0   50   100

Figure 10.10 Axially-planned church groups (iii). Exeter: after C.G. Henderson and P.T. Bidwell, 'The Saxon minster at Exeter', in *Early Church in W. Britain and Ireland*, ed. Pearce, fig. 10.3, with outline plan of the later cathedral added. Winchcombe: after Bassett, 'Probable Mercian royal Mausoleum'. Wells: after Rodwell, 'Churches in the landscape', fig. 6, and Rodwell, *Wells Cathedral: Excavations and Discoveries*. Rochester: early church and foundation (probably Roman) under S. aisle after W.H. St J. Hope, *The Architectural History of the Cathedral . . . of St. Andrew at Rochester* (1900); footing under north transept (just possibly Anglo-Saxon) plotted (approximately) after note by C.A.R. Radford in *Annual Report of the Friends of Rochester Cathedral* (1989). Glastonbury: after Fernie, *Architecture of the Anglo-Saxons*, fig. 48, and Radford, 'Glastonbury Abbey before 1184', figs. 2-4.
Conventions: as fig. 8.

and Paul and the other for St Mary, and probably wrote dedicatory poems for both of them.[106] According to Stephanus, the dilatory St Wilfrid was rebuked thus by the Archangel Michael: 'You have built churches (*domos*) in honour of the apostles St Peter and St Andrew, but for the blessed Mary, ever-virgin, who is interceding for you, you have built nothing. You must put this right by dedicating a church in her honour.'[107] At the minster of *De abbatibus* the founder, ealdorman Eanmund, built St Peter's, but the community had to wait for the fourth abbot, Sigbald, to build St Mary's; the fifth abbot contributed a tall cross.[108] Other common additions may have been specialized funerary buildings, such as the mausolea excavated at Repton (fig. 10.9), Whithorn and Gloucester,[109] the stone tomb containing six burials which Bishop Cuthbert built at Hereford,[110] or the mausoleum

106. William of Malmesbury, *De Gestis pontificum anglorum*, v.§197, v.§216, ed. N. E. S. A. Hamilton (Rolls Ser. 52 1870), 345, 361; Aldhelm, *Carmina Ecclesiastica*, i-ii, and *Aldhelm: The Poetic Works*, transl. Lapidge and Rosier, 38-9. For the wider context of epigrams on church dedications, see Sims-Williams, *Religion and Literature*, 350-2.
107. Stephanus, *Vita S. Wilfridi*, c.56. Wilfrid evidently obliged, since Bede wrote an epigram for his *porticus* of St Mary, probably at Hexham: M. Lapidge, 'Some remnants of Bede's lost "Liber Epigrammatum"', *Eng. Hist. Rev.* xc (1975), 804. Jean Hubert's remark on Gallic bishops ('"Cathédrales doubles" de la Gaule', 116) is apposite for Wilfrid and other English founders:

Ici et là, et plus ou moins tôt, pendant toute la période franque, du Ve au VIIIe siècle, des évêques ont jugé opportun de se conformer à des usages vénérables en faisant ériger un second sanctuaire près de leur cathédrale, et ils ont réalisé leur dessein avec plus ou moins d'adresse.

108. Æthelwulf, *De abbatibus*, lines 143-50, 431-72, 537-9 (ed. Campbell, pp. 12-15, 34-9, 43).
109. Biddle, 'Archaeology, architecture and the cult of saints', 14-22; P. H. Hill, *Whithorn 3: Excavations at Whithorn Priory, 1988-90* (Whithorn Trust, 1990), 11-14 (a small eighth-century rectangular building, immediately east of an apparent church, containing several coffined burials); C. Heighway and R. Bryant, 'A reconstruction of the 10th century church of St Oswald, Gloucester', in *The Anglo-Saxon Church*, ed. Butler and Morris, 188-95.
110. Sims-Williams, *Religion and Literature*, 341-3. As Sims-Williams points out, Bishop Cuthbert of Hereford may well be identical with Archbishop Cuthbert who was later to build at Canterbury a baptismal church intended to house the bodies of the archbishops (above, note 93).

postulated at Winchcombe.[111] On some sites the multiplication of churches continued throughout the Anglo-Saxon period, remaining the norm until the era of Romanesque rebuilding.[112]

Irish sources are disappointingly vague about church groups, and so few stone buildings can be dated earlier than the eleventh century that architectural evidence is of limited use.[113] Such information as we have indicates some similarities to the Gallic and English pattern, and no very striking differences. References to the burning of Clonmacnoise 'with its oratories' in 845 and Glendalough 'with its oratories' in 1020 show that at least the larger communities had multiple churches.[114] Stone churches existed on a few important sites in the seventh to ninth centuries, though they were probably not common until the tenth.[115] Some seventh-century churches had *exedrae*, equivalent to Anglo-Saxon *porticus*, entered from the main building through its side walls.[116] There was a pair of basilicas at Armagh, the southern one housing the relics of Roman saints, while the basilica at

---

111. Bassett, 'Probable Mercian royal mausoleum'.
112. E.g. at Kempsey in 868: Sims-Williams, *Religion and Literature*, 171; at Chester under Æthelflaed of Mercia: A. T. Thacker, 'Chester and Gloucester: early ecclesiastical organisation in two Mercian *burhs*', *Northern History* xviii (1982), 199–211; and at Bury St Edmunds in the eleventh century: R. Gem and L. Keen, 'Late Anglo-Saxon finds from the site of St Edmund's Abbey', *Proc. Suffolk Inst. of Archaeol. and Hist.* xxxv (1981), 1–2. At Worcester, St Oswald is said to have added a church of St Mary to the old cathedral of St Peter after the reform of the community in 961: C. Dyer, 'The Saxon cathedrals of Worcester', *Trans. Worcs. Archaeol. Soc.* 3rd ser. ii (1968-9), 34. This long tradition of adding new churches to minsters may have had some influence on the practice, widespread in eleventh-century East Anglia, of building two or even three churches in one churchyard: P. Warner, 'Shared churchyards, freemen church builders and the development of parishes in eleventh-century East Anglia', *Landscape Hist.* viii (1986), 39–52. A remarkable Manx example is Maughold, where a large churchyard contains a church, four chapels and several standing crosses: P. M. C. Kermode, *The Manx Archaeological Survey: a Re-Issue of the First Five Reports* (1968), 4th Report, fig. 7.
113. Two recent critical surveys show how little can really be relied upon: P. Harbison, 'Early Irish churches', in *Die Iren und Europa im Früheren Mittelalter*, ed. H. Löwe (Stuttgart, 1982), ii, 618–29; A. Hamlin, 'The study of early Irish churches', in *Irland und Europa: Die Kirche im Frühmittelalter*, ed. P. Ní Chatháin and M. Richter (Stuttgart, 1984), 117–26.
114. Hamlin, 'The study of early Irish churches', 118–19. Cf. A. Macdonald, 'Notes on monastic archaeology and the annals of Ulster, 650–1050', in *Irish Antiquity*, ed. D. Ó Corráin (1981), 305–9.
115. Harbison, 'Early Irish churches', 620; Hamlin, 'The study of early Irish churches', 119. There is one seventh-century reference to a stone church: the *dom liacc* (stone house) of St Cíannán, identified as Duleek, Co. Meath: Tírechán, *Vita S. Patricii*, c.27, ed. L. Bieler (*Script. Lat. Hib.* 10, 1979), 146. Quadrangular churches are mentioned in *ibid.*, cc. 35 and 44 (ed. Bieler, 150, 158).
116. Macdonald, 'Aspects of the monastery', 282–4; Macdonald, 'Notes on monastic archaeology', 308–9.

Kildare was divided longitudinally by a partition;[117] both recall Italian prototypes in their arrangement of churches side by side rather than end to end. In the early stages, Romanizing influences on the planning of major foundations may have been as important in Ireland as in England.[118]

So far I have considered churches grouped at close range, confined within the monastic or episcopal boundary. But some minster enclosures were merely the nuclei of diffuse constellations, or even extended lines, of churches and other related monuments.[119] Groups of this kind might include holy wells, cemeteries and other older ritual sites, as well as chapels of specialized function such as hermitages or retreat-houses. Bede mentions St Chad's *mansio remotior* not far from the main church at Lichfield, as well as a 'cemetery' near Hexham, dedicated to St Michael and surrounded by a ditch, which was also used for solitary prayer.[120] Other retreat-houses were further from their parent minsters, as were a wide range of dependent chapels of other kinds.[121] In topographical, ritual and perhaps sometimes legal terms, an important minster extended far out beyond its *uallum* into the territory around.[122]

There is probably no single explanation for the phenomenon of church groups in Anglo-Saxon England. Some of its features, such as the recurrence of churches dedicated to St Mary, link it through Merovingian to Italian and early Christian practice, but no evidence has been found in England (or indeed Gaul) for the ritual division of the year between summer and winter churches, or of the congregation between one church for the baptized and another for the catechumens. Explanations in terms of separate churches for the male and female communities (as at Wimborne and apparently at Barking),[123] for clergy and laity, or for different saints, may be valid in

---

117. Armagh, *Liber Angeli*, cc. 15-19 (ed. L. Bieler, *Script. Lat. Hib.* x (1979), 186-7); Cogitosus, *Vita S. Brigitae*, c.32 (*Acta Sanctorum*, Feb., i, 141). See also Thomas, *Early Christian Archaeology*, 145-6; Harbison, 'Early Irish churches', 624-9; Parsons, *Books and Buildings*, 20-1; C. Doherty, 'The basilica in early Ireland', *Peritia*, iii (1984), 310-13.

118. For Gallic and Roman influences, cf. Doherty, 'The basilica in early Ireland', especially the note of the *dedicatio bassilicae Sancti Pauli* at Druim Lias, Co. Antrim, in the Calendar of Willibrord (*ibid.* 311-12).

119. The pioneering work is again Rodwell, 'Churches in the landscape', 16-18. The main group at Saint-Denis had outlying chapels both to the west and to the east, possibly used as stations in processional liturgies: *Village au temps de Charlemagne*, 65 and fig. 12.

120. Bede, *HE* iv. 3 and v. 2 (ed. Colgrave and Mynors, 336-8, 456). Bede's account of Lichfield, which has the bishop alone in the *oratorium* while the brethren are in the *ecclesia*, suggests that the two were not far apart.

121. Cf. Blair 'Minster churches in the landscape', 50-5. Heiu established for herself a *mansio* at *Kaelcacaestir* (?Tadcaster) after the foundation of Hartlepool: Bede, *HE* iv. 23 (ed. Colgrave and Mynors, 406). For a possible retreat-house near Oxford, see Blair, 'Thornbury, Binsey', 18-20.

122. Cf. the references to 'a circuit of miles' in charters for Lindisfarne, Bobbio and Stavelot-Malmedy: P. Wormald, *Bede and the Conversion of England: the Charter Evidence* (the Jarrow Lecture, 1984), 17. There are later traditions of 'sanctuary zones' at Beverley and Ripon.

123. Rudolf, *Vita S. Leobae*, c.2, ed. G. Waitz (MGH, *Scriptores*, xv.1 1887), 123; Bede, *HE* iv. 7.

individual cases but are hard to apply universally.

The problem may exist only from a post-Romanesque perspective: early medieval liturgy was characteristically performed in sequences of small compartments, and the multiplication of these compartments around holy sites was the immemorial practice of the church. Adomnán's (or rather, Arculf's) account of the multifarious tombs, basilicas and oratories of the Holy Land, including the great line of churches on Golgotha, was known to Bede, probably to Wilfrid and to many of their contemporaries; its descriptions of holy cities presented a model for emulation.[124] Groups of churches in early medieval Europe were often ascribed a sacred, coherent character, heightened by the processional arrangements which bound them together in ritual cycles extending through the year.[125] The occasional references in English sources do little more than remind us that the day-to-day liturgical functions which church groups existed to serve are largely irrecoverable.[126]

THE BUILDINGS AND LAYOUT OF THE PRECINCT[127]

Whereas the churches can often be located, domestic and industrial buildings never remain standing and have rarely been excavated. There are, however, some descriptions, and retrieval of below-ground evidence has

---

124. Adomnán, *De locis sanctis*, ed. D. Meehan, *Script. Lat. Hib.* iii (1958), esp. pp. 42–51. For the likely influence of this text on Wilfrid, perhaps causing him to build his church of St Mary as a rotunda, see Gem, 'Towards an iconography of Anglo-Saxon architecture', 10–12.
125. For towns, see A. Havercamp, '"Heilige Städte" im hohen Mittelalter', in *Mentalitäten im Mittelalter: Methodische und Inhaltliche Probleme*, ed. F. Graus, *Vorträge und Forschungen*, 25 (Sigmaringen, 1987), esp. 131–5; I am grateful to Julia Barrow for this reference. Metz had a system of stational churches, organized on an elaborate cycle which covered the suburbs in turn while maintaining regular stations in the central area: T. Klauser, 'Ein Stationsliste der Metzer Kirche aus dem 8. Jahrhundert', in his *Gesammelte Arbeiten . . .*, ed. E. Dassmann, *Jahrbuch für Antike und Christentum*, Erg., 3 (Münster, 1974), 22–45. Cf. the 'cross of churches' at Utrecht: Hoekstra, 'City of Utrecht', 9–16. A splendidly full account of Rogation-tide processions from dependent townships to the main church is in Hariulf, *Chron. de Saint Riquier*, 296–306 (cf. Parsons, 'Pre-Romanesque church of Saint-Riquier', 29, 48–50). The role of multiple churches in processional liturgy is discussed further by C. Heitz, 'Architecture et liturgie processionnelle à l'epoque préromane', *Revue de l'art*, xxiv (1974), 30–47.
126. Especially the accounts of the departure of Ceolfrith from Monkwearmouth in 716: Bede, *Historia abbatum*, c.17 (*Opera Historica*, ed. Plummer, i, 381–2; cf. *ibid.*, 396–7). After mass had been said in both St Mary's and St Peter's churches the brethren assembled in St Peter's where Ceolfrith gave them the kiss of peace; then everyone processed, 'the sound of their weeping interrupting the litanies', to St Lawrence's chapel which adjoined the monks' dormitory. In *Regularis Concordia*, ed. Dom T. Symons (1953), 32–5, the arrangements for Ash Wednesday and Palm Sunday involve processing from the mother-church to a lesser church and back again. For liturgical processions in twelfth-century Winchester, see *Winchester in the Early Middle Ages*, ed. M. Biddle (Winchester Studies 1, 1976), 268–70.
127. For this section see also Foot, above, p. 212 no. 2.

now started to accelerate. At the same time, received characterizations of the 'Celtic monastery' have not stood up to criticism.[128] While it is still impossible to reconstruct the layout of any Anglo-Saxon minster with anything approaching completeness, there is scope for a new comparison with the Merovingian and Irish evidence which once again suggests more similarities than contrasts.[129]

In all three societies, religious settlements had strong affinities with ordinary secular settlements but were occupied more densely.[130] A large English minster was 'considerably more like a town than were most places'; it is no coincidence that so many of the small market towns of early medieval England, as of early medieval Ireland, originated as minsters.[131] Bede describes an approaching traveller's view of Coldingham (where the enclosure, fig. 10.1, still gives us some idea of scale), its 'public and private buildings' towering grandly up.[132]

Internal space must often have been heavily used and considerably subdivided, especially where a line of churches crossed the precinct. The male and female communities were segregated by walls at Wimborne (which seems to have been exceptionally strict), and apparently also at Æthelhild's minster near Partney.[133] The position of Wilfrid's cell at Oundle, projecting against the enclosure boundary, suggests that space was tight.[134] At Barking the second abbess had to have the dead sisters and brethren exhumed and reburied in a common tomb in St Mary's church *propter angustiam loci in quo monasterium constructum est*.[135] Excavation shows that some precincts contained mixed cemeteries which (to judge from their great size) must have served the laity,[136] but the graves of inmates were sometimes set apart; Barking had a nuns' cemetery to the

---

128. Contrast C. A. R. Radford, 'The Celtic monastery in Britain', *Archaeologia Cambrensis*, cxi (1962), 1-24, with C. D. Morris, *Church and Monastery in the Far North: an Archaeological Evaluation* (the Jarrow Lecture, 1989).
129. The standard survey is R. Cramp, 'Monastic sites', in *The Archaeology of Anglo-Saxon England*, ed. Wilson, 201-52. However, for parallels between Northumbria and Ireland, see R. Cramp, 'Northumbria and Ireland', in *Sources of Anglo-Saxon Culture*, ed. P. E. Szarmach and V. D. Oggins (Kalamazoo, 1986), 192-9.
130. For Gaul and Ireland, see James, 'Archaeology and the Merovingian monastery'; Macdonald, 'Aspects of the monastery', 284-97; *idem*, 'Notes on monastic archaeology', 310-14.
131. Campbell, *Essays*, 141. Blair, 'Minster churches in the landscape', 47-50, reviews the topographical characteristics of minster towns. For Ireland, see C. Doherty, 'The monastic town in early medieval Ireland', in *Comparative History of Urban Origins*, ed. Clarke and Simms, 45-75.
132. Bede, *HE* iv. 25 (ed. Colgrave and Mynors, p. 424).
133. Rudolf, *Vita S. Leobae*, c.2 (ed. Waitz, p. 123): 'duo monasteria . . ., muris altis et firmis circumdata . . ., unum scilicet clericorum et alterum feminarum'; Bede, *HE* iii. 11. Cf. Foot, *Anglo-Saxon Minsters*, 189.
134. Stephanus, *Vita S. Wilfridi*, c.67.
135. Bede, *HE* iv. 10.
136. For two cases, see P. Everson, 'Excavations in the vicarage garden at Brixworth, 1972', *JBAA*, cxxx (1977), 55-122; D. Allen and C. H. Dalwood, 'Iron Age occupation . . . Aylesbury, 1981', *Records of Buckinghamshire*, xxv (1983), 2, 6-8.

west of the *oratorium*, which stood on the south side of the complex, and a separate cemetery for the brethren.[137] The recurrent Irish arrangement of founder-saint's grave with a standing cross to its west is echoed by St Cuthbert, who requested burial 'near my oratory towards the south on the eastern side of the holy cross which I have erected there', and by Abbot Sigewine of *De abbatibus* who was laid 'by the figure of the tall cross which he himself had set up'.[138] Some Irish texts imply a relatively formal relationship between churches, cemeteries and main communal buildings: Adomnán's Life of St Columba mentions an open space or *plateola*, which may have had the principal church on its east side and the monk's sleeping-quarters on its west.[139]

The much-cited formality of Benedict Biscop's twin foundations needs to be seen in this context. His buildings are certainly (as Bede himself notes) of Gallic inspiration, in the mainstream of the European developments which culminated in the fully-fledged cloister.[140] Yet Wearmouth and Jarrow are not strikingly more regular in their layout than several of the church groups discussed above, or than the palace at Yeavering; while we are simply in no position to compare them with the layout of the principal buildings at Armagh or Iona, Canterbury or Coldingham. Rather than contrasting Roman regularity with Celtic confusion, it is more helpful to envisage a broad tradition of monastic planning in which formal main buildings coexisted with a high density of informal lesser ones.

The main domestic buildings would always have been those used for eating and sleeping. Jumièges had a *duplex . . . domus quiescendi*, evidently a large two-storey structure with stores and services on the ground floor and beds above.[141] Irish texts mention a 'great house' (*tech mór, magna domus, monasterium rotundum*) which seems to have been used for such varied activities as cooking, eating, reading, writing and teaching; the monks apparently slept in a large *domus* (possibly but not certainly a different building), circular or rectangular, divided into individual cubicles giving onto a central floor-space.[142] A curvilinear post-hole setting excavated at

---

137. Bede, *HE* iv. 7. Cf. discussion of Monkwearmouth cemeteries by Cramp, 'Monastic sites', 231-3.
138. Herity, 'Buildings and layout', 254-6; *idem*, 'The layout of Irish early Christian monasteries', in *Irland und Europa*, ed. Ní Chatháin and Richter, 106-7; Bede, *Vita S. Cuthberti*, c.37; Æthelwulf, *De abbatibus*, lines 537-9 (ed. Campbell, p. 43). For axial burials of Anglo-Saxon saints (which seem generally to be of the ninth and tenth centuries rather than earlier), see Biddle, 'Archaeology and architecture and the cult of saints', 11.
139. Macdonald, 'Aspects of the monastery', 293-7; Herity, 'Buildings and layout'; *idem*, 'Layout of Irish early Christian monasteries', 108-9.
140. Cf. E. Fernie, *The Architecture of the Anglo-Saxons* (1983), 48-53; James, 'Archaeology and the Merovingian monastery', 46-7. The plan of St Gall, with its apparently precocious claustral layout, was probably made after 826; see W. Jacobsen, review of W. Horn and E. Born, *The Plan of St Gall*, *Kunstchronik*, xxxv (1982), 89-96, at 93.
141. James, 'Archaeology and the Merovingian monastery', 37-40.
142. Macdonald, 'Aspects of the monastery', 284-9; *idem*, 'Notes on monastic archaeology', 310-11.

Iona has been plausibly interpreted as such a building.[143] No major specialized structure of this sort has yet been found on an English site, but the
aedificia . . . sublimiter erecta at Coldingham sound as though they could
have been storied.[144] In the Barking material preserved by Bede, a sick nun
comes out of her *cubiculum* and has a vision of the dying abbess lifted up *de
domo in qua sorores pausare solebant*, which suggests a large building divided up into cubicles on the Irish pattern.[145] Wimborne had a building big
enough to contain all the nuns when they were locked out of their church.[146]

Given the aristocratic lifestyle of many inhabitants of minsters, it would
not be surprising to find refectories which resembled secular halls. Even the
domestic ranges at Jarrow can be read as stone versions of contemporary
timber halls,[147] and the problem of distinguishing aristocratic from monastic
use is illustrated in acute form by the discoveries at Northampton (fig. 10.8).
Between St Peter's and St Gregory's churches, and axially aligned on the
former, lay an eighth-century timber hall which was rebuilt in stone in the
ninth century.[148] The interpretation of this hall as a royal palace cannot be
disproved, but neither is there written evidence to support it. Its location
between two Anglo-Saxon churches surely suggests, rather, that it served as
the minster refectory: a scene of those secular entertainments which so
annoyed Bede and Alcuin.[149]

Texts mention a variety of minor buildings: cells for reading and praying,
detached sleeping-huts, guesthouses, workshops.[150] Because of their sheer
numbers, it is mainly these small peripheral structures which archaeology
is now bringing to light. The recent publication of seventh- and eighth-
century buildings at Hartlepool is a landmark, not least because it helps to
make sense of the badly-recorded, but contemporary and closely similar,
features at Whitby.[151] By coincidence, the excavated areas at both sites are

143. Barber, 'Excavations on Iona, 1979', 299-303, 358.
144. Bede, *HE* iv. 25.
145. Bede, *HE* iv. 9. *Pace* Cramp, 'Monastic sites', 206, this passages does not show
    that 'there was a communal dormitory for the sisters but individual *cubiculi* for
    the aged and infirm nuns'. If the sick nun had a *cubiculum* the dying abbess
    would surely not have slept in an undivided dormitory, and the most natural
    explanation is that both ladies were in the same building, the *domus* being
    divided into *cubiculi*.
146. Rudolf, *Vita S. Leobae*, c.5 (ed. Waitz, p. 124).
147. A point made by Cramp, 'Monastic sites', 239.
148. J. H. Williams, M. Shaw and V. Denham, *Middle Saxon Palaces at Northampton*
    (1985).
149. Cf. Wormald, 'Bede, Beowulf and the conversion of the Anglo-Saxon aristocracy',
    42-5, 50-4.
150. Coldingham had *casas ac lectos* as well as *domunculae quae ad orandum vel
    legendum factae erant*, in all of which the nuns misbehaved themselves: Bede,
    HE iv. 25. See, James, 'Archaeology and the Merovingian monastery', 36-46 for
    Gaul, and Macdonald, 'Aspects of the monastery', 285-93 and 'Notes on monastic
    archaeology', 310-14 for Ireland. There are references to a guest-house at Ripon
    and at Æthelhild's minster (*Vita S. Cuthberti*, ii. 2; Bede, *Vita S. Cuthberti*, c.7;
    Bede, *HE* iii. 11), and to a monastic smith who preferred to stay in his workshop
    (*in officina sua*) day and night (Bede, *HE* v .14).
151. R. Daniels, 'The Anglo-Saxon monastery at Church Close, Hartlepool,
    Cleveland', *Archaeol. J.* cxlv (1988), 158-210; Cramp, 'Monastic sites', 223-9,
    453-62 (including a valiant attempt by Philip Rahtz to interpret the Whitby
    excavation records).

on the north-east edges of the precinct, with structures backing against and eventually spreading beyond the *ualla*. In each case there is a cluster of small rectilinear buildings (on stone footings replacing an earlier phase with earth-fast posts), fronting onto a more open area around the presumed site of the main church. The buildings seem denser and more complex at Whitby, though it is hard to separate the phases there on the available evidence. Whitby produced a collection of high-status personal objects including pins and writing styli, while debris from Hartlepool suggests workshops for high-quality metalwork.

A third eighth-century northern site, currently being excavated, is Whithorn. A line of buildings, including a church and a small mausoleum, stood on a stone terrace. South of this was a group of at least ten, perhaps many more, rectangular timber buildings separated by paths. As the excavator observes, there is a clear contrast with the Northumbrian 'palace' sites: 'Whithorn demonstrates more regular planning and more densely-packed buildings. The royal sites have larger halls, but Whithorn seems to have been a much larger settlement even though its full extent is unknown.'[152]

The common feature of Whitby, Hartlepool and Whithorn is the multiplication of small rectangular cells, not greatly differentiated in size.[153] It is as groups, not individually, that these structures are distinctive: in form and fabric they belong to the mainstream of English secular timber building,[154] stemming as clearly from their own vernacular tradition as do the round-houses and *clocháns* on Irish monastic sites.[155] Buildings of this kind have been revealed less extensively at Jarrow, Monkwearmouth and Tynemouth,[156] as well as other sites (such as Dorchester-on-Thames and Carlisle, figs. 10.3 and 10.1)[157] in close proximity to important minsters. Given their consistency both with the written sources and with the known monastic sites described above, the reluctance of many excavators to interpret such settlements as minsters is curious. A case which illustrates the problem of definition is the seventh- and eighth-century site at Brandon (Suffolk), on an island in the fens (fig. 10.11). It contains a later chapel (not yet excavated); it had a possible church, two cemeteries, and a close-packed huddle of small rectangular timber buildings which spread beyond a primary enclosure boundary. It has also produced a spectacular range of metal finds, including styli and a gold plaque bearing an Evangelist's symbol.[158] Brandon could be our best example so far of an

---

152. The fullest report at the time of writing is Hill, *Whithorn 3*.
153. Daniels, 'Monastery at Hartlepool', 203-8.
154. *ibid.*, 203-5; cf. S. James, A. Marshall and M. Millett, 'An early medieval building tradition', *Archaeol. J.* cxli (1984), 182-215.
155. Cf. Herity, 'Buildings and layout', 258.
156. Cramp, 'Monastic sites', 229-41, 217-20.
157. T. Rowley and L. Brown, 'Excavations at Beech House Hotel, Dorchester on Thames, 1972', *Oxoniensia*, xlvi (1981), 1-55; McCarthy, 'Thomas, Chadwick and Post-Roman Carlisle', 245-54.
158. R. D. Carr, A. Tester and P. Murphy, 'The Middle-Saxon settlement at Staunch Meadow, Brandon', *Antiquity* lxii (1988), 371-7. An apparently similar site at Flixborough is described briefly in *Current Archaeology*, cxxvi (Sept./Oct. 1991), 244-7.

Figure 10.11 A typical eighth-century minster? The excavated settlement at Brandon (Suffolk), reproduced by kind permission of R. Carr.

ordinary small minster, yet archaeologists are far from agreed that the site is a religious one. It is proving hard to defeat the insidious assumption that a seventh- or eighth-century site is unlikely to be a minster unless it is mentioned by Bede or other contemporary sources.

The places just discussed are all early and mainly northern; monastic settlement in southern England, and after the mid-eighth century, remains obscure. Our ignorance of the architectural consequences of reform, whether canonical in the ninth and eleventh centuries or Benedictine in the late tenth, is especially tantalizing, for Continental analogies suggest that it should have been substantial.[159] There is evidence for cloisters at Canterbury, Winchester, Glastonbury and Eynsham,[160] but so far no sign of the groups of canons' houses which must often have existed at more ordinary minsters,[161] nor of the quarters of strict-living cathedral canons in the eleventh century.[162] Many of the key sites are known, but archaeology has yet to fill this large gap in our knowledge.

CONCLUSION

I have argued that the planning of ecclesiastical sites in north-western Europe during the seventh to ninth centuries followed a single broad tradition of development. This tradition was, of course, articulated to local circumstances. Domestic buildings were rectilinear where Anglo-Saxon vernacular traditions prevailed, round where they did not; Roman forts and

---

159. The general English context is discussed by Blair, 'Secular minster churches', 116-25. For the creation of canons' precincts in French towns as a result of Carolingian reforms, and the urban reorganization and growth which resulted, see J. Hubert, 'Évolution de la topographie et de l'aspect des villes de Gaule du Ve au Xe siècle', in *Arts et vie sociale*, 23-31; Février, *Histoire de la France urbaine*, 541-5; Barral I Altet, *Paysage monumental*, 64-9; E. James, *The Origins of France* (1982), 63-9.

160. Cramp, 'Monastic sites', 208, 246-9; Fernie, *Architecture of the Anglo-Saxons*, 95-6, 110-11; Eynsham is currently (1991) being excavated by the Oxford Archaeological Unit.

161. Groups of canons' houses in France are discussed by J. Hubert, 'La vie commune des clercs et l'archéologie', in *Arts et vie sociale*, 126-9; this cites a diploma of Charles the Bald for the provost and canons of Brioude (Auvergne), giving dimensions of the canons' sixteen house-plots, each containing a court-yard, house and garden. Such arrangements could well have been common in England; possible cases are Wolverhampton (D. Hooke and T. R. Slater. *Anglo-Saxon Wolverhampton and its Monastery*, 1986), and Bampton (Blair, 'Secular minster churches', 139-40). Separate canons' houses grouped around minsters may be reflected in the post-Conquest traditions of 'twelve habitations and as many chapels' at Abingdon (Cramp, 'Monastic sites', 216), and of 'the old church of the place, and nine others which stood about the cemetery, together with certain houses of the canons which stood near the cemetery' at Christchurch, Hants. (Hase, 'Mother churches of Hampshire', 59).

162. The excavations at Wells revealed a corner of what may be the cloister built by Bishop Giso (1061-88) for his canons: Rodwell, *Wells Cathedral: Excavations and Discoveries*, 6-7. At Old Sarum a fragmentary quadrangular building north of the cathedral, partly overlain by a twelfth-century aisled hall, could be the cloister of the late eleventh-century canons.

villas were reused when available, but clearly could not be reused where they did not exist; churches aspired to *Romanitas* and architectural grandeur in so far as the wealth and contacts of their patrons allowed. These are very specific differences; the absence of broad and fundamental contrasts is much more striking. We have no grounds for thinking that an average minster in seventh-century England would have been distinguishable from one in Gaul, or that any of the topographical and architectural descriptions in Adomnán's Life of St Columba were less applicable to an English site than to an Irish one.

This is exactly what we should expect. Recent scholarship leaves us with no excuse to conceive 'national churches' as self-contained entities developing in isolation: contacts were maintained throughout the period, and in almost all directions. Mediterranean and Gallic influences were reaching south and east Ireland, Cornwall, Wales and north Britain through the fifth and sixth centuries, while the 'Class E' tableware suggests regular Gallic trade to Atlantic Britain and Ireland during the late sixth and seventh centuries.[163] In the south-west and west Midlands at least, the seventh- and eighth-century English found and assimilated an organized British church.[164] There were Irish ecclesiastics in Britain, including the southern and eastern English kingdoms, before the much better recorded links between Northumbria and Iona from the 620s onwards.[165] In the seventh century the Columbanian connection brought Irishmen to Gaul and England in large numbers, and stimulated numerous monastic foundations; it also took many Englishmen and Franks to Ireland.

For the present purposes, the channel of influence from Gaul to England is probably the most important. English minsters of the 650s onwards were built and ruled by men and women who had been brought up under the tutelage of the older, richer and more 'Roman' Gallic church, and would have looked to it automatically for their models.[166] To take an obvious

---

163. Thomas, *Early Christian Archaeology*, 11-28, 101-3; C. Thomas, 'East and west: Tintagel, Mediterranean imports and the early insular church', in *Early Church in W. Britain and Ireland*, ed. Pearce, 17-34; E. James, 'Ireland and western Gaul in the Merovingian period', in *Ireland in Early Medieval Europe: Studies in Memory of Kathleen Hughes*, ed. D. Whitelock, R. McKitterick and D. Dumville (1982), 362-86; C. Thomas, '"Gallici nautae de Galliarum provinciis": a sixth/seventh century trade with Gaul, reconsidered', *Med. Archaeol.* xxxiv (1990), 1-26.
164. S. Pearce, *The Kingdom of Dumnonia* (1978), 97-108, for the south-west; Steven Bassett's chapter in the present volume for the West Midlands. Cf. H. R. Loyn, 'The conversion of the English to Christianity: some comments on the Celtic contribution', in *Welsh Society and Nationhood: Historical Essays Presented to Glanmor Williams*, ed. R. R. Davies *et al.* (1984), 5-18.
165. For this and what follows, see Campbell, *Essays*, 51-62; D. L. T. Bethell, 'The originality of the early Irish church', *JRSAI* cxi (1981), 36-49; J. Campbell, 'The debt of the early English church to Ireland', *Irland und die Christenheit: Bibelstudien und Mission*, ed. P. Ní Chatháin and M. Richter (Stuttgart, 1987), 332-46.
166. Campbell, *Essays*, 56-62; M. Deanesly, 'Early English and Gallic minsters', *Trans. Royal Hist. Soc.* 4th ser. xxiii (1941), 25-69; Sims-Williams, *Religion and Literature*, 110f.

example, the great line of churches at Paris (fig. 10.6), ranged along the Roman river-front wall of the Île de la Cité and looming over the Seine, must have made a deep impression on any English visitor. If Arculf could sketch ground-plans of the Holy Places for Adomnán, might not other Gallic clergy have provided details of buildings nearer home?

The first conclusion about the early English church to be drawn from its sites and monuments is thus that it was cosmopolitan. The second is that far from being isolated, it was a major and integral part of the secular world. Minsters were frequented by the laity, and influenced their lives profoundly. In both Ireland and England they were among the most important local foci, centres for production and exchange and seedbeds of future growth.[167] As the English economy developed during the ninth and tenth centuries, the religious sites which I have described in this chapter became the towns which Gervase Rosser considers in the next. It is hardly surprising that they played a leading role in the practice of pastoral care.

---

167. Cf. Doherty, 'Monastic town in early medieval Ireland'.

11 The cure of souls in English towns before 1000

GERVASE ROSSER

> Let us speak therefore of those who live in cities and towns and see whether we can find anything like them in antiquity. It is written in the first book of Kings that Samuel said to Saul after he had joined him in his kingship: 'After that thou shalt come to the hill of the Lord, where the garrison of the Philistines is. And when thou shalt come there into the city, thou shalt meet a company of prophets coming down from the high place, with a psaltery and a timbrel, and a pipe and a harp before them; and they shall be prophesying, and the spirit of the Lord shall come down upon them and thou shalt prophesy with them and shalt be changed into another man.

On such a positive note does the early twelfth-century author of the 'Little book of the various orders and professions which there are in the church' open his discussion of the pastoral mission to the urban laity. This writer, himself a canon, observes that clerics of all kinds, whether secular or leading one of the forms of regular life known in his day, naturally undertake such work; and he insists on their right to material reward for their pains.[1] Before the millennium it was no less a presumption that clerics would involve themselves in pastoral work, and that this effort should be particularly concentrated in central places. The present contribution concerns those places in England which were distinguished by an urban, or proto-urban, character in the period c. 700 to c. 1000. Outside the cathedral towns, such sites were normally the locations of minsters. As other chapters in this book show, the distinction between monastic and clerical communities before the late tenth-century reform is hard to define.

---

1. *Libellus de diversis ordinibus et professionibus qui sunt in aecclesia*, ed. G. Constable and B. Smith (1972), 21, and see also 27, 41f., 75, 87f., 95, 97f. The author noted that regular monks in the lately reformed Benedictine houses might have preferred greater seclusion, but found themselves irresistibly importuned by demands for pastoral attention. Starting-points for this chapter are the following invaluable recent studies: C. N. L. Brooke, 'The church in the towns, 1000-1250', *Studies in Church History*, vi (1970), 59-83; J. Campbell, 'The church in Anglo-Saxon towns', *Studies in Church History*, xvi (1979), 119-35, repr. in *idem*, *Essays in Anglo-Saxon History* (1986), 139-54; and R. Morris, *Churches in the Landscape* (1989), ch. 5. In addition I am grateful to Jane Garnett and Richard Morris, and to the editors, John Blair and Richard Sharpe, for their advice and comments on an earlier version.

Whatever their precise observances, however, all of the middle-Saxon minster clergy (a minority of whom were in priests' orders) were expected by the legislation of the period to contribute to pastoral work.[2] The establishment of this framework by recent scholarship opens the way for closer examination of pastoral care in action. In what follows, the cure of souls in central places before 1000 will be illustrated principally from contemporary but also from later sources; for it will be argued that a degree of continuity in lay and clerical relations gives some retrospective value to subsequent testimony, which confirms the long-standing significance of pastoral contact in towns.

From its inception, the Christian mission to the population of England emanated outwards from a scatter of significant places. Many of these places had formerly, in the Roman period, been towns; most would from the tenth century onwards develop into permanently settled urban centres, large or small. In the intervening period their ecclesiastical function was, on the one hand, as bases from which pastoral tours of the rural hinterland could be launched, and on the other, as foci to which the laity were periodically drawn for a variety of purposes, of which spiritual welfare became one. The first of these two models is encapsulated in Bede's letter to Archbishop Ecgberht of York (AD 734), in which the pastor was exhorted to seek out his flock in the remote parts of his large diocese, preaching to them in the vernacular where Latin would not be comprehended.[3] Many holy men of the Anglo-Saxon period are known to have itinerated in this way: not only such seventh-century and later bishops as Cuthbert of Lindisfarne, Aldhelm of Sherborne and Oswald of Worcester, but also the seventh-century priors of a *monasterium* or minster such as that at Melrose.[4] It was on such a mission that Abbot Ecgwine of Evesham, early in the eighth century, was remembered as having preached to the townspeople of Alcester; but when the local smiths maliciously drowned his voice with their hammers, Ecgwine left the place with his effective

---

2. S. Foot, 'Parochial ministry in early Anglo-Saxon England: the role of monastic communities', *Studies in Church History*, xxvi (1989), 43-54; *idem*, pp. 212-25 above. On the minsters, see J. Blair, 'Minster churches in the landscape', in *Anglo-Saxon Settlements*, ed. D. Hooke (1988), 35-58; and *idem*, 'Local churches in Domesday Book and before', in *Domesday Studies*, ed. J. C. Holt (1987), 265-78.

3. *Councils and Ecclesiastical Documents Relating to Great Britain and Ireland*, ed. A. W. Haddan and W. Stubbs (3 vols., 1869-78), iii. 314-26.

4. Foot, 'Parochial ministry', 43; Bede, *Vita S. Cuthberti*, c.9, ed. B. Colgrave (1940), 184-7; William of Malmesbury, *Gesta pontificum Anglorum*, v. iii, ed. N. E. S. A. Hamilton, Rolls Series, 52 (1870), 382; Byrhtferth of Ramsey, *Vita S. Oswaldi*, pt. iii, in *The Historians of the Church of York*, ed. J. Raine (3 vols., Rolls Series, 71, 1879-94), i. 420-1; for Byrhtferth's authorship, see S. J. Crawford, 'Byrhtferth of Ramsey and the anonymous Life of St Oswald', in *Speculum Religionis, being Studies in Religion and Literature from Plato to Von Hügel Presented to G. M. Montefiore* (1929), 99-111.

curse upon its trade, which so impeded the word of God.[5] The second model - more properly the subject of this chapter - is exemplified by Aldhelm in his period as head of the religious community at Malmesbury during the last quarter of the eighth century. According to a celebrated story preserved in two early post-Conquest accounts, the inhabitants of the surrounding countryside knew little of the Christian faith, and although some were prepared to attend mass in the little town on Sundays, when merchants gathered there from outlying places to trade, none stayed for the sermon. Aldhelm therefore went on to the bridge which marked the boundary 'between the town and the country', and there intercepted the arrivals as they came to market. Having first arrested their attention by singing secular songs, he then proceeded to more elevated discourse. So the country people returned home doubly enriched by their journey to town.[6]

Aldhelm's address to a captive urban audience (later recalled in St Francis's theatrical performances in market squares) illustrates a general tendency of the ecclesiastical mission to exploit opportunities generated by economic activity. Legislation against Sunday markets indicates that these were common;[7] some communities of clergy owned their own markets;[8] and toll remissions conceded to particular churches underline the link between religion and trade.[9] Whether church or market-place had the strict chronological primacy in particular cases is of less significance than the fruitful association of commerce with the pastoral activity of ecclesiastical communities in the incipient towns of the early Middle Ages. At Malmesbury and certainly at many another such ecclesiastical centre, the clerics' promotion of a market was a means both to financial profit and to further the exposure of the laity to the evangelistic impetus of the religious house.

The extent of that evangelistic impetus in the tenth and earlier centuries has not yet been fully recognized. Admittedly, the primary aim behind the creation of an Anglo-Saxon minster may often have been the commemoration of its aristocratic founders rather than the pastoral care of the laity at

---

5. Dominic of Evesham, *Vita S. Ecgwini*, i, in *Chronicon abbatiae de Evesham*, ed. W. D. Macray (Rolls Series, 29, 1863), 24-6; this is the early thirteenth-century recension of Dominic's text by Thomas of Marlborough, who included this miracle as an addition of his own (*loc. cit.*, p. 23). The story therefore does not appear in the original text of Dominic's *Vita*, ed. M. Lapidge, *Analecta Bollandiana*, xcvi (1978), 65-104. See also M. Lapidge, 'The medieval hagiography of St Ecgwine', *Vale of Evesham Historical Society Research Papers*, vi (1977), 77-93, at 89.
6. William of Malmesbury, *Gesta pontificum*, i. 1 (p. 336); *Vita Aldhelmi Faricio Auctore*, i, ed. J. A. Giles, *Patrologia Latina*, lxxxix (1863), 67. Although filtered through terminology of c. 1100, the story conveys a truth about the earlier relation between church, town and countryside.
7. *Councils and Synods with Other Documents Relating to the English Church*, i, *AD 871-1204*, ed. D. Whitelock, M. Brett and C. N. L. Brooke (1981), 52, 321 (no. 19), 352.
8. E.g. the market owned before the Conquest by the community of canons of St Stephen's, Launceston, in Cornwall: P. Hull and R. Sharpe, 'Peter of Cornwall and Launceston', *Cornish Studies*, xiii (1985), 5-53, at 37.
9. R. Hodges, *The Anglo-Saxon Achievement* (1989), 93.

large. Nevertheless, the evidence of the later Anglo-Saxon period suggests that minsters commonly did perform such a pastoral function. The central location of many minsters and their own economic activities tended to generate a local need for pastoral provision amongst the population attracted to settle nearby. The response to that local and regional need became a part of the normal life of the late Anglo-Saxon urban minster clergy, whose pastoral efforts complemented those of the bishops.[10] The propaganda of the tenth-century monastic reform undoubtedly impedes appreciation of the pre-existing, looser patterns of clerical living in minster communities. But in addition post-reform Benedictinism has itself suffered from modern commentators imbued with a somewhat narrow vision of the monastic life.[11] The *Regularis concordia* may give relatively little space to discussion of pastoral matters - merely two chapters on almsgiving - yet the evidence not only of monastic charity but also of education and preaching by Benedictines in the later medieval centuries is proof that the liturgy, for all its importance, was only ever regarded as one aspect of the monastic vocation.[12] It is arguable, furthermore, that the pastoral strain in late medieval Benedictinism had roots before the reform.

The laity of the eleventh and later centuries enjoyed a remarkable liberty of admission to many churches of ancient foundation, despite institutional developments which might appear inimical to the continuance of such fraternization with the clergy. Even in the first flush of the establishment of the regular life, shortly after 1000, Bishop Æthelric of Dorchester could penetrate the monastery of Ramsey disguised as a lay traveller wishing to pray in the church, and wander about all the buildings to observe the monks at their daily tasks.[13] The *Regularis concordia* of c. 970 itself assumes a regular presence of lay parishioners at mass in the monastery; and indeed the scale and splendour of the houses rebuilt as a result of the reform implies as much.[14] Moreover, arrangements for lay access recorded

---

10. The absence of any evident pastoral impetus from aristocratic minster founda-
    tion charters is stressed by Patrick Sims-Williams, who also underlines the
    superior status, in the dioceses of Hereford and Worcester in the eighth century,
    of the bishops. P. Sims-Williams, *Religion and Literature in Western England
    600–800* (1990), 121-2 and ch. 6, *passim*.
11. David Knowles's great *The Monastic Order in England . . . 940-1216* (1940; 2nd
    edn., 1963) suffers from this defect. The basis of a more realistic assessment of
    monastic-lay relations at this period is provided by G. Constable, 'Monasteries,
    rural churches and the *cura animarum* in the early Middle Ages', *Settimane di
    studio del Centro italiano di studi sull'alto medioevo*, xxviii (1982), 349-95.
12. *Regularis concordia*, ed. T. Symons (1953), xxxvii, 61-2; Barbara Harvey, The
    Ford Lectures for 1989 (forthcoming).
13. *Chronicon abbatiae Ramesiensis*, ed. W. D. Macray (Rolls Series, 83, 1886),
    121-2.
14. *Regularis concordia*, 19. Cf. J. Hubert, 'La place faite aux laïcs dans les églises
    monastiques et dans les cathédrales aux XIe et XIIe siècles', *Miscellanea del
    Centro di studi medievali*, 5 (1968), 470-87, esp. p. 474. Note also the provision
    of monastic bell-towers, such as that added c. 1060 to St Oswald's church at
    Worcester by St Wulfstan, when prior, to gather the laity for sermons. William
    of Malmesbury, *Vita S. Wulfstani*, i. 8, ed. R. R. Darlington (Camden Soc., 3rd
    ser. 40, 1928), 15.

at somewhat later dates appear to have origins antedating the changes of the tenth century. Crowland Abbey in Lincolnshire was remembered by the monks living there around 1100 to have been founded as a minster, not long after the death of the patronal saint Guthlac in 751, by King Æthelbald of the Mercians. Following a rebuilding of 966 the house was reorganized as a Benedictine monastery. Yet in the later Middle Ages the lay parishioners of the district worshipped within the abbey church, in a chapel on the north side of the nave: an arrangement which may be suspected to recall one which had pertained before the tenth-century reform.[15] A similar history may lie behind the odd fact that in Hereford in the later medieval centuries the focus of the parish of St John, the parish which has a claim to be the primary or mother-parish of that town, was a chapel within the north transept of the cathedral church of St Æthelberht. By the fourteenth century both the cathedral canons and the lay parishioners were conscious of drawbacks to this arrangement, as each complained of disturbances to their respective services by the singing of the other body. The origin of the situation appears to have been an earlier relocation and enlargement of the cathedral church, probably the known rebuilding of c. 1100, as a result of which St John's, whose site lay significantly at the central crossroads of Anglo-Saxon Hereford, was subsumed within the new episcopal complex.[16] This pattern may be clarified further by a third example, that of Westminster. Here the parish church of St Margaret, which stands a few yards to the north of the choir of the abbey church, is first recorded in c. 1130, although a fourteenth-century tradition attributed its foundation to Edward the Confessor. The same fourteenth-century source, however, describes further how the parishioners used originally to attend services within the nave of the former abbey church, on the north side of that building; there 'they gathered for divine service and to receive the sacraments'. In the extant thirteenth-century north transept of the abbey church, a carving in the wall arcade shows St Margaret and her dragon: this sculpture may recall a hypothetical chapel of St Margaret formerly within the earlier abbey church, in the days when the parishioners were later remembered to have worshipped in the abbey, 'on the north side of the nave of the church'. The source is late and not entirely clear; but a plausible picture is given in which before the Conquest the lay inhabitants of Westminster received spiritual succour within the minster.[17] Crowland and Hereford evidently illustrate some such continuity at still later dates. So, too, does Beverley Minster, where in the late Middle Ages the canons shared responsibility for the parishioners of the town and a wide hinterland, who attended services at various altars in the mother-church.[18] In the monastery church of St Albans Abbey in the thirteenth century, a

---

15. *VCH, Lincs.*, ii (1906), 105-6; *Lincoln Record Society*, vii (1914), 36-7.
16. *Calendar of Patent Rolls, 1413-16*, 226; and see R. Shoesmith, *Hereford City Excavations: II* (CBA, Research Rep. 46, 1982), 13-20, 74-83.
17. G. Rosser, *Medieval Westminster, 1200-1540* (1989), 251-2.
18. *Memorials of Beverley Minster: The Chapter Act Book*, i, ed. A. F. Leach, Surtees Society, 98 (1897), lxxvi-lxxxii; *VCH, Yorkshire*, iii (1913), 355; *VCH, Yorkshire: East Riding*, vi (1989), 231ff.

number of altars appear to have stood against the piers of the nave, and seem likely also to have served lay congregations; once again, an earlier pattern may here have been sustained.[19] A similar sequence appears to be recorded at the former minster of St Frideswide in Oxford, where the location of the shrine and a parochial altar, in the north transept of the twelfth-century church, may indicate both the site of the Anglo-Saxon minster church and its pastoral function.[20]

The late eleventh-century Life of Edward the Confessor relates that the new abbey church of St Peter which he founded was begun on a site to the east of the then existing minster, in order not to disturb the divine services being offered there.[21] In this case the earlier church seems in due course to have been demolished to make way for the enlarged Romanesque abbey building. Elsewhere, however, dual or multiple churches continued to co-exist within the same architectural complex. This raises questions about the respective and perhaps complementary functions of these various churches in the Anglo-Saxon period.[22] At Malmesbury, for example, while the religious community treated first the church of Our Saviour, St Peter and St Paul, and then – from the late tenth century – that of St Mary as their principal base of operations, further churches of St Michael (adjoining St Mary's), St Andrew (apparently adjacent to Our Saviour's and used for the burial of successive abbots), and St Laurence (where John Scotus was first interred, after being murdered by his pupils) are also recorded. This complex at Malmesbury, sited at a major intersection of communications, has been likened to an Irish 'monastic city' such as Clonmacnoise.[23] At Worcester, even after Oswald's construction (or possibly reconstruction) of the church of St Mary had been brought to completion, in 983, the adjacent, episcopal church of St Peter stood until well into the following century.[24] St Peter's, the home of the secular clerks whom the Benedictine monks of the new foundation of St Mary's were intended to supersede in authority, may have continued to serve the laity in a pastoral role. Nor need the final destruction of St Peter's have left the neighbouring Worcester laity bereft; for their services may simply have been transferred within St Mary's. Crowland's parochial nave may illustrate the same process, as do the

---

19. The wall-paintings at St Albans, which are best interpreted as the traces of lost altars, are most recently discussed by P. Binski, 'The murals of the nave of St Albans Abbey', in the forthcoming Festschrift for C. N. L. Brooke.
20. J. Blair, 'St Frideswide's monastery: problems and possibilities', *Oxoniensia*, liii (1988), 255-8.
21. *Vita Ædwardi Regis*, vi, ed. F. Barlow (1962), 46.
22. Such complexes are also examined in John Blair's essay in this volume.
23. *VCH, Wiltshire*, iii (1956), 227-8; J. Haslam, 'The towns of Wiltshire', in *Anglo-Saxon Towns in Southern England*, ed. J. Haslam (1984), 87-147, at 115-17; Sims-Williams, *Religion and Literature*, 108-9.
24. Cf. William of Malmesbury, *Vita S. Wulfstani*, i. 4 (p. 9); J. A. Robinson, *St Oswald and the Church of Worcester*, British Academy Supplemental Papers, 5 (1919), 6; C. C. Dyer, 'The Saxon cathedrals of Worcester', *Trans. Worcs. Archaeol. Soc.* 3rd ser. ii (1968-9), 34; S. R. Bassett, 'A probable Mercian royal mausoleum at Winchcombe, Gloucestershire', *Antiq. J.* lxv (1985), 88, 98 n.55.

thirteenth-century parishioners of St Oswald's in Chester, who attended services at a chapel inside the reformed Benedictine abbey of St Werburh.[25] In such cases functions previously separated in distinct churches – churches which might be associated severally with parochial masses, burial and the monastic hours – may have been amalgamated under a single roof. To preserve the increasingly important sense of clerical difference, the presbytery would probably be sealed off by a screen: an early recorded example of such an addition is the *pulpitum* erected within Beverley Minster by Archbishop Ealdred in the 1060s.[26] Yet there remained ample opportunity for contact between parishioners and clergy. A slightly different pattern is exemplified at Sherborne in Dorset. Here the later medieval town church of All Hallows abutted the west end of the nave of St Mary's Abbey. The latter almost certainly stands on the site of St Aldhelm's cathedral church, founded in 705; All Hallows, erected on the same alignment, may originally have been a separate structure.[27] From the pastoral perspective, it is possible that the later parochial function of All Hallows continued an earlier role, while the abbey church may always, even before the late tenth-century reform, have been reserved principally for the calm recitation of the liturgy. Such a division may have been intended also at Winchester, where the foundation of the vast New Minster by King Alfred around 900 potentially provided for large congregations of the local laity, at a time of undoubted expansion in the urban population; the adjacent Old Minster may have been preserved for the primary use of the clergy.[28]

It must be allowed that the twin tendencies of the religious life, retreat from the world on the one hand, pastoral concern for the secular community on the other, have at all periods created tension. In the medieval period the potential for conflict was often explicitly recognized. The Sherborne refoundation charter of 998 makes candid reference to the possibility of future disagreements between the monks, as pastor, and their lay flock. Nor did this anxiety prove misplaced. Much later, in 1436, the townspeople attempted to transfer the town font, which at this period was in St Mary's, into their own church of All Hallows, to which they claimed the right of baptism anciently belonged. The escalation of hostilities led to an incendiary attack on the abbey church; but the parishioners were defeated. Until the dissolution of the monastery, they were compelled at the Easter service of baptism to pass through a door in the east end of their church to attend the ritual in the west part of St Mary's. Only at the Reformation did the townspeople gain victory when, on the expulsion of the monks, the abbey church was bought for parochial use; and All Hallows,

---

25. A. T. Thacker, 'Chester and Gloucester: early ecclesiastical organisation in two Mercian burhs', *Northern History* xviii (1982), 204.
26. *Historians of the Church of York*, ed. Raine, ii, 354; A. W. Clapham, *English Romanesque Architecture before the Conquest* (1930), 142; A. Vallance, *Greater English Church Screens* (1947), 133.
27. *VCH, Dorset*, ii (1908), 62-8.
28. M. Biddle, '*Felix urbs Winthonia*: Winchester in the age of monastic reform', in *Tenth-Century Studies*, ed. D. Parsons (1975), 131.

now redundant, was shortly afterwards demolished.[29] Monks, for their part, were correspondingly liable to feel overburdened by secular intrusions. In 1434 the Benedictines of Bardney in Lincolnshire grumbled that when the local laity came to services in their parish church, which like that of Sherborne stood adjacent to the abbey, they did not come and go discreetly but would 'wander and roam about in our said conventual church in time of divine service, and . . . hinder, molest, and disturb us in manifold ways during the divine offices by their noise and uproar'. The monks petitioned the bishop for the right to relocate the parish church farther off from the monastery, alleging that the parishioners had themselves requested the move for their own greater convenience.[30] Then and much earlier, there clearly existed the possibility of conflict. Nevertheless, the principle behind these various arrangements appears to be a complementary duality in the life both of the early minster and of the later monastery church complex, which served both intercessory and pastoral needs.

The extent to which the pastoral care offered by minster communities, in actual or nascent urban centres before 1000, was supplemented by small, local town churches is likely to have been limited. It is probable that more such subordinate urban churches existed before the late tenth century than are yet known. Nevertheless, most of the large numbers of medieval churches characteristic of the older English towns appear to have originated between c. 1000 and the mid-twelfth century. Both the increase in population together with the associated quickening of urban life, and the ending of direct lay control over the greater churches, doubtless contributed to this proliferation of lay foundations of secular churches. In so far as individual citizens and groups of neighbours had founded a few such private or street chapels before the millennium, they evidently met a demand for intimacy and independence in lay worship. All Saints', Oxford, which was created within a citizen's house, and St Mary's, Tanner Street, Winchester, in which the sole original door opened into a private dwelling, are excavated examples of this type of urban church.[31] Some collectively patronized *Kaufmanskirchen*, such as are recorded, for example, in the possession of groups of burgesses at Lincoln in 1086, may have antedated the year 1000.[32] Certain urban chapels, on the other hand, have been ascribed to a process of public planning: it has been suggested that the regular and prominent distribution of churches on the main streets and gates of Oxford formed part of Edward the Elder's plan for the city.[33] Once again, however, there is no certain evidence that any of these Oxford churches actually existed before the mid-eleventh century.[34] From the eleventh century

29. *VCH, Dorset, loc. cit.*
30. *Lincoln Record Society*, vii, 2, 5; cf. *VCH, Lincs.*, ii, 97.
31. Morris, *Churches in the Landscape*, 205; *Winchester in the Early Middle Ages*, ed. M. Biddle (Winchester Studies, 1, 1976), 332–3.
32. Campbell, 'Church in towns', *Essays*, 149; cf. P. Johansen, 'Die Kaufmanskirche im Ostseegebiet', in *Studien zu den Anfängen des Europäischen Städtewesens*, ed. T. Mayer, Vorträge und Forschungen (1958).
33. Morris, *Churches in the Landscape*, 192ff.
34. Blair, 'St Frideswide's', 224.

onwards the rapidly increasing number of such neighbourhood churches acquired more or less extensive parochial rights: that fewer of these were devolved in the towns of the south and west of the country than elsewhere may be attributable in part to a strong royal presence in those places, which would have sustained the claims of the royally endowed minsters to their monopoly of control, in particular over rights of sepulture.[35] But the motives for foundation were various, and not every small church erected before 1000 served the pastoral needs of the laity. When, for example, Abbot Wulsin of St Albans in *c.* 900 built churches at cardinal points around the little market town, to the north, south, and west, his purpose may have been to make a statement about clerical authority rather than to accommodate the lay population.[36] In no town before 1000 can the provision of pastoral care have been more than marginally affected by the then available local chapels.

Moreover, the establishment of local daughter-churches, which became marked after 1000, although it detracted from the jurisdictional prerogatives of the older minsters, did not remove their raison d'être as primary centres of lay attraction. In the later Middle Ages, notwithstanding the now more-or-less rigid limits of the local parishes laid down by 1300, those boundaries were constantly being crossed by a population whose mobility defied most principles of parochial conformity. Mobility led in many directions, but commonly a major pull continued to be exerted by the minster in the old town or central place. Many a late-medieval guild, whose focus of activity was a church of such ancient importance, drew its membership from a wide catchment area which transcended parish limits.[37] Again, in view of the continuities which have been identified between the organization of the Anglo-Saxon minsters and the priories of Augustinian canons of which so many were founded in the twelfth century, it is probably symptomatic of an earlier pattern that at an Augustinian house such as that of Thornton in Lincolnshire in the later Middle Ages the church was said on Sundays to be frequented by the laity of numbers of the surrounding local parishes.[38] Abbots of the Benedictine house of Bury St Edmunds were in the twelfth century chosen for their ability to preach to

---

35. The fact of geographical variation is recently discussed in Morris, *Churches in the Landscape*, 223.
36. *Gesta abbatum monasterii Sancti Albani*, ed. H. T. Riley (3 vols., Rolls Series, 28, 1867-9), i, 22. It should be noted, however, that the later chronicler, perhaps conditioned by his own preconceptions, suggests that the three churches were designed *both* for 'an ornament' *and* to serve the laity: 'tam ad ornatum quam utilitatem pagi'. There appears to be a close parallel between Wulsin's churches at St Albans and the 'cross of churches' laid out around the cathedral at Utrecht by Bishop Bernold (1027-54). In the Utrecht case the dedications of the churches and elements of their design indicate a primary concern to convey a political message (associating the bishop with the authority of Rome) rather than to meet pastoral needs: T. J. Hoekstra, 'The early topography of the city of Utrecht and its cross of churches', *JBAA*, cxli (1988), 9-17.
37. G. Rosser, 'Communities of parish and guild in the late Middle Ages', in *Parish, Church and People: Local Studies in Lay Religion*, ed. S. J. Wright (1988), 29-55.
38. *Lincoln Record Soc.* xxi (1929), 371.

the laity who gathered there on feast days.[39] From the point of view of the Christian layman, a daughter-church was not by any means a complete surrogate for the parent institution. The federation of village guilds in Devon in the late eleventh century, each based upon a village chapelry but collectively focused on the cathedral at Exeter, demonstrate the continuing attraction of the major church.[40] These enduring roles of former minsters point to an early tradition of active pastoral care amongst such churches.

The practical exercise of the pastoral office evidently depended upon the physical presence of the laity. The layman might be drawn within range of spiritual welfare by economic ties, as at Aldhelm's Malmesbury, or else by the attraction of a prestigious shrine. The miraculous powers of relics must have been for many the most notable feature of a major church; and the pastoral consequences of experiencing or witnessing a miracle could be profound. Hence the publicity generated by the keepers of the holy places. In the 970s the Winchester cult of St Swithun was described by Lantfred, a foreign monk then living at the Old Minster. Twenty years later Lantfred's account was rendered into verse by Wulfstan the cantor of Winchester, and around 1000 was drawn upon extensively by Ælfric of Eynsham in his *Lives of the Saints*, which was designed as a tool for preachers. These writers made their own substantial contribution to the draw of the thaumaturge, whose body had, shortly after 970, been translated to a new martyrium within the Old Minster.[41] The magnetic power of the saint is vividly conveyed in Ælfric's image of the cemetery which was 'filled with crippled folk, so that people could hardly get into the minster'.[42] Some of the pilgrims had covered long distances. Miracles of sight were a speciality of Swithun, and blind people made their perilous way to Winchester from as far afield as Essex, Bedford and the Isle of Wight.[43] Lantfred stressed Winchester's superiority to rival towns and shrines: the young man with poor vision was made worse by an ill-advised visit to Shaftesbury, but cured at Winchester.[44] Lantfred also listed triumphantly the many citizens of London who were healed at what evidently laid claim to be the kingdom's capital shrine, even as Winchester was the

---

39. *The Chronicle of Jocelin of Brakelond*, ed. H. F. Butler (1949), 12.
40. G. Rosser, 'The Anglo-Saxon gilds', in *Minsters and Parish Churches: The Local Church in Transition, 950-1200*, ed. J. Blair (Oxford University Committee for Archaeology, Monograph 17, 1988), 31-4; cf. Campbell, 'Church in towns', *Essays*, 152.
41. The texts: Lantfred of Winchester, *Translatio et miracula S. Swithuni*, ed. M. Lapidge (*Winchester Studies*, iv, forthcoming); *Frithegodi monachi breviloquium vitae Beati Wilfredi et Wulfstani cantoris narratio metrica de Sancto Swithuno*, ed. A. Campbell (1950); *Ælfric's Lives of the Saints*, ed. W. W. Skeat, ii (Early English Text Society, o.s. 82, 1885), 440-73. The cult: M. Biddle, 'Archaeology, architecture and the cult of the saints in Anglo-Saxon England', in *The Anglo-Saxon Church*, ed. L. A. S. Butler and R. K. Morris (CBA, Research Rep. 60, 1986), 22-5; M. Lapidge, 'The origin and development of the cult of St Swithun', in *Winchester Studies*, iv (forthcoming).
42. *Ælfric's Lives*, 451.
43. Lantfred, *Translatio et miracula S. Swithuni*, v, viii, xix.
44. *ibid.*, xxxvi. Cf. the cripple half-cured by St Augustine at Canterbury, made wholly better by St Swithun at Winchester. *ibid.*, xiii.

chief seat of the Wessex monarchy.[45] Not only medical healing, but reparation of justice was offered by the saint. The slave-girl wrongly punished by her master, a Winchester citizen, for the loss of his clothes (which had been stolen by robbers), escaped to the shrine; finding her there, the master miraculously perceived her innocence.[46] The potential ferocity of secular justice was likewise mitigated by the saint.[47] By the hagiographers all of the cures were celebrated as acts of spiritual as well as physical healing, which affected onlookers and hearers of the reports no less than the protagonists. They affirmed the primary pastoral status of the minster, even, in this case, during the period when local churches were beginning to spring up within its sphere of influence. These daughter-churches would never be able to compete with the other's tangible testimonies of power, the *ex votos* left by grateful penitents and pilgrims. The Winchester minster, where Swithun lay, 'was hung all round, from one end to the other on either wall, with crutches and with the stools of cripples who had been cured there, and not even so could they put half of them up'.[48]

Feast-days and relic-days, peak periods of pilgrimage, were opportunities for preaching to the gathered laity. Towards 1000 Ælfric reiterated the importance of basic teaching of the rudiments of the Christian faith (already enshrined in the canons of earlier councils) and of the vernacular exposition of the Gospel at Sunday services. His *Catholic Homilies* were designed to enable mass-priests and deacons (assumed to be literate) to accomplish these tasks.[49] Where a great church was not large enough to accommodate those drawn for spiritual succour, the pastoral endeavour could be transferred outdoors: at Worcester in the second half of the tenth century, Bishop Oswald preached to large audiences in the cemetery outside his cathedral church of St Peter.[50] Towards 1050 in the same city, St Wulfstan began his pastoral mission as a monk of the reformed house of St Mary. As prior, he preached on Sundays and feast-days, distributed alms and baptized for nothing the children of the poor in Worcester. Nor, then or later, did he mince words with the townsmen he addressed, castigating the merchants of Bristol, for example, for continuing to trade in

45. *ibid.*, ix, xi, xii, xiii.
46. *ibid.*, xxxviii; similar stories at *ibid.*, vi, xx, xxv, xxxi.
47. *ibid.*, xxvi.
48. *Ælfric's Lives*, 469.
49. *The Homilies of the Anglo-Saxon Church*, ed. B. Thorpe (2 vols., 1844-6), and for the second series see now *Ælfric's Catholic Homilies: The Second Series*, ed. M. Godden (Early English Text Society, suppl. ser., 5, 1979). See also Ælfric's pastoral letter for Wulfsige III of Sherborne, *Councils and Synods*, ed. Whitelock *et al.*, i. 208-9.
50. Robinson, *St Oswald*, 4-5.

slaves.[51] The (foreign) monk who criticized Wulfstan for preaching before his elevation to the episcopal office reflected the increasing prestige and prerogatives of bishops in the eleventh century; but the writings of Abbot Ælfric and of Archbishop Wulfstan (who was also a monk around 1000) clearly imply that anyone in priest's orders should preach as a matter of course.[52]

In his campaign to improve the effectiveness of the English pastoral mission, Ælfric drew on Carolingian exemplars, notably Paul the Deacon.[53] Ælfric differed from his continental sources, however, in his particular concern for preaching in the vernacular.[54] Here his clearest precedent, and obvious model, was the educational programme of King Alfred.[55] Ælfric's novelty was not his insistence on the importance of preaching by all priests, but his systematic and practical provision of the basic materials for others to use. Although he was a man of great learning, his constant premise was that 'One must speak to laymen according to their measure of understanding, so that they are not dismayed by the depth of meaning nor bored by the length.' Ælfric supplied further aids to the understanding of the laity, such as his notes on 'belief and prayer and blessing for laymen who know not Latin'.[56] But once again, the importance of Ælfric should not obscure the pre-existing tradition of homilistic teaching.

---

51. William of Malmesbury, *Vita S. Wulfstani*, ii. 17 (pp. 43-4). The texts of contemporary homilies tend not to specify the particular spiritual problems of the town-dweller. Yet they were doubtless written down in their generalized form in order to provide the basis for elaboration in delivery, as particular circumstances prompted. A general observable preoccupation in the texts with penitence and the last things is not an indication that everyday concerns were ignored in favour of eschatological oratory, but rather that the two were integrated in homiletic practice. The contrary claim of K. Greenfield, 'Changing emphases in English vernacular homiletic literature, 960-1225', *Journal of Medieval History*, vii (1981), 283-97, is tenuous.
52. William of Malmesbury, *Vita S. Wulfstani*, i. 8 (pp. 13-14), and see also the early abridgement of William of Malmesbury's, *Vita* vii (*ibid.*, 73-4); cf. D. Bethurum, *The Homilies of Wulfstan* (1957), 56-7 (Archbishop Wulfstan, a Benedictine), 85 (Saint Wulfstan, a monk and preacher). The evidence runs counter to Gatch's unfounded statement that in the mid-eleventh century 'the inhabitants of Worcester were not accustomed to hearing sermons, whether by monks or by seculars'. M. McC. Gatch, *Preaching and Theology in Anglo-Saxon England: Ælfric and Wulfstan* (Toronto, 1977), 47.
53. C. L. Smetana, 'Ælfric and the early medieval homiliary' *Traditio*, xv (1959), 163-204. Further on the importance of preaching on the Continent in the early period, see the remarks on Caesarius of Arles in H. J. G. Beck, *The Pastoral Care of Souls in South-East France during the Sixth Century* (Analecta Gregoriana, 51, 1950), 91.
54. P. A. M. Clemoes, 'Ælfric', in *Continuations and Beginnings: Studies in Old English Literature*, ed. E. G. Stanley (1966), 176-209; M. McC. Gatch, 'The achievement of Ælfric and his colleagues in European perspective', in *The Old English Homily and its Background*, ed. P. E. Szarmach and B. F. Huppe (1978), 43-73.
55. S. Keynes and M. Lapidge, *Alfred the Great* (1983), 25-36, 92-3, 124-7.
56. A. J. Frantzen, *The Literature of Penance in Anglo-Saxon England* (New Brunswick, 1983), 142-3; Gatch, *Preaching and Theology*, 58-9, 120; Clemoes, 'Ælfric', 187.

The Blickling and Vercelli collections of Anglo-Saxon homilies were both assembled in the mid-tenth century; both, like Ælfric and Archbishop Wulfstan later, stress the importance of penitence for sins, leading to a general moral reform of the individual layman.[57] Such addresses were clearly designed to lead to the confession of sins to the priest: a crucial context for the exercise of pastoral care. For it was in confession that the priest had the best opportunity to test the penitent's knowledge of the basic teachings of the church and to direct his behaviour in conformity with that model. This educational role of the confessional may have been all the more important since schools do not appear to have been numerous before the late tenth century.[58] Where these are recorded, they were located at the old minsters. In the late seventh century the young Willibrord was still a layman when he attended a school maintained by the clergy of Ripon minster.[59] St Dunstan received his first education, around 920, from the minster community at Glastonbury - having himself taken the tonsure, according to one of his later biographers, but amongst other sons of noblemen for whom a life of religion was evidently not anticipated.[60] At about the same time St Æthelwold in the city of Winchester began to study 'the sacred writings'; his teachers, however, are not specified.[61] Later, as bishop, Æthelwold would take delight in teaching boys, for whom he often had to translate the holy texts into English. Many, but clearly not all, of his pupils went on to become pastors in their turn, either as monks or secular priests. Indeed, Æthelwold's prize pupil was Ælfric of Eynsham himself.[62] The 'child-master' recorded at King Harold's mid-eleventh-century religious foundation of Waltham was evidently a figure long established at minster churches in general.[63]

Because the various duties of the Christian laity were not formalized for western Christendom as a whole before the Lateran Council of 1215, the degree to which churchmen in earlier centuries were clear about the religious responsibilities of the layman has sometimes been under-estimated.[64] Shortly before 1000, Wulfstan's *Canons of Eadgar* specified the

---

57. Frantzen, *Literature of Penance*, ch. 6. This is, in part, the catechetical thrust of these sermons, even though, as Gatch has emphasized, it is not entirely clear whether their immediate audience was of laymen or rather of clerics intended to mediate instruction to the laity. M. McC. Gatch, 'The unknowable audience of the Blickling Homilies', *Anglo-Saxon England* xviii (1989), 99-115.
58. D. A. Bullough, 'The educational tradition in England from Alfred to Ælfric: teaching *utriusque linguae*', *Settimane di studio del Centro italiano di studi sull'alto medioevo*, xix (1972), 453-94.
59. Alcuin, *Vita S. Willibrordi*, i. 3, in *Memorials of the Church of SS. Peter and Wilfrid, Ripon*, i (Surtees Society, 74, 1881), 1.
60. *Memorials of St Dunstan*, ed. W. Stubbs (Rolls Series, 63, 1874), 10-11 ('B'), 74-5 (Osbern).
61. Wulfstan, *Vita S. Æthelwoldi*, c.6, in *Three Lives of English Saints*, ed. M. Winterbottom (Toronto, 1972), 37.
62. Wulfstan, *Vita S. Æthelwoldi*, c.31 (ed. Winterbottom, 51).
63. W. Stubbs, *The Foundation of Waltham Abbey* (1861), xii.
64. E.g. by M. Chibnall, 'Monks and pastoral work: a problem in Anglo-Norman history', *J. Ecclesiastical History*, xviii (1967), 165-72.

requirements of the laity to learn the Creed and Pater Noster, to give alms and pay tithes, and to eschew adultery and pagan practices.[65] But from long before, from at least the period of the council of *Clofesho* (AD 747), the people had been directed to come often to communion, and were admonished on those occasions to reform their lives.[66] The clergy, meanwhile - whether bishops, local priests or members of religious communities - were no less often urged to use the pastoral methods both of teaching and example. That example was to be based upon a certain clerical difference: from *Clofesho* onwards, clerks (whether priests or not) were instructed not to allow themselves to be corrupted by contact with secular society.[67] Much of the legislation on clerical standards implies the great difficulty of establishing and sustaining that difference. Repeated prohibitions of marriage for priests were still flouted in the twelfth century;[68] and Wulfstan's code of c. 1000 known as the *Northumbrian Priests' Law* suggests that at least in York, there was little to distinguish the priest from his lay flock.[69] The particular problems of clerical income in towns, where the tithe can never have amounted to much, seem to be indicated in such rules as that which forbade the priest to supplement his income by performing songs in taverns.[70] While forbidding also the practice of a usurious merchant, the roughly contemporary *Canons of Eadgar* urged priests to learn an honest trade.[71] The aim at this period was evidently not to make of the local clergy a distinct caste, set above the laity by its privileges and avoidance of manual toil - that would come later - but rather that they should exercise their pastoral duty, first and foremost, through their personal example of life *within* lay society. Inevitably, a fine line divided the presentation of a worthy model from a descent into worldliness. No doubt the lifestyle of Anglo-Saxon priests gave a sometimes excessive intimacy to pastoral relations. Abbot Brihtwold II of Malmesbury, who died in c. 1052 during a drinking bout in the town, was not the only Anglo-Saxon cleric to be seduced by the world.[72] Yet for all this, at least some of the clergy set examples of Christian living which were not without effect upon secular society. Bede wrote of Cuthbert, when the latter was bishop of Lindisfarne, that 'he protected his flock committed to him by constant prayer on their behalf, by wholesome admonition and - which is the real way to teach - by example first and precept later.'[73]

---

65. *Councils and Synods*, ed. Whitelock *et al.*, 321 (no. 17), 322 (no. 22).
66. Haddan and Stubbs, *Councils*, iii, 370.
67. *ibid.*, iii, 374-5; *Councils and Synods*, ed. Whitelock *et al.*, 331 (no. 52).
68. J. Barrow, 'Hereford bishops and married clergy, c. 1130-1240', *Historical Research*, lx (1987), 1-8.
69. *Councils and Synods*, ed. Whitelock *et al.*, 449-68; cf. Brooke, 'Church in the towns', 80.
70. *Councils and Synods*, ed. Whitelock *et al.*, 333 (no. 59).
71. Ælfric's first Old English letter for Wulfstan: *Councils and Synods*, 296 (no. 185); 'Canons of Edgar': *ibid.*, 318 (no. 11), 319 (no. 14); Ælfric's pastoral letter for Wulfsige III: *ibid.*, 212 (no. 77).
72. William of Malmesbury, *Gesta pontificum*, v. 4 (pp. 411-12); and, for the date, *The Heads of Religious Houses in England and Wales 940-1216*, ed. D. Knowles, C. N. L. Brooke and V. C. M. London (1972), 55.
73. Bede, *Vita S. Cuthberti*, c.26 (ed. Colgrave, 240-3).

One element, in particular, of this edifying example was concentrated in towns: the sacrifice of charity. In c. 900 Abbot Leofric of St Albans brushed aside the murmurings of some of his fellow monks in order to distribute to the humble people treasures, including classical gems, which had been gathered for the monastic buildings.[74] At Winchester a few decades later Æthelwold performed the same model sacrifice to mitigate the effects of a famine on the local population.[75] In his translation of St Benedict's *Rule*, Æthelwold gave his own additional emphasis to the monks' duties towards the poor.[76] The example of charity in the ideal Anglo-Saxon priest, as successive councils and pastoral letters reiterated, was to be part of a style of life which in all respects inspired emulation and spiritual renewal in the lay population.[77] The impact of the example is reflected in the aristocratic wills of the period, such as that of the ætheling Æthelstan, who in 1015 provided for 100 poor people to be fed each year at Ely, on the feast-day of St Æthelthryth.[78] All of these instances illustrate the concentration of charitable distributions in central places, at the major ecclesiastical centres; a phenomenon which in the later Middle Ages would continue to attract assemblies of the needy from the urban hinterland.

The reform of the clerical life was no less a lay than an ecclesiastical concern. Once the ministrations of the priest had become a desirable commodity, certain standards of behaviour were demanded. The value set in particular on intercessory masses at this period has yet to be fully explained, although the harshness of the penitentials must form part of the background. The early eleventh-century aristocrat, Wulfin, who paid the monks then established in Gloucester Abbey to pray for him, had his humbler counterparts in the members of the guilds who offered up collective prayers and who doubtless, like later medieval fraternities, regularly supported and supervised their own spiritual ministers.[79] Ælfric denounced the competition among priests for possession of a newly dead corpse, that commodity of such potential value in its requirement of commemorative prayers.[80] The urban clergy's lack of financial security gave scope for extensive lay control over what would later be called chantry priests, and indeed guilds of laymen in the later Middle Ages hired and fired their ministers as a matter of course; it seems probable that such relationships

---

74. *Gesta abbatum*, 29-30. The prototype and ultimate justification for this was the similar behaviour of the third-century Roman deacon St Laurence. The tradition is discussed in C. Rudolph, *The 'Things of Greater Importance': Bernard of Clairveaux's Apologia and the Medieval Attitude to Art* (Philadelphia, 1990), 80-4.

75. Wulfstan, *Vita S. Æthelwoldi*, c.29 (ed. Winterbottom, 50).

76. M. Lapidge, 'Æthelwold as scholar and teacher', in *Bishop Æthelwold: His Career and Influence*, ed. B. Yorke (1988), 89-117, at 101.

77. Wulfstan, 'Institutes of Polity', in *Die 'Institutes of Christian Polity, Civil and Ecclesiastical'*, ed. K. Jost (Schweizer Anglistiche Arbeiter, 47, 1959), 84, 98. On the Continent in the mid-eighth century, Theodulf, bishop of Orleans, stands out for his insistence on the same argument: R. McKitterick, *The Frankish Church and the Carolingian Reforms, 709-895* (1977), 53-4.

78. D. Whitelock. *Anglo-Saxon Wills* (1930), 59.

79. W. Dugdale, *Monasticon Anglicanum* (6 vols., 1817-1830), i, 545.

80. *Councils and Synods*, ed. Whitelock *et al.*, 218 (no. 111), 295-6 (nos 182, 184).

were anticipated in Anglo-Saxon central places. Burial, also, was a matter which concerned lay allegiance even more than it did clerical jurisdiction or fiscality. To a large extent – and particularly in the west – mother-churches before 1000 retained their monopoly of burial rights. Here again, guilds of laymen played a part in sustaining the pre-eminence of the minster cemetery. The surviving statutes of the pre-Conquest guilds provide for the collection of the body of a deceased member, to be brought back to 'the minster' for due interment among his ancestors; the living members of the guild of Abbotsbury in Dorset would travel up to 60 miles from home on this mission. Similar burial provisions recur in the ordinances of later town guilds, enshrining a perennial lay preoccupation.[81]

To carry a body to burial was a recognized alms-deed; so, too, were other imperatives expressed in the statutes of the Anglo-Saxon guilds of laity: pilgrimage to the holy places, and the distribution of cash sums to the poor. Complementing this charitable impulse, the guilds evinced in addition a particular concern with peace, and the reconciliation of enemies. The same call for social peace is found in the vernacular homilies preached by the clergy of the period:

> If your nearest friend offend you in any matter, entreat him lovingly to make amends. If he will not, summon two others of your friends and, with them, ask him again. If he still refuses, take your complaint to the church, that is to the priest and the congregation. If neither priest nor church can induce him to behave rightly, let him be held to be a criminal and a heathen.[82]

It would be hard to say whether the desire for Christian peace, expressed here at similar periods both in the statutes of secular guilds and in the injunctions of the priests, received its critical impulse from one source or from the other. What is evident is a reciprocal relationship between the two. There is always a danger in religious history of underestimating the ability of laymen to understand and even to initiate complex ideas. It must be allowed that Wulfstan's *Sermo Lupi ad Anglos* presupposes a lay audience of no mean powers of comprehension.[83] Ælfric refers to the circulation, doubtless among a minority, of religious books in the vernacular. His own works of translation were largely motivated by a desire to rectify the damage caused by lay reading of corrupt or heretical texts.[84] Ælfric's aristocratic patron Æthelmær, who sat in on divine service at his

---

81. Rosser, 'The Anglo-Saxon gilds'.
82. *Old English Homilies*, ed. R. Morris, 2 vols., i (Early English Text Society, o.s. 34, 1868), 16–17 (twelfth century). The invitation to refer disputes to the joint arbitration of the priest and the lay congregation deserves emphasis.
83. Wulfstan, *Sermo Lupi ad Anglos*, ed. D. Whitelock (1939).
84. For Ælfric's concern about the potential dangers of making vernacular texts available to an evidently wide potential market, see his conclusion to his translation of *Genesis*, in *Select Translations from Old English Prose*, ed. A. S. Cook and C. B. Tinker (1908), 149–51. Further on Anglo-Saxon literacy in the vernacular, see S. Kelly, 'Anglo-Saxon lay society and the written word', in *The Uses of Literacy in Early Medieval Europe*, ed. R. McKitterick (1990), 36–62, esp. 54–62.

monastic foundation at Eynsham and for whom Ælfric may have provided devotional writings for private prayer, was surely exceptional.[85] Nevertheless, these are hints of the existence of an intelligent, aware, and demanding lay culture, to which the reforms of the late Old English church should in part be seen as a response. And an urban emphasis was a key to this. It was the urban minster which was the principal religious focus for most laymen before the millennium. The associated difference in degrees of cultural sophistication between town and country was expressed in the monk Byrhtferth of Ramsey's *Manual* for priests of 1011. The work is written in both Latin and English, explications being patiently inserted at every point for the sake of ignorant *suburbani clerici : uplendiscean preostas :* 'backwoods priests'.[86] The implication of the phrase is stirring: that against the rustic world of ignorance and heathendom is set the town, bastion of wisdom and orthodoxy. Here the minster community presented to lay society not only the priestly sacraments but, above all, a visible example of Christian living.

If the Christian pastoral mission depended at all times on the involvement of the laity at large - by whom, indeed, the very character of that mission was to a significant extent determined - the particular relations of the church with secular authority were also important. From at least the date of the Roman mission, the church in England was closely bound up with lay power; and the concentration of each in central places underlined their interrelationship. Pope Gregory himself, in his *Pastoral Care*, had made plain the political implications of Christian obedience: 'When we offend against our lords we offend against the God who created authority.' This sentiment goes some way to explain the attraction of the *Pastoral Care* to King Alfred;[87] and under Alfred's successor Eadgar the same point was made by Wulfstan the homilist: 'Should the Christian faith weaken, the kingship will immediately totter.'[88] The inclusion in royal law codes from the ninth century onwards of injunctions to obey the priests and pay their dues served the interest of political and social control.[89] The development of the ecclesiastical coronation ritual as a prop for the monarchy is echoed at the local urban level in the use by the civic elders of York of a public sermon by St Oswald to stage an impressive entrance before the gathered public.[90] Yet this was never more than a small part of the story. The roles assigned to bishops and priests in Anglo-Saxon (and indeed later) royal legislation were functions to which ecclesiastics were already accustomed. That bishops, for example, should be custodians in the towns of standard weights and measures was no more than a formalization of their

85. Gatch, *Preaching and Theology*, 48-9.
86. *Byrhtferth's Manual (AD 1011)*, ed. S. J. Crawford (Early English Text Society, o.s. 177, 1929), esp. 16-17, 114-15, 132-3. Note the use of the Latin word *suburbanus* to mean both 'remote from' and 'beneath' the town.
87. A. J. Frantzen, *King Alfred* (Boston, Mass., 1986), ch. 3.
88. Wulfstan, 'Institutes of Polity' (ed. Jost, p. 58).
89. E.g. *Councils and Synods*, ed. Whitelock *et al.*, 33 (no. 40.2) (laws of Alfred), 62 (no. 2) (laws of Edmund), 97-102 (laws of Eadgar).
90. Byrhtferth of Ramsey, *Vita S. Oswaldi*, pt. v, in *Historians of the Church of York*, ed. Raine, i, 454-5.

natural duty to guard justice and protect the weak from exploitation.[91]

Nearly all priests and clerks in minor orders living in England between 700 and 1000 were based in central places: actual or nascent towns. They resided in those communities generally called minsters; but whether they followed some elements of a daily rule, or were simply the more common clerical team ministries, their status and organization did not segregate them definitively from the laity of the immediate environs and surrounding hinterland. On the contrary; for they were the inheritors of the dual tradition of Christianity: that of the recluse who flees the corruption of the world, and that of the imitator of Christ's life on earth.[92] While the Christian Church has always held the former in high regard, the latter has, since apostolic times, continued to be recognized as the more widely relevant model. Holy men and women are often forced to strike a balance between the two types of life, if their impact is to be felt outside themselves. The clerical communities of Anglo-Saxon England were in many cases located at points of maximum visibility. As urban life gathered momentum in these central places, the increasing concourse of the laity ensured that the teaching and practical example of the clergy would act as a leaven throughout secular society.

---

91. *Councils and Synods*, ed. Whitelock *et al.*, 419; W. Ullmann, 'Public welfare and social legislation in the early medieval councils', *Studies in Church History*, vii (1971), 17–18.
92. In general: B. E. Daley, 'The ministry of disciples: historical reflections on the role of religious priests', *Theological Studies*, xlviii (1987), 605–29. A valuable case-study: C. Stancliffe, 'Cuthbert and the polarity between pastor and solitary', in *St Cuthbert, his Cult and his Community to AD 1200*, ed. G. Bonner, D. Rollason and C. Stancliffe (1989), 21–44.

Index

DATE DUE

DATE DUE			
APR 1 4 1995			
MAY 0 6 1999			

Pastoral care before the
parish